Between 1641 and 1649, for the first time befo
by the international community as an indepe
Cromwellian conquest of 1649, followed by a
and the restoration of the Stuart monarchy
Catholic Ireland's revolution, it nevertheless ranks as one of the most
successful revolts in early modern history.

This interdisciplinary collection of essays examines how the tumultuous
events of the 1640s and 1650s transformed the course of Ireland's history.
Apart from a chronological account of the civil war and of the collapse of the
Cromwellian régime in 1659–60, the essays are thematic and cover such
diverse issues as the early stages of the 1641 insurrection, the impact of
continental military technology on Irish warfare, confederate foreign policy,
Anglo-Irish relations and the formulation of Irish policy at Westminster
during the later 1640s, the wartime economy, the land settlement and the
proliferation of radical sects during the 1650s. Other chapters examine
the respective divisions within the Catholic and Protestant communities, the
nature of Irish royalism and the evasive concept of national identity.

The contributors consider why Restoration Ireland was·such a different
world from that of the early Stuart era. Was the change simply due to the
passage of twenty years; or to war in the 1640s followed by English
occupation in the 1650s? During these decades did active forces of change
outweigh those of continuity in shaping Irish society, identities, warfare,
religious beliefs, economic and tenurial practices? Finally these essays seek to
set Ireland in its wider European and British contexts.

IRELAND FROM INDEPENDENCE TO OCCUPATION, 1641–1660

IRELAND
FROM INDEPENDENCE
TO OCCUPATION
1641–1660

EDITED BY

JANE H. OHLMEYER

Yale University

CAMBRIDGE
UNIVERSITY PRESS

PUBLISHED BY THE PRESS SYNDICATE OF THE UNIVERSITY OF CAMBRIDGE
The Pitt Building, Trumpington Street, Cambridge, United Kingdom

CAMBRIDGE UNIVERSITY PRESS
The Edinburgh Building, Cambridge CB2 2RU, UK
40 West 20th Street, New York NY 10011–4211, USA
477 Williamstown Road, Port Melbourne, VIC 3207, Australia
Ruiz de Alarcón 13, 28014 Madrid, Spain
Dock House, The Waterfront, Cape Town 8001, South Africa

http://www.cambridge.org

First published 1995
First paperback edition 2002

A catalogue record for this book is available from the British Library

Library of Congress Cataloguing in Publication data
Ireland from independence to occupation, 1641–1660 /
edited by Jane H. Ohlmeyer.
p.   cm.
Includes bibliographical references and index.
ISBN 0 521 43479 3
1. Ireland – History – 1649–1660. 2. Ireland – History – 1625–1649.
I. Ohlmeyer, Jane H.
DA944.4.I74   1995
941.506–dc20   94-16542   CIP

ISBN 0 521 43479 3 hardback
ISBN 0 521 52275 7 paperback

CONTENTS

     interpretation   181
     KEVIN MCKENNY

10   *Radical religion in Ireland, 1641–1660*   201
     PHIL KILROY

11   *The Protestant interest, 1641–1660*   218
     T. C. BARNARD

12   *1659 and the road to Restoration*   241
     AIDAN CLARKE

13   *Conclusion. Settling and unsettling Ireland: the Cromwellian and*
     Williamite revolutions   265
     T. C. BARNARD

     Select bibliography   292
     Index   310

ILLUSTRATIONS

PLATES

MAPS

TABLES

CONTRIBUTORS

DR JOHN ADAMSON has written extensively on the English peerage during the mid-seventeenth century. His essay 'The baronial context of the English civil war' in *Transactions, Royal Historical Society*, fifth series, 40 (1990) won the Alexander prize in 1990. He is a Bye-Fellow of Peterhouse, Cambridge and is currently editing the *History of Parliament: the Commons 1640–60* for the History of Parliament Trust.

DR T. C. BARNARD has published *Cromwellian Ireland: English government and reform in Ireland 1649–1660* (Oxford, 1975), and *The English republic* (London, 1982). With Jane Clark he edited *Lord Burlington: architecture, art and life* (London, 1994), and he is editing a collection of essays on scholars, learning and the transmission of ideas in medieval and early modern Ireland. The author of numerous articles on Irish history and Anglo-Irish topics, he is engaged on a study of the origins, ideologies and characteristics of Irish Protestant society between 1641 and 1760. Since 1976 he has been a fellow and tutor of Hertford College, Oxford.

PROFESSOR NICHOLAS CANNY is author of *The Elizabethan conquest of Ireland* (New York, 1976), *The upstart earl: A study of the social and mental world of Richard Boyle, first earl of Cork, 1566–1643* (Cambridge, 1982) and *Kingdom and colony. Ireland in the Atlantic world 1560–1800* (Baltimore, 1988) together with numerous articles on the history of early modern Ireland and colonial America published both in anthologies and conference proceedings and in such journals as *Past and Present, Irish Economic and Social History* and *Irish Historical Studies*. He also co-edited *The westward enterprise: English activities in Ireland, the Atlantic and America 1480–1650* (Liverpool, 1978) and *Colonial identity in the Atlantic world 1500–1800* (Princeton, 1987), and has edited a volume entitled *Europeans on the move: studies of European migration, 1500–1800* (Oxford, 1994). Dr Canny, who is Professor of Modern History at

University College, Galway, is currently completing a comprehensive study of British settlement in Ireland and the Irish response to that presence which will be published by Oxford University Press under the title *Ireland in the English colonial system, 1550–1650*.

PROFESSOR AIDAN CLARKE, author of *The old English in Ireland 1625–1642* (Ithaca and London, 1966) and *The Graces* (Dundalk, 1968), has contributed articles on the earl of Antrim, Sir Piers Crosby, Bishop Bedell, Ireland and the 'General Crisis', the Ulster plantations, the Irish rebellion of 1641 and the 1641 depositions to *Irish Sword, Past and Present, Irish Historical Studies, Proceedings of the Royal Irish Academy* and to a host of edited volumes, including volume III of *A new history of Ireland*. Professor Clarke is Erasmus Smith's Professor of Modern History at Trinity College, Dublin and a past president of the Royal Irish Academy.

DR RAYMOND GILLESPIE is author of *Colonial Ulster: the settlement of East Ulster 1600–1641* (Cork, 1985) and *The transformation of the Irish economy, 1550–1700* (Dundalk, 1991) and co-editor of regional studies on Counties Mayo, Longford and Galway. He has written numerous articles on the early modern Irish economy and on the origins of the 1641 rebellion. Dr Gillespie is a lecturer in History at St Patrick's College, Maynooth and is currently working on a book on popular religion in early modern Ireland.

DR PHIL KILROY is author of *Protestant dissent and controversy in Ireland 1660–1714* (Cork, 1994). She has contributed articles on 'Women and the Reformation' to Margaret MacCurtain and Mary O'Dowd, *Women in early modern Ireland* (Dublin, 1991) and on 'Protestantism in Ulster, 1610–1641' to Brian Mac Cuarta (ed.), *Ulster 1641* (Belfast, 1993). She is currently writing a scholarly biography of the French educationalist, Madeleine Sophie Barat, 1779–1865.

DR KEVIN MCKENNY, using an extensive computer database, has completed his dissertation on the 'North West Ulster settlers and their Lagan army, 1641–1685'. He is author of 'Charles II's Irish Cavaliers: the 1649 officers and the restoration land settlement', *Irish Historical Studies* (November, 1993) and is an adjunct lecturer in the departments of Irish Studies and History at the City University of New York, Queen's College.

PROFESSOR ROLF LOEBER, author of *A biographical dictionary of architects in Ireland, 1600–1720* (London, 1981) and *The geography and practice of English colonisation in Ireland from 1534 to 1609* (Dublin, 1991), has written several articles on the activities of the Dutch in seventeenth-century Ireland and on early modern Irish architecture. He is Professor of Psychiatry, Psychology and Epidemiology at the University of Pittsburgh and is currently working on the geography of Gaelic lordships and the North American ventures of Puritans who settled in seventeenth-century Ireland.

DR JANE OHLMEYER, author of *Civil war and restoration in the three Stuart kingdoms: the career of Randal MacDonnell, marquis of Antrim 1609–83* (Cambridge, 1993), has also contributed articles on the marquis of Antrim, Irish privateers and the Irish Civil War of the 1640s to *The Historical Journal, History Today* and *Mariner's Mirror*. She teaches Irish History at Yale University and is currently working on a monograph on the Irish Civil Wars and on aristocratic culture and indebtedness in early modern Ireland.

DR MICHELLE O RIORDAN, author of *The Gaelic mind and the collapse of the Gaelic world* (Cork, 1990), has also written several articles on early modern Irish literature. She is the publications officer at the School of Celtic Studies in Dublin.

PROFESSOR GEOFFREY PARKER has written extensively on early modern European history. His works on military history include *The army of Flanders and the Spanish road 1567–1659: the logistics of Spanish victory and defeat in the Low Countries' wars* (Cambridge, 1972; 3rd edn., 1989), *The Thirty Years War* (London, 1984) and *The military revolution: military innovation and the rise of the west, 1500–1800* (Cambridge, 1988). Professor Parker is Robert A. Lovett Professor of Military and Naval History at Yale University and is currently completing a study of the grand strategy of Philip II of Spain.

DR SCOTT WHEELER, author of 'Logistics and supply in Cromwell's conquest of Ireland' in Mark Charles Fissel (ed.), *War and government in Britain 1598–1650* (Manchester and New York, 1991) and 'The logistics of the Cromwellian conquest of Scotland, 1650–1651', *War and society* (1992), is an Associate Professor of History at the US Military Academy, West Point.

ACKNOWLEDGMENTS

Like so many other recent works on early modern Irish history, this collection of essays arose from a conversation with Raymond Gillespie in the summer of 1990. I am especially grateful to Dr Gillespie for prompting me to edit this volume and for his advice and input, especially in the planning stages. Aidan Clarke, Tom Connors and Kevin Whelan have also been particularly supportive of this project and, from the outset, have allowed me to draw upon their expertise. I am deeply indebted to them and to Toby Barnard for reading early drafts of each essay and for making numerous helpful and incisive comments and to Nicholas Canny for casting an eagle eye over the introduction, chronology and bibliography. I am very grateful to Ian Gentles and Geoffrey Parker who read the entire manuscript in its final form and made a number of invaluable suggestions for improvement. My thanks also to William Davies at Cambridge University Press who was, as always, a delight to work with, and to Frances Nugent for her meticulous copy-editing. However, my greatest debt of gratitude is to the contributors and I would like to take this opportunity to thank them for their co-operation, for their endless patience with my editing and for their general enthusiasm for the project. Last but not least I would like to say a special word of thanks to my mother, Shirley, whose baby-sitting skills remain unsurpassed, and to my children, Richard and James, who have distracted and delighted me as I edited this volume.

CHRONOLOGY OF EVENTS,
1639–1660

(Major military encounters are indicated in **bold**) [1]

Date	Ireland	Scotland and England	The continent
1639	21 May: Proclamation of the 'black oath'	May–June: First Bishops' War (ended by Treaty of Berwick, 18 June)	
	Aug: Poor harvests (since 1636)		
			Oct: Dutch destroy Spanish fleet at the battle of the Downs
			Dec: *c.* 1,300 Irish troops serving in Flanders (under Owen Roe O'Neill)
1640			Feb: Strafford asks Spain for assistance
	16 Mar–17 June: first session of Charles I's second Irish Parliament		
	1 Apr: Irish parliament adjourns to 1 June	13 Apr–5 May: Short Parliament in England	

[1] This is based on the relevant sections of T. W. Moody, F. X. Martin and F. J. Byrne (eds.), *A new history of Ireland*, VIII: *A chronology of Irish history to 1976* (Oxford, 1982) and on material in the following chapters.

Date	Ireland	Scotland and England	The continent
			May: Revolt of Catalonia (until 1652)
		June: Alonso de Cárdenas becomes Spanish ambassador in London (until Oct 1655)	June–Aug: Owen Roe O'Neill defends Arras against the French
	July: Wentworth's 'New Army' assembles at Carrickfergus		July: Olivares offers Charles I financial assistance
		20 Aug: Scottish army crosses the Tweed; beginning of Second Bishops' War (ended by Treaty of Ripon, 21 Oct)	
	1 Oct–12 Nov: second session of Charles I's second Irish Parliament		
		3 Nov: Meeting of the 'Long Parliament'	
		11 Nov: Strafford impeached	
			Dec: Revolt of Portugal (until 1668)
1641			Gennep (governor Thomas Preston) surrenders to Dutch after a bitter struggle during which the Irish troops distinguished themselves
			Francisco de Melo becomes governor of the Spanish Netherlands

Date	Ireland	Scotland and England	The continent
	26 Jan–5 Mar: third session of Charles I's second Irish Parliament	30 Jan: Articles of impeachment against Strafford sent to House of Lords	Jan: Catalonia accepts French protection
		15 Feb: Triennial Act	
		22 Mar: Beginning of Strafford's trail	
	11 May–17 Nov: fourth session of Charles I's second Irish Parliament	12 May: Strafford executed; unsuccessful plans for use of force against Parliament	May: Mary Stuart marries William, prince of Orange
			June: Portugal and France sign a mutual aid treaty
			Portugal and Netherlands sign 10-year truce
			Treaty of Hamburg between France and Sweden
			July: Soissons conspiracy in France
		Aug: Charles I leaves London for Edinburgh	Aug: French fleet arrives in Lisbon to help Portuguese rebels
		Sept: Peace concluded with Scots	
	22 Oct: Outbreak of the Ulster rebellion	28 Oct: Scottish Parliament offers to send an army of 10,000 to crush the Ulster rising	
	23 Oct: Alleged attempt to seize Dublin thwarted		

Date	Ireland	Scotland and England	The continent
	26 Oct: Sir Phelim O'Neill captures Armagh		
	4 Nov: Sir Phelim O'Neill issues commission purporting to be from the king	22 Nov: Publication of Grand Remonstrance	
	11 Nov: Ormond appointed lieutenant-general of the king's army		
	16–17 Nov: Brief meeting of Irish Parliament		
	21 Nov: 'Rebels' attack and plunder Lord Moore's residence at Mellifont		
	21 Nov: 'Rebels' begin siege of Drogheda (raised in Mar 1642)		
	28 Nov: 'Rebel' attack on Lisburn repulsed		
	29 Nov: Army, sent to relieve Drogheda, defeated at Julianstown, County Meath; Irish insurgents open negotiations with Old English		
	End Nov: Sir Charles Coote garrisons Newcastle, County Wicklow and relieves Wicklow Castle		

Date	Ireland	Scotland and England	The continent
	1 Dec: Coote skirmishes with 'rebels' at Kilcoole before returning to Dublin	1 Dec: Charles I presented with Grand Remonstrance	
	3 Dec: Antrim and lords of Pale summoned to a conference in Dublin on 8 Dec; they refuse		
	15 Dec: Coote attacks Santry and Clontarf		
	30 Dec: Sir Simon Harcourt and 1,100 foot arrive in Dublin from England		
	Dec: Alliance between Old English and Ulster insurgents; Counties Roscommon, Mayo, Sligo, Kilkenny and Tipperary join the rising		
1642	c. 22–37,000 Protestant and c. 11–23,000 Catholic troops in arms	1642: Publication of Henry Jones, *A remonstrance of divers remarkable passages concerning the church and kingdom of Ireland* (London)	
	Dublin administration and Confederates strike coinages		
	Jan: Catholics in Counties Antrim, Limerick and Clare join the rising	Jan: Attempt to arrest the Five Members; Charles I leaves London; passage of the Militia Ordinance	Jan: England unofficially recognizes Portugal's independence
	Early Jan: Coote routs 'rebel' forces at Swords		
	11 Jan: O'Neill's attempt to take Drogheda fails		

Date	Ireland	Scotland and England	The continent
	11 Jan–9 Feb 1647: fifth session of Charles I's second Irish Parliament		
	1–3 Feb: Ormond burns Newcastle and takes Naas, County Kildare		Feb: Henrietta Maria travels to Dutch Republic for assistance
	12 Feb: Lord Lambert defeats Wicklow 'rebels' and clears Dublin of insurgents		
	Mid-Feb: Rebellion spreads to County Kerry		
	20 Feb: 1,500 foot under Col. Monck arrive in Dublin from England		
	End Feb: Viscount Muskerry and County Cork Catholics join the insurrection; a further assault on Drogheda fails		
	Mar: Siege of Drogheda raised	19 Mar: 'Adventurers' Act'	
	Lords Justice later allege that by 16 March 154,000 Protestants have been killed by 'rebels' (more realistic figure is c. 4,000)		
	19 Mar: Town of Galway declares for the 'rebels' and besieges Galway fort (to June 1643)		
	End Mar: Henry Tichborne retakes Ardee and Dundalk		

Date	Ireland	Scotland and England	The continent
	2 Apr: Ormond campaigns in County Kildare and relieves Borris, Birr and Knockmenease	Apr: Gates of Hull shut against the king	
	15 Apr: Ormond defeats insurgents at at Kilrush; a Scottish army under Monroe lands at Carrickfergus		
	29 Apr: Skirmish between Scots and forces of Sir Phelim O'Neill's at Kilwarlin Wood, near Lisburn, County Down		
	End Apr: Siege of Cork raised; Muskerry besieges Limerick Castle; Coote relieves Castlegeasal and Castlejordan and captures Philipstown and Trim		
	May: Scots recapture Newry and clear County Antrim of insurgents		**May: Spanish Army of Flanders defeats the French at Honnecourt**
	Early May: Tichborne seizes Carlingford		
	7 May: Insurgents fail to recapture Trim but Coote 'received his ticket to hell'		
	10–13 May: Meetings of Catholic clergy and laity at Kilkenny		

Date	Ireland	Scotland and England	The continent
	End May: Government offensive grinds to a standstill for want of victuals and supplies; two English regiments arrive in Munster		
	June: Confederate Oath of Association drawn up and provisional Supreme Council nominated	19 June: Charles I rejects Nineteen Propositions	
	Scots march on Lisnagarvey, Armagh and Charlemont		
	Insurgents besiege Limerick		
	Alleged 'massacre' of Protestants at Kilmore		
	10 June: First meeting of Presbytery of the Scottish army at Carrickfergus		
	July: Owen Roe O'Neill and some veterans from Flanders land at Doe Castle, County Donegal		
	10,000 Scots now in Ulster		
	25 Aug: Inchiquin's victory at Liscarroll, County Cork	22 Aug: Outbreak of First English Civil War	Aug: French take Perpignan (Catalonia) from Spain
	Sept: Thomas Preston lands at Wexford		
	Sept: Good local harvests		

Date	Ireland	Scotland and England	The continent
	24 Oct–21 Nov: First confederate General Assembly	**23 Oct: Battle of Edgehill (royalist victory)**	
	Nov: Inchiquin wins battle of Bandonbridge		24 Nov/4 Dec: Cardinal Richelieu dies; succeeded by Mazarin as French chief minister (until 1661)
			Dec: Confederates appoint representatives in Spanish Netherlands (Bourke); Paris (O'Hartegan); Rome (Wadding); Madrid (Magennis and Talbot)
			Dec 1642–Feb 1643: Confederate agents issue c. twenty letters of marque; by end of 1642 the confederate navy allegedly comprised c. 30 ships, rising to c. 40–50 warships by the mid-1640s
1643	c. 27–35,000 Protestant and c. 14–22,000 Catholic troops in arms		1643: French agents disseminate anti-Spanish propaganda in Naples
			Jan: Fall of Olivares
	Feb: Preston takes Barre	1 Feb: Oxford Propositions	
	18 Mar: Ormond, after failing to take New Ross, defeats Preston near Old Ross		

Date	Ireland	Scotland and England	The continent
	23 Apr: King orders Ormond to treat with the Confederates		
	20 May–19 June: Second confederate General Assembly		4/14 May Louis XIII of France dies; succeeded by Louis XIV (until 1715)
	May: Ormond's troops mutiny in Dublin		
			9/19 May: Habsburg defeat at battle of Rocroi
	13 June: Owen Roe O'Neill defeated by Sir Robert Stewart at Clones, County Monaghan		
	20 June: Fort of Galway surrenders to Confederates		
	24 June: Truce negotiations between Ormond and the Confederates begin		
	July: Papal agent, Pier Francesco Scarampi, arrives at Kilkenny	1 July: Westminster Assembly (sat until 1649)	
	July: Owen Roe O'Neill's forces defeat English at Trim	14 July: 'Doubling Ordinance' passed by English Parliament	
		26 July: Royalists capture Bristol	

Date	Ireland	Scotland and England	The continent
	6 Aug: Town of Galway joins the Confederates		Aug: Negotiations at Westphalia to end the Thirty Years War begin (until 1648)
	15 Sept: One-year cease-fire concluded between the Royalists and Confederates	25 Sept: Solemn League and Covenant between the English Parliament and the Scots	
	Sept: Disastrous harvests		
	7 Nov–1 Dec: Third confederate General Assembly		
	13 Nov: Ormond appointed lord lieutenant by Charles I		
	Nov 19: Confederates nominate seven delegates to meet Charles I at Oxford		
1644	*c.* 19–25,000 Protestant and *c.* 18–24,000 Catholic troops in arms		Opening of peace talks with French in Münster
	Inchiquin strikes a coinage (further issues in Cork, 1645 and 1646) and expels Catholics from Cork		Marquis of Castel Rodrigo becomes governor of Spanish Netherlands
			c. 1,230 Irish mercenaries arrive for service in Spain; by 1652 *c.* 22,200 had left Ireland for Spanish service; and by 1649 *c.* 7,000 more had left for service in France

Date	Ireland	Scotland and England	The continent
	Jan: Charles I authorizes Antrim to request arms, men and supplies from the Confederates	19 Jan: Scots army invades England 25 Jan: Royalist defeat at battle of Nantwich	
	Jan: Foissotte (Spanish agent, until early 1652) and de la Monnerie (French agent, until Feb 1646) arrive		
	Mar: Preston captures Duncannon	24 Mar: Confederate agents arrive at Oxford to negotiate with Charles	
		1 Apr: Charles I grants plenary powers to Glamorgan	
		Apr: Inchiquin visits the king in Oxford; denied the lord presidency of Munster	
	14 May: Monroe seizes Belfast		
	June: Confederates allow French and Spanish to recruit 2,000 Irish troops	29 June: Royalist victory at Cropredy Bridge	June: Dutch unofficially 'recognize' Parliament
	24 June: Ormond instructed to continue negotiations with the Confederates		
	27 June: Antrim sends c. 2,000 Irish troops to fight in Scotland with Montrose		

Date	Ireland	Scotland and England	The continent
	17 July: Inchiquin abandons royalist cause and declares for Parliament	**2 July: Charles I defeated at Marston Moor**	July: Innocent X succeeds Urban VIII as Pope
	20 July–31 Aug: Fourth confederate General Assembly		
	End July: The earl of Castlehaven's confederate army reaches Armagh		
	July–Oct: O'Neill and Castlehaven campaign in Ulster; stalemate at Charlemont		
		Aug: Parliament lose forty heavy guns to the king at Lostwithiel	Aug: French occupy Alsace
			c. 600 Irish troops serving in Flanders (under Patrick O'Neill)
	Sept: Confederates abandon siege of Youghal	**1 Sept: Montrose's victory at Tippermuir, near Perth**	
		22 Oct: Newcastle falls to Parliamentarians	
		24 Oct: English Parliament's 'no-quarter' ordinance for Irishmen captured in England or Wales	
		24 Nov: Uxbridge Propositions	Nov: Henrietta Maria arrives in Paris

Date	Ireland	Scotland and England	The continent
		19 Dec: Self Denying Ordinance (leads to creation of New Model Army)	31 Dec: Richard Bellings seeks continental aid for the Confederates
1645	*c.* 18–25,000 Protestant and *c.* 14–20,000 Catholic troops in arms		French capture ten towns in the Spanish Netherlands
			Publication of Conor O'Mahony, *Disputatio Apologetica* (Lisbon)
	20 Jan: Preston invests Duncannon fort (taken 19 Mar)	Jan: Parliament appoints Inchiquin as lord president of Munster	
		2 Feb: Montrose's victory at Inverlochy	
			Mar: Edward Tirrell replaces O'Hartegan as confederate agent in Paris
			Habsburg defeat at battle of Jankov makes German peace more likely
	15 May–31 August: Fifth confederate General Assembly	**9 May: Montrose's victory at Auldearn, near Nairn**	
	End June: Glamorgan arrives in Ireland	**14 June: Charles I defeated at Naseby**	June: Turks besiege Crete leading to war with Venice (until 1664)
	8 July: A parliamentary force under Sir Charles Coote takes Sligo	**2 July: Montrose's victory at Alford**	

Date	Ireland	Scotland and England	The continent
	25 Aug: Secret treaty between Glamorgan and the Confederates	**15 Aug: Montrose's victory at Kilsyth**	**Aug: French victory at Alerheim**
		10 Sept: Parliament takes Bristol	
		13 Sept: Montrose defeated at Philiphaugh	
	12 Oct: Papal nuncio Rinuccini arrives in County Kerry with Massari		
			10/20 Nov: Treaty between Innocent X and Sir Kenelm Digby signed at Rome
	20 Dec: Second secret treaty, dictated by Rinuccini, between Glamorgan and the Confederates		
	26 Dec: Glamorgan arrested by Ormond (released 22 Jan 1646)		
1646	*c.* 16–25,000 Protestant and *c.* 15–23,000 Catholic troops in arms	Publication of Sir John Temple's, *The Irish rebellion* (London)	*c.* 140 Irish mercenaries arrive for service in Spain
	Ormond strikes a gold coinage in Dublin		
	Jan: De la Torre (Spanish agent) arrives (until late 1649)	26 Jan: Parliament appoints Philip Sidney, Viscount Lisle as commander-in-chief for projected Irish campaign	Jan: Dutch Republic's negotiators arrive in Münster

Date	Ireland	Scotland and England	The continent
	7 Feb–4 Mar: Sixth confederate General Assembly	3 Feb: Chester falls to Parliament	
	19 Feb: Confederates prolong truce with king to 1 May		
	Late Feb: Dumolin (French agent) arrives		
	28 Mar: Peace agreed between Confederates and Ormond		
		15 Apr: Parliament appoints Philip Sidney as lord lieutenant of Ireland for one year	
		5 May: Charles I surrenders to Scots near Newark	
	5 June: Confederate victory over the Scots at Benburb, County Tyrone	25 June: Oxford surrenders	
	June: Roscommon surrenders to Preston, who fails to move against Sligo		
	14 July: Capture of Bunratty Castle, County Clare, by Confederates	July: Charles I rejects the Newcastle Propositions	July: Congress of Münster; provisional peace articles signed by Dutch and Spaniards
	30 July: Proclamation of the 'First Ormond Peace' in Dublin (3 Aug in Kilkenny)	July: Brothers Bellièvre appointed by France to mediate between the king and Parliament (until Apr 1649)	

Date	Ireland	Scotland and England	The continent
	12 Aug: Rinuccini's legatine synod declares Confederates adhering to the Ormond Peace to have broken the oath of association		Summer: *c*. 200 Irish troops serving in Army of Flanders (under Patrick O'Neill)
	1 Sept: Rinuccini's synod excommunicates all who favour the Ormond Peace	3 Sept: Montrose leaves Scotland for Norway	Sept: Franco–Imperial preliminary peace
	18 Sept: Rinuccini returns to Kilkenny to dictate terms to the Supreme Council		
	26 Sept: New Council nominated under presidency of Rinuccini		
	Sept: Ormond announces his intention of surrendering Dublin to Parliament		
	Sept–Nov: Confederate offensive against Dublin (8–10,000 Confederates versus 3–4,000 Royalists) fails to take the city		
		Oct: Publication of *Ormonds curtain drawn* (London)	**Oct: French take Dunkirk**
		26 Nov: Completion of Westminster Assembly's confession of faith	
	Late 1646: Confederates allow Spain to recruit two regiments and France one		Dec: Peace of Vienna between Habsburgs and Transylvania

Date	Ireland	Scotland and England	The continent
1647	c. 18–26,500 Protestant and c. 20–30,000 Catholic troops in arms		500 Irish mercenaries arrive for service in Spain
	Early 1647: La Monnerie returns (until Jan 1649) with Du Talon		
	10 Jan–4 Apr: Seventh confederate General Assembly	30 Jan: Scots hand Charles I over to Parliament	Jan: Spanish–Dutch truce (until 1648)
	2 Feb: Declaration of the confederate assembly against the 'First Ormond Peace'		c. 1,147 Irish troops serving in Flanders (largely under Patrick O'Neill and John Murphy)
	Feb: Lisle arrives in Munster		
	Mar: New oath of association adopted by the confederate assembly	12 Mar: Parliament refuses to pay Scottish army in Ulster	
		Mar: Parliament dismisses Lisle	
			Apr: Archduke Leopold becomes governor of the Spanish Netherlands
	May: Dungarvan falls to Inchiquin	May–June: Covenanters regain the Isles	May: Revolt of Sicily against Spain (until Apr 1648)
	7 June: Parliamentary force of 2,000 under Colonel Michael Jones lands near Dublin	4 June: Charles I seized by parliamentary army at Holmby, Northants	

Date	Ireland	Scotland and England	The continent
	19 June: Ormond surrenders Dublin to Parliament		
	End June: Parliamentary commissioners recommend that the Dublin clergy replace the Book of Common Prayer with the Directory of Worship		
	28 July: Ormond withdraws to England		July: Revolt of Naples against Spain
	8 Aug: Jones defeats Preston at Dungan's Hill, near Trim	1 Aug: *Heads of the Proposals*	
	Aug: O'Neill's army fails to take Sligo then mutinies	6 Aug: New Model Army occupies Westminster	
		Aug: Ormond confers with king at Hampton Court	
	14 Sept: Inchiquin sacks Cashel		
	Oct: Jones campaigns against O'Neill and clears northern Leinster of confederate strongholds	Late Oct–early Nov: Putney debates	Oct: Spain declares bankruptcy
	Nov: O'Neill fails to recapture lost garrisons and to take Dublin	11 Nov: King escapes from army	

Date	Ireland	Scotland and England	The continent
	12 Nov–24 Dec: Eighth confederate General Assembly	15 Nov: Leveller-inspired mutiny in army suppressed	
	13 Nov: Inchiquin defeats confederate army of Munster at Knocknanuss, near Mallow (County Cork) and captures major towns in Munster (except Limerick, Clonmel and Waterford)		
	Nov: O'Neill campaigns in Leinster; withdraws when Jones pursues		
		26 Dec: King and Scots sign an 'Engagement'	Dec: French fleet arrives to help Neapolitans (until Jan 1648)
1648	c. 14–38,000 Protestant and c. 18–24,000 Catholic troops in arms		
	Outbreaks of smallpox and dysentery		
	Spring: Talks between Parliamentarians and nuncio's followers begin		
		Jan: Parliament breaks off negotiations with king	20/30 Jan: Peace of Münster between Dutch Republic and Spain (ratified 5/15 May)
	Feb: Inchiquin begins negotiations with Confederates		Feb: Confederate envoys sent to France and Rome

Date	Ireland	Scotland and England	The continent
	3 Apr: Inchiquin and Supreme Council sign a cease-fire	28 Apr: English Royalists take Berwick	
	4 Apr: Ulster Council of War accepts the Engagement	29 Apr: English Royalists take Carlisle	
	20 May: Declaration of truce between Inchiquin and Confederates	May–Aug: Second Civil War in England	May: Outbreak of Fronde in France
			19/29 May: French take Ypres
	27 May: Rinuccini excommunicates supporters of 'Inchiquin Truce'		
	31 May: Supreme Council appeals to Rome against the excommunication		
		27 June: Publication of Westminster Confession of Faith	
		June: Scottish Committee of Estates prepared to make common cause with Inchiquin and Confederates	
		8 July: Hamilton, with 9,000 Scottish engagers, crosses into Cumberland	
	Aug: Owen Roe O'Neill in direct contact with Michael Jones	**17 Aug: Oliver Cromwell defeats Scottish Royalists at Preston, Lancs and invades Scotland**	**10/20 Aug: French defeat Spain at battle of Lens**

Date	Ireland	Scotland and England	The continent
			Aug: Chmielnicki's revolt in Ukraine (until 1654)
	Sept: Belfast and Coleraine surrender; Monck takes Carrickfergus		
	4 Sept–17 Jan 1649: Ninth and final confederate General Assembly		
	30 Sept: Ormond lands at Cork		
	8 Oct: Antrim leads a rebellion against Ormond; quickly crushed		14/24 Oct: Peace of Westphalia ends war in Germany (began 1618)
	21 Nov: Confederate envoys return from Rome		
		2 Dec: Army occupies Westminster	
		6 Dec: Colonel Pride's purge of Parliament	
		Mid-Dec: Negotiations between Independents and Old Irish begin in London (until Aug 1649)	
	End 1648: Confederation virtually bankrupt		
1649	c. 25–38,000 Protestant and c. 18–28,000 Catholic troops in arms		Spain recovers Ypres

Date	Ireland	Scotland and England	The continent
	Early 1649: Count of Berehaven (Spanish agent) arrives		*c.* 2,200 Irish mercenaries arrive in Spain
	17 Jan: Declaration of 'Second Ormond Peace'; Confederates to raise 18,000-man army	20 Jan: Instrument of Government drawn up 30 Jan: Charles I executed	Jan: French court leaves Paris for St Germain Dutch delegates sent to London to plead for king's life
	23 Feb: Rinuccini leaves for continent	5 Feb: Charles II proclaimed king by Scots	
	Late Feb: Rupert and twelve royalist warships arrive at Kinsale	6 Feb: Abolition of House of Lords 7 Feb: Abolition of monarchy 13 Feb: Council of State appointed	
		30 Mar: Cromwell approved as commander-in-chief in Ireland	Mar: Treaty of Rueil and temporary end to Fronde; French court returns to Paris
	1 Apr: Derry besieged by Ulster Scots; relieved by Owen Roe O'Neill (8 Aug)		Apr: Imperial cities admit religious parity
	May–June: Jones reinforced from England	14 May: Defeat of Leveller mutineers at Burford	
	8 May: Truce concluded between Monck and O'Neill	19 May: England declared a 'Commonwealth'	

Date	Ireland	Scotland and England	The continent
		May: Publication of John Milton, *Observations* (London)	
	June–July: Confederates advance on Dublin	5 June: Parliamentary army ordered to leave for Ireland	
	July: Plague reaches Galway from continent (until 1652)	10 July: Cromwell leaves London for Ireland	
	2 Aug: Ormond's army defeated by Jones at Rathmines		
	15 Aug: Cromwell lands near Dublin		
	11 Sept: Fall of Drogheda		
	11 Oct: Fall of Wexford		
	19 Oct: Surrender of New Ross		
	20 Oct: Treaty between Ormond and Owen Roe		
	2 Nov: Scots surrender Carrickfergus to Parliament		Nov: Prince Rupert and royalist fleet take refuge off Lisbon
	6 Nov: Death of Owen Roe O'Neill		
	20 Nov: Fall of Carrick-on-Suir		
	24 Nov: Waterford invested (siege raised 2 Dec)		

Date	Ireland	Scotland and England	The continent
	Late 1649–1652: *c.* 13,000 Irish soldiers leave for service in the Habsburg armies		
1650			Fronde flares up again
	3 Feb: Fethard, County Tipperary surrenders		
	24 Feb: Cahir surrenders		
	18 Mar: Heber MacMahon succeeds Owen Roe O'Neill	Mid-Mar: Montrose arrives in Orkney with 1,200 continental mercenaries	Mar: Robert Blake and Commonwealth navy blockade royalist fleet off Lisbon
	27 Mar: Kilkenny surrenders		
	10 Apr: Parliamentary victory at battle of Macroom, County Cork		
	10 May: Clonmel surrenders	May: Montrose executed; last royalist stronghold in Scotland falls to Parliament	
	26 May: Cromwell leaves Ireland; replaced by Henry Ireton		
	21 June: Parliamentary victory at battle of Scarrifhollis, County Donegal destroys Army of Ulster	June: Cromwell returns from Ireland. Beginning of the 'Third Civil War' in Britain	
	24 July: Carlow surrenders	July: Cromwell leads army into Scotland	

Date	Ireland	Scotland and England	The continent
	6 Aug: Waterford surrenders		
	12 Aug: Ormond repudiated by Catholic bishops		
	14 Aug: Charlemont fort surrenders		
	17 Aug: Duncannon surrenders		
	15 Sept: Catholic bishops excommunicate supporters of Ormond	**3 Sept: Scots defeated by Cromwell at battle of Dunbar**	
	26 Nov: Assembly of the Catholic laity at Loughrea, County Galway		
	6 Dec: Ormond appoints the marquis of Clanricard as his deputy		Dec: Philip IV of Spain recognizes the English Commonwealth
	11 Dec: Ormond leaves Ireland for France		
1651			1651/2: *c.* 1,120 Irish mercenaries arrive in Spain
	Jan–June: Efforts by Protestant clergy to preach in Irish	1 Jan: Charles II crowned at Scone	
	26 Feb: Stephen de Henin, ambassador of Charles, duke of Lorraine arrives to treat with Confederates		Feb: Mazarin goes into temporary exile

Date	Ireland	Scotland and England	The continent
			May: Anthony Ascham murdered in Madrid by Royalists
	4 June: Limerick invested (surrenders 27 Oct)		
		3 Sept: Defeat of Charles II at Worcester ends 'Wars of the Three Kingdoms'	
		9 Oct: First Navigation Act	
	26 Nov: Ireton dies; replaced by Edmund Ludlow		
1652	English standing army of *c.* 30,000 stationed in Ireland	Publication of Gerard Boate, *Ireland's naturall history* (London)	*c.* 4,500 Irish mercenaries arrive in Spain
		Feb: Act of Indemnity and Oblivion	
	12 Apr: Galway surrenders		
	28 June: Clanricard surrenders		
	July: Lorraine sends pinnace to Innishbofin Island	8 July: Outbreak of First Anglo-Dutch war (ends 5 Apr 1654)	
		9 July: Charles Fleetwood appointed commander–in–chief in Ireland (arrived 10 Sept)	
		12 Aug: Act for Settlement of Ireland passed	

Date	Ireland	Scotland and England	The continent
			Sept: Blake destroys French squadron off Dunkirk; France recognizes the Commonwealth
			Oct: Barcelona submits to Philip IV
			Nov: Dutch Admiral Tromp defeats Blake
1653			End of Fronde
			c. 9,000 Irish mercenaries arrive in Spain; many travel on to Flanders
			1653/4: *c.* 2,250 Irishmen serving in Army of Flanders (largely under D. Costello, J. Kannan and P. O'Reilly)
	6 Jan: Catholic priests to be expelled from Ireland		
	4 Feb: Sir Phelim O'Neill captured (executed 10 Mar)		18–21 Feb: Blake defeats Tromp at battle of Portland
	Apr: Surrender of Cloughoughter completes Cromwellian conquest of Ireland	20 Apr: Cromwell expels 'rump' of Long Parliament	
	23 May: Order for transplantation of Ulster Presbyterians		

Date	Ireland	Scotland and England	The continent
		20 June: Drawing of lots for adventurers' lands in London	2–4 June: Blake defeats Tromp; Dutch ask for peace (rejected)
		22 June: Order authorizing the 'Gross', 'Civil' and 'Down' surveys	
	1 July: Order for transplantation of vagrants to America	4 July–12 Dec: 'Little' or 'Barebones' parliament (six Irish MPs and five Scottish MPs)	31 July: Blake defeats Tromp off Scheveningen; peace negotiated
	2 July: Order for transplantation of native Irish to Connacht or Clare (by 1 May 1654)		
		26 Sept: Act of Satisfaction	
		15 Dec: 'Instrument of Government' accepted by Cromwell	
		16 Dec: Cromwell becomes lord protector	
1654			France briefly launches another anti–Spanish expedition to Naples
			c. 3,500 Irish mercenaries arrive in Spain
	6 Jan: Appointment of Loughrea commissioners to allot land to transplanted Irish		

Date	Ireland	Scotland and England	The continent
			Feb: Spaniards arrest Charles, duke of Lorraine
		Mar–Sept: Glencairn's rising in Scotland	
	14 Apr: Order directing 'Civil Survey' to be undertaken		Apr: Treaty of London ends war with Dutch Republic; alliance signed
	27 June: Ordinance in favour of Munster Protestants who supported Cromwell in 1649		
	2 Aug: Act of Bangor		
		3 Sept: Meeting of First Protectorate Parliament (dissolved 22 January, 1655); thirty Irish MPs	
	20 Oct: Irish Catholics prohibited from entering Scotland		
	30 Nov: All 'transplantable persons' ordered to move by 1 Mar 1655		
	11 Dec: William Petty ordered to survey land forfeited for soldiers ('Down Survey')		Dec: c. 1,700 Irishmen serving in the Army of Flanders (under John Murphy and P. O'Reilly)
	28 Dec: Appointment of Athlone commissioners to decide claims of transplanted Irish		

Date	Ireland	Scotland and England	The continent
1655	Quakers arrive in Ireland in significant numbers		Alexander VIII succeeds Innocent X as Pope
		Jan: Publication of Vincent Gookin, *The great case of transplantation in Ireland discussed* (London)	
		Mar: Publication of Richard Lawrence, *The interest of England in the Irish transplantation stated* (London)	
		Mar–May: Penruddock's rising in England	
			Apr: Vaudois Protestants massacred in Piedmont
			10–17 May: Jamaica seized from Spain by English
	9 July: Arrival of Henry Cromwell		
		Aug–Oct: Rule of Major-Generals in England (until Jan 1657)	
			Oct: Peace between England and France; Charles II to be expelled
		Oct: England declares war on Spain	

Date	Ireland	Scotland and England	The continent
1656	Henry Cromwell considers raising a militia in Ireland; vetoed by Oliver Cromwell		
		17 Sept: Second Protectorate Parliament (dissolved 4 Feb 1658)	Sept: Capture of Spanish treasure ships off Cadiz
1657	English standing army of *c.* 9,000 serving in Ireland		*c.* 1,200 Irishmen serving in Army of Flanders
		23 Feb: Proposal to make Cromwell king	
		31 Mar: 'Humble Petition and Advice' presented to Cromwell	Mar: Treaty of Paris – England and France undertake the reconquest of Mardyk, Dunkirk and Gravelines (operations begin in May)
			Apr: Blake's victory against Spain off Cadiz
		8 May: Cromwell refuses crown	May: Anglo-French treaty – Cromwell to help France recover Catalonia
	26 June: 'Act for the attainder of the rebels in Ireland'		
	17 Nov: Henry Cromwell appointed lord deputy (lord lieutenant, 6 Oct 1658)		

Date	Ireland	Scotland and England	The continent
1658			1658: Philip IV offers his daughter, Maria Teresia, in marriage to Louis XIV
	23 Apr: Convention of ministers meets in Dublin		
			May: Dunkirk besieged by French and English
			4 June: Battle of the Dunes followed by fall of Dunkirk to English
		3 Sept: Oliver Cromwell dies; Richard Cromwell proclaimed protector	
1659		27 Jan–22 Apr: Third Protectorate Parliament	
	Mar: Convention advocated tithe-supported ministry	Mid-Mar: Royalist overtures made to Monck	
		6 (or 7) May: 'Rump' of Long Parliament reassembles	
		24 May: Richard Cromwell resigns the Protectorate	
	7 June: Henry Cromwell recalled and replaced by commissioners nominated by the English Parliament		

Date	Ireland	Scotland and England	The continent
	18 July: Edmund Ludlow appointed commander–in–chief		
	Summer: Irish army purged and remodelled	Aug: Booth's rebellion in northwest England	
	18 Oct: Ludlow sets sail for England	13 Oct: Army expels members of Rump	
		27 (or 26) Oct: Committee of Safety takes control	
			Nov: Peace of Pyrenees between France and Spain
	Dec: Council of Officers (led by Coote, King and Jones) assume control	4 Dec: Army establishes a provisional government in Portsmouth	
	13 Dec: Dublin Castle seized in name of Parliament	12 Dec: Attempt by army to take Tower of London fails	
	30 Dec: Ludlow returns to Ireland		
		26 Dec: Rump returns to power	
1660		1660: Publication of Sir William Petty, *Reflections upon some persons and things in Ireland* (London)	
		1 Jan: Monck enters England	
		3 Feb: Monck reaches London	

Date	Ireland	Scotland and England	The continent
		16 Feb: Declaration in favour of readmission of secluded members	
		20 (or 21) Feb: Monck readmits secluded members	
	2 Mar: Convention opens in Dublin	16 Mar: Long Parliament dissolves itself	Mid-Mar: Royalist overtures to Monck in London; to the Cootes and Sir John King in Dublin
	8 Mar: Civil government devolved to commissioners (Broghill, Coote, Bury, Clotworthy)		Late-Mar: Royalist overtures to Broghill
	24 Apr: Convention issues order for poll-tax	25 Apr: Convention Parliament assembles	4/14 Apr: Charles II's declaration at Breda
	4 May: Day of thanksgiving in Dublin for restoration of king	8 May: Charles II proclaimed king	
		29 May: Charles II enters London	
	14 May: Charles II proclaimed king in Dublin		
	28 May: Convention adjourns		
		29 Aug: 'An act of free and general pardon'	
		13 Sept: Navigation Act	

Date	Ireland	Scotland and England	The continent
		30 Nov: Charles II's declaration confirming land title of Cromwellian soldiers and Adventurers and providing for 'innocent papists'	
	31 Dec: Eustace, Boyle and Coote sworn in as Lords Justice		

ABBREVIATIONS

BL	British Library, London
Add. MSS	Additional Manuscripts
Bodl.	Bodleian Library, Oxford
Cal. S P Ire.	*Calendar of state papers relating to Ireland, 1633–47* [etc] (London, 1901–)
DNB	*Dictionary of national biography*, ed. Sir Leslie Stephen and Sir Sidney Lee (66 vols., London, 1885–1901; reprinted with corrections, 22 vols., 1908–9)
HMC	Historical Manuscripts Commission
IHS	*Irish Historical Studies*
IMC	Irish Manuscripts Commission
NA	National Archives, Dublin (formerly the PROI)
NLI	National Library of Ireland, Dublin
ns	new series
NUI	National University of Ireland
os	old series
PRO	Public Record Office, London
SP	State Papers
PRONI	Public Record Office of Northern Ireland, Belfast
RO	Record Office
TCD	Trinity College, Dublin

CHAPTER I

INTRODUCTION.
A FAILED REVOLUTION?

JANE OHLMEYER

AT THE height of the 'General Crisis' which gripped Europe during the middle decades of the seventeenth century, one English preacher in 1643 informed the House of Commons that 'These are days of shaking and this shaking is universal: the Palatinate, Bohemia, Germania, Catalonia, Portugal, Ireland, England'.[1] He could have added Scotland and the Netherlands to his list and, by the end of the decade, Naples, Sicily and the Ukraine as well for, as Voltaire later concluded in his *Essai sur les moeurs et l'esprit des nations* (1756), this 'was a period of usurpations almost from one end of the world to the other'.[2] Of these 'usurpations' only Portugal, the Dutch and the Ukraine succeeded. Even though Catholic Ireland failed to win lasting political autonomy within the context of a tripartite Stuart monarchy, its rebellion of the 1640s nevertheless ranks as one of the most successful revolts in early modern history, for, between 1642 and 1649, the Confederation of Kilkenny enjoyed legislative independence and Irish Catholics worshipped freely.

Unlike the Dutch and Portuguese, the Irish made no bid for national self-determination during these years. On the contrary, the Confederates consistently touted their loyalty to Charles I and hoped that Ireland would remain an integral part of the Stuart monarchies, albeit with greater religious and political freedom. Therefore, even during the 1640s, Ireland should be viewed as a state within a 'composite' or 'multiple' monarchy which can be superficially compared to the dominions of the Austrian Habsburgs, of the Spanish Habsburgs, of the triple state of

---

[1] Jeremiah Whittaker, quoted by H. Trevor-Roper, 'The general crisis of the seventeenth century', in T. S. Aston (ed.), *Crisis in Europe 1560–1660* (London, 1965), p. 59. I am grateful to Toby Barnard, Nicholas Canny and Geoffrey Parker for reading an earlier draft of this chapter and for making numerous incisive comments and helpful suggestions for improvement.

[2] Cited in Geoffrey Parker and Lesley M. Smith (eds.), *The general crisis of the seventeenth century* (London, 1978), p. 3.

Poland–Lithuania–Ukraine or, even, of the Swedish crown.[3] Certainly the Stuarts encountered problems in handling Ireland (and, for that matter, England and Scotland as well) similar to those experienced by Philip IV in Catalonia, in Flanders or in Naples or by John Casimir in the Ukraine. In these 'peripheral states' the forces of conservatism and provincialism outweighed those of change and centralization, cultural and linguistic boundaries meant more than national and geographic ones, and religious divisions – whether within the Protestant and Catholic faiths or between them – repeatedly challenged the principle of *cuius regio eius religio*.[4]

Recently Michael Perceval-Maxwell and Conrad Russell have high-lighted the problems involved in running a multiple kingdom and, together with John Morrill and others,[5] have drawn attention to the British and Irish context of the origins and course of the 'Wars of the Three Kingdoms'.[6] However this does not necessarily mark any novel departure, for many scholars of mid-seventeenth-century Ireland, like Donal Cregan writing in

---

3   For the Polish Commonwealth see William Hunt, 'A view from the Vistula on the English Revolution', in Bonnelyn Young and Dwight D. Brautigam (eds.), *Court, country and culture. Essays on early modern British history in honor of Perez Zagorin* (Rochester, New York, 1992), pp. 41–53.

4   For Ireland see Aidan Clarke, 'Ireland and the general crisis', *Past and Present*, 48 (1970), pp. 79–99; Michael Perceval-Maxwell, 'Ireland and the monarchy in the early Stuart multiple kingdom', *The Historical Journal*, 34 (1991), pp. 279–95; Ciaran Brady, 'The decline of the Irish kingdom', in Mark Greengrass (ed.), *Conquest and coalescence. The shaping of the state in early modern Europe* (London, 1991), pp. 95–115. Also see the seminal essay by H. G. Koenigsberger, 'Dominium regale or dominium politicum et regale', reprinted in *Politicians and virtuosi: essays in early modern history* (London, 1986). For an interesting, comparative overview of the causes of early modern revolutions see Perez Zagorin, *Rebels and rulers 1500–1660* (2 vols., Cambridge, 1982).

5   Perceval-Maxwell, 'Ireland and the monarchy'; Conrad Russell, *The causes of the English Civil War* (Oxford, 1990), *The fall of the British monarchies 1637–1642* (Oxford, 1991) and *Unrevolutionary England, 1603–42* (London, 1990), part IV; John Morrill (ed.), *The Scottish national covenant in its British context 1638–51* (Edinburgh, 1990). Also see Ronald Asch (ed.), *Three nations – a common history? England, Scotland, Ireland and British history c. 1600–1920* (Arbeitskreis Deutsche England-Forschung vol. XXIII, Bochum, 1993), especially the introduction and part II; Ronald Hutton, *Charles II, king of England, Scotland and Ireland* (Oxford, 1989); Peter Donald, *An uncounselled king. Charles I and the Scottish troubles 1637–1641* (Cambridge, 1990), David Stevenson, *Scottish covenanters and Irish confederates: Scottish-Irish relations in the mid-seventeenth century* (Belfast, 1981); Jane H. Ohlmeyer, *Civil war and restoration in the three Stuart kingdoms. The career of Randal MacDonnell, marquis of Antrim, 1609–1683* (Cambridge, 1993).

6   However, others remain sceptical of the New British History and, with some justification, fear that this reinvention of the wheel will merely perpetuate the anglocentrism characteristic of the study of early modern English history. For as one Scottish historian noted recently 'It is all very well to have our subject treated as "serious history" by the Anglo-American establishment, there is also a danger in reaching out too eagerly for what could be a poisoned chalice' (Keith Brown, 'British history: a sceptical comment', in Asch (ed.), *Three nations*, p. 117). Nicholas Canny has expressed similar concerns, see *ibid.*, p. 82. In this volume the term 'Britain' refers to England, Scotland and Wales, but does not include Ireland. Though Ireland can be viewed as one of the Stuart kingdoms, it was never part of Britain and technically speaking 'British' history excludes Ireland.

1944, have been careful 'to take account of the cross-Channel situation'.[7] Similarly Hugh Hazlett's detailed investigation on the armies fighting in Ireland during the 1640s (largely written in the late 1930s and 1940s), John Lowe's first-rate articles on Anglo-Irish relations (published in the early 1960s), and the more recent studies by Karl Bottigheimer, T. C. Barnard, David Stevenson, Michael Perceval-Maxwell and Jane Ohlmeyer show special sensitivity to the complex interrelations between the three Stuart monarchies.[8] Nevertheless, even though all of these works, together with the rather unwieldy and sometimes partisan accounts by eighteenth- and nineteenth-century scholars such as Thomas Carte, C. P. Meehan and J. P. Prendergast, and Patrick Corish's seminal chapters in *A new history of Ireland*, have shed much light on the history of the 1640s and 1650s, a recent, analytical, comprehensive study of the Civil War and its aftermath is entirely lacking.[9]

---

[7] Donal F. Cregan, 'Some members of the confederation of Kilkenny', in S. O'Brien (ed.), *Measgra i gCuimhne Mhichíl Uí Chleirigh* (Dublin, 1944), p. 34. Also see Cregan, 'The confederation of Kilkenny: its organization, personnel and history' (unpublished PhD thesis, NUI, 1947). Parts of the thesis have appeared in Cregan, 'Some members of the confederation of Kilkenny' and 'The confederation of Kilkenny', in Brian Farrell (ed.), *Irish parliamentary tradition* (Dublin, 1973).

[8] Hugh Hazlett, 'A history of the military forces operating in Ireland, 1641–9' (unpublished PhD thesis, Queen's University, Belfast, 1938) is extremely valuable, as are his articles on 'The financing of the British armies in Ireland, 1641–9', *IHS*, 1 (1938), pp. 21–41 and 'The recruitment and organization of the Scottish army in Ulster, 1642–9', in H. A. Cronne, T. W. Moody and D. B. Quinn (eds.), *Essays in British and Irish history in honour of James Eadie Todd* (London, 1949). For John Lowe see 'The negotiations between Charles I and the confederation of Kilkenny, 1642–9' (unpublished PhD thesis, University of London, 1960) and the following articles which are derived from his thesis: 'The earl of Antrim and Irish aid to Montrose in 1644', *Irish Sword*, 4 (summer, 1960), pp. 191–8, 'Some aspects of the war in Ireland, 1641–1649' in *ibid.*, 4 (winter, 1959), pp. 81–7, 'Charles I and the confederation of Kilkenny, 1643–9', *IHS*, 14 (1964), pp. 1–19, 'The Glamorgan mission to Ireland 1645–6', *Studia Hibernica*, 4 (1964), pp. 155–96. For more recent studies see Karl Bottigheimer, *English money and Irish land. The 'Adventurers' in the Cromwellian settlement of Ireland* (Oxford, 1971),'English money and Irish land. The "Adventurers" in the Cromwellian settlement of Ireland', *Journal of British Studies*, 7 (1967), pp. 12–27; T. C. Barnard, *Cromwellian Ireland. English government and reform in Ireland 1649–1660* (Oxford, 1975); Stevenson, *Scottish covenanters;* Perceval-Maxwell, 'Ireland and the monarchy' and 'Ulster 1641 in the context of political developments in the three kingdoms', in Brian Mac Cuarta (ed.), *Ulster 1641* (Belfast, 1993), pp. 93–106; Ohlmeyer, *Civil war and restoration*. Also see Robert Elkin, 'The interactions between the Irish rebellion and the English civil wars' (unpublished PhD thesis, University of Illinois at Urbana-Champaign, 1961) and the various articles by John A. Murphy in *Journal of the Cork Historical and Archaeological Society*, especially 'The politics of the Munster Protestants, 1641–1649', 76 (1971), pp. 1–20.

[9] Thomas Carte, *History of the life of James, first duke of Ormonde* (second edn., 6 vols., Oxford, 1851); C. P. Meehan, *The confederation of Kilkenny* (Dublin, 1860); J. P. Prendergast, *The Cromwellian settlement of Ireland* (revised edn., London, 1870; third edn., Dublin, 1922); Patrick Corish's four chapters in T. W. Moody, F. X. Martin and F. J. Byrne (eds.), *A new history of Ireland*, III: *Early modern Ireland 1534–1691* (Oxford, 1978), chapters 11–14. The 'standard' political account of the years 1603–90 remains Richard Bagwell, *Ireland under the Stuarts and during the Interregnum* (3 vols., London, 1909–16; reprint, 1963). T. L. Coonan, *Irish Catholic confederacy and the Puritan revolution* (Dublin, London and New York, 1954) is hopelessly inadequate – see J. C. Beckett's

This is somewhat surprising given the number of primary printed sources relating to these decades (largely published under the auspices of the Irish Manuscripts Commission and the Historical Manuscripts Commission), the accessibility of Ormond's extensive archive which contains a wealth of detail pertinent to the conflict, and the amount of material relating to Ireland housed among the State Papers (Public Record Office, London).[10] Perhaps this relative dearth of scholarship can be attributed to the destruction, in 1711 and 1922, of so many official records, especially the archive of the Confederation of Kilkenny.[11] Certainly the loss of these seminal documents has forced Irish historians to adopt several approaches. First they are increasingly willing to turn to other disciplines – Irish literature, historical geography, archaeology and anthropology – for insights.[12] For instance, recent work by historical geographers, especially William Smyth, has offered a novel perspective on the study of seventeenth-century Irish society and of the land settlement;[13] while discussions of contemporary

devastating review in *IHS*, 11 (1958), pp. 52–5. Interestingly the origins of the rebellion have stimulated intense recent historical interest, see chapter 2, footnotes 6 and 7 below, Mac Cuarta (ed.), *Ulster 1641* and M. Perceval-Maxwell, *The outbreak of the Irish rebellion of 1641* (Dublin, 1994).

[10] The more important source compilations include Sir J. T. Gilbert (ed.), *A contemporary history of affairs in Ireland from A.D. 1641 to 1652* (3 vols., Irish Archaeological Society, Dublin, 1879) and *History of the Irish confederation and the war in Ireland, 1641–3* . . . (7 vols., Dublin, 1882–91); Mary Hickson (ed.), *Ireland in the seventeenth century* (2 vols., London, 1884); [E. Hogan (ed.)], *The history of the warr in Ireland* . . . (Dublin, 1873); J. Hogan (ed.), *Letters and papers relating to the Irish rebellion* (IMC, Dublin, 1935); Brendan Jennings (ed.), *Wild Geese in Spanish Flanders 1582–1700* . . . (IMC, Dublin, 1964); Robert Dunlop (ed.), *Ireland under the Commonwealth: being a selection of documents relating to the government of Ireland, 1651–9* (2 vols., Manchester, 1913); John Lowe (ed.), *Letter-book of the earl of Clanricarde, 1643–7* (IMC, Dublin, 1983). Also the works listed in footnotes 17 and 18 below. Ormond's archive is divided between the Bodleian Library in Oxford (the Carte papers) and the National Library of Ireland in Dublin. The more important material relating to the war has been printed in Carte, *Ormond*, VI; Gilbert (ed.), *A contemporary history* and *Irish confederation*. Also see HMC, *Calendar of the manuscripts of the marquis of Ormonde*, ns (8 vols., London, 1902–20) and HMC, *The manuscripts of the marquis of Ormonde*, os (2 vols., London, 1895–9).

[11] T. C. Barnard has also drawn attention to the lasting influences of the highly partisan contemporary accounts and the tendency by later historians to treat them as 'gospel'. See T. C. Barnard, 'Crises of identity among Irish Protestants 1641–1685', *Past and Present*, 127 (1990), pp. 39–83; Barnard, '1641: a bibliographical essay' in Mac Cuarta (ed.), *Ulster 1641*, pp. 173–86; and Barnard, 'Irish images of Cromwell', in R. C. Richardson (ed.), *Images of Cromwell: essays by and for Roger Howell* (Manchester, 1993), pp. 180–206.

[12] For instance see Pádraig Lenihan, 'Aerial photography: a window on the past', *History Ireland*, 1 (summer, 1993), pp. 9–13 and footnotes 13 and 14 below.

[13] William J. Smyth, 'Society and settlement in seventeenth-century Ireland: the evidence of the "1659 census"', in William J. Smyth and Kevin Whelan (eds.), *Common ground. Essays on the historical geography of Ireland presented to T. Jones Hughes* (Cork, 1988), pp. 55–83; Smyth, 'Territorial, social and settlement hierarchies in seventeenth century Kilkenny', in William Nolan and Kevin Whelan (eds.), *Kilkenny: history and society* . . . (Dublin, 1990), pp. 127–60; Smyth, 'Property, patronage and population. Reconstructing the human geography of mid-seventeenth-century County Tipperary', in William Nolan and Thomas G. McGrath (eds.), *Tipperary: history and society* (Dublin, 1985). Also see P. J. Duffy, 'The evolution of estate properties in South Ulster 1600–1900', in Smyth and Whelan (eds.), *Common ground*, pp. 84–109.

literature and poetry enhance our understanding of early modern Irish culture, national identities and loyalties.[14] Comparing the wartime experiences of Ireland with those of other countries is equally valuable and helps explain phenomena such as the spread of the 'Military Revolution' in Ireland or the growth of war-weariness and provincialism. Third, historians of the 1640s and 1650s have no alternative but to make extensive use of more fragmentary sources – land surveys, estate records, parish and taxation registers, correspondence, proclamations and newsletters – which have survived. For example, Nicholas Canny's imaginative treatment of 'eye witness' accounts gleaned from the '1641 depositions' enables him to examine the conduct and progress of the insurrection in the localities and to unravel 'the complex of motivations that the Protestants attributed to their assailants'.[15] Equally important (and, as yet, largely unexploited) are the remarkably complete archives of the continental countries involved in Irish affairs during the mid-seventeenth century.[16] The papers of governments in Paris, Madrid and Brussels contain a wealth of tantalizing information: despatches, memoranda, reports and correspondence of their agents in Ireland and of their ambassadors in London and Edinburgh.[17] Similarly rewarding are the Roman archives and the personal papers of the

[14] See especially Breandán Ó Buachalla, 'James our true king. The ideology of Irish royalism in the seventeenth century', in D. George Boyce, Robert Eccleshall and Vincent Geoghegan (eds.), *Political thought in Ireland since the seventeenth century* (London and New York, 1993), pp. 7–35. Also see Brendan Bradshaw, Andrew Hadfield and Willy Maley (eds.), *Representing Ireland: literature and the origins of conflict, 1534–1660* (Cambridge, 1993); T. J. Dunne, 'The Gaelic response to conquest and colonization: the evidence of the poetry', *Studia Hibernica*, 20 (1980), pp. 7–30; Michelle O Riordan, *The Gaelic mind and the collapse of the Gaelic world* (Cork, 1990); O Riordan, 'The native Ulster *mentalité* as revealed in Gaelic sources 1600–1650', in Mac Cuarta (ed.), *Ulster 1641*, pp. 61–91; Bernadette Cunningham, 'Native culture and political change in Ireland, 1580–1640', in Ciaran Brady and Raymond Gillespie (eds.), *Natives and newcomers: essays on the making of Irish colonial society, 1534–1641* (Dublin, 1986), pp. 148–70; Bernadette Cunningham and Raymond Gillespie, 'The East Ulster bardic family of Ó Gnímh', *Eigse*, 20 (1984), pp. 106–14; Nicholas Canny, 'The formation of the Irish mind: religion, politics and Gaelic Irish literature', *Past and Present*, 95 (May, 1982), pp. 91–116. Also see chapter 6 below.
[15] See pp. 27–8 below.
[16] Robert A. Stradling, *The Spanish monarchy and Irish mercenaries: the Wild Geese in Spain, 1618–68* (Dublin, 1994), especially chapters 2–6, demonstrates how important foreign – and, in this instance, Spanish – sources are for the study of civil war in Ireland. I am grateful to Dr Stradling for making his manuscript available to me in advance of publication.
[17] A considerable amount of Irish material from the Paris archives is available in print. For the Bibliothèque Nationale, see the National Library of Ireland, *Report of the trustees 1949–50* (Dublin, 1950) and *1950–1* (Dublin, 1951). A number of letters from the Ministère des Affaires Etrangères have been reproduced in Gilbert (ed.), *Irish confederation*. For the Archives Générales du Royaume, Brussels, see Brendan Jennings (ed.), *Wild Geese in Spanish Flanders, 1582–1700* . . . (IMC, 1964). Sadly there is no adequate listing of the Irish material in the A[rchivio] G[eneral,] S[imincas, Spain].

papal nuncio, Giovanni Battista Rinuccini, and his second-in-command, Dionysius Massari, dean of Fermo.[18] These commissioned essays demonstrate that sufficient source material has survived for further research at the regional and national levels at home, as well as abroad. For instance, relatively little is known about key military leaders such as Sir Phelim O'Neill,[19] Thomas Preston, James Touchet, earl of Castlehaven[20] or Sir Charles Coote; or about prominent political figures, especially James Butler, marquis of Ormond,[21] Theobald Taaffe, later earl of Carlingford,[22] Ulick Burke, earl of Clanricard,[23] Murrough O'Brien, Lord Inchiquin,[24] Arthur Annesley, earl of Anglesey and Richard Talbot, later earl of Tyrconnell.[25] Despite innovative studies by Donal Cregan, John Lowe and Hugh Hazlett, much remains to be done

[18] See especially B. Millet, 'The archives of the congregation de propaganda fide', *Irish Catholic Historical Committee* (1956), pp. 20–7 and 'Catalogue of Irish material . . . ', *Collectanea Hibernica*, 10–12 (1967–9). Also see Cathaldus Giblin (ed.), 'Vatican Library: MSS Barberini Latini . . . ', *Archivium Hibernicum*, 19 (1955), pp. 67–144 and 'Catalogue of material of Irish interest in the collection Nunziatura di Fiandra, Vatican archives', *Collectanea Hibernica*, 1 (1958), pp. 7–125. For Rinuccini and Massari see R. O'Ferrall and R. O'Connell, *Commentarius Rinuccinianus*, ed. Revd S. Kavanagh (IMC, 6 vols., Dublin, 1932–49); G. Aiazza, *The embassy in Ireland of Monsignor G. B. Rinuccini* . . . , translated by Annie Hutton (Dublin, 1873) and Dionysius Massari, 'My Irish campaign', *The Catholic Bulletin*, 6 (1916), 7 (1917), 8 (1918), 9 (1919), 10 (1920).

[19] Jerrold Casway, 'Two Phelim O'Neills', *Seanchas Ardmhacha*, 11 (1985), pp. 331–41 and John J. Marshall, 'Sir Phelim O'Neill 1604–1652[-3]', *Ulster Journal of Archaeology*, second series, 10 (1904), pp. 145–50.

[20] For his memoirs see, James Touchet, earl of Castlehaven, *Memoirs . . . his engagements and carriage in the wars of Ireland* (London, 1680; later editions 1681, 1684; reprinted New York, 1974).

[21] The best account of Ormond's career remains Carte's biography (footnote 9 above). Even though Ormond has received some recent historical attention – J. C. Beckett, *The cavalier duke. A life of James Butler first duke of Ormond 1610–1688* (Belfast, 1990) and Billy Kelly, '"Most illustrious cavalier" or "unkinde desertor", James Butler, first duke of Ormond', *History Ireland*, 1 (summer, 1993), pp. 18–22 – his specific contribution to the Irish Civil War still needs further analysis.

[22] The only recent account is in Harold O'Sullivan, 'Land ownership changes in the County of Louth in the seventeenth century' (unpublished PhD thesis, TCD, 1992), chapter 5.

[23] The bulk of Clanricard's personal papers are available in print, see Lowe (ed.), *Letter-book*; Ulick de Burgh, marquis of Clanricarde, *The memoirs of Ulick, marquis of Clanricarde . . .* (London, 1757) and *Memoirs of . . . Clanricarde . . . relating to the treaty between the duke of Lorraine and the Irish commissioners* (London, 1722). The excellent studies by Bernadette Cunningham, 'Political and social change in the lordships of Clanricard and Thomond, 1569–1641' (unpublished MA thesis, NUI, Galway, 1979) and Tom Connors, 'The impact of English colonial expansion on Irish culture: the Protestant reformation, popular religion, and the transformation of the family in early modern Connacht' (unpublished PhD thesis, University of Illinois at Urbana-Champaign, 1994) focus on the sixteenth- and early seventeenth-century earls of Clanricard.

[24] The recent biography of Inchiquin by Ivar O'Brien, *Murrough the burner* (Whitegate, County Clare, 1991) is inadequate. See instead John A. Murphy, 'Inchiquin's changes of religion', *Journal of the Cork Historical and Archaeological Society*, 72 (1967), pp. 58–68.

[25] J. Miller, 'The earl of Tyrconnell and James II's Irish policy, 1685–1688', *The Historical Journal*, 20 (1977), pp. 802–23 and James Maguire, 'Richard Talbot, earl of Tyrconnell (1603–91) and the Catholic Counter-Revolution', in Ciaran Brady (ed.), *Worsted in the game. Losers in Irish history* (Dublin, 1989), pp. 73–83.

on the Confederation of Kilkenny, especially its organization in the provinces (how did the Confederates raise troops and money; how did they discipline unruly or disaffected citizens?) and the role played by various interest groups (namely the lawyers, the clergy, the aristocracy and the merchant community) in shaping confederate policy.[26] More analysis too is required of the confederate, royalist and parliamentary armies fighting in Ireland;[27] of the Catholic church and the religious orders and the role played in the conflict by clerics (especially by prominent figures like Rinuccini[28] or the Irish bishops Heber MacMahon,[29] Hugh O'Reilly,[30] David Rothe,[31] Malacy O'Queely,[32] and Oliver Darcy).

In stark contrast to England, where regional studies of the Civil Wars abound, relatively little is known about the impact the rebellion, ten years of fighting and two decades of heavy taxation had on the various localities and on individual family fortunes.[33] We need to investigate further the

---

[26] See especially the pioneering studies by Cregan listed in footnote 7 above and by J. C. Beckett, 'The confederation of Kilkenny reviewed', in Michael Roberts (ed.), *Historical Studies*, II (London, 1959), pp. 29–41. The confederate lawyer Patrick Darcy has attracted some attention, see Liam O'Malley, 'Patrick Darcy, Galway lawyer and politician, 1598–1668', in Diarmuid Ó Cearbhaill (ed.), *Galway: town and gown 1484–1984* (Dublin, 1984), pp. 90–109 and C. E. J. Caldicott (ed.), 'Patrick Darcy. An argument' in *Camden Miscellany XXXI* (Camden fourth series, vol. XLIV, London, 1992), pp. 193–320.

[27] The work of Hugh Hazlett, much of which remains unpublished, is invaluable, see footnote 8 above. Also see Ian Ryder, *An English army for Ireland* (London, 1987), Jerrold Casway, *Owen Roe O'Neill and the struggle for Catholic Ireland* (Philadelphia, 1984), Nicholas Perry, 'The infantry of the confederate Leinster army, 1642–1647', *Irish Sword*, 15 (1983), pp. 232–41 and Jane Ohlmeyer, 'The war of religions', in Keith Jeffery and Tom Bartlett, *A military history of Ireland* (Cambridge, forthcoming). Pádraig Lenihan is currently completing a doctoral thesis at University College, Galway on 'The armies of the Irish Catholic confederation 1641–9'.

[28] For Rinuccini see Michael J. Hynes, *The mission of Rinuccini, 1645–49* (Louvain, 1932) which is essentially a summary of *Commentarius Rinuccinianus*; Patrick Corish, 'Ireland's first papal nuncio', *Irish Ecclesiastical Record*, 81 (1954), pp. 172–83 and Andrew Boyd, 'Rinuccini and civil war in Ireland, 1644–9', *History Today*, 41 (Feb. 1991), pp. 42–8. Tadgh Ó h Annracháin is currently completing a dissertation on the Irish mission of Rinuccini at the European University Institute in Florence.

[29] Séamus Ó Mórdha, 'Heber MacMahon, soldier bishop of the confederation of Kilkenny', in Joseph Duffy (ed.), *Clogher record album. A diocesan history* (Monaghan, 1975); Ó Mórdha, 'Ever MacMahon', *Studies*, 40 (1951), pp. 323–33 and 41 (1952), pp. 91–8 and J. E. McKenna, *Heber MacMahon in the confederate wars (1641–1650)* (Dublin, 1908).

[30] Séamus Ó Mórdha, 'Hugh O'Reilly (1581?–1653), a reforming primate', *Breifne*, 4 (1970), pp. 1–42 and 6 (1972), 345–69.

[31] Maureen Hegarty, 'David Rothe', *Old Kilkenny Review. Journal of the Kilkenny Archaeological Society*, ns, 2 (1979), pp. 4–21.

[32] Richard J. Kelly, 'Dr O'Queely, archbishop of Tuam. A great statesman and prelate', *Irish Ecclesiastical Record*, 17 (1905), pp. 247–53.

[33] Nicholas Canny has suggested that the 'true character of the revolt . . . will be better understood when the depositions for each locality and region are studied and correlated', Nicholas Canny, 'The 1641 depositions as a source for the writing of social history: County Cork as a case study', in Patrick O'Flanagan and Cornelius G. Buttimer (eds.), *Cork: history and society* (Dublin, 1993), p. 277. Also see Nicholas Canny, 'The marginal kingdom: Ireland as a problem in the first

survival strategies adopted by beleaguered Protestants during the 1640s and the accommodations made, during the 1650s, by Catholics who remained *in situ*.[34] Similarly the issue of indebtedness among the Irish natives and newcomers merits analysis. Did, for example, the crushing debts accumulated during the course of the 1640s represent more of a threat to Irish landlords than harsh governmental legislation or religious persecution? An anonymous Gaelic poet lamented how the war had interrupted traditional aristocratic pursuits and 'studies in the liberal arts and languages'; yet, apart from T. C. Barnard's enlightening account of the mental world of leading Old Protestants (see chapter 11), we lack any comprehensive scholarly analysis of wartime popular and élite culture, marriage and education patterns.[35] More attention must also be devoted to the continuities – especially the intellectual, cultural and political ones – with the pre- and post-war years. For as John Adamson notes in his essay on the three kingdoms context of Viscount Lisle's lieutenancy of Ireland (chapter 7), it is easy 'to overlook the fact that there were strong continuities, in both policy and personnel, between the Straffordian interest of 1639–40 and the junto which emerged in control of parliamentarian Irish policy at the end of the First Civil War'. Both T. C. Barnard and John Adamson call attention to the extensive clientage and patronage networks that spanned the Irish Sea and provided vital points of contact between the centre and the periphery. Yet we need to examine further the role played by Irish men and women in influencing government policy and in articulating Irish

British empire', in Bernard Bailyn and Philip D. Morgan (eds.), *Strangers within the realm: cultural margins of the first British empire* (Chapel Hill, 1991), pp. 35–66. The depositions have also been used extensively by Hilary Simms, 'Violence in County Armagh, 1641', in Mac Cuarta (ed.), *Ulster 1641*, pp. 123–38; Thomas Fitzpatrick, *The bloody bridge and other papers relating to the insurrection of 1641* (Dublin, 1903; reissued, 1970), Fitzpatrick, 'The Ulster civil war, 1641. "The king's commission" in the County Fermanagh', *Ulster Journal of Archaeology*, second series, 13 (1907), pp. 133–42, 155–9 and Fitzpatrick, 'The wars of 1641 in County Down: the deposition of High Sheriff Peter Hill (1645)', *ibid.*, 10 (1904), pp. 73–90. Local studies of the civil war in England are too numerous to list in full. See, for instance, Alan Everitt, *The community of Kent and the Great Rebellion, 1640–1660* (Leicester, 1966); John Morrill, *Cheshire 1630–60: A county government during the English Revolution* (Oxford, 1974); B. G. Blackwood, *The Lancashire gentry and the great rebellion, 1640–1660* (Manchester, 1978) and Ann Hughes, *Politics, society and civil war in Warwickshire, 1620–1660* (Cambridge, 1987).

34 Some inroads have been made by Raymond Gillespie, 'A question of survival: the O'Farrells of Longford in the seventeenth century' in Raymond Gillespie and Gerard Moran (eds.), *Longford: essays in county history* (Dublin, 1991), pp. 13–29; Ohlmeyer, *Civil war and restoration*, especially chapters 9 and 10; O'Sullivan, 'Land ownership'.

35 Also see Barnard, 'Crises of identity', pp. 39–83. Under the influence of the *Annales* school numerous works were published during the 1970s and 1980s which attempted to unravel the *mentalité* of early modern people. See, for instance, David Underdown, *Revel, riot and rebellion. Popular politics and culture in England, 1603–1660* (Oxford, 1987) and Peter Burke, *Popular culture in early modern Europe* (London, 1978). However, none covered Ireland.

grievances at the royalist court, whether in London, Oxford or on the continent, or at Westminster in the years after 1641.[36]

Finally, the Irish migrant community – whether in Britain, North America, the West Indies or on the continent – would be equally worthy of closer analysis.[37] What, for example, became of the hundreds of Protestant refugees who fled to England, Wales and Scotland after the outbreak of the rebellion?[38] Even though the passage of Irish troops to and from Europe and the activities of Irish privateers have been the subjects of recent studies, other aspects of Ireland's relationship with the continent – especially with regard to commerce – deserve attention.[39] For instance certain Spanish municipal archives, such as the Archivo del Consulado de Bilbao, hold registers of ships entering and leaving the port (libros de averia), together with details of their destination and cargo;[40] while the notarial archives in the Gemeentearchief in Amsterdam contain information on merchants trading with, and vessels travelling to, Carrickfergus, Cork, Derry, Galway, Limerick, Portrush, Waterford and Wexford during the 1640s and 1650s.[41] Louis Cullen has used French regional archives extensively in his work on eighteenth-century trade and perhaps a careful examination of the notarial records of La Rochelle, St Malo, Nantes and Bordeaux could shed light on trade with Ireland, on the passage of Irish troops, and on the activities of those Irish privateers who frequented these ports during the 1640s.[42] While,

[36] Inroads have been made by Bottigheimer, English money and Donal Cregan, 'An Irish cavalier: Daniel O'Neill', Studia Hibernica, 3 (1963), pp. 60–100, 4 (1965), pp. 104–33 and 5 (1965), pp. 42–76. For the earlier period see P. S. J. Little, 'Family and faction: the Irish nobility and the English court, 1632–1642' (unpublished MLitt thesis, TCD, 1992).

[37] Hilary Beckles, 'A riotous and unruly lot: Irish indentured servants and freemen in the English West Indies, 1644–1713', William and Mary Quarterly, 47 (1990), pp. 503–22 and '"Black men in white skins": The formation of a white proletariat in West Indian slave society', The Journal of Imperial and Commonwealth History, 15 (1986), pp. 5–21.

[38] For the earlier period see the fascinating study by Patrick Fitzgerald, '"Like Crickets to the crevice of a brew-house". Poor Irish migrants in England, 1560–1640', in Patrick O'Sullivan (ed.), The Irish world wide history, heritage, identity, 1 Patterns of migration (New York, 1992), pp. 13–35.

[39] Jane H. Ohlmeyer, '"The Dunkirk of Ireland": Wexford privateers during the 1640s', Journal of the Wexford Historical Society, 12 (1988–9), pp. 23–49 and 'Irish privateers during the civil war, 1642–50', Mariners' Mirror, 76 (1990), pp. 119–33. See especially Stradling, Spanish monarchy.

[40] See especially Registros de memoriales y representaciones, provisiones reales, libros de decretos y elecciones. These sources were all used by T. Guiard y Larrauri, Historia del consulado y casa de contratación de Bilbao (3 vols., fac. edn., Bilbao, 1972). Material relating to trade with Ireland also exists in the Vizcayan regional archive (Archivo de la Diputación de Vizcaya in Bilbao), especially in the correspondence between the crown and the senior officials of the province (Corregimiento). I am grateful to Miguel Angel Echevarria Bacigalupe for bringing this material to my attention.

[41] I am grateful to Rolf Loeber for bringing this to my attention.

[42] See especially Louis Cullen, 'Galway merchants in the outside world, 1650–1800', in Ó Cearbhaill, Galway, pp. 63–89. La Rochelle's notarial records are housed in the Archives Départementales de la Charente Maritime, La Rochelle; for Nantes and Bordeaux see the relevant collections held by the Archives Départementales de la Loire Atlantique and the

as the recent work by Gráinne Henry on the 'Wild Geese' in Flanders prior to 1641 demonstrates, military records, hospital reports, wills and parish registers can be used to reconstruct the military and merchant communities resident in Flanders, Spain, France and even the Netherlands, which, by the mid-1650s, may have exceeded 40,000 people (the equivalent of Dublin's pre-war population).[43]

Even though this volume falls far short of being a comprehensive history of these two turbulent decades, it nevertheless draws attention to how the events of the 1640s and 1650s transformed the course of Ireland's history. Apart from a chronological account of the Civil War and of the collapse of the Cromwellian régime in 1659–60 (chapters 3 and 12), the essays are thematic and cover such diverse issues as the early stages of the 1641 insurrection (chapter 2), the impact of continental military technology on Irish warfare (chapter 4), confederate foreign policy (chapter 5), Anglo-Irish relations and the formulation of Irish policy at Westminster during the later 1640s (chapter 7), the wartime economy (chapter 8), the land settlement (chapter 9) and the proliferation of radical sects during the 1650s (chapter 10). Finally chapters 6 and 11 examine the respective divisions within the Catholic and Protestant communities, the nature of Irish royalism and the evasive concept of national identity.[44]

Throughout the contributors consider why Restoration Ireland was such a different world from that of the early Stuart era. Was the change simply due to the passage of the twenty years; or to war in the 1640s followed by English occupation in the 1650s? During these decades did active forces of change outweigh those of continuity in shaping Irish society, identities, warfare, religious beliefs, economic and tenurial practices? Finally these chapters seek to set Ireland in its wider European context. What was the relationship between independent Ireland and France, Spain and the Papacy and what influence did events and ideas in Europe have on Irish politics and warfare? Particular attention is also paid to the triangular relationship between Ireland, England and Scotland. Recent scholarship

Archives Départementales de la Gironde respectively. For details on the notarial archives in Nantes, albeit in the sixteenth century, see Jean Tanguy, *Le commerce du port de Nantes au milieu du XVIe siècle* (Paris, 1956). For St Malo see the relevant collections in Archives Départementales d'Ille-et-Vilaine and J. Delumeau, *Le mouvement du port de Saint-Malo . . .* (Rennes, 1966), pp. vii–xiv, 217–21.

[43] Gráinne Henry, *The Irish military community in Spanish Flanders, 1586–1621* (Dublin, 1992) and 'Ulster exiles in Europe, 1605–1641' in Mac Cuarta (ed.), *Ulster 1641*, pp. 37–60. Also see Stradling's account of the 'Ulster army' in Cantabria, *Spanish monarchy*, chapters 7 and 8 and Jerrold Casway, 'Irish women overseas, 1500–1800', in Margaret MacCurtain and Mary O'Dowd (eds.), *Women in early modern Ireland* (Dublin, 1991), pp. 112–32.

[44] Also see the 'chronology of events' at pp. xv–l above.

has firmly rooted the origins of the 1641 rebellion, in Nicholas Canny's phrase, 'within the broad context of political developments in England, Scotland and Ireland'.[45] The same may be said for the restoration of Charles II, which, as Aidan Clarke notes, was facilitated by external intervention from Scotland and, to a lesser extent, Ireland. But what of the intervening years? Certainly Charles I, Charles II, Oliver Cromwell and the Westminster Parliament remained acutely sensitive to the interrelations between the three kingdoms: during the 1640s the Stuarts hoped to use Irish troops against their rebellious British subjects; while the English Parliament turned to the Scottish Covenanters for assistance in the belief that 'unlesse we doe fully vindicate these malicious papists [in Ireland], these two kingdomes both Scotland and England, cannot sleepe long in security'.[46] As the war progressed Ireland became sucked into the British political and military arena and, after 1648 and the outbreak of the Second English Civil War, actually became an extension of it.

I

According to accounts left by Protestant contemporaries, the Ulster rebellion of 1641 came as a total surprise: the County Tyrone MP, Audley Mervin, for one, could hardly believe that it was 'conceived among us, and yet never felt to kick in the wombe, nor struggle in the birth'.[47] Nevertheless the rising, which began on 22 October, plunged Ulster, and within a short time all of Ireland, into a decade of total war. Sir Phelim O'Neill and his co-conspirators succeeded in taking the key strongholds of Charlemont, Mountjoy Castle, Tandragee and Newry; only Derry, Coleraine, Enniskillen, Lisburn and Carrickfergus escaped capture. From Ulster the revolt quickly 'diffused through the veines of the whole kingdome'; by the spring of 1642 it had engulfed almost the entire country, wrecking havoc on the militarily impotent Protestant population.[48]

The unexpected nature of the rising, combined with political unrest in Britain, proved critical to its initial success. Charles I, already exhausted by the Bishops' Wars of 1638 and 1639–40 against the Scottish Covenanters, became embroiled in his own struggle with the Westminster Parliament and failed to act decisively against the Irish insurgents. Had the English king accepted the 'Grand Remonstrance' (December 1641) and somehow reconciled his differences with Parliament, there can be little doubt that the

---

[45] See p. 26 below.
[46] *The Lord Balmerino's speech in the high court of Parliament in Scotland . . .* (London, 1641), p. 3.
[47] *An exact relation of all such occurences . . .* (London, 1642), p. 1.   [48] *Ibid.*

revolt in Ireland could have been quashed with relative ease; but any hope of dealing quickly with the 'Irish Problem' was thwarted by the outbreak of the First English Civil War in August 1642 which dramatically reduced the amount of English money and the quantity of supplies and soldiers available for Ireland and allowed the Catholic insurgents, now bonded by an oath of association,[49] to organize themselves into a formal confederation, modelled on the English Parliament, with its 'capital' at Kilkenny.[50]

This wholesale Catholic involvement also greatly increased the rebellion's chances of success. Initially, as Nicholas Canny points out, the revolt had taken the form of a popular rising directed 'against the Protestant farming population which had come into possession of better tenancies' during the first half of the seventeenth century.[51] In this respect it clearly resembled the Normandy rebellion of the Nu-pieds in 1639 or the insurrections which broke out in 1647 in the Habsburg kingdoms of Naples, Sicily and Andalusia, where rural unrest and urban misery created conditions ripe for revolt. However these 'anguished and spontaneous outbursts' were, according to John Elliott, doomed 'to disappointment' because the ruling classes failed to back them.[52] And indeed, given the initial lack of support by the earl of Antrim, an influential Ulster magnate, and of the Old English community who were, in the words of their apologist, John Lynch, horrified by 'this sedition' stirred up by 'the dregs of people, the rabble of men of ruined fortunes or profligate character',[53]

---

[49] Interestingly this oath resembled the Scottish National Covenant and 'other religious bonds that so often united the insurgents in early modern revolutions', Zagorin, *Rebels*, II, p. 47.

[50] Similar circumstances facilitated the success of other early modern revolts. For example, Portugal's rebellion against Habsburg rule in December 1640 could, according to John Elliott, not have come at a 'more opportune moment' because Spain, reeling from the Dutch destruction of the Spanish fleet at the battle of the Downs (October 1639), was next surprised by the outbreak of a major revolt in Catalonia in May 1640; John Elliott, 'The Spanish monarchy and the kingdom of Portugal 1580–1640', in Greengrass (ed.), *Conquest and coalescence*, p. 65.

[51] See p. 31 below.

[52] J. H. Elliott, 'Revolts of the Spanish monarchy', in Robert Forster and Jack P. Greene (eds.), *Preconditions of revolution in early modern Europe* (Baltimore and London, 1970), p. 127. Also see Zagorin, *Rebels*, I, p. 19.

[53] Quoted on p. 122 below. Contemporary writers and later historians have grouped Ireland's inhabitants under three principal headings: the Old English, descendants of Norman settlers who remained Catholic; the Old, or native, Irish, who were also Catholic but were of Gaelic descent and culture; and the 'New English' Protestant colonists who settled in Ireland after the Reformation. For further details see *A new history of Ireland*, III, pp. xlii–xliv. However as one historian has recently noted 'In fact matters were not always so straightforward. "Old English" was in practice a cultural label, extending to some families of Gaelic Irish origin who had become wholly anglicized. The so-called "New English", equally, included some, like . . . Ormond, whose family had been in Ireland for centuries but who were Protestants', S. J. Connolly, *Religion, law and power. The making of Protestant Ireland 1660–1760* (Oxford, 1992), p. 114. Also see footnote 82 below.

the Irish insurrection might have suffered a similar fate. However, as the rebellion gained momentum, the leading Catholic aristocrats temporarily sank their economic, cultural and religious differences and, in December 1641, the Old English lords concluded an uneasy alliance with the Ulster insurgents.[54] From this point on the Irish conflict enjoyed many similarities with the other great struggles for political autonomy raging during the 1640s in Catalonia, Portugal, Britain, the Ukraine and the Dutch Republic. Why then did the Catholic insurgents fail to take advantage of this unique set of favourable circumstances in order to win freedom of religious worship and lasting political autonomy within a tripartite Stuart monarchy?

Part of the explanation lay in the huge investment in a massive but fragmented war-effort. At the height of the Irish Civil War (also known as the Confederate or Eleven Years' War) four separate armies operated in the field (see chapter 3). The absence of reliable quantitative data makes it impossible to estimate accurately the size of these forces; but the few surviving musters and the numerous qualitative sources (letters, ambassadorial despatches, intelligence reports, contemporary pamphlets and newsheets) indicate that at least 45,000 men constantly served in arms throughout the decade. Scott Wheeler has estimated that shortly after the outbreak of the rebellion between 33,000 and 60,000 men fought in the confederate, royalist and Scottish armies; and that by 1649 this figure had risen to between 43,000 and 66,000 soldiers. These totals are striking, given that Ireland's population has been estimated at around 2.1 million people. If roughly 20 per cent (or 9,000 men) of this force of 45,000 were 'foreign' (largely English or Scots), one could argue that, prior to 1649, seventeen Irish men out of every thousand inhabitants, or nearly 7 per cent of the adult male population, served in the armed forces. If accurate this would indicate that as many Irishmen, in relation to total population, bore arms in the 1640s as served in the armies of Louis XIV during the 1690s, where the military participation ratio stood at 17.6 for every thousand inhabitants and where society was much better prepared for lengthy and costly combat.[55]

Larger armies were merely one feature of the 'Military Revolution' which transformed early modern European warfare; other key developments included the artillery fortress, the naval broadside, reliance on

[54] Beckett, 'Confederation of Kilkenny'. For further details on this uneasy alliance see Aidan Clarke, *The Old English in Ireland 1625–1641* (Ithaca and London, 1966), chapters 10–12.

[55] The population of France at this point numbered *c.* 19 million; while the size of Louis XIV's army stood at *c.* 333,000. For details see John A. Lynn, 'Recalculating French army growth during the *grand siècle*, 1610–1715', *French Historical Studies* (fall, 1994). I am grateful to John Lynn for sharing his expertise on this issue with me.

firepower in combat, and the application of strategies that deployed several armies in concert. The evidence presented below by Scott Wheeler, Rolf Loeber and Geoffrey Parker (chapters 3 and 4) makes it clear that, although these innovations scarcely influenced Irish warfare before 1641, all were firmly in place only a few years later and that Ireland's military leaders mastered remarkably quickly continental techniques and technology by both land and sea, and for both offence and defence.

However any advantage which up-to-date military methods brought the combatants was soon lost because neither the Confederates, the Royalists nor the Parliamentarians (prior to 1649) appeared to possess a 'grand strategy' for winning the war. On the contrary little or no co-operation linked the various commanders. For example, just as in the early stages of the English Civil War, the armies fighting in Ireland acted as independent units, advancing, retreating and offering battle as the opinion of the commanders and local circumstances dictated, while the leading confederate generals constantly feuded and bickered with one another over trivial, personal matters. Inept leadership by Owen Roe O'Neill, Castlehaven and Thomas Preston prevented the exploitation of opportunities for strategic success against forces loyal to England in 1643–4 and 1646–7, and eventually gave first Michael Jones and then Oliver Cromwell the opportunity to win major battles in 1647 and 1649. Had the Confederates secured overall military victory prior to 1646, as they came so close to doing, the costs of reconquest in 1649 might have seemed too high, paving the way for a mediated political solution. Thus, Scott Wheeler concludes, 'A failure of confederate leadership, not "Cromwell's Curse", dashed Irish Catholic hopes for religious toleration and political autonomy'.[56]

Military impotence alone, however, cannot explain why the Confederates ultimately lost the war. A complex combination of economic, diplomatic, political and religious factors also contributed to this failure. As Nicholas Canny, Raymond Gillespie and Kevin McKenny have shown, economic considerations – especially poor harvests, endemic indebtedness and the loss of property through plantation, mortgage or the practice of primogeniture – drove the Irish to take up arms in the first place. A lengthy war then exacerbated the situation by sparking a series of devastating commercial crises which crippled Irish trade and drained the economy of much needed specie (see chapter 8). However, as Raymond Gillespie demonstrates, the disruption varied from region to region, affecting urban areas, especially Dublin, more than the countryside and the more prosperous

[56] See p. 65 below.

counties in the south and east. Naturally the economic downturn influenced the conduct of the war. On the one hand, an inability to generate sufficient food, clothing and cash undermined the Protestant war-effort and left the anti-Catholic coalition totally dependent for their survival on inadequate and sporadic English and Scottish handouts. On the other, even though the Confederates tried to alleviate their mercantile problems by minting their own coinage and encouraging trade with continental powers, their inability to place Catholic Ireland on a stable economic foundation ultimately doomed to failure their bid for autonomy. By the end of 1648 the Confederates teetered on the verge of bankruptcy, unable to raise money 'from a country so totally exhausted, and so lamentably ruined'.[57] Finally the outbreak of plague after 1649 laid to rest any hopes of an economic revival. In this respect Ireland enjoyed much in common with Catalonia, where a shortage of coin was compounded by the fact that the revolt interrupted commerce with Catalonia's largest pre-war trading partner, Castile, and where the plague of 1650–4 'destroyed any lingering chances Catalonia may still have had of preserving its independence from the Spanish Crown'.[58] In contrast to this, a buoyant domestic economy, abundant specie and extensive overseas empires served as invaluable assets in the Dutch and Portuguese struggles for independence; while the English Parliament's control over London and the capital's merchant community, together with its monopoly on trade, proved critical in its struggle against the king.[59]

Nevertheless timely foreign aid could occasionally resuscitate a wasted domestic economy or, at least, provide military hardware, veteran troops and international recognition. Thus external intervention undoubtedly contributed to the success of the revolts in the Ukraine, Portugal and the Netherlands; while Scottish assistance allowed the Westminster Parliament to win the First English Civil War in 1646 and Dutch leadership facilitated another revolution in 1688. Ultimately Spanish manpower and money did not enable the prince of Condé to seize power in France after 1649, but it prolonged the Fronde and effectively crippled France's ability to interfere in European affairs. Even though no continental armies actually fought on Irish soil, as they did during the 'War of the Three Kings' (1689–91), interference from abroad played a critical role in shaping the Irish revolt. English and Scottish supplies throughout the 1640s helped to sustain the

---

[57] Gilbert (ed.), *Irish confederation*, VI, p. 271.
[58] J. H. Elliott, *The revolt of the Catalans. A study in the decline of Spain 1598–1640* (Cambridge, 1963, paperback, 1984) p. 539, also p. 538.
[59] Robert Brenner, *Merchants and revolution. Commercial change, political conflict, and London's overseas traders, 1550–1653* (Cambridge, 1993), especially part III.

Protestant cause, while decisive English intervention after 1649 reduced Ireland to English control. While there is no evidence linking any of the continental Catholic powers with the outbreak of the 1641 rebellion, one recent Habsburg historian has suggested that 'Spain played the role of an inadvertent accessory in the Irish conspiracy. Madrid's desperation in the quest for mercenary troops which might be reliable both in terms of military value and religious orthodoxy, had in practice conduced to the maturation of the uprising, by allowing Strafford's army to be kept in being – fed, trained and even (to some degree) armed – until the right moment arrived.'[60] Certainly by 1642/3, Spain had become a confederate pay-master. As Jane Ohlmeyer shows, the Irish insurgents desperately needed financial and material assistance and, to that end, sent envoys to several European capitals and received accredited diplomats in Kilkenny (see chapter 5). As the 1640s progressed, however, the desire to become Ireland's 'protector' and to interfere directly in Irish politics became an aim of French, Spanish and papal diplomacy. This totally destabilized domestic politics and further divided the Irish political nation into the 'Francophiles' (largely Old English and pro-Ormond), who wanted to aid Charles I in return for the best political, religious and tenurial concessions they could extort, and those (largely Gaelic Irish) who favoured Spain and advocated abandoning the king altogether and making Catholic Ireland, with the aid of foreign powers, impregnable to invasion from England. Thus, to some extent, Ireland had become an international battleground, a minor theatre in the Thirty Years War then raging on the continent. Once again, Ireland's experience of revolt closely resembled that of Catalonia where French intervention initially divided the rebels into those who favoured some contact with Philip IV and those determined to place the region under the sovereignty of Louis XIV. However as it became increasingly clear that France intended to use Catalonia to further her own strategic interests, continued intervention provoked widespread hostility and anti-French riots, greatly undermining the Catalan war-effort, until 'the strains that came from divided loyalties, especially among nobles, ecclesiastics and businessmen still benefiting from the Spanish connection' resulted in defeat.[61]

Perhaps effective political leadership and domestic harmony could have helped to overcome the formidable problems faced by the Confederates

[60] Stradling, *Spanish monarchy*, p. 39.
[61] Elliott, 'The Spanish monarchy and the kingdom of Portugal', p. 65. Also see Elliott, *Revolt*, pp. 534–9 and J. Sanabrè, *La acción de Francia en Cataluña* (Barcelona, 1956). I am grateful to Geoffrey Parker for drawing the latter reference to my attention.

during the 1640s. Certainly a tradition of autonomy and the leads taken by the duke of Braganza in Portugal and the house of Orange in the Netherlands enabled the Portuguese and Dutch 'rebels' to take on and defeat Habsburg Spain, an early modern superpower.[62] Conversely the failure of the Fronde can be attributed to a weakness of leadership and to the total lack of unity amongst the leading aristocratic, bureaucratic and judicial insurgents.[63] Similarly in Scotland religious differences, increasing disillusionment with Argyll's leadership and deep divisions over whether to support the king or the English Parliament as the best means of furthering the revolution proved fatal for the Covenanters.[64] After 1646 domestic discord in Scotland stemmed in part from English politicking over how best to conduct the reconquest of Ireland (see chapter 7). Some Westminster politicians favoured a campaign which included the Scots and involved a negotiated settlement with Ormond; while others, mainly supporters of the earl of Northumberland and the 'Independents', advocated an entirely English offensive which pointedly ignored the interests of the Scots and of the Irish Protestants. For a brief period between 1646 and 1647 these 'hardliners' triumphed and their anglocentric policy elicited, as John Adamson demonstrates, a dramatic response in all three kingdoms: it alienated key Parliamentarians in Ireland and made possible an alliance between the commander there, Lord Inchiquin, and the Confederates in the spring of 1648; it pushed many Scottish Covenanters, who, quite reasonably, feared that Parliament was intent on reasserting English dominance throughout the British Isles, towards the royalist cause (an 'Engagement' was signed in December 1647); and, finally, by providing Charles I with the Scottish manpower and resources he so desperately needed to continue his own struggle against Parliament, it resulted in the outbreak of the Second Civil War in England (May–August 1648). Ironically the defeat of the Scottish Royalists at the battle of Preston, instead of fostering unity among Parliamentarians, exacerbated the factional animosities between the 'Presbyterians' and 'Independents' and only a determination by the army to bring Charles Stuart 'that man of blood, to an account for that blood he had shed, and mischief he had done . . . against the Lord's cause and people in these poor nations'[65] facilitated the constitutional revolution of 1648–9. However, throughout

---

[62] Zagorin, *Rebels*, II, pp. 209, 221.

[63] A. Lloyd Moote, *The revolt of the judges* (Princeton, 1971).

[64] David Stevenson, *Revolution and counter-revolution in Scotland 1644–1651* (London, 1977), pp. 211, 215.

[65] Quoted in Ian Gentles, 'The impact of the New Model Army', in John Morrill (ed.), *The impact of the English civil war* (London, 1991), p. 99.

the 1650s, competition between the army and the politicians for control at Westminster continued to destabilize English affairs. The struggle discussed by Aidan Clarke (chapter 12), between those who believed in rule by 'a single person and parliament', the Cromwellians, and those Republicans who remained committed to the 'good old cause' of the Long Parliament (which had been expelled by Cromwell in April 1653) reached its climax in the months after the protector's death in September 1658 until, in March 1660, the Long Parliament dissolved itself, paving the way for the return of Charles II and the end of the 'English Revolution'.

Similarly in Ireland internal dissension arising from divided loyalties, racial rancour and religious differences help to account for the failure of the revolution there. Despite the fact that the Confederates (like the English Parliamentarians) blatantly violated the king's royal prerogatives and consistently refused to obey his instructions, they nevertheless referred to themselves as 'loyal subjects' and, as Nicholas Canny points out, the majority operated 'within the context of loyalty to the Crown'.[66] The confederate oath of association contained the phrase 'I further swear that I will bear faith and allegiance to our sovereign lord King Charles . . . and that I will defend him . . . as far as I may, with my life, power and estate'; while the confederate seal of office bore the inscription *Pro Deo, Rege et Patria, Hibernia Unanimis.*[67] However, reaching a political and religious arrangement acceptable to all parties proved predictably difficult. The General Assembly may have been at pains to ensure that 'there shall be no distinction or comparison made betwixt old Irish, and old and new English, or betwixt septs or families, or betwixt citizens and townsmen and countreymen, joyning in union, upon pain of the highest punishment', but in practice the Catholics remained as divided as ever.[68] As the war progressed, some Confederates, especially those of 'Old English' descent, often Ormond's kinsmen or clients, proved increasingly eager to conclude a settlement with the king, even if it jeopardized the future safety of the Catholic religion. This group dominated the Supreme Council, the confederate executive body responsible for carrying out the orders of the General Assemblies and for supervising the Catholic war-effort, and clashed constantly with those who favoured complete freedom for the Catholic religion as the inevitable price of any compromise with the Royalists. These Confederates, usually of 'Old Irish' or Gaelic descent,

---

[66] See pp. 29–30 below.
[67] Cited in Clarke, *The Old English in Ireland,* pp. 179–80 and Gilbert (ed.), *Irish confederation,* I, p. lxv, II, p. 85.
[68] Beckett, 'Confederation of Kilkenny', p. 36.

tended to predominate in the confederate General Assemblies and, after 1645, turned to Rinuccini and, to a lesser extent, to Owen Roe O'Neill, for guidance. Yet, as Michelle O Riordan's study of contemporary Gaelic verse highlights, traditional labels such as 'Old English', 'Old Irish', 'Ormondist' or 'nuncioist' inadequately describe the 'complex nexus of allegiances and values held by Irish Catholics during these years'. For many Catholics, like their Old Protestant compatriots after 1660, had no wish to divorce Ireland from Stuart control; on the contrary, the 'political' poems she discusses 'were written with the conviction that devotion to Catholicism and recognition of Charles I's position as sovereign of Ireland were in no way incompatible'.[69] As another Gaelic scholar has recently noted, for the majority of Irishmen 'Charles I was still their rightful king – "this good tho'" unfortunate king", the Irish were *sliocht Shéarlais*, "Charles's people"'.[70]

Nevertheless, after the conclusion of a temporary cease-fire in September 1643, the vast majority of Confederates faced the dilemma of how to reconcile this loyalty to the king with their devotion to the church and to formulate a moderate settlement which would, in the words of the earl of Clanricard, not cut 'too deep an incision . . . into old sores'.[71] However it proved impossible to 'staunch and heal the bleeding wounds of this unhappy kingdom'[72] largely because religious differences formed the main stumbling block to the conclusion of any permanent peace between the Confederates and the Royalists which, in turn, undermined any real chance of defeating their common enemy, the English Parliament. In January 1645 Charles I, desperate for Irish aid, instructed the earl of Glamorgan, a prominent Catholic noble from Wales, to secure Irish troops for royalist service in return for religious concessions and, the following August, the Confederates and Glamorgan agreed upon a secret treaty which involved sending 10,000 Irish troops, arms and munitions to England. Almost at once Rinuccini rejected the 'Glamorgan Treaty' on the grounds that insufficient provision had been made for the Catholic religion and that Glamorgan lacked the power to implement those concessions he had granted; while the following year, for similar reasons, the nuncio found yet another peace agreement, known as the 'First Ormond Peace', unacceptable and first excommunicated and then exiled from Kilkenny those Confederates who favoured it. Defeat on the battlefield exacerbated these factional divisions within the ranks of the Catholic party and left an already fragmented country divided into 'a woeful spectacle, cantonized into

---

[69] See p. 113 below.
[70] Ó Buachalla, 'James our true king', p. 23.
[71] Lowe (ed.), *Letter-book*, p. 41.   [72] *Ibid.*

severall sundry factions, drawing all divers waies, and driveing on several interests'.[73]

Matters deteriorated further in the spring of 1648 when the parliamentary commander Lord Inchiquin declared for the king and forged an alliance with the more moderate Confederates. Rinuccini responded by excommunicating the supporters of the 'Inchiquin Truce', who in retaliation appealed directly to Rome against his censure.[74] Catholic Ireland was thus more polarized than ever before, and the battle lines between the 'moderate', pro-Ormond party and the 'extreme', pro-nuncio faction were formalized on 11 June when Owen Roe O'Neill and the Army of Ulster declared war on the Supreme Council. These internecine quarrels mystified foreign observers, who could not understand the myopia of the Irish:

> What really surprises the majority of those who contemplate the affairs of Ireland [the French ambassador in London reported back to Paris] is to see that people of the same nation and of the same religion – who are well aware that the resolution to exterminate them totally has already been taken – should differ so strongly in their private hostilities; that their zeal for religion, the preservation of their country and their own self interest are not sufficient to make them lay down – at least, for a short time – the passions which divide them one from the other.[75]

Similarly, frustrated Gaelic poets repeatedly bemoaned the nation's lack of military and political unity and, like John Lynch writing in 1662, wondered: 'Are not five hundred years powerful enough to make one people of the English and the Irish?'[76]

II

Amidst the conflict and confiscations of the mid-seventeenth century the forces of continuity, and of change within continuity, are apparent. For instance, in a recent discussion of Irish royalism Breandán Ó Buachalla convincingly demonstrates that the seventeenth century as a whole

[73] *A letter from Sr Lewis Dyve to the lord marquis of Newcastle* . . . (The Hague, 1650), p. 5.
[74] *Commentarius Rinuccinianus*, III, pp. 70–1, 73; Aiazza, *Embassy*, pp. 376–9, 380–1; Patrick Corish, 'Rinuccini's censure of May 22 1648', *Irish Theological Quarterly*, 18 (Oct. 1951), pp. 323–9; Corish, 'Bishop Nicholas French and the second Ormond peace, 1648–1649', *IHS*, 6 (Sept. 1948), pp. 90–100; Corish, 'The crisis in Ireland in 1648: the nuncio and the supreme council: conclusions', *Irish Theological Quarterly*, 22 (Jan. 1955), pp. 230–57 discusses the contemporary controversy over the excommunication. Also see chapters 3 and 6 below.
[75] Bellièvre to Brienne, 3/13 November 1648 (Archives du Ministère des Affaires Etrangères, Correspondance politique, Angleterre, Côte 57, fos. 314–15).
[76] Cited on p. 123 below.

represented a watershed in Irish intellectual developments and 'for the hereditary learned classes in particular' it marked 'the beginning of the end of their privileged position in Irish society, as the socio-economic system on which their status depended slowly gave way'. However he adds that the passing away of the bardic order 'should not be interpreted . . . as the demise of a culture, language or society' for these years also witnessed 'a major period of literary diversification and of reorganization'.[77] In chapter 6 Michelle O Riordan draws attention to this new intellectual order of Catholic Ireland and to the works of poetry and prose penned by an emerging literary class of prose writers and priest poets who were not necessarily schooled in the bardic tradition and who used English and Latin as well as Irish to convey their message.

Yet the fact remains that the Irish rebellion of the 1640s and the land settlement to which it gave birth had a dramatic and permanent impact on the course of Ireland's history. In the conclusion to this volume T. C. Barnard outlines the 'revolutionary' legacies of these years – on the owner-ship of land, on the distribution of political power, and on attitudes and the sense of distinctive identities within particular ethnic and confessional communities. Apart from a brief interlude after 1685, it was 1922 before Catholics again dominated Ireland's political and diplomatic structures. Cromwellian occupation and direct rule from Westminster also ushered in a new phase in Anglo-Irish relations which, thanks to the failure of the Irish Parliament to meet between 1666 and 1689, continued after the Restoration as the London government and the Stuart court extended their control over Irish appointments, finances, defence and the church. Even though the radical sects, especially the Baptists, Quakers and Independents, which had flourished during the 1650s were marginalized after the Restoration, as Phil Kilroy points out in chapter 10, 'old religious paradigms had changed radically'. In particular Presbyterianism, which had been critically shaped by the war and had taken even deeper root in Ulster, continued to thrive and became a permanent, disruptive feature on the Irish religious scene. However it took the established church 'over a century to grasp that several distinct, dissenting influences had taken root in Ireland, and that they could not conform to the Restoration Church Settlement'.[78]

While the 'forces of change were not compressed into the 1640s and 1650s', Kevin McKenny argues in chapter 9 that the tenurial upheavals of these years helped to transform Ireland 'from a tribal kingdom into a

---

[77] Ó Buachalla, 'James our true king', p. 9.   [78] See p. 217 below.

recognizably "modern" state'.[79] The revolution in Irish landholding, which began with the plantations of the early seventeenth century, had by 1688 reduced the Catholic share of land from 59 per cent in 1641 to 22 per cent. Admittedly these tenurial upheavals led to the creation of more efficient estates; but they also reconfigured Irish society by accelerating the destruction of the economic foundations of the old Gaelic order. Many low-ranking Gaelic and, to a lesser extent, Old English families suffered an all-encompassing calamity which deprived them of their estates, status and power and forced others to seek service in one of the Catholic continental armies. However, according to McKenny's detailed study of West Ulster, this revolution in landholding has been somewhat distorted. On the one hand, key sources (especially the Books of Survey and Distribution) which deal with the transfer of land, tend to inflate the amount of property held by Catholics prior to 1641 and thereby misrepresent the number of acres actually lost by them during the 1650s. On the other, some historians have perhaps overstated the sectarian nature of the land transfer and failed to appreciate that significant numbers of Catholics, especially higher-ranking nobles with contacts at court or with extensive estates in remote areas, survived the social, economic and political turmoil caused by the Civil War with their lands and power largely intact.[80]

Despite these caveats, the events of the mid-seventeenth century 'transformed the landed class of Ireland in a way which the English and French Revolutions failed to do'.[81] Moreover the fact that it was the pre-war Protestant settler community which benefited the most from the land transfers helped to facilitate the emergence of a 'Protestant ascendancy' in Ireland. T. C. Barnard outlines the mental worlds and traces the fortunes of prominent Old Protestants and demonstrates how the war divided them into those, most notably James Butler, marquis and, after 1660, duke of Ormond and Sir George Lane, who aligned unquestionably behind the Stuarts; and others, including Roger Boyle, Lord Broghill, Sir Charles Coote and Arthur Annesley, who equated 'popery with treachery' and sided first with Parliament and then with Cromwell (chapter 11).[82] However many of those who took up arms against the king or collaborated often did so reluctantly. Similarly, after 1660, even though many Old Protestants

---

[79] See p. 198 below.
[80] This is not the case with all historians, see footnote 34 above.
[81] See p. 181 below.
[82] Contemporaries described the pre-war Protestant settlers as 'Old Protestants' and the Protestants who settled in Ireland after 1641 as 'soldiers' or 'adventurers'. Historians use the term 'New English' to describe the Protestant colonial element which settled in Ireland after 1534 and do not distinguish between the pre- and post-war Protestant settlers.

found the Stuart proclivity for 'popery' odious and resented their eagerness to interfere in the Irish boroughs, law courts, land settlement and army, few wanted to sever links with the crown. Thus, according to Barnard, the Convention of 1660 did not mark 'the dawn of Irish Protestant "colonial nationalism"'; nor should the 'circumstances and attitudes' of seventeenth-century Protestants be linked with the revolutionary 1790s. They simply wanted more political autonomy and greater control over the army, judiciary and administration *within* the context of the Stuart monarchy. As Barnard and Aidan Clarke point out, the real significance of the 1660 Convention lay in the fact that it was the first exclusively Protestant assembly which claimed to represent Ireland. To be sure intermarriage, the survival of Catholic landholders and conversions to Protestantism often blurred ethnic and religious divisions, but, in the final analysis, 'the divisive forces released by conquest, dispossession and legalized degradation, tended to . . . intensify sectarian fissures' and, increasingly, made religion 'the surest touchstone of reliability'.[83]

The events of the 1640s and 1650s thus intensified a brand of sectarianism and religious bigotry which has lasted in parts of Ireland until the present day. The '1641 Ulster massacres' mean as much to the Protestant tradition as Cromwell's 'atrocities' at Drogheda in 1649 do to Catholic popular culture.[84] The French Religious Wars, the Dutch Revolt, the Thirty Years War and, some would argue, the Civil Wars of England and Scotland demonstrate that wars of religion were commonplace in early modern Europe.[85] Clearly Ireland was no exception. But whereas elsewhere in early modern Europe after the 1640s religion no longer dominated international relations, confessional divisions and animosities continued to play a prominent role in shaping Ireland's history. The German Civil War may well have been the last continental conflict fought over 'religion', but in Ireland the hostilities of the 1640s marked only a beginning.

---

[83] See pp. 282, 237 below. Also see Ó Buachalla, 'James our true king', pp. 8–9.

[84] Mac Cuarta (ed.), *Ulster 1641*, especially p. 1 and Kevin McKenny, 'The Cromwellian storm of Drogheda, 11 September 1649: the invention of Irish national identity' (unpublished paper presented to the American Conference of Irish Historians, April 1993). I am grateful to Kevin McKenny for allowing me to read his paper in advance of publication.

[85] See especially John Morrill, 'The religious context of the English Civil War', *Transactions, Royal Historical Society*, fifth series, 34 (1984), pp. 155–78 and Geoffrey Parker, *The Thirty Years War* (London, 1984), pp. 215–26.

CHAPTER 2

WHAT REALLY HAPPENED IN IRELAND
IN 1641?

NICHOLAS CANNY

THAT THE rising of 1641 was one of the critical moments in Irish history, equal in importance with the insurrection of 1798, or the Land War of the nineteenth century, or the Northern Ireland troubles of today, seems beyond dispute. Yet, in spite of its acknowledged importance, the rising has been surprisingly little studied, and this in itself calls for an explanation. The reluctance of academic historians to come to grips with the subject stems primarily from the fact that Protestant apologists appropriated the episode, and the sources that relate to it, within a few short years of the rising. The most effective was Sir John Temple, an official in the Dublin government when the insurrection happened: his *The Irish rebellion*, published in an extensive form in 1646, advanced a coherent explanation of what had happened only five years previously. According to Temple the insurrection, and an associated pre-meditated massacre of the Protestant settlers in Ireland, had been planned by the Catholic leaders in the country long before 1641. He asserted that the Old English politicians of Anglo-Norman descent figured prominently at this planning stage, and that they had been egged on by the Catholic clergy in order to recover Ireland for the pope's interest. Events in Ireland therefore formed part of a broader Catholic attack upon Protestantism, and success in Ireland would have led to an immediate assault against the Protestant populations of England and Scotland with a view to restoring Catholicism as the religion of both those kingdoms. The Gaelic lords of Ulster who were known to have been first and most prominent in the action were, in a sense, excused by Temple as but the pliant instruments of wily priests and treacherous Old English lawyers and landowners.[1]

---

[1] John Temple, *The Irish rebellion: or the history of the beginning and first progress of the general rebellion raised within the kingdom of Ireland upon the three and twentieth day of October 1641* (London, 1646). There has been no recent edition of Temple's *Rebellion* but extracts from it have been published in the *Field*

Temple claimed authority for his version of events first by describing it as a history, and second by his liberal citation from contemporary evidence to support his various propositions. The material most frequently cited came from the sworn statements known to historians as the '1641 depositions', collected from the survivors of the assault during the months immediately after the insurrection.[2] Besides these depositions Temple was also in a position to draw upon the official correspondence of the Dublin government both immediately before and after the October insurrection (also see chapter 11 below).

At the time Temple wrote, the Catholics he accused were in no position to defend themselves from his barbs. Consequently, *The Irish rebellion* assumed the status of an official interpretation almost from the moment of its publication. It also soon became the standard Protestant interpretation, and its publication record through the eighteenth and even into the nineteenth century reveals that fresh editions appeared whenever Protestant control of Irish government and society was threatened by Catholic demands for a recovery of some of their lost power.[3] Under these circumstances it was difficult for those who sympathized with the position in which Catholics had found themselves in the 1640s to respond. Instead of countering it with an interpretation of their own, those who were uneasy with Temple's version of events strove to discredit the authority on which it was based by asserting that the 1641 depositions were so biased in their reportage that they could not be admitted as evidence.[4]

One consequence of this stand-off was that the Protestant explanation of 1641 stood alone, and in so far as Catholic writers responded at all it was by

day *anthology of Irish writing* ed. Seamus Deane *et al.* (Derry, 1991), I, pp. 221–5. This chapter is a modified and expanded version of an essay, entitled 'In defense of the constitution? The nature of Irish revolt in the seventeenth century' and published in L. Bergeron and L. M. Cullen (eds.) *Culture et pratiques politiques en France et en Irlande XVIe–XVIIIe siècles. Actes du Colloque de Marseille, 28 Septembre–2 Octobre 1988* (Paris, 1991), pp. 23–40. I was persuaded by Dr Jane Ohlmeyer to recast that paper for inclusion in this volume and I am indebted to her for helpful editorial advice.

[2] Aidan Clarke, 'The 1641 depositions', in Peter Fox (ed.), *Treasures of the library of Trinity College, Dublin* (Dublin 1986), pp. 111–22; Máiréad O'Keeffe, 'The politics of Irish Protestants, 1641–1660' (unpublished MA thesis, University College, Galway, 1991), pp. 1–101.

[3] *Ibid.* and T. C. Barnard, 'Crises of identity among Irish Protestants, 1641–1685', *Past and Present*, 127 (May 1990), pp. 39–83, especially pp. 53–5; Barnard, 'The uses of 23 October 1641 and Irish Protestant celebrations', *English Historical Review*, 106 (1991), pp. 889–920; Thomas Bartlett, 'Review article: A new history of Ireland', *Past and Present*, 116 (August 1987), pp. 206–19, especially p. 214.

[4] The historians who were uneasy with Temple's interpretation were both those who wrote in the Catholic tradition and those who drew their inspiration from nineteenth-century liberals. On the origins of Catholic historiography see Thomas Bartlett, *The fall and rise of the Irish nation: the Catholic question, 1690–1830* (Dublin, 1992), pp. 50–5; and the fount for the liberal tradition is W. E. H. Lecky, *A history of Ireland in the eighteenth century* (5 vols., London, 1892), I.

looking to the later Cromwellian atrocities at Drogheda and Wexford as the source for their own martyrology. Academic historians of the present century, in their concern to appear objective, have also avoided analysing what happened in 1641, and their entry into the realm of controversy has been only to question the theory of a pre-meditated massacre of Protestants and to suggest that the claims made in the Protestant accounts of the numbers actually slaughtered in 1641 are implausible.[5] The thrust of the scholarly endeavour has been to explain why 1641 occurred rather than to consider what happened, and in the course of advancing their explanations authorities have situated the events leading to the outburst of the rising on 23 October 1641 within the broad context of political developments in England, Scotland and Ireland. The most persuasive of these high-politics accounts was formulated by Aidan Clarke and has largely been integrated into Conrad Russell's *The fall of the British monarchies 1637–1642*.[6] This focuses attention on the difficulties experienced by King Charles and his closest associates in governing three kingdoms, and suggests that disturbances or contention in any one had unforeseen but nonetheless inevitable consequences for the other two. The Irish rising of 1641 was, according to this interpretation, triggered by political dislocations in Scotland and England, while the events in Ireland further exacerbated relations between the monarch and powerful sections of the political nation in the other two kingdoms. Raymond Gillespie also favours this three-kingdoms context in offering an explanation for the 1641 rising, but he has added an economic and religious dimension which accounts for the popular aspect to the insurrection.[7]

Despite these very considerable advances in our understanding of what precipitated the rising of 1641, a detailed narrative of the course of events in the months immediately following its outbreak is still lacking, as is an

---

[5] Aidan Clarke, 'The 1641 depositions'; Walter Love, 'Civil war in Ireland', *Emory University Quarterly*, 22 (1966), pp. 57–72.

[6] Aidan Clarke, 'The genesis of the Ulster rising of 1641', in Peter Roebuck (ed.), *Plantation to partition* (Belfast, 1981), pp. 29–45; Conrad Russell, *The fall of the British monarchies, 1637–1642* (Oxford, 1991), pp. 373–400. It should be noted that Russell is suspicious of the neat manner in which the Irish revolt has been fitted into a 'British' model and he suggests (pp. 373–4) that this may be due to a bias in the surviving documentation. The high-politics model is further developed in Michael Perceval-Maxwell, 'Ireland and the monarchy in the early Stuart multiple kingdom', *The Historical Journal*, 34 (1991), pp. 279–95, and in Jane H. Ohlmeyer, *Civil war and restoration in the three Stuart kingdoms: the career of Randal MacDonnell, marquis of Antrim, 1609–1683* (Cambridge, 1993), pp. 10–17, 77–102.

[7] Raymond Gillespie, 'The end of an era: Ulster and the outbreak of the 1641 rising', in Ciaran Brady and Raymond Gillespie (eds.), *Natives and newcomers : the making of Irish colonial society, 1534–1641* (Dublin 1986), pp. 191–213; Gillespie, 'Harvest crises in early seventeenth-century Ireland', *Irish Economic and Social History*, 11 (1984), pp. 5–18.

identification of those individuals who led the disturbances and those social groups that were engaged in action in various parts of the country. Only a close study of the depositions can reveal this information.[8] There can be little doubt that the thirty-two volumes of sworn statements, collected from those Protestant settlers in Ireland who endured the onslaught that had been launched against them in the autumn of 1641, is a body of material which is emotional and which seeks to represent Irish Catholics in the worst possible light. However, despite these apparent biases this Protestant testimony cannot be ignored, because it represents the only detailed evidence of what happened in Ireland in and after October 1641.[9] A close study of the depositions also suggests that they might prove more useful than would at first appear because the deponents themselves, and those who collected the information from them, were concerned to identify those who had attacked them, and they recorded the gist of the justifications for the onslaught offered to them by their assailants. In the course of these summaries the deponents sought to distinguish between political, religious and economic legitimizations, and the more thoughtful reflected back on their previous relations with their Catholic neighbours in search of evidence, which had not then seemed significant, that an assault was long being planned. This retrospective analysis led to the conclusion that a conspiracy, involving the more prominent Irish Catholic political leaders and the Catholic clergy, precipitated the assault of October 1641, but successive deponents also acknowledged that the attack, when it did come, was a complex movement and that different individuals became involved with different ends in view. One of the attractions therefore of the depositions as a historical source is that they make it possible for us to unravel the complex of motivations that the Protestants attributed to their

[8] Several recent studies have made use of the depositions, collected in 1641 and 1642, to shed light on the course and character of the 1641 rising. See especially Nicholas Canny, 'The Irish background to Penn's experiment', in Richard S. Dunn and Mary Maples Dunn (eds.), *The world of William Penn* (Philadelphia 1986), pp. 139–56; Canny, The marginal kingdom : Ireland as a problem in the first British empire', in Bernard Bailyn and Philip D. Morgan, (eds.), *Strangers within the realm: cultural margins of the first British empire* (Chapel Hill, N.C., 1991), pp. 35–66; Canny, 'The 1641 depositions as a source for the writing of social history : County Cork as a case study', in Patrick O'Flanagan and Cornelius G. Buttimer (eds.), *Cork: history and society* (Dublin, 1993), pp. 249–308; Mary O'Dowd, 'Women and war in Ireland in the 1640s', in Margaret MacCurtain and Mary O'Dowd (eds.), *Women in early modern Ireland* (Edinburgh, 1991), pp. 91–112; O'Dowd, *Power, politics and land: early modern Sligo, 1568–1688* (Belfast, 1991), pp. 105–31; Michael Perceval-Maxwell, 'The Ulster rising of 1641 and the depositions', *IHS*, 21 (1978) pp. 144–67.

[9] The origin, character and potential use of the depositions, as well as the difference between those depositions collected in the 1641–3 period and those collected in the 1650s have all been considered in Aidan Clarke, 'The 1641 depositions', and Nicholas Canny, 'The 1641 depositions as a source for the writing of social history'.

assailants, and to suggest explanations for the involvement of different social elements from within the Irish Catholic community in this common assault upon the Protestant population in the country. Moreover a study of the depositions clearly indicates that the colourful depictions of atrocity that were quoted so liberally in Protestant 'histories' of 1641,[10] were usually the product of rumours that circulated among the settlers after they had found shelter in one of the towns or fortified positions that remained in Protestant hands. This hearsay material clearly differs from the narrations which the deponents gave of their personal experiences. The eye-witness accounts are so clinical in detail as to be entirely plausible.

Several deponents from different parts of the country presented testimony which provides corroborating evidence for the high-politics explanation of the outbreak of the revolt favoured by Aidan Clarke and Conrad Russell. Such statements make reference to the involvement of Irish Catholic leaders in the constitutional politics of Ireland and England during the years previous to 1641; they allude to the special interest that these political figures took in the military activities of the Scottish Covenanters; and they suggest that the Catholic leaders in 1641 intended to follow the example of the Scots by seizing upon the principal fortified positions in the country so that they could dictate terms to the king in such matters as establishing Catholicism as the official religion of the state and having only Irish Catholics appointed to senior positions in government and as justices of the peace. These deponents further testified that the insurgents justified their ambitions to them either on the grounds that they had been wrongly deprived of positions of trust because of their religion, or that they feared a further move against Catholicism was being planned by English Parliamentarians and their sympathizers in Ireland.[11]

Those Protestants who recorded these 'justifications' could not disguise their contempt for them; but they could not deny the validity of the fears of Irish Catholics; first because spokesmen for the Protestant interest had inveighed consistently against the tacit toleration of Catholicism that had been permitted in Ireland by the king, and second because the animosity in the English Parliament towards Catholicism in general and towards the queen's Catholic chaplain and courtiers in particular was well known. The deponents were therefore ready to concede some plausibility to the insurgents' claim that they had risen to defend the queen, but Protestants were deeply offended and annoyed by the further assertion that their

---

[10] See, for example, Mary Hickson, *Ireland in the seventeenth-century* (2 vols., London, 1884).
[11] Deposition of Dr Robert Maxwell, Rector of Tinon, County Armagh (TCD, MS 809, fos. 5–12); deposition of Edward How (TCD, MS 835, fo. 29).

actions enjoyed the sanction of the king and that one of their purposes was to defend the royal prerogative. Some deponents sought to counter this argument by suggesting that the parchment with a great wax seal dangling from it which Sir Phelim O'Neill had flourished before his followers was in fact a forgery.[12]

Deponents were especially concerned to discredit the contention of the insurgents that their actions enjoyed royal approval, because in all such statements from the insurgents the Protestant leaders in Ireland were depicted as Puritans and 'rebels', and the insurgents themselves were represented as loyal subjects of the crown.[13] More immediately, the deponents were anxious to expose as fraudulent the idea that the insurrection enjoyed royal approval because this claim had apparently proven convincing for many Scottish settlers in Ulster who, as several deponents testified, remained neutral when Sir Phelim O'Neill and his associates captured the fortified positions at Charlemont, Mountjoy, Dungannon and Armagh.[14] And the deponents also seemed convinced that the rebels' claims that their actions enjoyed prior royal approval also facilitated their efforts to solicit further support from within the Catholic community.

While seeking to undermine the arguments advanced by the Catholic leaders, the deponents were tacitly admitting that the purpose of those who had risen in arms was not to return to the Gaelic order that had been overthrown at the end of the sixteenth century, nor even to cancel the plantation that had been established in Ulster, but rather to make Ireland a Catholic kingdom under the jurisdiction of King Charles I. The deponents' concern with O'Neill's assertion that his action had been sanctioned by the king shows also that they assumed that substantial elements of the Catholic population would never have engaged in military action unless they had been convinced that it enjoyed royal approval. In addition, several deponents testified that the leaders of the insurrection continued to proceed cautiously and to function within the context of

---

[12] In her deposition Katherin Maddison reported that she had 'often heard' it reported by the rebels that they had risen 'because the queen's confessor was murdered in her arms' (TCD, MS 835, fo. 210); on the issue of the supposed royal sanction see Clarke, 'The genesis of the Ulster rising', and the deposition of George Fletcher (TCD, MS 835, fo. 105); that of Edward Slacke (TCD, MS 835, fo. 170); that of John Right (TCD, MS 835, fo. 158).

[13] Thomas Ashe, a deponent from County Meath, testified that he heard one of the rebels state that 'the king was deposed, the palsgrave [Charles Lewis, the Elector Palatine and Charles I's nephew] crowned and that the king had given the Catholics of Ireland direction to rebel lest they [Irish Protestants] should assist the Puritans in England' (TCD, MS 816, fo. 90).

[14] See, for example, the deposition of Henry Boine of Mullaghtean, County Tyrone (TCD, MS 839, fo. 1).

loyalty to the crown even after their initial successes in capturing several of the garrisons in Ulster.

One John Kerdiff, who had been rector of Desereagh in County Tyrone and who was taken prisoner in the early stages of the revolt, stated that he had then heard Sir Phelim O'Neill profess that he had a commission for his actions 'not only from most of the chief of the nobility of this kingdom but also from his Majesty . . . [and] also letters to that purpose from the earl of Argyll. And that these instructions were only for the liberty of their religion and for the recovery of those lands which should appear by the law of the land to be unjustly held from them, and for the king's prerogative'.[15] Another clergyman who had been captured in the early stages of the revolt was given a similar explanation by Sir Phelim O'Neill who had further informed him of plans to capture Dublin and other fortified positions and that this strategy had been resolved 'amongst the lords and gentry of this kingdom for the preservation of his Majesty's prerogative and their own religion and liberties against the Puritan faction in England, Scotland and Ireland who intended (as the said Sir Phelim averred), to enact such laws whereby the inhabitants of Ireland should conform in religion . . . and otherwise to be deprived of life, liberty and estates'.[16] Consistent with these assertions was the further statement by Turlough O'Neill, after he had captured the town of Armagh, that 'he would surrender the town to the English army if he was requested to do so in the name of the king but that he would refuse to do so if requested in the name of parliament'.[17]

While such statements bore witness to the prudence with which the Catholic leaders in Ulster proceeded, deponents also testified that this caution was not shared by all the insurgents and that some became involved for less worthy motives than those articulated by the leaders. Charity Chappell, for example, mentioned that one Preston, a son-in-law to Sir Phelim O'Neill, had informed her 'that the gentry of Ireland on their side did think much that the scum of England should be here to overtop them'.[18] It may have been some of these gentry, jealous of the success of the settlers, who enquired of Jane Grace 'and other English what they did in this land, for the land of Ireland was theirs and therefore they would have the English goods'.[19] For some of the Ulster Catholics recovery of their property could only have been accomplished by a reversal of the plantation in Ulster, and William Duffeild testified that the rebels who had attacked

15 Deposition of John Kerdiff (TCD, MS 839, fo. 2).
16 Deposition of William Fitzgerald, clerk (TCD, MS 836, fo. 82).
17 Deposition of Charity Chappell, wife of Richard Chappell, Esq. (TCD, MS 836, fo. 44).
18 Ibid.
19 Deposition of Jane Grace (TCD, MS 836, fo. 52).

him claimed authority from England 'to win their lands again and inhabit them if they could'. Even more specifically, he identified among the leaders one 'Toole McCann that came of another country and claimed the land of Clancan'.[20]

Such specific references to remembered losses that derived from the Ulster plantation are rare, and most insurgents seem to have recognized that a formal reversal of the plantation would do nothing to resolve their problems. What concerned those of the insurgents who gave expression to their economic grievances by actions, if not by words, was that they had been reduced to an inferior position within the social order that had come into being during the course of the seventeenth century. The extent of such resentment does not appear to have been appreciated by Sir Phelim O'Neill and the other leaders of the insurrection who seem to have been taken by surprise when their own challenge to the existing political authority precipitated a popular onslaught against the Protestant farming population which had come into possession of the better tenancies. These attacks were apparently aimed at the expulsion of those Protestants with whom Catholics had previously lived amicably as neighbours, and they extended to the estates of the Catholic proprietors (including the estates of Sir Phelim O'Neill himself) who had rented out much of their property to English, improving tenants.[21] There is some mention in the depositions that the rebel leaders attempted to halt this breakdown into chaos, especially when it involved attacks upon the English tenants they had settled on their own properties. All such efforts proved futile, however, either because of the panic of the English settlers who would not trust their Irish landlords to protect them, or because of the animus of the popular onslaught against those particular tenants.[22] Interventions by the Catholic landowners thus exacerbated an already difficult situation, and frequently resulted in the proprietors themselves being accused of leading the assault as, for example, the charge made by George Burne of Dungannon against John O'Neill that he had killed his own servants.[23]

The popular attacks did not usually result in loss of life, nor were they intended to. However they were always gruesome affairs because they

[20] Deposition of William Duffeild (TCD, MS 836, fo. 48).
[21] Francis Leiland (TCD, MS 836, fo. 98) mentioned that his brother Thomas Leiland 'had been a workman to Sir Phelim O'Neill'. Also Joan Constable in listing those Protestants killed included 'Sir Phelim O'Neill's own nurse and her husband and one child' (TCD, MS 836, fo. 87).
[22] The way in which the revolt complicated relationships between an Irish Catholic landlord and his English Protestant tenants has been detailed in the case of James Condon of County Cork in Canny, 'The 1641 depositions as a source', pp. 273–5.
[23] Deposition of George Burne of Dungannon (TCD, MS 839, fo. 7).

involved face-to-face confrontations between individuals who had long known each other. The typical offensive usually involved an armed group of Irish descending upon a Protestant settler family and demanding, at knife point, that they remove themselves from their house and farm. Killings usually occurred only where the Protestants resisted, but Protestants who refused to divulge where they had hidden their money were frequently tortured.[24] The greed for money also led the insurgents to strip their adversaries, and Jane Grace for example complained that many English were put naked in stocks in frost and snow 'until they confessed money'.[25] Not satisfied with depriving the settlers of their farms, money, clothes and possessions, the insurgents also turned their attention to the various legal documents that were kept in the settlers' houses. The most valued of such records would have been the leases which gave the settlers title to their farms. These were certainly taken or destroyed by the rebels but so also were bonds and specialities that bore testimony to native indebtedness.[26] The concern of the insurgents to find and destroy such evidence indicates how widespread was their concern over the level of their indebtedness. The leaders could see that debt had been responsible for the loss of control over their property, much of which had slipped into alien possession as a result of their inability to meet their commitments. The most conspicuous losses were those suffered by less efficient Catholic landowners who had negotiated loans either with more enterprising Protestant landowners or with English or Old English moneylenders in Dublin and other Irish towns. These lenders would have insisted on land being mortgaged as a security but land also passed away from Catholic management whenever the proprietors placed English tenants on a large block of their property in return for a high entry fine and a low rent.[27] On the popular level, concern over debt would have related to the series of small obligations contracted by farmers within their own localities, and usually with their Protestant neighbours. It was evidence of these debts which was systematically sought out and destroyed in the thousands of house raids that occurred initially

---

[24] Margaret Phillips of Kilmore, County Armagh, witnessed the ears of a neighbour being cut off 'to make him confess money' (TCD, MS 836, fo. 66).
[25] Deposition of Jane Grace (TCD, MS 836, fo. 52).
[26] The following depositions all contain such references and these from one county alone (TCD, MS 835, fos. 84, 117, 119, 170, 181).
[27] The shift in the ownership of land through commercial transactions has been detailed in several local studies; see especially Breandán O Bric, 'Galway townsmen as owners of land in Connacht, 1585–1641' (unpublished M.A. thesis, University College, Galway, 1974); O'Dowd, *Power, politics and land*, pp. 89–104; Michael MacCarthy Morrogh, *The Munster plantation: English migration to Southern Ireland, 1583–1641* (Oxford, 1986), pp. 151–71; Raymond Gillespie, *Colonial Ulster: the settlement of East Ulster, 1600–1641* (Cork, 1985), pp. 28–46, 84–111.

in Ulster and then everywhere that settlers had established themselves in Ireland (also see chapters 8 and 9 below).

Several deponents, such as Henry Boine of Mullaghtean, County Tyrone, said of the insurgents that 'their chief malice was against churchmen' even during the early days of the revolt.[28] This animosity may be explained as much by the ministers' heavy involvement in money-lending transactions as by their religious profession, and this is certainly suggested by a study of the depositions for County Fermanagh which shows how several Protestant clergymen had acquired substantial properties through keen financial dealings within their communities.[29] Debt collectors were similarly isolated for attack, and one who had the misfortune to fall into the rebels' hands had his bills 'taken by those that robbed him and torn in pieces with many oaths and testations of the rebels that there should never be debt paid in this kingdom any more'.[30]

Such instances point to the motivation of some of the attacks on individual Protestants that took place within all localities once the insurrection had broken out. Taken together they do not explain why the revolt happened, nor do the short-term economic causes of the revolt, to which Raymond Gillespie has alluded, explain all such individual assaults because, as already noted, the grievances of some of the Irish were long established and derived from such basic matters as the Ulster plantation. Even where such fundamental issues were invoked to justify their actions the insurgents remained restrained in their actions and kept physical violence to a minimum. Indeed whatever loss of life occurred during the course of these house-raids usually happened when the settlers presented armed resistance to their assailants. The situation changed however once the Protestants began to form themselves into armed groups for the purpose of mutual defence or to recover what had been lost. The settlers everywhere were remarkably slow to unite, and in Ulster the Scots were repeatedly charged by the English with a refusal to make common cause with them in providing for their mutual defence.[31] However once the Protestants did mobilize themselves they proved reasonably effective in defending themselves in those parts of the country where settlement was thick on the ground. The ensuing conflict between armed bands resulted in heavy casualties, sometimes on both sides. Where this loss of life was on the

[28] Deposition of Henry Boine (TCD, MS 839, fo. 1).
[29] Canny 'The marginal kingdom', pp. 51–2 and 58.
[30] Deposition of Christian Stanhawe (TCD, MS 836, fo. 75); deposition of Lieutenant Thomas Bromley of Dublin City (TCD, MS 810, fo. 121).
[31] Raymond Gillespie, 'The end of an era', Gillespie, 'Harvest crises'; the testimony of Henry Boine (TCD, MS 839, fo. 1).

Catholic side it precipitated the revenge killings for which the 1641 disturbance is notorious. In the case of central Ulster, where the revolt first began, the two most gruesome incidents – the drowning of Protestants at the bridge over the Bann at Portadown and the burning of Protestants in a thatched cottage in the parish of Kilmore – were recognized by Protestants to have been in revenge for the first Protestant victory at Lisnagarvey (now part of Lisburn). There, according to one deponent, the assembled settlers succeeded not only in defeating the rebel forces but in killing seven hundred of them, and the rage of the English in attack was such that even their horses deliberately trampled down the rebels and 'took pikes in their mouths' to hack at them.[32] Whatever the zeal of their horses, the bloody-mindedness shown by the settlers at Lisnagarvey in December 1641 made a deep impression upon the Irish, and one deponent, Thomas Tuckes of Drogheda, remarked that the 'slaughter of the English' could be dated from that battle.[33]

According to William Clarke, who recorded the most credible account of the episode at Portadown, about one hundred Protestants (men, women and children) from the parish of Loughgall in County Armagh who were already prisoners in the hands of the rebels then suffered repeated tortures such as 'strangling and half-hanging'. Afterwards they were 'driven like hogs' six miles to the river Bann, being forced by the rebels 'to go fast' with swords and pikes which they thrust 'into their sides'. Three had already been murdered by the time they had reached the river at Portadown and the remainder were stripped naked and forced with pikes and swords on to the bridge which had been 'cut down in the midst'. In this way they were 'thrust headlong' into the water, and those who sought to save themselves were shot at by the rebels. All, according to Clarke, were killed, except for himself, who had given £15 to the rebels 'for which money's sake they promised him many kindnesses' most of which they failed to fulfil.[34]

The incident at Kilmore also concerned prisoners. This group was being detained in a thatched cottage which was then deliberately put on fire by Jane Hampson, the wife of a settler Henry Hampson, and herself 'formerly a Protestant'. However, as one deponent put it, Jane Hampson was really 'a mere Irish-woman and lately turned to Mass' who by her actions proved herself 'a bloody virago' and 'the most forward and cruellest rebel'.[35]

Repeated reference to these two incidents in the depositions from mid-Ulster suggests that such wanton slaughter of Protestants was greater than

[32] Deposition of Katherin Cooke (TCD, MS 836, fo. 92).
[33] Deposition of Thomas Tuckes (ibid., fo. 16).
[34] Deposition of William Clarke (ibid., fos. 2–3).
[35] Deposition of Margaret Clarke (ibid., fo. 35); deposition of Joan Constable (ibid., fo. 87).

it actually was. They remain the only two such recorded episodes from the central Ulster area, although deponents also testified to a small number of similar occurrences, that might be depicted as 'massacres', from other areas in Ulster as well as from Sligo, from Shrule Castle on the border between Counties Mayo and Galway, and from Silvermines in County Tipperary.

We can take it that such episodes, which bear all the hallmarks of insubordination among the ranks of the rebel forces, did not have the approval of the initial leaders of the revolt. The fact that discipline broke down so quickly and so readily suggests that relatively few of the minor officers of the rebel forces shared the lofty objectives and the high sense of moral purpose that was articulated by the leaders. A number of deponents, from several parts of the country, detected this in their conversations with their captors. One of the more plausible reports of such dialogues comes from Joan Constable from County Armagh who 'frequently' asked the rebels 'how they durst do and commit the outrages and cruelties for fear of the king's majesty and his laws'. In response 'they would and did answer always (in most base, contemptuous and obscene manner) that they cared not a fart for the king and his laws', and Joan Constable mentioned specifically that Turlogh O'Corr, 'a base devilish fellow' wished he 'had the king's head' in his possession. Confirming that such outbursts marked a departure from official rebel policy, Joan Constable further reported that O'Corr and others made such shocking pronouncements only when 'they were put to any want or distress or were commanded by Sir Phelim O'Neill to go where they thought they should meet with any resistance and be put in any danger'.[36]

Incidents, also depicted as atrocities by the deponents, which did enjoy the endorsement of the rebel leaders occurred when Protestant groups retreated to defensible buildings such as churches and castles. These bands of armed Protestants were identified as a security threat by the insurgent leaders and their places of refuge were subjected to sustained military assault. Whenever these buildings were surrendered it was on terms of life only and with a promise of safe conduct for Dublin or the nearest exit port for Britain. On the occasions when their defences fell, many of the refugees were put to death, and these executions, as well as the lives lost during the siege, were readily depicted by the deponents as massacres.[37] Those who surrendered and were granted safe passes frequently fared no better

---

[36] Deposition of Joan Constable (*ibid.*, fo. 87).
[37] One of the more detailed reports of a siege was that of Ballyaly Castle in County Clare. The original deposition was later published in pamphlet form and reprinted as 'The Siege of Ballyaly Castle in the county of Clare by Maurice Cuffe, Esq.' in T. Crofton Croker (ed.), *Narratives illustrative of the contests in Ireland in 1641 and 1690* (London, 1841).

because several of the insurgent captains who were given responsibility for conveying the survivors made their task easier by slaughtering them. Other insubordinate junior officers brought their charges only part of the distance to a designated safe haven, and then left them in mid-passage to the mercy of marauding bands who stripped, tortured and taunted these unfortunates as they wended their weary way almost naked in the winter cold.[38]

Those freebooters who engaged in attacks on the refugees were seen by their victims to have been still different in character and motivation from their earlier assailants. Unlike those who had put a start to their cycle of troubles by attacking them in their homes, the brigands were usually strangers to the Protestants whom they attacked. Whether known to them or not they were frequently identified as masterless men or wood-kernes who had never reconciled themselves to settled conditions, or as uncles or younger brothers of landowners or tenants who had been left destitute of land once inheritance by primogeniture had become the sole legal mode of succession to property.[39] These soldier–assailants were frequently described as cruel and bloody by the deponents and some suggested that they even looked more ferocious than the rest of the Irish population. Mary Sillyard for one, described her attacker, who had stripped her naked and robbed her of money that she had hidden in her shoes, as a 'tall black man and hath his beard and face very hairy'.[40] Not all were men. Several deponents testified that these marauders included women and even children among their ranks, and several contended that their female assailants were more fierce and merciless than the men.[41] Whatever their sex, all freebooters seem to have conversed more frequently in the Irish language between themselves and to their victims than did the more settled Irish. Elizabeth Price testified that when the Protestants requested time to pray before their execution they were denied this opportunity with the words 'Cur do anim in Dwell' which we can take to be a phonetic rendering of the Irish malediction *Cuir do anam don Deabhall* [Send your soul to the Devil].[42] The ability to respond to these assailants in their own language was no guarantee of immunity or leniency to the settlers, and Joan Constable mentioned that her sister who could speak Irish had been specifically left exposed to frost and snow because the rebels feared she would divulge their secrets.[43]

---

[38] The most frequent such episodes occurred in County Armagh for which see TCD, MS 836.
[39] One deponent, Frances Knight, actually identified her assailant Cormack Oge as a 'former wood-kerne' (TCD, MS 835, fo. 126).
[40] Deposition of Mary Sillyard (*ibid.*, fo. 248).
[41] Deposition of Elizabeth Price, wife of Captain Price, parish of Armagh (TCD, MS 836, fo. 101).
[42] *Ibid.*   [43] Deposition of Joan Constable (*ibid.*, fo. 87).

Any attempt such as this to categorize the several different kinds of attack made upon Protestant settlers in Ireland during the early stages of the 1641 rising is bound to be excessively rigid. The depositions clearly point to the various kinds of assault that have been described above, and those who testified drew a special distinction between the behaviour of those assailants of their previous acquaintance who displayed some restraint in their actions, or who even apologized for the attack, and those strangers who acted with brutal violence. At the same time, however, deponents were anxious to show that some of those who, at the outset of the revolt, sought to legitimize their actions within the context of loyalty to the crown subsequently engaged in promiscuous assault upon Protestants. The effort at categorization also breaks down because the nature of the attacks made upon Protestants varied from one part of the country to another and the variation seems to be explained in part by the character of the settlement in the different areas.[44] Another factor which renders categorization difficult is that revolt did not occur simultaneously everywhere in the country, and disturbances in some areas were aggravated or even precipitated by military incursions from outside.[45]

Classification is also difficult because several deponents believed that they had been attacked simply because they were Protestants and that the assault had been planned in advance. Francis Sacheverall from County Armagh drew special attention to the animosity shown by Catholic clerics towards the Protestants during the course of the insurrection. This was made especially manifest, he said, because they had refused Protestants the right of burial or baptism in the churches that came under their control, which was sufficient proof for him that the rebellion had been plotted by Irish clergy on the continent six years previously.[46] Several deponents also alluded to the presence of priests at the moment of particular atrocities and some suggested that these priests had encouraged the rebels in their bloody efforts, and they reported rebel boasts 'that the priests and friars were the cause of their killing and putting to death the English and Scottish Protestants'.[47] Such assertions were given great play by later Protestant polemicists but when we look more closely at references made by successive deponents to the actual role played by priests in the insurrection it appears that it was more complex than is suggested by the more simplistic accounts.

[44] Canny, 'The marginal kingdom'.
[45] O'Dowd, *Power, politics and land*, pp. 105–30; Canny 'The 1641 depositions as a source', pp. 276–7.
[46] Deposition of Francis Sacheverall (TCD, MS. 836, fo. 107).
[47] Canny, 'The marginal kingdom', pp. 55–6; Deposition of Margaret Bromley (TCD, MS 836, fo. 40).

All references to Catholic clerics in the depositions suggest that they supported the insurrection in its early stages, and many deponents alleged that priests and bishops in Ireland had been advocating some form of military action long before the first challenge to the government's authority. The consistency of these reports makes it clear that Catholic spiritual leaders in Ireland were unhappy with the position that had obtained before 1641, and one can presume that clerical discontent derived either from the threats to religious freedom made by English Parliamentarians or from their dissatisfaction with the nature of religious toleration permitted by the government of King Charles I. To this extent the clergy were perceived to be advocates or even agents of change, but the accumulation of such references does not support the case that they either planned or approved what actually took place. Indeed most references to the involvement of particular priests in the insurrection would suggest that they were the first to realize that the action taken had gone wildly astray and that they then tried to get it back on to a more reasonable course. For example Joan Constable, in referring to the thatched cottage atrocity at Kilmore, mentioned that while most of the rebels exulted in the action taken by the notorious Jane Hampson, one O'Corr 'a dignitary priest' upbraided them for their actions in the 'deponent's hearing' and pronounced that 'without doubt God cried out for vengeance against them, and that neither corn nor grass would ever grow nor any thing prosper where they did any of these bloody acts'.[48] Several deponents also attributed their survival to the intervention of clerics who had rescued them from the hands of undisciplined rebel captains, and some others acknowledged that they had been entertained by priests after they had made their escape from the hands of their would-be assassins.[49] The Reverend John Kerdiff attributed his escape to the help provided him initially by Colonel Plunkett and later by Friar Malone of Skerries in County Dublin who had provided him with food and shelter after he had made his escape there. Even in acknowledging this assistance, Kerdiff still found reason to complain that the friar had admitted that he had been employed for sixteen years 'to bring this design to pass' and Kerdiff found 'only this (besides the rebellion) condemnable in him [Friar Malone] that he took the poor men's bibles which he found in the boat and cut them in pieces and cast them into the fire with these words

[48] Deposition of Joan Constable (TCD, MS 836, fo. 87).
[49] John Wisdome from Armagh mentioned that after his escape by sea from Carlingford to Howth in County Dublin he was 'kindly entertained by one John Moore, a friar' (TCD, MS 836, fo. 14).

that he would deal in like manner with all Protestant and Puritan bibles'.[50]

This reference is especially valuable because it indicates that the friar wished to direct the animosity of the revolt against Protestant objects rather than persons. For the Catholic clergy it seems that the presence of Protestants within their community was offensive not because most of them were foreign settlers who had acquired Irish land through a variety of means, but because they upheld Protestant religious worship which, in the eyes of the Counter-Reformation, was a malignant presence. Most of the priests mentioned in the depositions appear to have been concerned as Christian leaders to protect the British from murder and robbery, and it seems to have been on their insistence that many settlers were given the opportunity to 'turn to Mass' before being expelled from the community. Such an invitation held little appeal for most settlers, and many deponents detailed, with some grim satisfaction, how those who took advantage of this opportunity and became infidels had subsequently suffered loss of goods and even life at the hands of the rebels.[51] When they so testified, the deponents were really admitting that the moral authority of priests within the Catholic community was sustained only while they were themselves present to direct the course of events. However these episodes suggest that, where priests were concerned, it was the religious profession of individuals rather than their national origin which determined their right of belonging to the community. And to emphasize their definition of community further, as we learn from repeated depositions from all parts of the country, the Catholic clergy directed the venom of the insurgents against the symbols of Protestantism. It was apparently at their insistence that traditional places of Christian worship were recovered for Catholic use, and were cleansed of the contamination of Protestant heresy by the ritual desecration of Protestant bibles and prayer books and by the exhumation of Protestant corpses from the graves within the confines of the churches.[52]

Such fine distinctions between an assault against Protestant objects and Protestant persons were frequently lost on their victims, who interpreted these symbolic attacks to mean that the revolt had been religiously inspired. Further support for this interpretation arose as the rebellion proceeded, because as the initial leaders of the revolt lost control of the course of events they, and their subordinates, seized upon the religious imperative as the

---

[50] Deposition of John Kerdiff (TCD, MS 839, fo. 2).
[51] Canny, 'The 1641 depositions as a source', p. 278.
[52] See the depositions of Robert Flack (TCD, MS 835, fo. 201); of Elizabeth Taylor (*ibid.*, fo. 176); of Elizabeth Dewsbury (*ibid.*, fo. 100) and of Margaret Farmony and Margaret Leadly (*ibid.*, fo. 104).

only one which would provide a justification for their actions. Thus as
the claim for royal endorsement lost its credibility, so the insurgents
emphasized the Catholic dimension of their endeavour to the point where
they represented their action as an undisguised attempt to eradicate
Protestants as well as Protestantism from the land. Presumably the clergy
and indeed the leaders of the initial revolt abhorred this confusion of
objectives, but this provided scant consolation to the Protestants who were
confronted by such pronouncements as that 'it was no more pity to kill
English than to kill dogs, calling the English heretics and saying they were
God's enemies . . . [and] saying further what right have the English in
Ireland to do anything there? They had been there long enough and that
the king was no king for the Parliament would not suffer him to do any
thing – no more than one of them could do'.[53] Those rebels who adopted
such an extreme position were further convinced that none but 'were
christened at Mass were Christians', and that those English who died in the
action would go to hell whereas for any of themselves who were killed in
battle 'their souls would go to God'.[54] From there it was but a short step to
pronouncing that the events had been foreordained, and some of the more
aggressive soldiers were alleged to have made reference to the prophecies
of popular Irish saints to provide assurance that victory would be theirs and
that Protestantism would be swept from the land.[55]

It will be evident from what has been said that different elements of the
Irish population responded differently to the break-down in social order
precipitated by the actions taken by the Ulster leaders of the revolt in
October 1641. Deponents repeatedly inferred that the variety of responses
was related to the grievances which the several elements of the population
had had with the *status quo*. Differences in behaviour and ambition became
more difficult to distinguish once 'the business' became 'spoiled' by
'bloodshed and robbery', but even at the height of the confusion deponents
could distinguish those of the insurgents 'that were more merciful' from the
remainder.[56] The Ulster leaders sought to regain control of the forces they
had unleashed by persuading the Catholic landowners in the other
provinces to join the action. When they did receive such support it came,
however, at the point when the authority of these proprietors had been
undermined by the outbreak of inchoate popular disturbances associated
with attacks upon the Protestant settlers within their own areas. Thus it was

53 Deposition of Margaret Bromley (TCD, MS 836, fo. 40).
54 Deposition of Briget Drewrie (*ibid.*, fo. 46).
55 Deposition of Richard Bourk, minister (TCD, MS 835, fo. 238).
56 The quotation on the spoiling of the revolt was attributed by Dr Robert Maxwell to the earl of
   Antrim (TCD, MS 809, fos. 5–12); deposition of George Burne (TCD, MS 839, fo. 7).

borne in upon the leaders that they could only recover the initiative by soliciting the support of the Catholic clergy to bolster their moral authority and by enlisting military assistance from their kinsmen who held commissions within the Spanish Army in Flanders. Support was forthcoming from both these sources and some semblance of order and discipline was restored to those areas that remained under Catholic control. As it was established, however, the political initiative passed to the Catholic clergy and to the returned military officers, and it was they who then sought to dictate the course of events on the Catholic side and to determine fresh objectives. At this point it might be said that the insurrection of 1641 was a spent force, and we enter upon the Irish phase of 'The Wars of the Three Kingdoms'.

The return to Ireland of emigré officers and men (chapter 4 below) seemed to confirm the belief of several Protestant deponents that the 1641 rising had been originally planned to coincide with an invasion from without, and this proposition was readily assumed by Sir John Temple in *The Irish rebellion*.[57] However, while the testimony of the deponents does prove that some Irish rebels hoped for aid from their kinsmen on the continent it does not establish that they had previously conspired to negotiate support. The case for the 1641 uprising being part of an international movement, spearheaded by the pope, thus remains unproven, at least by this source. To say this is not to deny the fact that the very existence of Irish soldiers abroad was a source of political instability in Ireland and was perceived to be such by government officials. They had frequently noted the possible dangers of the departure of Irish soldiers for continental service, and their comments were made not only in the months leading up to 1641 but at all times of political tension during the previous four decades. Whenever they commented on this emigration it was with a view to having the government in England put an end to this human traffic, but these sentiments were never followed through once the crisis had passed.[58]

The failure of the Dublin officials to persist with their objection may be explained by their recognition that the outflow of young fighting men eased the social tensions that would otherwise have resulted from the

[57] Temple, *The Irish rebellion*; more significantly Henry Jones, the prime mover behind the collection of the depositions, articulated this conspiracy theory as early as 3 March 1642 (TCD, MS 809, fos. 1–4).

[58] Ohlmeyer, *Civil war and restoration*, pp. 14–17 and 152–73, and Gráinne Henry, *The Irish military community in Spanish Flanders, 1585–1621* (Dublin 1992); for some examples of official concern over the continental regiments see Chichester to Salisbury, 26 Jan 1607 (PRO, SP 63, vol. 221, no. 11); Fenton to Salisbury, 12 February 1607 (*ibid.*, vol. 221, no. 19); Aidan Clarke, *The Old English in Ireland, 1625–1642* (Ithaca and London, 1966), pp. 28–43.

simultaneous inflow of Protestant migrants from England and Scotland, who settled not only on lands that were formally planted but on estates everywhere in Ireland.[59] Since this inflow of people, which numbered at least 100,000 during the years 1603–41, was considered necessary to promote the better civility of Ireland, it seems reasonable to assume that the officials weighed one possible evil against the other and concluded that it was better to have young Irish Catholic men make careers for themselves on the continent rather than become a disruptive influence at home. Any such calculations would have proceeded from the assumption that a large-scale movement of men and munitions from Flanders to assist a disturbance in Ireland could not have escaped the detection of the English government. The factor that escaped attention was the possibility that the English authorities would be so divided and preoccupied with their own internal affairs that they would be unable to prevent the passage of continental help to insurgents in Ireland. It was the occurrence in 1642 of this unforeseen circumstance which explains how a popular uprising in Ireland became a war which all but extinguished the British and Protestant interest in Ireland.

---

[59] Nicholas Canny, *Kingdom and colony: Ireland in the Atlantic world, 1560–1800* (Baltimore, Md., 1988), pp. 69–102; L. M. Cullen, 'The Irish diaspora of the seventeenth and the eighteenth centuries', in Nicholas Canny (ed.), *Europeans on the move: studies of European migration, 1500–1800* (Oxford, 1994). This paper was in final form well before the appearance of Michael Perceval-Maxwell, *The outbreak of the Irish rebellion of 1641* (Dublin, 1994) which now carries the high-politics interpretation furthest (see p. 26 note 6 above). The collection *Ulster 1641* (Belfast 1993), edited by Brian Mac Cuarta, also appeared too late to be taken into account.

CHAPTER 3

FOUR ARMIES IN IRELAND

SCOTT WHEELER

THE IRISH rebellion of October 1641 both ignited ten years of vicious warfare in Ireland and destabilized the political and military situation in England and Scotland. By 1644 four armies or, more accurately, groups of armies, scattered throughout the country in 300–400 small garrison towns and castles, actively participated in the Irish Civil War:[1] first, the Scots Army, based largely in County Antrim and under the command of Major-General Robert Monro; second, select 'British' forces in Ulster and a further three regiments in Munster loyal to the Westminster Parliament; third, troops devoted to the king's service under the jurisdiction of James Butler, marquis of Ormond; and finally, the confederate provincial armies of Ulster, Leinster and Munster under the respective commands of Owen Roe O'Neill, Thomas Preston and Theobald, Viscount Taaffe. From the summer of 1642 the Irish Confederates, who controlled the bulk of the country, not only possessed sufficient military force to defeat their domestic enemies, whether parliamentary, Scottish or (prior to September 1643) royalist, but also to despatch expeditionary forces to Britain. However they failed to use their military superiority effectively when presented with opportunities for strategic victory. This chapter considers why the Confederates proved unable to exploit their numerical, tactical, and geographical advantages to restore Catholicism to its pre-Reformation position in Ireland, to win lasting Irish political autonomy within a tripartite monarchy and, after the

---

[1] Bodl., Carte MSS 18, fos. 215–29 provides lists of the regimental and company quarters of Preston's Leinster Army. Ian Gentles, *The New Model Army in England, Ireland, and Scotland, 1645–1653* (Oxford, 1992), p. 544, n. 163, citing Carte MSS 67, fo. 238 and Bulstrode Whitelocke, *Memorials of the English affairs from the beginning of the reign of Charles I to the happy restoration of King Charles II* (later edn., 4 vols., Oxford, 1853), III, p. 461.

cease-fire of 1643, to help facilitate a royalist victory in the British Civil Wars.[2]

I

During the winter of 1641–2 the English and Scottish governments, united by a common desire to extirpate the Irish rebellion, enjoyed significant military advantages over their opponents. Protestant units from the peace-time standing army, nearly 3,000 men in all, garrisoned the key ports in Leinster and Munster, such as Drogheda, Cork, and most importantly Dublin; while British settlers in Ulster, of English and Scottish descent, formed regiments (totalling over 4,000 men) which held Enniskillen, Derry and Belfast. With the arrival in Dublin and Drogheda of 3,000 English reinforcements in March 1642, quickly followed by the despatch of 10,000 Scottish veterans to East Ulster in April and July, the reconquest of Ireland became an attainable goal.[3]

The influx of English and Scottish manpower enabled the Protestant forces, commanded by Ormond, to raise the siege of Drogheda in March 1642 (despite being heavily outnumbered by the Catholic 'rebels' led by Sir Phelim O'Neill), to take the port of Carlingford (County Louth) and in April to win an important encounter at Kilrush (County Kildare). In August Ormond went on to relieve Athlone (County Westmeath) and recapture a number of key castles in County Kildare. Meanwhile on 29 April the Scottish and British troops defeated Sir Phelim's forces at Kilwarlin wood, near Lisburn (County Down), and in May recaptured Newry and cleared County Antrim of 'rebels'. While none of these actions proved decisive in quelling the rebellion they did prevent the insurgents from dominating the Pale and much of Ulster.

However Protestant triumphs in the spring and summer of 1642 also stemmed from Sir Phelim's inability to arm, train and discipline his unruly recruits and to the fact that his forces depended for victuals on the nomadic

[2] Conrad Russell, *The fall of the British monarchies, 1637–1642* (Oxford, 1991), p. 378; Aidan Clarke, 'Ireland and the general crisis', *Past and Present*, 48 (1970), pp. 79–99; Brendan Fitzpatrick, *Seventeenth century Ireland: the wars of religion* (Dublin and New Jersey, 1989), pp. 170–2, 175.

[3] Ian Ryder, *An English army for Ireland* (London, 1987), pp. 14–17; David Stevenson, *Scottish covenanters and Irish confederates: Scottish-Irish relations in the mid-seventeenth century* (Belfast, 1981), pp. 72, 98; Thomas Birch (ed.), *A collection of the state papers of John Thurloe, esq.: secretary first to the council of state, and afterward to the two protectors Oliver and Richard Cromwell* (7 vols., London, 1742), I, pp. 16, 17, 32–3; BL, T[homason] T[racts] E134 (26), *A proclamation of the Lords Justices*, 8 February 1642, mentions 'British', a term used by the Anglo-Scottish settlers in Ulster when referring to themselves; see also E118 (23), *The last true and joyful news from Ireland*, 22 September 1642, for lists of British commanders. All tracts were printed in London unless otherwise indicated.

Irish cattle herders, known as 'creaghts', who lacked sufficient resources to sustain sieges or large field armies on extended campaigns.[4] In an attempt to compensate for these grave weaknesses Sir Phelim resorted to Fabian tactics which aimed to control local food supplies and populations and to wear down his enemies with ambushes. Although such schemes had failed in Ulster during the Nine Years War of the 1590s, they might prove effective against an enemy unable to sustain a long foreign war. However as long as the Scots in Ulster and Ormond's troops in Leinster continued to receive supplies from Britain through the seaports on the east coast this strategy offered little hope for Catholic victory.[5] By the autumn of 1642 over 35,000 Protestant troops were deployed in Ireland and had civil war not broken out in England in August the Irish rebellion could have been suppressed with relative ease.[6]

The onset of hostilities across the Channel, however, forced the anti-Catholic coalition in Ireland to adopt a defensive stance, keeping its field army garrisoned in key ports and castles, such as Derry, Carrickfergus, Belfast, Newry, Drogheda, Trim, Cork and Youghal, and mounting occasional campaigns into the Catholic-controlled hinterland in order to destroy crops, livestock and shelter. The Scottish commander in Ulster, Monro, like Ormond in Dublin and Murrough O'Brien, Lord Inchiquin, the Protestant commander in Munster, also periodically strove to bring the insurgents to battle and to destroy their logistical base.[7] But much to their disgust, 'the Irish rebels never stood to fight'. Instead they ambushed Protestant columns in closed terrain and at river crossings and raided garrison towns, burning and destroying crops and buildings, and stealing

---

[4] Even Owen Roe O'Neill would find these men difficult to train when he assumed command of the Ulster Irish.

[5] TT, E133 (14), *Good and true news from Ireland*, 24 January 1642, p. 4; TT E134 (11), *Admirable news from Ireland*, 24 January 1642, p. 4; E100 (28), *A letter sent to William Lenthal . . . from the mayor of Bristol*, 5 May 1643, providing details on several ships ready to sail with supplies to Munster.

[6] Exact troop strength is impossible to determine. Ryder's *An English army for Ireland* estimates anti-Catholic troop strength at 42–44,000 men in the summer of 1642. His sources do not consistently support this estimate. *Cal. S P Ire., 1633–1647*, p. 369, lists thirty-seven infantry regiments and thirty troops of cavalry as the forces in Parliament's pay in Ireland in July 1642 excluding the Scots. *Ibid.*, p. 433 indicates that there were ten British foot regiments in Ulster in 1642–4, and there were only ten foot regiments in Parliament's direct pay in 1642. If the regiments were at full strength of 1,000 men each, then Ryder could be right. But contemporary sources do not support this assumption. A more realistic strength figure would be 80 per cent strength for the units, with a total estimate being 24,000 infantrymen and 1,440 horsemen on Parliament's 1642 establishment; thus, with the Scots, roughly 36,000 men. Many expected a relatively rapid victory in 1642 see TT, E113 (18), *Special passages*, 16–23 August 1642, p. 13; E124 (14), *Special passages*, 18–25 October 1642, p. 96; and E134 (26) *A true copy of a letter from Dublin*, 8 February 1642, p. 13: 'Had they put at Dublin a considerable supply of men, money, and munitions [in February] by God's assistance they would soon rout the rebels thereabouts'.

[7] For example see TT, E131 (35), *A perfect relation of . . . the Irish rebellion*, 1642, p. 2.

'our cattle from us, within the liberties of our city [Dublin] by night'.[8] The English could only break this pattern by increasing their armies to a size large enough to seize and garrison the castles of the interior but the outbreak of civil war in England, in addition to putting pressure on the uneasy Protestant coalition in Ireland which until this point had been loosely obedient to Charles I, also ensured that the Westminster Parliament diverted all available resources into the struggle against the king on the reasonable premise that 'if the kingdom [England] be not preserved . . . there can be no help for Ireland'.[9] The lack of support from England forced Ormond both to abandon his siege of New Ross in March 1643 and to retreat to Dublin despite defeating Preston in an encounter near Old Ross shortly afterwards. Unable to pay his mutinous troops, Ormond had no alternative but to restrict his operations to the Dublin area and, although victorious in isolated skirmishes, his forces could not prevent the insurgents from foraging within three miles of the city later that year.[10] Morale in the capital fell steadily and constant shortages aggravated the situation further. Late in September the Lords Justice complained that 'powder and match of which there is so great want . . . hath so many weeks laid at Chester . . . Coats, caps, stockings, and shoes which were coming over thither from the Parliament . . . were stayed in their way . . . by the king's warrant . . . The rebels came within these few days, and took ninescore head of cattle from under the walls of Dublin'.[11]

Logistical problems likewise crippled the Protestant war-effort elsewhere. Even though Inchiquin's army in Munster won a major victory at Liscarroll (25 August 1642), together with a number of skirmishes (such as the one at Bandonbridge, near Cork, late in November) his troops remained poorly supplied, fed and paid.[12] In January 1643, Inchiquin reported to Parliament that 'without relief ... our army will disband; the soldiers have eaten all we had, and now forsake us . . . The soldiers also grow very unruly; want of pay loseth their obedience'.[13] Despite some aid from Bristol, by April shortage of munitions and victuals kept his men confined to their lodgings. The Scottish forces in Ulster also lacked the

---

[8] TT, E125 (5), *Special passages*, 11–18 October 1642, p. 87.
[9] TT, E113 (18), *Special passages*, 16–23 August 1642, p. 13.
[10] TT, E116 (24), *Exceeding happy news from Ireland*, 9 September 1642, pp. 3–5; E125 (5), *Special passages*, 11–18 October 1642, p. 87. TT, E110 (9), *Letter from Hugh Colme to the Speaker of the House of Commons*, dated 4 August 1642, 11 August 1642, p. 4.
[11] TT, E118 (45), *Special passages*, 20–7 September 1642, pp. 1–2. Also see chapter 8 below.
[12] TT, E125 (15), *A journal of the most memorable passages in Ireland*, 19 October, 1642, pp. 1–3; E128 (29), *Certain and true relations of a great and glorious victory in Ireland . . . by Lord Inchiquin*, pp. 3–8. TT, E128 (16), *Special orders of the Lords and Commons*, 26 November 1642, p. A4.
[13] TT, E86 (38), *Special passages*, 24–31 January 1643, pp. 206–7.

supplies and equipment necessary to conduct effective campaigns into enemy-held territory. Towards mid-1643 it was clear that 'notwithstanding the good success which the Protestants have had against the rebels, yet by reason of the present distractions in England, the Protestants in many places are much distressed for want of necessaries'.[14]

If changing circumstances in England greatly weakened the Protestant war-effort in Ireland, they simultaneously presented the Confederates with a unique opportunity for military victory. Two key developments further transformed the Catholic cause. First, the creation of the Confederation of Kilkenny late in 1642 meant that a Supreme Council now co-ordinated Catholic military strategy; while four provincial councils oversaw the daily conduct of tactical operations.[15] Second, the return from Flanders over the summer of 1642 of Owen Roe O'Neill and Thomas Preston, professional soldiers well versed in the latest military technology and techniques, together with roughly a thousand Irish veterans, breathed fresh life into the Catholic struggle.[16] Both Preston, commander of the Army of Leinster, and O'Neill, commander of the Army of Ulster, immediately reorganized their troops and took active steps to bring their poorly disciplined soldiers up to continental standards (see chapter 4 below). Within a relatively short period of time these forces could hold their own against the anti-confederate armies: by the spring of 1643 Preston had driven Ormond's garrisons out of Queen's County and was closing in on Dublin, while Owen Roe's troops in Ulster had achieved the cohesion and discipline lacking under Sir Phelim and, in July 1643, defeated a substantial Protestant force near Armagh.[17] By the summer of 1643, as map 1 shows, the Confederates controlled most of the country while the Protestant coalition only held Dublin and the Pale, Counties Antrim and Louth, parts of Counties Down and Cork, together with numerous isolated enclaves in and around Derry, Dungannon, Enniskillen, Boyle, Loughrea, Portumna and Carlow.

As the Catholic war-effort in Ireland gained momentum, the struggle between the king and Parliament in England degenerated into a stalemate which could only be broken by foreign intervention. And so, in the spring of 1643, as Parliament approached the Scots for assistance (the Solemn

---

[14] TT, E130 (33), *The last true intelligence from Ireland*, December 1642, p. 3.

[15] For further details see Patrick Corish, 'The rising of 1641 and the Catholic Confederacy, 1641–45', in T. W. Moody, F. X. Martin and F. J. Byrne (eds.), *A new history of Ireland, III: Early modern Ireland, 1534–1691* (Oxford, 1976), pp. 298–303.

[16] Stevenson, *Scottish covenanters*, pp. 120–2; Nicholas Perry, 'The infantry of the confederate Leinster army', *Irish Sword*, 15 (winter 1983), pp. 233–5; Jerrold Casway, *Owen Roe O'Neill and the struggle for Catholic Ireland* (Philadelphia, 1984), p. 63.

[17] TT, E89 (17), *Special passages*, 7–14 February 1643, p. 222; TT, E89 (31), *Newest intelligence . . . from Ireland*, 1 February 1643, pp. 1–2; TT, E132 (22), *Condition of Ireland*, 9 January 1643, p. 4.

League and Covenant was finally signed in September), Charles I badgered Ormond to send Irish recruits for immediate service in England and, to this end, pressured him to conclude a cease-fire with the Confederates.[18] From the outset the problem of securing a religious settlement acceptable to all parties hampered the truce negotiations which began in late June. At one end of the confessional spectrum stood hard-line Catholics who, acutely aware of their military edge, would only consider a cessation in return for freedom of worship, the retention of recaptured churches, and official recognition of a Roman hierarchy.[19] At the other end, the staunchly Presbyterian Scots in Ulster refused to consider a compromise on the reasonable grounds that an armistice would allow the Irish to strengthen their forces while the exodus of troops to the English theatre of war would further weaken the Protestant position on all fronts.[20]

Even though Ormond found the task of negotiating with the Confederates distasteful, he realized that no alternatives remained if he were to salvage the royalist cause in both Ireland and Britain. In a similar vein the more moderate, predominately Old English members of the confederation believed that the best means of securing their new-found religious and political gains was by winning formal royal recognition for their cause. Accordingly a one-year cessation of arms was signed on 15 September. Despite the fact that it contained no religious concessions, the truce represented *de facto* royal recognition of the Confederation of Kilkenny.

II

In the long term this temporary end of hostilities proved disastrous for the Confederates, for instead of pursuing their strategic advantages and focusing their efforts on driving their parliamentary and Scottish opponents out of Ireland, they became involved in lengthy negotiations with the king (a lasting peace settlement was not reached until January 1649). Had the Catholics concentrated on domestic victory the English reconquest of Ireland in 1649–52 would have been more difficult and the course of the 'Wars of the Three Kingdoms' very different.

In the short term, however, the Confederates benefited from the truce

---

[18] Samuel R. Gardiner, *History of the great civil war, 1642–1649* (new edn., 4 vols., London, 1893; reprint ,1987), II, p. 125: Corish, 'The rising of 1641', p. 306; Bodl., Carte MSS 6, fo. 13.

[19] Corish, 'The rising of 1641', p. 305; TT, E37 (31), A manuscript titled 'The motives and reasons occasioning the Catholic subjects to take up arms' (written 'immediately after cessation, 1643'), pp. 10–13.

[20] Bodl., Carte MSS 6, fos. 118–19, 277, 328.

Map 1 Ireland on the eve of cessation of arms, September 1643

Table 3.1. *Estimates (in ranges) of Protestant troop strength*[21]

Year	Leinster	Connacht and Munster	'British' in Ulster	Scots in Ulster	Total
1642	[a]4–6,000	2–6,000	6–?11,000	10,000	22–37,000
1643	[a]4–7,000	4–6,000	8–?12,000	c. 9–10,000	27–35,000
1644	[a]3–5,000	2–3,000	8–?10,000	6–7,000	19–25,000
1645	[a]3–5,000	2–5,000	8–9,000	5–6,000	18–25,000
1646	[a]2–4,000	4–5,000	5–9,000	5–6,000	16–25,000
1647	[b]7–8,000	4–6,000	5–9,000	2–3,500	18–26,500
1648	[b]7–9,000	4–6,000	5–8,000	c. 2,000	14–38,000
1649	[c]16–24,000	4–6,000	5–8,000	?	25–38,000

[a] = Ormond's forces
[b] = Jones's forces
[c] = Cromwell's forces

because it temporarily shifted the balance of power in Ireland in their favour. On the one hand, it shattered the uneasy Protestant alliance between Ormond's forces and the Scots in Ulster. On the other, it paved the way for the dispatch of approximately 5,000 Protestant troops for service with the English Royalists which, as tables 3.1 and 3.2 illustrate, gave the Confederates in Leinster and Munster a clear advantage: by November 1645 only 15–20,000 Protestant soldiers remained in Ireland – of the 37,000 men of the autumn of 1642 – and by January 1646 anti-Catholic troop strength fell to 16–25,000 men.[22]

Since Inchiquin's and Ormond's forces could do little more than hold the Protestant enclaves in Munster and Leinster in the king's name, the Confederates, who met at Waterford in November 1643, decided to turn their attention to ridding Ulster of the Scottish army of occupation. To begin with the General Assembly endorsed a proposal by Randal

---

[21] The figures in table 3.1 are based on numerous sources. *Cal S P Ire., 1633–1647*, pp. 369, 420, 433–4, 631, 693, for Parliament's and Preston's forces; Pádraig Lenihan, 'The Leinster army and the battle of Dungan's Hill, 1647', *Irish Sword*, 71 (1991), pp. 141–2 for Preston and Jones; Henry Cary (ed.), *Memorials of the great civil war in England from 1646 to 1652* (2 vols., London 1842), I, pp. 360–3; II, pp. 152–4, 159–62; numerous Carte MSS references including MSS 8, fo. 243; MSS 18, fos. 255–8; MSS 19, fos. 9, 143; MSS 21, fos. 371–3; MSS 24, fos. 795–7; MSS 26, fos. 14, 68; Stevenson, *Scottish covenanters*, for Scottish strength in Ulster; numerous Thomason Tracts such as E417 (14) *A mighty victory in Ireland obtained by the Lord Inchiquin . . .* 13 November 1647; E46 (22), *News from Dublin . . .* 22 November 1647; E468 (3) *The proceedings of the army under the command of . . . Jones*, September 1648; Casway, *Owen Roe O'Neill*, for O'Neill's Ulster Army strength over the years; Ian Gentles, *The New Model Army*, chapter 11; and Ryder, *An English army for Ireland*.

[22] TT, E252 (13), *Perfect diurnal*, 25 December 1643–1 January 1644, p. 182. Six regiments were sent to Flintshire by November 1643, but many soldiers deserted their royalist commanders and sought service with Parliamentary units. *Cal. S P Ire., 1633–47*, pp. 369, 420, 431–4.

Table 3.2. *Estimates (in ranges) of Catholic troop strength*

Year	Ulster (O'Neill)	Leinster (Preston)	Munster (Taaffe)	Connacht (Clanricard)	Total
1642	3–8,000	4–8,000	2–5,000	c. 2,000	11–23,000
1643	3–6,000	5–7,000	4–7,000	c. 2,000	14–22,000
1644	5–7,000	6–7,000	5–8,000	c. 2,000	18–24,000
1645	3–5,000	5–7,000	4–6,000	c. 2,000	14–20,000
1646	5–7,000	4–7,000	4–6,000	2–3,000	15–23,000
1647	6–8,000	6–8,000	4–8,000	4–6,000	20–30,000
1648	7–8,000	3–5,000	5–7,000	3–4,000	18–24,000
1649	5–8,000	[a]10–15,000		3–5,000	18–28,000

[a] = Confederate forces under Ormond's command

MacDonnell, earl of Antrim, to send an expeditionary force directly to Scotland which was not only supposed to draw the Scots out of Ulster but to reduce Scottish assistance for the Parliamentarians in England.[23] Accordingly, in June 1644, two Irish regiments landed in the Western Isles where they became the core of the marquis of Montrose's triumphant army, which for more than a year tied down as many as 12,000 Scottish Covenanters and prevented reinforcements from marching to aid the Parliamentary forces in England.[24] From a confederate perspective Antrim's gambit enjoyed limited success, for only about 2–3,000 of Monro's troops retreated across the North Channel to protect their farms and families, leaving a sizeable number in East Ulster; however had the Confederates sent reinforcements to Scotland in the winter of 1643–4, as Antrim urged them to do, they might well have caused the recall of the remaining Scottish forces from Ulster and indeed from northern England.[25] Their failure to follow this through constituted a major strategic mistake and missed opportunity.

In addition to sending an expeditionary force to Scotland, the General Assembly resolved to reinforce O'Neill's Ulster army of 5,000 with a further 4,000 infantry and 300 cavalry. However instead of placing these recruits under the experienced O'Neill the Supreme Council offered them, together with supreme command of the Army of Ulster, to James Tuchet, earl of

---

[23] John Lowe, 'The earl of Antrim and Irish aid to Montrose in 1644', *Irish Sword*, 4 (1960), pp. 191–8; Jane H. Ohlmeyer, *Civil war and restoration in the three Stuart kingdoms: the career of Randal MacDonnell, marquis of Antrim, 1609–1683* (Cambridge, 1993), pp. 159–70.

[24] TT, E47 (30), *Perfect occurrences*, 10–17 May 1644, p. A1; C. Ó Danachair, 'Montrose's Irish regiments', *Irish Sword*, 4 (1959), pp. 61–7.

[25] *Calendar of state papers and manuscripts, relating to English affairs, existing in the archives and collections of Venice, 1643–47*, pp. 15, 30, 32, 39.

Castlehaven.[26] Castlehaven proved to be an unfortunate choice: on the one hand, he lacked military experience and basic leadership skills; on the other, his appointment alienated Owen Roe O'Neill, the earl of Antrim and Thomas Preston – all of whom nurtured hopes of being created lord general of the confederate army in the north.[27] Sure enough when Castlehaven and his combined army of nearly 10,000 arrived in County Armagh towards the end of July, instead of engaging the Scottish forces in battle, he rashly allowed O'Neill's troops to disperse in order to take advantage of the summer grazing; while he, with about 5,000 men, built a camp near Cromore.[28] Only the approach of Monro with 6,000 Scots, early in August, forced the Confederates to regroup and concentrate their forces in entrenchments near Charlemont, where they remained for the next seven weeks.[29] Then scarcity of provisions, combined with poor weather, forced Castlehaven and O'Neill to withdrew and return to Leinster for separate winter quarters.[30] This humiliating retreat ended major operations in Ulster until 1646.[31]

Confederate failure to execute a timely campaign against the Scots early in 1644 and a general unwillingness by O'Neill and Castlehaven to seek aggressively to destroy Monro's army when offered the chance highlight the inherent leadership weaknesses which plagued the Confederation of Kilkenny. None of the commanders could put the Catholic cause before personal pride, and none seemed able to develop a coherent military strategy to win the war. There can be little doubt that Monro's defeat on the battlefield in the summer of 1644 would have ended his ability to campaign and to supply his garrisons. This could have opened the way for Irish domination of Ulster and, coupled with Montrose's victories, forced the Scots to withdraw their troops from Ireland and England in order to defend Scotland from Irish attack, changing the balance of power in all three Stuart kingdoms. Moreover while the Confederates wasted their chance to control the north, they suspended military operations elsewhere. Initially Inchiquin had supported Ormond's decision to sign the cessation,

[26] *Cal. S P Ire., 1633–47*, pp. 403–4; John Lowe (ed.), *Letter-book of the earl of Clanricarde, 1643–47* (IMC, Dublin, 1983), p. 17. As it was, no major operation could be undertaken against Ulster until late spring 1644 since the nomadic Ulster creaghts refused to support a winter campaign, *ibid.*, pp. 20–5.

[27] Stevenson, *Scottish covenanters*, p. 191; Casway, *Owen Roe O'Neill*, pp. 102–4; Ohlmeyer, *Civil war and restoration*, pp. 137, 140–1.

[28] [E. Hogan (ed.)], *The history of the warr in Ireland . . . by a British officer of the regiment of Sir John Clotworthy* (Dublin, 1873), p. 38.

[29] *Ibid.*, pp. 39, 108–9; Bodl., Carte MSS 12, fos. 101, 405, and 446.

[30] [Hogan (ed.)], *The history of the warr*, pp. 40–1.

[31] O'Neill remained in quarters in northern Leinster throughout the summer of 1645.

even though it meant switching to the royalist side and thus forfeiting logistical support from London, and he had obeyed Charles I's orders to deploy Protestant regiments to England, leaving fewer than 2,000 men in the Munster garrisons.[32] However, in the spring and early summer of 1644, three factors forced Inchiquin to reassess his loyalties: first, during a trip to England in February and March 1644 he was not only snubbed by the king in Oxford, but denied the presidency of Munster; second, Ormond's inability to prevent Irish raids against Munster Protestants infuriated him; and, finally, Charles I's defeat at Marston Moor (2 July) convinced him of the need to return to the parliamentary fold in mid-July.[33] Inchiquin's defection had a dramatic impact on the course of the war: on the one hand, it gave Parliament important bridgeheads (Cork, Duncannon and Youghal) in Munster; on the other, it created an effective military stalemate since none of the major protagonists now fighting in Ireland possessed the strength to destroy their opponents.

Inchiquin's volte-face also took the Confederates, preoccupied with Castlehaven's Ulster campaign, completely by surprise and forced them to face another active front in the southwest. As a result they failed to act decisively against him until 1645 when Preston captured Duncannon (March) and Castlehaven campaigned in western Munster, clearing the Blackwater valley by July.[34] Even then they lacked the cannon and logistics necessary to assault or besiege the other walled towns held by Inchiquin. This, combined with the fact that Preston flatly refused to serve under Castlehaven, enabled Inchiquin's deputy, Roger Boyle, Lord Broghill, to break the siege of Youghal in September, forcing the Confederates to withdrew and disperse their troops prematurely.

In part confederate disunity on the battlefield stemmed from the failure of the Supreme Council to co-ordinate the actions of their generals; but it also reflected deep-seated tensions within the Confederation over how best to prosecute the war with some members favouring continued negotiations with the king, while others pushed for an outright victory on the battlefield. The arrival in October 1645 of the papal nuncio Giovanni Battista Rinuccini, archbishop of Fermo, further exacerbated an already tense situation because he not only refused to condone a secret peace agreement concluded in August with the Catholic Royalist Edward Somerset, earl of Glamorgan, but also rejected a treaty concluded with Ormond the

[32] Bodl., Carte MSS 6, fos. 54, 235; Ryder, *An English army for Ireland*, pp. 31–3.
[33] C. V. Wedgwood, *The king's war* (New York, 1959), pp. 292–4; TT, E50 (19), *The spy . . . from Oxford*, 30 May–6 June 1644, p. 15. Bodl., Carte MSS 11, fos. 5, 533–4, 599–600; MSS 12, fo. 30.
[34] Bodl., Carte MSS 14, fo. 317; Gardiner, *Civil war*, III, p. 31.

following March and excommunicated anyone who adhered to it. Then, in September 1646, the nuncio purged the Supreme Council of those members who favoured a negotiated settlement with the king and took personal control of confederate politics.[35]

Rinuccini's intervention in Catholic affairs could not have come at a worse time for Charles I, who became increasingly desperate for Irish support both in England and Scotland after his army's defeat at Marston Moor in July 1644. However, even if an acceptable peace had been signed in the winter of 1646 or spring of 1647, few troops could have been spared for service in England from an Ireland still threatened by the Scots in Ulster, and by Inchiquin in Munster. As it was, the parliamentary triumph at Naseby (14 June 1645) quickly followed by Montrose's defeat at Philiphaugh (13 September) ended any hope of a royalist victory in Britain and for a *politique* settlement in Ireland.[36] Although some, notably Glamorgan, still tried to secure a large Irish Catholic army for service in England, it soon became apparent that the king had lost the First Civil War.[37]

Even as it undermined chances for a royalist victory in Britain and for the formation of an anti-parliamentary alliance in Ireland, Rinuccini's arrival in the autumn of 1645 brought new energy and resources to Catholic efforts in Ulster. By March 1646, the nuncio had given O'Neill enough money to recruit seven infantry regiments and seven troops of cavalry: able to pay his soldiers regularly for the first time, O'Neill could count on their obedience in an extended campaign.[38] In late May, he learned that Monro was planning a rendezvous near Benburb and a sweep through the Catholic-held regions in mid-Ulster and so, in order to prevent the possible juncture of Protestant forces, O'Neill moved north to Benburb where he selected good defensive positions near a crossing-point of the Blackwater river.

On 5 June, after a ten-hour march, Monro, with over 3,000 men, moved aggressively against O'Neill, fully expecting him to withdraw. Instead O'Neill waited for the Scottish onslaught. At approximately 7 p.m., after five hours of skirmishing, O'Neill, reinforced by a fresh reserve of 1,000

---

[35] Fitzpatrick, *Seventeenth century Ireland*, pp. 189–90. The 'First Ormond Peace', as this was later known, was not made public until the summer.

[36] Bodl., Carte MSS 15, fos. 330–6; Wedgwood, *King's war*, p. 455.

[37] Glamorgan eventually received permission from the confederate Supreme Council to recruit and ship 3,000 men to England; however the fall of Chester on 3 February 1646 closed the last royalist port in the west to Irish reinforcements, Wedgwood, *King's war*, p. 538.

[38] [Hogan (ed.)], *The history of the warr*, pp. 43–4; Stevenson, *Scottish covenanters*, pp. 225–6, 230, 234; Bodl., Carte MSS, 17, fo. 367.

men, surprised Monro by ordering an attack. The unexpected Irish charge shattered Monro's exhausted units, killing roughly 1,800 men and routing the rest. This was the most successful Irish battle of the entire decade, made possible by the nuncio's money, O'Neill's continental experience and boldness, and Monro's over-confidence. Benburb destroyed the Scottish army as an independent military force in Ulster, but O'Neill failed to pursue his advantage, missing an opportunity to annihilate Monro's units in the field and possibly to seize his bases quickly.[39] Instead, he withdrew to Charlemont and dispatched columns to forage in Protestant areas before moving south in August to Kilkenny in order to support Rinuccini's political *coup d'état* the following month.[40] Except for isolated foraging raids, Ulster remained quiet for the next year.[41]

During the summer of 1646 the Confederates also enjoyed military successes elsewhere. In June, Preston, with his army of 6,000, campaigned into Connacht where he laid siege to Roscommon, which surrendered after a small Protestant force failed to relieve the town.[42] However, rather than move against the outnumbered British in Sligo, Preston withdrew and remained inactive for the rest of the summer, claiming that logistical shortages prevented him from keeping 'our men together longer than eight days'.[43] Nevertheless in July the Confederates managed to take Bunratty Castle, near Limerick from forces loyal to Parliament, but no co-ordinated efforts were made to destroy either the Scots in Ulster or Inchiquin in Munster. Instead, they turned their attention to Ormond and the capture of Ireland's commercial and administrative centre, Dublin.

For the remainder of 1646 Preston and O'Neill focused their efforts on trying to prevent Ormond, horrified by the confederate rejection of his peace treaty and alarmed by Rinuccini's domination of the Supreme Council, from surrendering his powerbase in and around Dublin to forces loyal to Parliament.[44] However, even though their combined armies of 8–10,000 men stood unopposed in the field neither general attempted to use artillery to batter down the walls of Dublin, defended by a force of 3–4,000 Royalists. Moreover throughout the abortive offensive they refused to work together (in fact Preston actively conspired with the enemy) and in November, when supplies ran low, the Catholic armies returned to quarters. This allowed Colonel Michael Jones, the son of an Irish bishop

---

[39] [Hogan (ed.)], *The history of the warr*, pp. 44–51; Stevenson, *Scottish covenanters*, pp. 225–35.
[40] [Hogan (ed.)], *The history of the warr*, pp. 52–3; Gardiner, *Civil war*, IV, pp. 57, 155–6.
[41] Bodl., Carte MSS 17, fo. 374.
[42] Bodl., Carte MSS 17, fo. 370; MSS 18, fos. 216–19 for account of the muster of Preston's Leinster Army, 8 May 1646; [Hogan (ed.)], *The history of the warr*, pp. 54–6.
[43] Bodl., Carte MSS 18, fo. 343.   [44] *Ibid.*, fos. 590–5, 604, 658.

who had abandoned the king's cause in Ireland after the cessation of 1643 and joined the parliamentary army in England, together with three infantry and one cavalry regiments, which had been freed for service in Ireland by Charles I's defeat and represented the first major English reinforcements sent to Ireland in three years, to land near Dublin in June 1647. The following month Ormond handed the capital over to Jones. Thus, without firing a shot, Parliament gained control of the most important strategic city in Ireland, thereby paving the way for the reconquest of the island.

After 1646, only outright Catholic military victory in Ireland could have saved the Irish from an increasingly powerful Parliament, but this would have required the confederate armies to abandon their defensive tactics and to destroy the Protestant armies, as O'Neill had done at Benburb, with aggressive campaigns. Only such a strategy could have cleared Ireland of enemy bridgeheads and thus prevented the Westminster Parliament from dealing so effectively with its 'Irish Problem' after August 1649.

III

On 1 August 1647 Jones prepared to leave Dublin for his first foray into the Catholic-dominated hinterland with 4,300 soldiers, seven cannon and enough carts and pack horses to haul the 26,000 pounds of meal and cheese needed every four days to re-supply his army.[45] Protestant garrisons from Drogheda and Ulster joined his onslaught, raising his force to over 5,000 infantry, 1,500 cavalry, and nine cannon (see map 2). On 7 August, as his troops neared Trimbleston, Jones learned that Preston's army was near Portlester, between his army and Dublin. Early the next morning he daringly took the offensive. The battle of Dungan's Hill opened with an ineffectual exchange of artillery fire, followed by a mid-morning English attack; by noon, Jones's cavalry had broken both flanks of Preston's army, allowing the infantry to attack the Irish centre.[46] Preston's six infantry regiments broke and fled into a nearby bog which Jones then surrounded and methodically cleared, leaving 3,000 dead (or so it was rumoured) and many officers, including five out of six regimental commanders, together with Preston's correspondence, in English hands. Parliamentary casualties were minimal and one contemporary Protestant historian argued that Dungan's Hill was 'the greatest and most signal victory the English ever had

---

[45] *Ibid.*, MSS 21, fos. 371–3, 'A diary and relation of passages in and about Dublin from the first of August 1647 to the 10th'. These victuals represent part of 240,000 pounds of meal and £4,000 worth of cheese sent to Dublin from England in the summer, see *ibid.*, fo. 215 for list of supplies.

[46] Bodl., Carte MSS 21, fo. 372.

Map 2 The parliamentary campaigns of 1647 and 1649–52

in Ireland'.[47] On 10 August Jones sent his troops from Ulster back to their garrisons while his main force cleared eastern Leinster of the enemy before returning to Dublin on 17 August.[48] His brief campaign, focused on the destruction of the enemy's army, shifted the military balance against the Catholics in Leinster.

O'Neill, meanwhile, ravaged northeastern Connacht and attempted to take Sligo from Sir Charles Coote's Protestant forces. However he moved too slowly to seize the town by a *coup de main* and lacked the supplies and artillery needed to besiege or storm it.[49] In August, his army mutinied for lack of pay, rendering O'Neill powerless to act decisively when Jones, with 7,700 men, took the field again on 2 October. The parliamentary commander began his new campaign with an attack on Castlejordan before turning to Athboy, where he put most of the defenders to the sword.[50] He proceeded to clear northern Leinster of Catholic enclaves, placing his own men into strategically important strongholds along the river Boyne before returning to Dublin on the 19th.[51]

The following month, O'Neill, who had finally regained control of his troops, retaliated and led a force of 8,000 to within seven miles of Dublin. However heavy rains prevented him from bringing along his artillery and consequently he failed to recover the lost garrisons. When supply shortages forced O'Neill to withdraw, Jones sortied from Dublin to force him to fight. The Irish refused battle, retreating, instead, by forced marches to western Leinster and, after a futile chase, Jones returned to winter quarters.[52]

During the spring and summer of 1647, English supplies and reinforcements also reached Inchiquin in the southwest, enabling him to lead 4,500 troops against Dungarvan (which fell in May) and Cashel (which he sacked in September).[53] Then, in early November, Inchiquin received intelligence that Theobald Taaffe was in the field with an army of 7,000 foot and 1,200 horse near Mallow. Inchiquin, together with 4,000 infantry, 1,200 cavalry and three cannon, immediately taunted Taaffe, who had placed his army on Knocknegoall or Knocknanuss Hill, to meet him in battle and on the 13th moved his troops to the base of the hill. After placing his artillery on the left side of the Catholics in an attempt to gall them into attacking down the hill, Inchiquin launched his cavalry against them and, after two hours

47 Edmund Borlase, *History of the execrable Irish rebellion (1641–1662)* (London, 1680; later edn., Dublin, 1743), p. 242.
48 Bodl., Carte MSS 21, fo. 373; Lenihan, 'The Leinster army', pp. 139–53.
49 Casway, *Owen Roe O'Neill*, pp. 184–7.
50 Gardiner, *Civil war*, IV, pp. 184–6; Bodl., Carte MSS 118, fo. 33a.
51 *Ibid.*, fos. 33–4.
52 *Ibid.*, fo. 34b.   53 Corish, 'The rising of 1641', p. 324.

of heated combat, sent a cavalry reserve against Taaffe's right flank, routing his forces. The battle of Knocknanuss, which allegedly claimed 4,000 lives, not only destroyed the confederate Army of Munster but allowed Inchiquin to capture all the major towns in the province except Limerick, Waterford and Clonmel.[54]

The parliamentary victories at Dungan's Hill and Knocknanuss, which wiped out two of the three Catholic armies, can be attributed to the restoration of adequate logistical support from England in the wake of Charles I's defeat and capture, as well as to the aggressive leadership of Jones and Inchiquin. However the outbreak of hostilities in England during the spring of 1648 and of the Second English Civil War in May prevented Parliament from sending sufficient resources to their commanders in Ireland for the remainder of the year. Initially Jones and Inchiquin responded by conducting short foraging campaigns into enemy-held territory, thus denying resources to their foe and increasing the supply areas available to themselves.[55] Neither O'Neill nor Preston responded to these incursions: instead they retaliated by withdrawing supplies from Protestant reach.[56] Within a short period of time Inchiquin believed that if aid and money did not reach his troops in four to six weeks, he would be forced to take desperate action.[57] As he reached the end of his logistical tether in late March, a Catholic army moved towards his headquarters in Cork, preventing his forces from living off the land.[58] This threat, along with Inchiquin's antipathy to the Independent faction in Parliament, led him abruptly to change sides yet again; on 3 April, he signed a cease-fire (a truce was concluded on 20 May) with the confederate Supreme Council which paved the way for the formation of a royalist coalition in Ireland against Jones – and also against Owen Roe O'Neill, who paradoxically condemned the reconciliation[59] (see chapter 8 below).

O'Neill's persistent refusal to rejoin the Confederation ensured that instead of devoting its precious military resources to the defeat of the Parliamentarians, the Supreme Council spent most of their energies in 1648

---

[54] Cary, *Memorials*, 1, pp. 360–6; TT, E417 (14), *A mighty victory in Ireland obtained by the Lord of Inchiquin near Englishman's Hill*, 29 November 1647; Richard Bagwell, *Ireland under the Stuarts and during the Interregnum* (3 vols., London, 1906–16), 11, p. 158.

[55] For example, early in 1648 Jones seized Wicklow and sent a task force to Westmeath to ravage O'Neill's main supply area.

[56] TT, E425 (11), *Moderate Intelligencer*, 27 January–3 February 1648, pp. 1147–8.

[57] TT, E431 (10), *The Kingdom's Weekly Intelligencer*, 29 February–7 March 1648, pp. 858–9.

[58] TT, E434 (21), *The Kingdom's Weekly Intelligencer*, 28 March–4 April 1648, pp. 893–6.

[59] TT, E452 (10), *Declaration of the Protestant army . . . in Munster* (Cork, 1648) pp. 1–3; TT, E435 (33), *Papers presented to the Parliament against Lord Inchiquin . . . and the Lord Inchiquin's declaration . . . read in both Houses of Parliament*, 15 April 1648, pp. 4, 6.

defending Leinster and Connacht from the Army of Ulster.[60] To make matters worse, in the autumn of 1648 O'Neill concluded a temporary cease-fire with Jones, who was now desperately short of supplies and anxious to preserve his own hold on the Pale, and even supplied the Parliamentarians with beef in return for powder.[61]

In fact Jones had little to fear from his enemies since they lacked the unity of command necessary to exploit their numerical advantages. While Jones had roughly 8–10,000 men, counting troops in Ulster, the Confederates could muster an army of 10–15,000 including Inchiquin's Munster forces, but excluding O'Neill's men (see tables 3.1 and 3.2). But Inchiquin refused to allow his troops to serve with Taaffe or Preston; while the earl of Clanricard remained primarily interested in defending Connacht from the raids of the small Protestant garrison in Sligo.[62] Consequently, Jones continued to expand the radius of his garrisons around Dublin and to campaign in Catholic areas in order to destroy the harvest, while in September George Monck seized Carrickfergus, Belfast and Coleraine in Ulster from their small Scottish garrisons.

Just as the Catholic cause looked hopeless, Ormond returned to Ireland at the end of September with instructions from the royalist court in exile to conclude a compromise settlement with the Confederates. By January 1649 he had negotiated a treaty, known as the 'Second Ormond Peace', whereby the Confederates, in return for a verbal promise of religious toleration, formally recognized the king's authority and, together with Inchiquin, agreed to raise an 18,000-man army.[63] If handled aggressively by a single commander, such a force could have made real headway against Jones. Moreover in February 1649 Prince Rupert arrived in Kinsale with a small royalist navy of twelve warships from Holland to join forces with the Irish privateers operating against English and Scottish vessels in the Irish Sea and elsewhere.[64] This put additional pressure on Jones in Dublin, since at

---

[60] TT, E444 (9), *Moderate Intelligencer*, 18–25 May 1648, p. 1259; TT, E446 (28), *ibid.*, 1–8 June 1648, p. 1384;. TT, E463 (16), *Moderate Intelligencer*, 7–14 September 1648; TT, E468 (17), *ibid.*, October, 1648, p. 1695.

[61] TT, E476 (9) *The Kingdom's Weekly Intelligencer*, 5–12 December 1648, p. 1184.

[62] Taaffe, Clanricard and Preston were to raise 4,000 foot and 800 horse in Munster, Connacht and Leinster respectively, while Inchiquin was to raise 3,000 foot and 600 horse in Munster. TT, E464 (13), *Two letters from Cork*, 19 September 1648, pp. 3–5; TT, E464 (18), *The Kingdom's Weekly Intelligencer*, 12–19 September 1648, p. 1088; for Jones's strength see Bodl., Carte MSS 118, fo. 44, list of army strength, May 1648.

[63] TT, E527 (30), *Perfect summary of exact passages of Parliament*, 26 February–5 March 1649, p. 50, which refers to a letter from Colonel Jones in Dublin to Parliament.

[64] TT, E476 (15), *Perfect weekly account*, 6–13 December 1648, p. 305; TT E476 (39), *The Kingdom's Weekly Intelligencer*, 12–19 December 1648, p. 1191; also see Jane H. Ohlmeyer, 'Irish privateers during the civil war, 1642–50', *Mariner's Mirror*, 76 (May 1990), pp. 125–31.

least ten English supply ships were seized in December alone by Irish privateers (see chapter 4 below). These naval forces allowed the Royalists to isolate enemy coastal enclaves and contributed to a new wave of successes enjoyed by the anti-parliamentary coalition. By June 1649 only Dublin, Drogheda and Derry remained outside confederate control; in July, Drogheda fell and Ormond prepared to besiege Dublin with the 16–20,000 men of the combined forces of Taaffe, Preston and Inchiquin.[65] But it was too late: events in England once again dramatically impinged upon the situation in Ireland.

IV

The New Model Army's victory in the Second Civil War in August 1648, followed by Pride's Purge in December 1648 and the execution of Charles I on 30 January 1649, resolved a power struggle which had gone on between the Independents and Presbyterians since 1647 and from this point on the solution of the 'Irish Problem' became a top priority on the agenda of the recently formed Council of State.[66] For the first time since 1642 the efforts of the English government focused on the defeat of the Irish insurrection; the royalist and Catholic causes in Ireland were doomed.

Parliament swiftly raised taxation to unprecedented levels and sold large amounts of property, both to pay off the £3 million owed to their forces and military suppliers and to finance the Irish offensive. At the end of March 1649 it selected Oliver Cromwell to command an expeditionary force of 12,000 New Model Army veterans and put at his disposal a large train of artillery, nearly 100 ships and, above all, a war chest of over £100,000.[67] In addition four infantry regiments, together with tons of supplies, left at once for Ireland and their timely arrival frustrated Ormond's offensive against Dublin.[68]

Throughout the war Ormond's strength as a commander had been patience in the face of adversity. Now, for the first time in the decade, he controlled an army superior to its enemy. The only way he could have exploited this advantage was to have moved immediately against Dublin – still poorly defended (see plate 2) – in the spring of 1649, rather than picking off the outlying garrisons like Drogheda and Trim. Such a direct approach, however, was a method of warfare unfamiliar to Ormond, whose

---

[65] Cary (ed.), *Memorials*, II, pp. 152–4; Stevenson, *Scottish covenanters*, pp. 273–4.
[66] *Journals of the House of Commons* (London, 1803), VI, p. 138–9.
[67] Whitelocke, *Memorials*, III, pp. 89–90.
[68] *Calendar of state papers, domestic series, 1649–50*, pp. 61, 66–7, 572–3; PRO, SP 25/118, pp. 19–24.

prior military experience remained confined to positional warfare around limited objectives.[69] Thus when he finally marched against Dublin in August, intending to isolate Jones's troops from their local supply area and to cut off the city from seaborne assistance, he did so too late. Had he begun his siege in March, Ormond, along with Rupert's efforts to cut off communications between Dublin and England, might have taken the capital and, consequently, the outlying towns as well.[70] Unfortunately for the Irish, the lord lieutenant lacked the vision and experience to do so.

The first wave of English reinforcements, which arrived at Dublin in May and June, raised Jones's field strength to over 8,000 men, enabling him to take the offensive. On 2 August he launched a surprise attack on Ormond's outpost at Baggarath, within a mile of Dublin, and overwhelmed 1,500 Royalists. The rout spread to Ormond's main force at Rathmines, already weakened by Inchiquin's withdrawal to defend Munster from a rumoured English landing, and resulted in the loss of c. 4,000 Royalists and six cannon.[71] This victory also broke the siege of Dublin, allowing Cromwell, together with 12,000 New Model Army veterans, to land unmolested near the capital on 15 August and forcing Ormond to disperse his dispirited troops and to adopt Fabian tactics. Presumably he hoped that Parliament would either fail to supply Cromwell with the manpower and logistics needed to seize and occupy the Irish hinterland, with its hundreds of castles and fortified towns, or would once again be diverted from the conquest of Ireland by events in Britain.[72]

Ormond's expectations foundered, however, for the Parliamentarians never seriously lacked victuals and reinforcements during the next two years. From the summer of 1649 the Commonwealth sent a steady flow of supplies, money and manpower to its army in Ireland enabling Cromwell and his subordinates to campaign with well-stocked columns in Leinster, Ulster and Munster for the next year, with only a short rest in winter quarters in December and January.[73] As the bloody attacks against Drogheda (September) and Wexford (October) highlight, the Parliamentarians maintained the initiative throughout the offensive, used artillery well, and supplied their columns regularly. Elsewhere they allowed

[69] Bodl., Carte MSS 118, 44b.

[70] Cary (ed.), *Memorials*, ii, p. 160; TT, E527 (38), *Perfect diurnal*, 12–19 March 1649, carried a report that Ormond ordered Rupert to blockade Dublin, Bodl., Carte MSS 24, fos. 795–7.

[71] Cary (ed), *Memorials*, ii, pp. 159–62, Jones to the Speaker of the House of Commons, 6 August 1649; Samuel R. Gardiner, *History of the commonwealth and protectorate 1649–1660* (4 vols., London, 1903; reprinted, 1988), i, pp. 99–101.

[72] Bodl., Edward Edwards, Calendar of Carte MSS, 24, p. 60.

[73] J. S. Wheeler, 'Logistics and supply in Cromwell's conquest of Ireland', in Mark Fissel (ed.), *War and government in Britain 1598–1650* (Manchester and New York, 1991), pp. 44–53.

Protestant royalist garrisons in Ulster and Munster, such as Cork, Youghal, and Carrickfergus, to return to the parliamentary camp, and Catholic warlords like the marquis of Antrim to cut deals that salvaged life and property in exchange for persuading enemy towns to surrender.[74]

To a large extent Cromwell's success depended on the support of the Commonwealth's navy. In January 1649, just before Rupert's royalist fleet arrived in Kinsale, the London government overhauled the command and financial structures of the navy, ensuring effective leadership and adequate administration of large maritime forces.[75] By May 1649, a parliamentary naval squadron, led by Robert Blake and Edward Popham, had blockaded Rupert's ships in Kinsale, and another under Richard Deane protected convoys sailing from England to Dublin. The navy also cut the Royalists off from French support.[76] Blake maintained the blockade of Kinsale until late October, when bad weather drove his vessels off station and although Rupert was then able to flee with nine of his ships to Lisbon, Cromwell's supply lines were secured, allowing a steady flow of support to Ireland.[77] Any further threat to this life line ended with the capture of Wexford and the destruction of the Irish privateering fleet on 11 October.

The ability of Cromwell, Jones and Henry Ireton (Cromwell's successor in Ireland in May 1650) to sustain their forces for long periods of time on campaign can be attributed on the one hand to the steady flow of material from England and, on the other, to superior logistical technique in Ireland. Of course whenever possible ships and boats were used to haul supplies and cannon along the coasts and rivers for the army's columns;[78] but the key to tactical mobility in the crucial interior counties remained adequate land transport. In 1647 Jones drew attention to the fact that:

> there are few or no carts or carriages in this town [Dublin] for carriage of ammunition or victuals . . . [and] that was . . . the only bane and destruction of all our designs for which our men have been drawn forth . . . Soldiers are easily got together to march, but carriages not to be provided on a sudden ready. And to have steel mills ready to grind corn [was necessary here], this country not being like England full of villages and towns replenished with victuals; but slenderly inhabited, wasted barren without victuals.[79]

---

[74] Ohlmeyer, *Civil war and restoration*, pp. 230–9.

[75] J. S. Wheeler, 'The administrative, financial, and logistical foundation of British naval power, 1649–1654' (unpublished Naval War College thesis, Newport, 1991), chapter 1.

[76] R. C. Anderson, 'Naval operations, 1648–52', *English Historical Review*, 31 (1916), p. 414.

[77] PRO, SP 25/118 and SP 63/281 indicate that, by September 1650, 7,000 soldiers, over £51,000 worth of food, £33,000 worth of clothing and £300,000 cash had been sent to Ireland together with £3.5 million in soldiers' pay by 1656.

[78] PRO, SP 28/139, part 27, fos. 280–3.

[79] Bodl., Carte MSS 118, fo. 41.

Cromwell had obviously heeded Jones's remarks for in 1649 each English unit came equipped with carts and at least two wagons for the transport of food, tents and munitions and with handmills for grinding grain. Infantry regiments received twelve horses to pull these carts and the artillery train had 900 horses to haul cannon, powder, and numerous items of ordnance repair equipment.[80] Consequently, English columns operated simultaneously in Ulster, Leinster and Munster, rapidly reducing the royalist support base.

Despite shortages of food, munitions and money, Ormond spent the autumn of 1649 trying to co-ordinate the defence of various walled towns like Kilkenny, Waterford, and Galway into which he had dispersed his troops after the débâcle at Rathmines. Late in October he also reconciled his differences, and joined forces, with Owen Roe O'Neill. However the general's untimely death the following month left the command of the Army of Ulster in the inexperienced hands of Ever MacMahon, bishop of Clogher, who did not enjoy the confidence of O'Neill's soldiers and failed to prevent their annihilation at the battle of Scariffhollis in Donegal on 21 June 1650. This ended effective organized Irish resistance in the north. Then late in 1650 Ormond gave up his command for a second time and retired to France, leaving the earl of Clanricard in a hopeless situation in the west.

The nearly unbroken string of Parliamentary victories sapped Irish morale. The Irish defensive successes at Waterford in late 1649 and Clonmel in May 1650 proved the exceptions to the rule of Cromwellian superiority, but they also indicate that more aggressive royalist leadership in August 1649 would have made a significant tactical difference. After the destruction of O'Neill's army in June 1650, only guerrilla operations remained as an Irish option outside of Connacht. One place after another fell: Kilkenny (March 1650), Carlow (June), Waterford (August), Limerick (November 1651) culminating in the surrender of Galway in April 1652. These defeats stemmed partly from English military supremacy, but the Irish continued to let their personal differences undermine their cause 'as if they are not interested in the danger of the kingdom. Their stupidity [is] so generally incredible as that either they apprehend no danger near them or [are] so desperately defeated as scarce any will afford a helping hand to their own preservation'.[81]

The successful Dutch and Portuguese revolts demonstrate that, wars, even between a great power and a small state, never have inevitable

80 PRO, SP 25/118, pp. 88–91.
81 Clanricard to Ormond, 19 February 1650 (Bodl. Carte MSS 26, fo. 772).

outcomes. Yet was there real hope for Irish victory in the 1640s? Without doubt both the Royalists and the Confederates missed numerous opportunities to win the Irish Civil War and, thereby, to alter the outcome of the 'Wars of the Three Kingdoms'. To begin with Catholic political and military leadership remained poor throughout the 1640s; but it was the confederate failure to unite their forces under a single commander which proved so disastrous. Inept leadership by O'Neill, Castlehaven and Preston prevented the exploitation of opportunities for strategic success in 1643–4 and 1646–7, and eventually gave Jones and Cromwell the opportunity to win major battles in 1647 and 1649. Credit for parliamentary victory in Ireland belongs to Ormond, Jones and Cromwell: ironically Ormond maintained England's cause in its darkest days in 1643–6 and handed Dublin over to the English Parliament in 1647; Jones conducted successful holding operations in 1647 and won the important battles of Dungan's Hill and Rathmines; finally, Cromwell triumphed in the Second English Civil War which freed the Commonwealth to concentrate its resources on the defeat of the Irish rebellion. However without a steady outpouring of men, money and supplies from England the style of warfare favoured by Jones and Cromwell, which concentrated on the battlefield defeat of their enemy's army, would have been doomed to failure. This had been the case between 1643 to 1646 when events across the Channel crippled the English war-effort in Ireland and almost facilitated a Catholic victory. Had the Irish managed to drive the Parliamentarians out of Ireland during this critical period, the costs of reconquest in 1649 may have proved too high, paving the way for a mediated political solution. A failure of Irish leadership, not 'Cromwell's Curse', dashed Catholic hopes for religious toleration and political autonomy.

CHAPTER 4

THE MILITARY REVOLUTION IN
SEVENTEENTH-CENTURY IRELAND[1]

ROLF LOEBER AND GEOFFREY PARKER

EVERYONE IN Ireland understood the military significance of the rebellion of October 1641. Almost immediately the Lords Justice warned that without immediate intervention from Britain

> [This] kingdom will be utterly lost and all the English and Protestants in Ireland destroyed, and so England instead of subjects will have enemies here, who will continually disturb the peace of that Kingdom, as well from hence as from foreign powers . . . and then of necessity England must be forced to undertake a new conquest of this Kingdom, for a politic reformation will then become impossible; and to make a new conquest will be now more difficult and chargeable than in former times, in regard the ports and inland towns and the principal strengths will be immediately lost, as some of them already are . . . and the people better disciplined in the rules of war, besides many other advantages they have as well by the return hither of commanders of the Irish who served in foreign nations . . . Besides all the mere Irish now in the service of the King of Spain will undoubtedly return hither to join with the rebels.[2]

The Dublin administration perceived with remarkable prescience that the conflict would be qualitatively different from any of the earlier revolts in Ireland because it would dislodge thousands of British settlers and their families, undo English control over large areas of the country, and provoke an unprecedented arms race.

Historians, however, seem to have missed this point. Although the major military innovations in early modern continental warfare have received detailed study, their transfer to Ireland during the first half of the

---

[1] The authors are much indebted to Paul Kerrigan, Jane Ohlmeyer and Robert Stradling for making available to them published and unpublished material. The authors are grateful for comments by Magda Stouthamer-Loeber on an earlier draft of this chapter.

[2] HMC, *Calendar of the manuscripts of the marquis of Ormonde*, ns (8 vols., London, 1902–20), II, p. 10.

seventeenth century has not. Four key developments, sometimes termed the 'Military Revolution' are at issue: the artillery fortress, the naval broadside, the reliance on firepower in combat, and the application of strategies that deployed several armies in concert. All four appeared in Ireland during the 1640s, and transformed the nature of the conflict.[3]

Warfare in Ireland before 1641 followed two basic patterns. Traditionally the Irish excelled in skirmishes, ambushes, capturing settlers' strongholds and, occasionally, building earthworks. The English, by contrast, concentrated on the control of towns from which they tried to dominate the surrounding countryside. Although many English settlements without walls were burnt by the Irish, formal sieges were rare and even small fortified towns remained relatively impregnable. The capture of Athenry (County Galway, 1576) and Kilmallock (County Limerick, 1583) proved the exception, and even they were soon recovered.

Admittedly artillery was used both to attack and defend towns before 1500, and it became increasingly common thereafter; but, thanks to the rarity of roads and the ubiquity of bogs, heavy guns tended to be used only against coastal or riverside fortresses – at Carrigafoyle in 1579, at Smerwick in 1580, at Dunluce in 1584, and most notably at Kinsale in 1601-2. Most of these strongholds boasted 'Italian-style' defensive systems with low, thick walls and quadrilateral bastions protected by artillery. The earl of Kildare built the first artillery fortress recorded in Ireland at Maynooth (County Kildare) in about 1533, defended by numerous heavy guns and a garrison of 100, of whom 60 were gunners. The first Gaelic Irish known to have used siege artillery were the O'Donnells, who took Sligo Castle with a French gun in 1515.[4]

Some settlers in the Munster plantation in the later sixteenth century, at Mallow in County Cork, and at Castle Island and Castlemaine in County Kerry, also brought artillery and constructed gun platforms; while newcomers in Ulster after 1610 did the same – Sir Thomas Ridgeway at Augher (County Tyrone); Sir Oliver St John at Ballymore (County Armagh) and Sir Thomas Phillips at Limavady (County Londonderry) – but they formed a minority. Elsewhere, only a few plantation centres seem to have received artillery. Thus Richard Boyle, earl of Cork, provided his new town of Bandon (County Cork) with six pieces of ordnance for its defence in 1642,[5]

---

[3] See Geoffrey Parker, *The military revolution: military innovation and the rise of the west, 1500–1800* (Cambridge, 1988). For Ireland see C. Falls, *Elizabeth's Irish wars* (New York, 1970) and P. Kerrigan, 'Fortifications in Tudor Ireland', *Fortress*, 7 (1990), pp. 27–39.

[4] G. A. Hayes-McCoy, 'The early history of guns in Ireland', *Galway Archaeological Society Journal*, 18 (1938–9), pp. 54–5; A. M. Freeman (ed.), *The annals of Connacht* (Dublin, 1983), p. 631.

[5] George Bennett, *The history of Bandon* (Cork, 1862), p. 67.

and an early plan of the settlement showed bulwarks designed to carry artillery and, in an unusual design, the long curtain walls built on a shallow V-plan, rather than straight, so that the guns could be fired parallel to the walls without hitting the next bastion.[6] Derry, the largest new town in Ulster, must have been supplied with cannon in the early part of the century by the London Companies, although Lord Deputy Strafford caused their 'best and most useful ordnance be carryed away' before the rebellion (presumably for the campaign in Scotland in 1640).[7]

New-style defences were exceptional, however. By and large, artillery in Ireland before 1641 remained confined to the older cities, even though most lacked walls capable of carrying them. Shortly after the outbreak of the rebellion, for example, the Lords Justice complained that Dublin was in a 'very weak condition to make any defence' with 'the suburbs having no walls and the city walls . . . being made four hundred years ago are very much decayed and have no flankers on them, nor places for men to fight on'. If the city fell, moreover, they feared that Dublin Castle would soon follow, 'having been built four hundred years ago, and having on it no modern fortification and the towers being very crazy and in danger of falling, especially when they come to be shaken with the shooting of the ordnance now mounted thereon'.[8] The best improvements to existing fortifications in Ireland were those added at Limerick in about 1590 (most of them still in place during the siege of 1651: plate 1). A late sixteenth-century plan indicates a star-shaped redoubt outside the city walls, at least seven new bastions, and a fortified bridgehead.[9] Elsewhere, improvements in fortifications mostly remained limited to gun platforms attached to older walls. However a number of towns on the south and west coasts with a predominantly Catholic population (including Galway, Limerick, Cork and Waterford) received a citadel, which had the dual purpose of denying access to an invading force and dominating the town. Thus a drawing of the new stronghold at Waterford, dating from 1624–6, shows a gun platform with four cannon facing the settlement.[10] Likewise, Limerick Castle was given a polygonal bastion facing the town with a platform for artillery.[11] A citadel could be a mixed blessing, however, because if an enemy occupied it, the adjoining town and port could more easily be bombarded and thus

[6] P. O'Flanaghan, *Bandon* (Dublin, 1988), map. 6.
[7] J. Hogan (ed.), *Letters and papers relating to the Irish rebellion between 1642–46* (IMC, Dublin, 1936), p. 4.
[8] HMC, *Ormonde MSS*, ns, II, p. 33.
[9] Kerrigan, 'Fortifications', p. 35.
[10] G. A. Hayes-McCoy (ed.), *Ulster and other Irish maps, c. 1600* (IMC, Dublin, 1964), plate XVI.
[11] BL, Add. MSS 24,200, survey by Nicholas Pynnar, 1624.

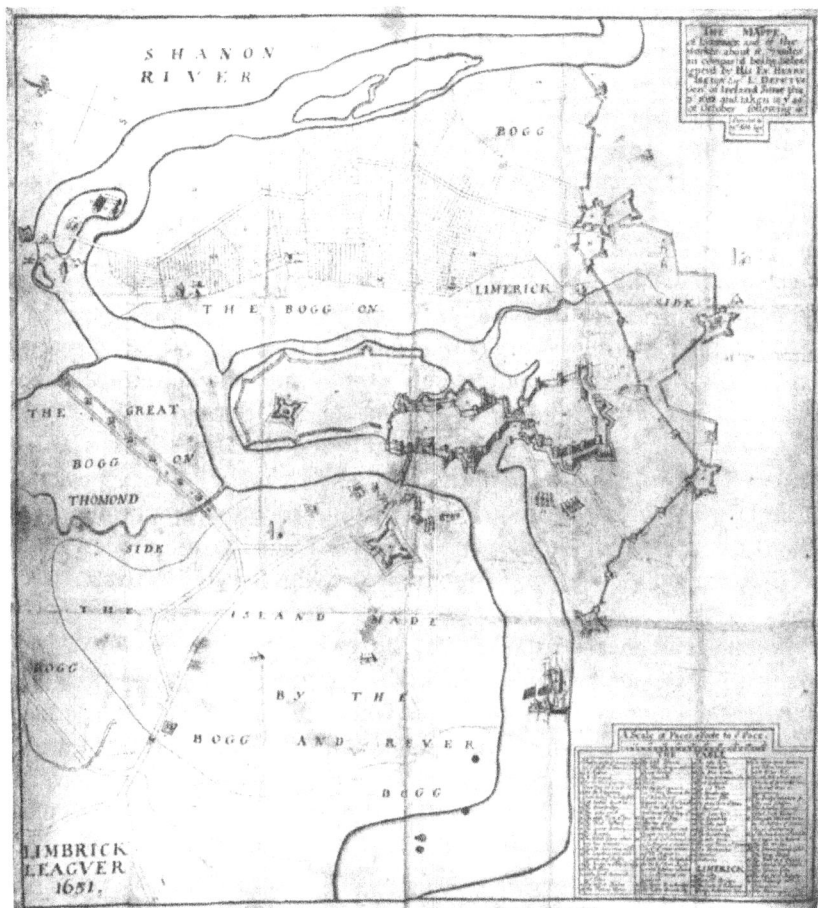

Plate 1 The siege of Limerick by Ireton's forces, 1651

forced to surrender.[12] Finally another military innovation occurred in late sixteenth-century Ireland: building artillery fortresses on estuaries leading to ports. Duncannon Fort, a splendid structure commanding the east shore of the approach to Waterford harbour, built in 1587–9, by 1642 housed several 'great pieces of battery and other ordnance'.[13] The star-shaped

---

12 M. D. O'Sullivan, 'The fortification of Galway in the 16th and early 17th century', *Journal of the Galway Archaeological and Historical Society*, 16 (1934), p. 34.
13 P. M. Kerrigan, 'Irish castles and fortifications in the age of the Tudors, part 2 – 1558 to 1603', *An Cosantóir* (1984), p. 276. It was built under the supervision of Geoffrey Fenton, who presumably had some knowledge of warfare since he had translated Guicciardini's *Wars of Italy* (London, 1579); Hogan (ed.), *Letters*, p. 151.

fortification at Castle Park, dominating the entrance to Kinsale, completed in 1604, also possessed strong defences.

The proliferation of artillery fortresses placed a new premium on the ability to manufacture heavy guns locally, rather than depend on imports from abroad. However, cannon-founding, whether in iron or bronze, required large capital investment and highly skilled craftsmen, and cannon are known to have been cast in privately owned furnaces at only two sites in pre-war Ireland. Richard Boyle, earl of Cork established the first at Cappoquin (County Waterford) in 1626.[14] His weapons were probably of medium calibre, since he placed them in the forts of Cork and Waterford to defend the Munster plantation against foreign invaders.[15] The second site lay at Ballinakill (County Laois) where ten (probably iron) three-pounder 'minions' were cast in 1633. The foundry belonged to Sir Thomas Ridgeway, but Lord Deputy Wentworth (and probably others) owned shares.[16] The iron may have been mined locally, but until 1641 specialists from Liège in the Low Countries operated the foundry. Wentworth, after witnessing a successful trial of the minions at Kilmainham outside Dublin in 1633 praised them as 'the smoothest, and with the closest Grain I ever saw'.[17]

Foreign influence on the military affairs of pre-war Ireland was not confined to architecture and artisans: several foreign military treatises also entered the kingdom. Thus a copy of Gutiérrez de la Vega's *De re militari* was pillaged from a Spanish soldier killed at Smerwick in 1580, and formed the basis for Nicholas Lichefild's translation, published in London two years later; while the defeated commander of Kinsale, Don Juan del Aguila, presented Sir George Carew, lord president of Munster, with a book on fortifications.[18] A few catalogues of private libraries shed some light on the military books available in seventeenth-century Ireland. For instance the marquis of Ormond, who played a crucial military role in the civil wars, in 1684–5 owned several relevant early works, including the *Artillery master* (no known place or date) and J. Perret, *Des fortifications et artifices d'architecture*

[14] *Cal. S P Ire., 1625–32*, p. 110.

[15] J. Bruce (ed.), *Letters and papers of the Verney family* (London, 1853), p. 125.

[16] W. Knowler (ed.), *Letters and dispatches of the Earl of Strafforde* . . . (2 vols., London, 1739), i, pp. 128, 145, 163; A. B. Grosart (ed.), *The Lismore papers* (10 vols., London, 1886–8), first series, iii, p. 209; H. F. Kearney, 'Richard Boyle, ironmaster', *Journal, Royal Society of Antiquaries of Ireland, 82–3* (1952–3), p. 161; Sir A. Vicars, *Index to the prerogative wills of Ireland* (Dublin, 1897) p. 37.

[17] Knowler (ed.), *Letters*, I, p. 163; W. Nolan, 'The historical geography of the ownership and occupation of land in the barony of Fassadinin, Kilkenny, c. 1600–1850' (PhD thesis, University College, Dublin, 1975).

[18] K. Duncan-Jones, *Sir Philip Sidney, courtier poet* (New Haven, 1991) p. 229; R. Loeber, 'Biographical dictionary of engineers in Ireland, 1600–1730', *Irish Sword*, 13 (1977–9), p. 31.

et perspective (Paris, earliest edition, 1594).[19] The Irish 'master gunner', Samuel Molyneux, who served in Ormond's army and later in the parliamentary army, may have owned several other volumes, which survived in the library of his descendants, such as Nicholas Goldman's *La nouvelle fortification* (Leiden, Elsevier, 1645), and Mattias Dögen's *Architectura militaris moderna* (Amsterdam, Ludovic Elzevir, 1647).[20] Roger Boyle, Lord Broghill (and later earl of Orrery), author of an excellent military treatise that drew extensively on his experiences during the wars in Ireland, probably owned Adam Freitag's *Architectura militaris nova et aucta* (first published at Leiden in 1630).[21] In addition, interested Irish readers enjoyed access to the military books, over 150 in number, published in England before 1641.[22] Nevertheless only one Irishman is known to have brought out a military handbook during the period: Garret Barry, a kinsman of the earl of Barrymore, who served in the Spanish Army of Flanders and at the outbreak of the rebellion returned to Ireland, in 1634 published in Brussels *A discourse of military discipline*, with fourteen tables and diagrams, whose third part bore the mysterious title 'Of Fire-wourckes of rare executions by sea and lande, as alsoe of firtifasions[sic]'.[23]

Nevertheless, although the Military Revolution thus scarcely touched Ireland directly, many Irishmen came into contact with it in other ways. To begin with, countless Irish soldiers received training in the English army,

[19] HMC, *Ormonde MSS*, ns, VII, pp. 514–15.

[20] TCD (printed books) vvi, 45.

[21] He copied many of its illustrations for his own book, entitled *A Treatise of the art of war* (London, 1677). The link with Freitag initially became evident to Rolf Loeber from the mention of Freitag's work in Orrery's play 'Mr. Anthony'.

[22] M. J. D. Cockle, *A biography of English military books up to 1642, and of contemporary foreign works* (second edn., London, 1900).

[23] Barry also published a translation, in similarly barbarous English, of the official history of Spinola's victorious siege of Breda: see Herman Hugo, *The seige* [sic] *of Breda* (Leuven, 1627). Remarkably, the end of the Irish wars did not spawn a spate of publications similar to those celebrating the end of the Eighty and the Thirty Years War on the continent in 1648. Only a few military commanders who had served in Ireland thought it worthwhile to publish military tracts after 1660, most notably Roger Boyle, later earl of Orrery, who published *A treatise of the art of war* (London, 1677), and Sir James Turner, who wrote *Pallas armata. Military essays of the ancient Grecian, Roman and modern art of war* (London, 1683). Another exception was master gunner Samuel Molyneux, who published an educational treatise on gunnery and ballistics. This work, of which only one copy appears to have survived (at Trinity College, Dublin, lacking its title page and date of publication), relied on trigonometry and exemplified the empirical and statistical basis of the 'New Learning' which emerged in the 1650s. It is interesting to note that officers who had served during the Irish civil war and in the subsequent Down Survey – Miles Symner, Samuel Molyneux, William Petty, Benjamin Worsley – formed the core of the Dublin Philosophical Society. Although civilians eventually also contributed to this Irish equivalent of the Royal Society of London, military officers took the initiative. See T. C. Barnard, 'The Hartlib circle and the origins of the Dublin Philosophical Society', *Irish Historical Studies* 19 (1974), pp. 56–71.

sometimes abroad – in the Netherlands, France and Brittany – but above all with the English forces stationed in Ireland. According to Barnaby Riche in 1615, Irish had outnumbered English soldiers by a ratio of three to one during the Nine Years War (1594–1603). With a sense of foreboding he wrote, 'I have never reade of any such polycy wher a rebellyous people, that wer every day redy to revolt from ther dutyes to ther soveraygnes, shuld be admytted to the exercyse of chevallry: or shuld be Ineured in the practyse of armes . . .'[24] After the war, many of these soldiers left Ireland to join the continental armies, above all the Spanish Army of Flanders.

Some also doubted the wisdom of thus providing former rebels with expert military training, but the victorious English commander, Lord Mountjoy, offered the reassurance that 'it hath ever been seen that more than three parts of the four of these countrymen do never return, being once engaged in any such voyage'.[25] He was wrong: by 1640 the Army of Flanders included some 1,300 Irish troops and senior officers, such as Owen Roe O'Neill and Thomas Preston, and both of these commanders, together with several hundred of their veteran compatriots, returned in 1641–2.[26] There they joined not only the thousand or so Irish veterans who simultaneously returned from service in France and Spain,[27] but also the Catholic troops mobilized and trained by Strafford in 1640 as the 'New Army' destined to serve the king in England. According to their commanding officer, these men were not 'poor stinking rascally sneaks[;] thes are brave gallant fellows . . . there cloaths are better, theire persons [are] better and there mettell is better'. He later added: 'I doe not care whoe sees them . . . noe prince in the Christian world hath . . . better men, nor

---

[24] E. M. Hinton, 'Rych's "An Anatomy of Ireland" with an account of the author', *Publications of the Modern Language Association of America*, 55 (1940), p. 96.

[25] Mountjoy to Privy Council, 1 May 1601, quoted in R. D. FitzSimon, 'Irish swordsmen in the imperial service in the Thirty Years War', *Irish Sword*, 9 (1969–70), p. 22.

[26] In January 1640 the eighteen companies of Irish infantry (in a single tercio) serving in the Army of Flanders numbered 199 officers and 1,071 men, see the Memorial of Pieter Roose, 18/28 January 1640 (Archives Générales du Royaume, Brussels, Conseil Privé Espagnol 1574, fos. 81–99). Interestingly, according to this document the Irish units had changed from arquebus to musket in 1633–4, but the English still carried the lighter arquebus. Although by 1640 only one Irish regiment served in the Spanish Netherlands, there had been four in 1636: B. Jennings, *Wild Geese in Spanish Flanders 1582–1700* . . . (IMC, Dublin, 1964), pp. 8–14; and R. A. Stradling, *The Spanish monarchy and Irish mercenaries: the Wild Geese in Spain 1618–68* (Dublin, 1994), pp. 164–5. For an account of the Irish military community in Flanders see G. Henry, *The Irish military community in Spanish Flanders, 1586–1621* (Dublin, 1992); and Henry, 'Ulster exiles in Europe, 1605–41', in B. Mac Cuarta (ed.), *Ulster 1641* (Belfast, 1993), pp. 37–60.

[27] Precise numbers are elusive, but the Irish units serving in Spain fell to one regiment in 1643, and in the French army from seven regiments in 1641 to one in 1643. It must be presumed that many of these 'missing' troops returned to their native land: personal communication from Robert Stradling.

more orderly'.[28] Many of them joined the rebellion and formed the backbone of the confederate armies. To make matters worse, the Dublin government, still trusting the Old English and, trying to contain the rebellion, sent out thousands of arms to these Catholic landowners in Leinster. Since many of them later joined the rebellion, most of the weapons fell into enemy hands.[29] Equally serious, from the government's point of view, Irish society on the eve of the rebellion was considerably less militarized than ever before. In the nine counties of Ulster, for example, whereas in 1619 one settler in eight owned a musket, only one in thirty-three did so in 1630 – a mere 700 among over 13,000 adult males; whilst in 1631 Carrickfergus and Derry boasted only twenty muskets apiece for their defence. Throughout the country, landowners abandoned fortified castles in favour of stately manor houses. As a Kerry gentleman, forced by the events of October 1641 to seek refuge in the earl of Cork's stronghold, lamented: 'My house I built for peace, having more windows than walls.'[30]

Yet within a few months several relatively well-equipped armies, trained and commanded by professionals with continental experience, clearly outclassed the English forces ranged against them. Eventually they also surpassed the Scots: at the battle of Benburb in 1646 the confederate Army of Ulster, under Spanish-trained commanders, used the defensive techniques perfected by Habsburg troops to defeat a Scottish force, under Swedish-trained leaders, using the offensive tactics pioneered by Gustavus Adolphus.[31]

At first, to be sure, the rebels lacked artillery; but this defect was partially remedied when they captured several English strongholds. For example, at Newry (County Down) they acquired powder and three heavy guns, which they immediately used to attack Lisburn (County Antrim) in late November 1641. They 'apeared drawn up in Batalia . . . and sent out two

[28] St. Leger to [Ormond], 21 July and 17 August 1640 (Bodl., Carte MSS 1, fos. 214, 231).
[29] H. Hazlett, 'A history of the military forces operating in Ireland, 1641–9' (unpublished PhD thesis, Queen's University, Belfast, 1938), p. 117. Strafford made a substantial arms purchase in Holland in 1638 (Wentworth to Boswell, 26 October 1638, Sheffield City Library, Wentworth Woodhouse Muniments xi a. 126) and boasted in February 1639 that 'our standing army of one thousand horse and two thousand foot will be in very good condition; besides we have eight thousand spare arms and twelve field pieces, and eight greater for battery, ready upon their carriages', Wentworth to Newcastle, 10 February 1639, Knowler, *Letters*, ii, p. 281. (Our thanks go to Michael Perceval-Maxwell for these references.)
[30] Examples taken from R. Gillespie, 'Destabilizing Ulster, 1641–2', in Mac Cuarta (ed.), *Ulster 1641*, pp. 107–21, at pp. 110–11. Also see BL Add. MSS 4770, fo. 283, listing the settlers and their weapons in c. 1630: the 13,092 'men' listed in the nine counties possessed 7,226 swords, 3,085 pikes, 700 muskets, 384 calivers, 836 snaphances (a light flintlock), 69 halberds and 11 lances.
[31] Stradling, *Spanish monarchy*, p. 91.

devisions, of about six or seaven hundr[ed men] apeece, to compass the Towne, and placed their field-peeces on the high-way to it . . . '[32] In the event the Irish failed, and the newly acquired weapons lay abandoned in a bog hole; but they still had in Newry 'a great Iron Battering peece . . . which was left in an old Turret in the towne, throwne off the carriages'.[33] This suggests that the Irish may not yet have possessed the expertise to handle such a gun (or at least to fix it to a gun carriage) but the returning veterans soon provided the missing knowledge. For instance, at the siege of Limerick in June 1642, the Irish under Colonel Garret Barry (see above), captured 'three pieces of ordnance, whereof one of them weighted neer 8000 weight [eight cwt] mounted', a 'battering piece of such large dimensions, that it took twenty-five oxen to remove it' and fired a thirty-two pound shot.[34] It must have been either a whole or a demi-cannon. Some foresaw that 'with the advantage of his Majesty's ordnance' the rebels 'would fall upon such holds and castles as were then possessed by the English, both in Munster and this county of Clare . . . ', and indeed the rebels soon brought a demi-cannon by water and took Askeaton Castle 'and all the castles and houlds that were invested by the English' in the county of Limerick. Most places were not besieged at all but instead surrendered in advance because they could not have withstood battery.[35]

An early, though unconfirmed, reference to confederate cannon-founding occurred in 1642, when news reached Irish supporters on the continent that 'Colonel Richard Plunquet [Plunkett] is at the Earl of Fingall's house making powder and casting artillery'.[36] This could have been either at Fingall's house at Virginia (County Cavan) or, more likely, at Killeen (County Meath). Scattered references also exist to the manufacture of cannon in the midlands. For instance, a smith at Athboy (County Meath), not far from Killeen, is said to have manufactured for the Irish 'a great piece of ordnance' from 140 pots and pans collected in the locality. Scarcely surprisingly, the gun burst when discharged against the walls of Geashill (County Offaly) in 1641. However another piece of Irish manufacture (called a 'Master-Piece') was effectively employed at the siege

[32] I. Ryder, *An English army for Ireland* (London, 1987), p. 8; Hazlett, 'Military forces', pp. 114, 119; 'The battle of Lisnegarvey, a.d. 1641', *Ulster Journal of Archaeology*, 1 (1853), pp. 242–3.

[33] Cited in T. Fitzpatrick, *The bloody bridge and other papers relating to the insurrection of 1641* (Dublin, 1903, reissued Port Washington, N.Y., 1970), pp. 121–2, 124; Sir James Turner, *Memoirs of his own life and times* (Edinburgh, 1829), p. 20.

[34] *A more exact relation of a great victory . . .* (London, 1642), p. 3–3v; Bennett, *Bandon*, p. 82.

[35] Hogan (ed.), *Letters*, pp. 117–18; T. C. Croker, *Researches in the south of Ireland* (London, 1824), pp. 40–1.

[36] HMC, *Reports on the Franciscan manuscripts preserved at the convent, Merchants' Quay, Dublin* (Dublin, 1906), pp. 121–2.

of Castle Coote (County Roscommon).[37] Moreover the Irish were able to operate iron works at Artully (near Kenmare, County Kerry) around 1645, and at Lissan (County Tyrone), where existing works seized by Niall O'Quinn in 1641 subsequently produced pike heads for the Irish Army in Ulster.[38]

The Irish also augmented their stock of artillery with cannon recovered from ships. For example, at the end of 1642, a French vessel unable to enter the Shannon and blockaded by a parliamentary flotilla landed three pieces of ordnance, sank two ships and recovered eight cannon from them. Shipwrecks provided other opportunities to retrieve artillery: in 1642 a Dutch East Indiaman foundered in foul weather at Dungarvan (County Waterford) and yielded five pieces of ordnance; the *Hopewell*, cast away off Wexford while sailing from London to Dublin, produced five more.[39]

Finally munitions also arrived intermittently from abroad. One ship, probably sent over from Spanish Flanders and almost captured in October 1642, arrived safely in Wexford with 'two hundred barrels of powder, some muskets, and three pieces of bronze [artillery]' with 'balls of iron'. A continental supporter wrote that these pieces 'will serve to batter the castles in which the heretics make their quarters and defence, and are field pieces as neat as have been seen . . . '[40] At Easter 1643, more ships arrived with ammunition, hand weapons and artillery, paid for by Spain.[41] This, or another shipment, included two iron twenty-four pounders and a Spanish iron mortar.[42] A further consignment of four demi-cannon from Spain is mentioned in 1648.[43] By then, some towns had assembled considerable arsenals: Wexford, a major confederate port, together with its fort, contained at the time of its surrender to Cromwell in 1649 'near a hundred cannon'.[44]

Most of this information, however, comes from Leinster. The position of the confederate Army of Ulster was very different. A report in October 1642

---

[37] W. A. McComlish, 'The survival of the Irish castle in an age of cannon', *Irish Sword*, 9 (1969–70), p. 17.

[38] D. Massari, 'My Irish campaign', *The Catholic Bulletin*, 4 (1916), p. 218; Eileen McCracken, 'Charcoal-burning ironworks in seventeenth and eighteenth century Ireland', *Ulster Journal of Archaeology*, 20 (1957), p. 134.

[39] HMC, *Franciscan MSS*, p. 229; Hogan (ed.), *Letters*, p. 88; *La courageuse resolution d'une dame irlandoise* (Paris, 1642), p. 6.

[40] HMC, *Franciscan MSS*, pp. 199, 206.

[41] J. T. Gilbert (ed.), *A contemporary history of affairs in Ireland (1641–1652)* . . . (3 vols., Irish Archaeological Society, Dublin, 1879), I, p. 32; Gilbert, *History of the Irish confederation and war in Ireland* (7 vols., Dublin, 1882–91), II, p. 331.

[42] Gilbert, *Irish confederation*, I, p. 151.

[43] Gilbert, *Contemporary history*, I, p. 184.

[44] T. Carlyle (ed.), *Oliver Cromwell's letters and speeches* (5 vols., London, 1870), II, p. 197.

lamented Owen Roe O'Neill's shortage of artillery in Ulster, noting that if he were to have 'but two pieces of battery and four or five field pieces with store of arms, he would clear all Connaught and Ulster in three months, leaving never a Puritan, English or Scotch, in either Province'.[45] Lacking a major port to which supplies could be directed, Owen Roe probably possessed little or no artillery until, four years later, he captured six to nine pieces, perhaps two of them siege cannon, from the Scots at the battle of Benburb (County Tyrone) in 1646.[46]

Elsewhere armies campaigned, almost certainly for the first time in Ireland, with their own artillery trains. A confederate train in Leinster was first noted in 1643, and by 1646 it consisted of a brass cannon, a brass culverin, two quarter-cannon, carriages and a sleigh.[47] When Thomas Preston's army was defeated at Dungan's Hill in 1647, Colonel Michael Jones captured 'four demiculverins, each carrying a twelve-pound bullet, and 64 fair oxen attending the train', which were added to Jones's seven cannon.[48] On the Protestant side, the outbreak of the First English Civil War prevented the dispatch in August 1642 of artillery intended for the English army in Ireland.[49] However shortly afterwards, a train for the Scottish forces landed in the north with ninety-six officers and artificers (up to that point, the Scots had to make do with a small cannon taken from Carrickfergus Castle).[50] By February 1643 the Scots artillery possessed six 'battering pieces', while Ormond had seven.[51] By contrast, the train brought to Ireland by Cromwell contained eleven siege guns and twelve field pieces, which both in magnitude and fire-power exceeded all the others operating in Ireland combined![52]

Cromwell also enjoyed far better logistical support (see chapter 3 above). Although in 1647 Owen Roe O'Neill managed to lead his army over the Curlew mountains from Boyle to Sligo because 'his pioneers were at work five or six weeks through Rockey mountains to make way for his

45 HMC, *Franciscan MSS*, p. 206.
46 C. Hollick, 'Owen Roe O'Neill's Ulster army of the confederacy, May–August 1646', *Irish Sword*, 18 (1991), pp. 224, 226; Gilbert (ed.), *Contemporary history*, I, p. 116; G. A. Hayes-McCoy, *Irish battles. A military history of Ireland* (Belfast, 1989), pp. 174–99.
47 HMC, *Ormonde MSS*, I, p. 58; Gilbert (ed.), *Irish confederation*, VI, p. 84.
48 C. H. Firth, *Cromwell's army* (London, 1902, reprinted London, 1992), p. 150. Also see chapter 3 above.
49 Ryder, *English army*, p. 22.
50 D. Stevenson, *Scottish covenanters and Irish confederates: Scottish-Irish relations in the mid-seventeenth century* (Belfast, 1981), p. 72; Gilbert (ed.), *Contemporary history*, I, p. 419.
51 C[ambridge] U[niversity] L[ibrary], MS Ee.3.39, fo. 1; see also Stevenson, *Scottish covenanters*, pp. 321, 323–4. A listing of the artillery train in Munster in 1645 can be found in CUL, MS Ee.3.40, fos. 4v–5v; C. MacNeill (ed.), *The Tanner letters . . .* (IMC, Dublin, 1943), p. 315.
52 Firth, *Cromwell's army*, p. 169, n.1.

Guns',[53] their achievement paled in comparison with the pontoon bridge built by Cromwell's engineers across the river Barrow near New Ross which, according to a writer of the time was 'a stupendious worke' and 'a wonder to all men, and understood by none'.[54] Nevertheless even Cromwell strove to transport his artillery as much as possible by water: for the 1649 campaign he shipped his battery from Dublin first to Drogheda and then to Wexford.[55]

Access to a seaport was also essential for landing, storage and transfer of supplies; as a safe haven for privateering and other shipping; as winter and training quarters for a garrison; and as the point of departure and return for campaigns to dominate the hinterland. The Irish therefore stood at a serious disadvantage, for in Ulster they lacked any major port (such as Derry or Carrickfergus); in Leinster they never held Dublin, and lost Dundalk and Carlingford; and in the south they also failed to obtain a permanent foothold at Cork, Kinsale, Youghal or Bandon, although for much of the civil war they held Waterford, Wexford, Limerick and Galway. However even these key harbours required constant protection from parliamentarian ships and this could only be accomplished effectively in three ways. First, confederate ships could patrol the mouth of the harbour and keep it open for sorties by privateers and merchantmen loyal to their cause. Second, a bulwark capable of dominating the approaches with its artillery could be built. Thus, at Rosslare Point, near Wexford harbour, a fort, equipped with about seven 'great' guns, was built under the supervision of Captain Antonio Vanderipen from Spanish Flanders.[56] Finally, a chain could be stretched from one bank of the harbour to the other in order to prevent ships from getting through, as at Galway in 1643 (although after a blockade of seven weeks the citadel, St Augustine's fort, depleted of supplies, capitulated).[57] Likewise, during the siege of Drogheda in 1642, Sir Phelim O'Neill used a chain to close off the river, but it was later rammed by an incoming ship and broke. Eventually, the besiegers were forced to withdraw.[58]

[53] [Hogan, E., (ed.)], *The history of the warr in Ireland . . . by a British officer of the regiment of Sir John Clotworthy* (Dublin, 1873), p. 58.

[54] Gilbert (ed.), *Contemporary history*, II, pp. 55, 102.

[55] In contrast, the confederate army rarely made use of shipping to transport cannon, possibly because of the provincial division of its forces, although Preston shipped his guns from Athy (County Kildare) to Carlow on the river Barrow, a distance of about twelve miles, Gilbert (ed.), *Contemporary history*, I, p. 262.

[56] [J. Lodge], *Desiderata curiosa Hibernica* (2 vols., Dublin, 1772), II, p. 159; Carlyle (ed.), *Cromwell*, II, p. 191.

[57] P. Walsh, 'Rinmore Fort: a seventeenth century fortification at Renmore, Galway', *Journal of the Galway Archaeological and Historical Society*, 41 (1987–8), pp. 120–1.

[58] Hogan (ed.), *Warr in Ireland*, p. 16.

Artillery fortresses only proliferated in Ireland after the war began. The largest defensive earthworks were made around Dublin: the Down Survey (plate 2) shows earthen ramparts encircling most of the suburbs to the south and north of the city, reinforced by at least eighteen bastions positioned at regular intervals. A description of these fortifications, dating from 1646, speaks of half-moons before the gates, palisades to strengthen the earthworks, and the destruction of houses outside of the walls to prevent the enemy from taking shelter.[59] Perhaps fortunately, Dublin never underwent a full siege. Soon after the beginning of the rebellion, the Boyle family and its associates in Munster reinforced several towns, including an entrenchment and four gates, probably wooden, at Tallow (County Waterford) in 1643 and improvements at the town walls of Youghal (County Cork) in 1644.[60] In Leinster, Duncannon Fort (County Wexford) received 'brave rampiers' in 1645 under the direction of General Thomas Preston.[61] Pierce Fitzgerald, commissary-general of the confederate horse, built a full bastioned fort (plate 3) with a water-filled moat and various earthworks around nearby villages, at Ballyshannon (County Kildare),[62] while Lieutenant Colonel Walter Cruise's fort at Ardlonan, four miles from Kells (County Meath) was deemed by the New Model Army 'a verie strong place haveing 3 walls within one another, two of them beinge of earth the 3[r]d of stone, all regularly fortified'.[63]

A few Ulster towns also received new defences. At Antrim, in 1642 men and women made 'a Ditch of about 8 feet broad without any Breastwork only the Flankers and Rounds . . . ' The appearance of 4,000 Irish, however, interrupted the works and the town and its outer defences were assaulted and burnt in 1649 by the Scots (although they were unable to destroy 'the Mount and Castle . . . being a place that is not for a Running party to attack').[64] At Belfast, a bastioned enceinte was built in 1643, for which Lord Chichester was granted £1,000: 'He planted cannon in the

59 NLI, MS 4617 unfol.
60 Grosart (ed.), *Lismore papers*, first series, v, p. 221; second series, v, p. 120; Loeber, 'Biographical dictionary of engineers in Ireland, 1600–1730', *Irish Sword*, 13 (winter, 1977), p. 106; R. Caulfield (ed.), *The council book of the corporation of Youghal* (Guildford, 1878), pp. 546–7, 550.
61 Gilbert (ed.), *Contemporary history*, I, p. 102–3.
62 Gilbert, *Irish confederation*, VI, p. 84; Lord W. FitzGerald, 'The FitzGeralds of Ballyshannon (County Kildare), and their successors thereat', *County Kildare Archaeological Society Journal*, 3 (1899–1902), pp. 425–52.
63 R. M. Young (ed.), 'Diary of the proceedings of the Leinster army under Governor Jones', *Ulster Journal of Archaeology*, 3 (1897), pp. 153–61, quote at p. 157; HMC, *Tenth report, appendix IV* (London, 1885), p. 87; D. F. Cregan, 'Some members of the confederation of Kilkenny', in S. O'Brien (ed.), *Measgra I gCuimhne Mhichíl Uí Chléirigh* (Dublin, 1944), p. 43; M. J. Moore, *Archaeological inventory of County Meath* (Dublin, 1987), p. 117.
64 Hogan (ed.), *Letters*, pp. 20, 95.

Plate 2 Detail of the Down Survey showing the fortifications of Dublin

works, and did begin to cut off the highway that enters Carrickfergus port'. Nevertheless the town was surprised twice, in 1644 and 1648, indicating the limitations of the improvements.[65] The fortifications erected at Limerick in the 1590s received considerable additions during the 1640s, leading the

[65] *Cal. S P Ire., 1633–47*, pp. 393, 561; HMC, *Tenth report, appendix IV*, p. 92.

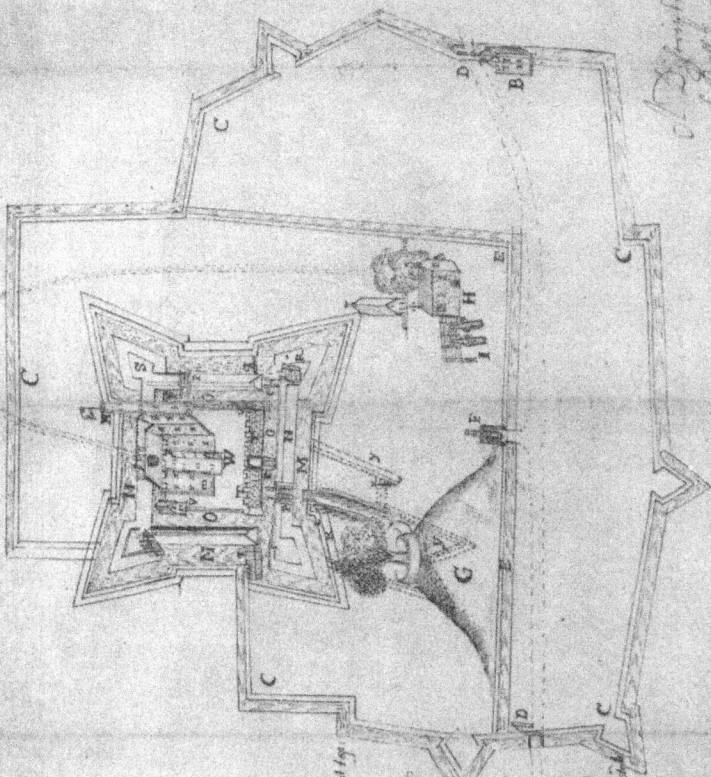

Plate 9 The siege of Ballyshannon, County Kildare 1648

Frenchman La Boullaye-Le-Gouz in 1644 to call it, probably correctly, 'the strongest fortress in Ireland', while Dean Massari wrote a year later that 'it is almost impregnable, being surrounded with a triple wall, the three walls in turn being protected by water'.[66]

Limerick was one of the record number of towns besieged by Cromwell's forces between 1649 and 1652. They rarely used circumvallation, which was time-consuming and labour-intensive, preferring instead a shock approach, by first erecting batteries and bombarding weak segments of town walls or adjacent structures, followed by a general assault. At both Drogheda and Wexford, Cromwell first identified a tall structure near the town wall (a church in Drogheda, a castle at Wexford), and then concentrated on seizing that structure. This gave his soldiers some protection against counterattack and a high vantage point from which to advance upon the town itself. In both cities this strategy proved decisive. Limerick, however, provided a far more serious challenge. In 1651, Cromwell's son-in-law and successor, Henry Ireton, erected an extensive circumvallation (see plate 1). Two major forts were constructed (Fort Cromwell and Fort Ireton), forming part of the chain of circumvallation, and a battery of twenty-eight guns and four mortar pieces (one of which is said to have thrown a projectile weighing two hundredweight) arrived by sea. Ranged against them, behind the formidable defences, stood experienced troops and at least thirty-four guns, including two demi-cannons. Eventually a breach was made at a point where the Irish had not reinforced the town wall, yet even Limerick might have held out longer but for treachery within the garrison.[67]

A characteristic feature of Irish warfare during the 1640s was the interdependence of cities and nearby castles. Castles, especially those situated at strategic points such as bridges or fords across rivers, could both safeguard access to the town and give the alarm when enemy forces approached. A location on a river could also prove of economic importance, because one or more mills might be able to operate under the protection of the castle and thus provide much-needed corn, which often could not be ground in the city itself. For example, in 1642, the defenders of Kinsale garrisoned Arcloyne Castle and its mill, about one mile outside of the town, 'which lyeth under command of the Castle, and hope we shall keepe it; we had not

---

[66] J. Hill, *The building of Limerick* (Cork, 1991), p. 31; Massari, 'Campaign', p. 221.
[67] J. G. Simms, 'Hugh Dubh O'Neill's defence of Limerick, 1650–1651', *Irish Sword*, 3 (1957), pp. 115–23; Gilbert (ed.), *Contemporary history*, III, pp. 238–9, 253. For a brief account see Ian Gentles, *The New Model Army in England, Ireland and Scotland, 1645–1653* (Oxford, 1992), pp. 377–80.

the use of any Mill these three weeks till now, which caused us (though we have store of Corne) to want [= lack] bread.'[68]

The interdependence of a town and its nearby castles became evident when the town surrendered to the enemy. Surrounding strongholds toppled like a pack of cards because, besides the loss of support from the centre, the large forces mobilized to capture a town usually threatened to engulf all the small garrisons in their path.[69] Even before the town fell, nearby fortifications could also prove a liability when seized by an enemy and it was therefore common for the defenders of an endangered town to rase castles in the immediate vicinity. For instance, as the Irish approached Drogheda in 1642, the earl of Ormond (who did not leave Dublin) ordered its garrison to waste neighbouring strongholds and villages.[70] Surrounding castles might also be destroyed after a siege was raised, either to improve overall defensive capacity or to take revenge on the gentry who had aided the besiegers.[71] However, to hold down territory it was necessary to occupy all available fortifications. Thus even after the Cromwellians had overrun the country, they felt obliged to maintain a profusion of garrisons: one contemporary source listed 350 of them by early 1652 and estimated that another hundred were still required for total security.[72]

The need to occupy so many strongholds caused many complications. First, with the large number of troops dispersed in garrisons, it became impossible to concentrate an effective field army; second, with some exceptions, since most castles were small, their ability to hold out in the face of an attack remained limited; third, the wide distribution of fortifications often strained the supply network to excess. These drawbacks, however, had to be set against major strategic advantages. Possession of a network of fortified points came in useful when campaigns ended, since most of the armies operating in Ireland lacked large fortified bases for winter quarters. Moreover, they also enabled the occupants to plant corn and keep cattle in

[68] J. F. Fuller, 'Kinsale in 1641 and 1642', *Journal of the Cork Historical and Archaeological Society*, 13 (1907), p. 2. See also chapter 8.
[69] For example, when Galway fell in 1651, all surrounding castles also surrendered or were abandoned, Robert Dunlop (ed.), *Ireland under the commonwealth* . . . (2 vols., Manchester, 1913), II, p. 616.
[70] Gilbert (ed.), *Contemporary history*, II, pp. 247–8.
[71] R. Cox, *Hibernia Anglicana, or the history of Ireland from the conquest thereof by the English to this present time* . . . (2 vols., London, 1689–90), II, p. 92; N. Barnard, *The whole proceedings of the siege of Drogheda* (London, 1642), p. 71; Grosart (ed.), *Lismore papers*, first series, v, p. 102. For instance, when the town of Bandon became an isolated enclave, men from the town assailed seven castles in its neighbourhood, some of which they burnt and slighted, while others they subsequently maintained for the outlying defence of the town.
[72] C. H. Firth (ed.), *The memoirs of Edmund Ludlow lieutenant-general of the horse in the army of the commonwealth of England 1625–1672* (2 vols., Oxford, 1894), I, p. 497.

the adjoining countryside for their own upkeep, and to raise contributions, thus reducing their dependence on supplies of food from central depots (although they remained heavily dependent on them for ammunition).[73] In this respect, however, Ireland resembled the continent. There too, despite exposure to the Military Revolution for over a century, strategy in most theatres of war continued to revolve around the capture of major fortresses and their penumbra of strong points; garrisons normally tied down one half, if not more, of each state's armed forces (even in wartime); and, almost everywhere, sieges outnumbered battles.

It is true that some areas of Ireland remained totally unaffected by military innovation. Even in 1652, after all major confederate forces had surrendered, English officials lamented the existence of numerous 'crannogs': 'vaste great boggs in the middest of which there are firme woody grounds like islands, into which they have passes or casewayes through the boggs where noe more then one horse can goe a breast, which passes they can easily mainteine, or suddainely break up soe as noe horse can approach them, and being inured to live in cabbins and to wade through those boggs they can fetch prey from any part of the countrey to releive themselves and prosecute their designes which are to robb and burne those places that yeild our forces subsistance'. The officials explained that the 'fastnesses being unpassable for horse, and into which foote cannot goe without some experience and hardship to wade in water and tread the bogg . . . Their fastenesses are better to them in point of strength then walled towns'.[74] Yet such 'no go' areas became less numerous than ever before in Irish history, thanks to the ability of pioneers to drive roads and bridges through previously impassable country, opening up new areas to artillery and exposing to destruction strongholds that had formerly been invulnerable. Only the relative scarcity of heavy calibre weapons before 1649 allowed so many fortifications constructed before the gunpowder revolution to retain a military role.[75]

The 'modern' defences of Ireland required, and received, modern techniques of siegecraft, however: the blockade of Limerick, although the largest, was far from unique. After September 1642 at Castle Forbes (County Longford), the Irish dug many trenches,[76] while at Castle Coote (County Roscommon) in the next year the engineer Saint Loo, 'an

---

[73] BL, Egerton MSS 81, fos. 21 fol. Agreements of surrender to the Cromwellians make this abundantly clear and show widespread evidence of soldiers who were active farmers.

[74] Firth (ed.), *Ludlow*, I, p. 498.

[75] This, too, was true on the continent, where old-style fortifications in remote fortresses could still defy the full force of the Military Revolution, see Parker, *Military revolution*, p. 8.

[76] J. Lodge, *The peerage of Ireland*, ed. M. Archdall (7 vols., Dublin, 1789) II, pp. 141–3n.

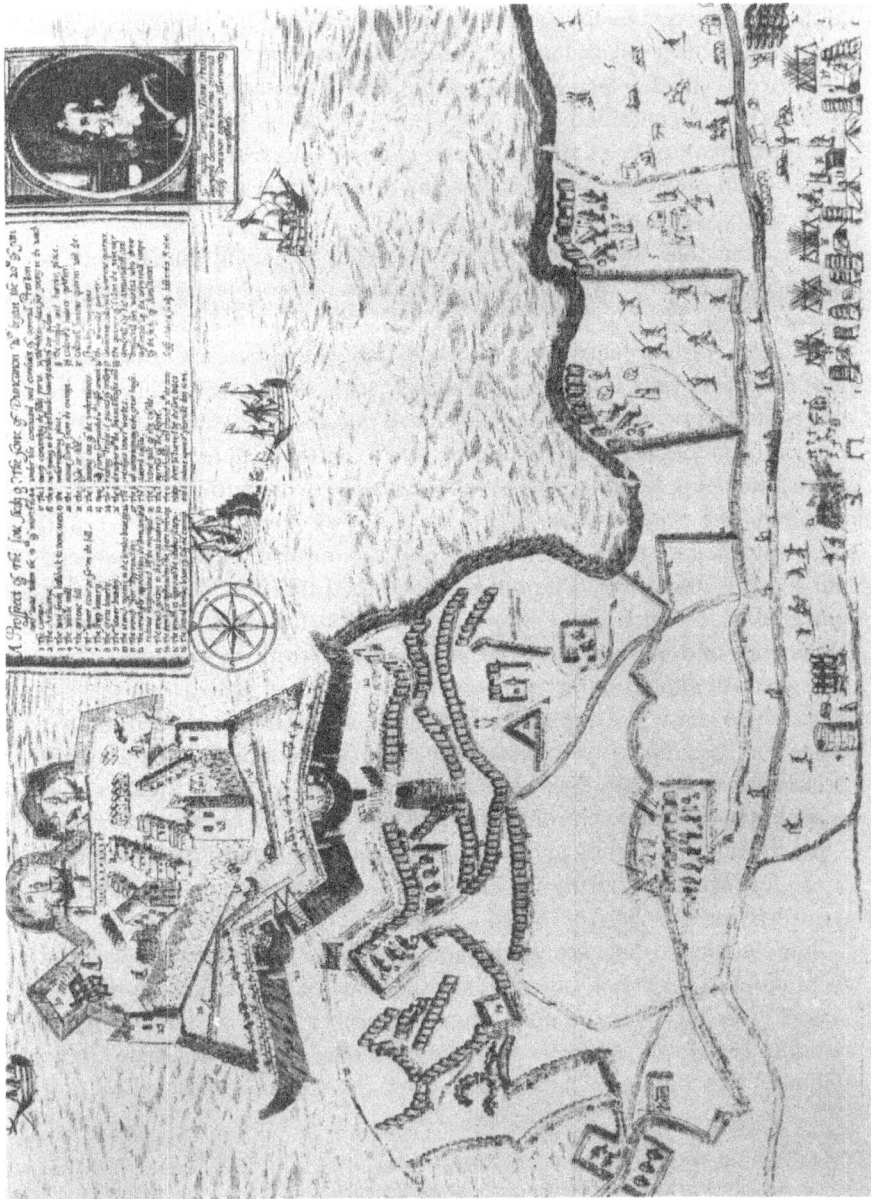

Plate 4 The siege of Duncannon Fort, County Wexford, by General Preston, 1645

experienced Low-Country soldier', made a 'regular circumvallation about the castle; yet the garrison so nobly attacked each redoubt, as greatly disappointed the besiegers'.[77] When Thomas Preston besieged Duncannon Fort (County Wexford) in 1645, he 'made trenches a farr off, and by degree both daie and night, by triangle and quadrangle worke, came a pistol shott neere the fort . . . ' (plate 4). According to a contemporary writer it was 'the verie best siedge that was yett in Ireland . . . the ordinance and bombs going very thicke', and an engraving shows that Preston commanded seventeen guns and two mortars.[78] At other sieges the Irish dug mines and counter-mines (as at Limerick in 1642 and at Birr the following year). They also used 'sows', an apparatus pushed against the walls to shield the miners attempting to bring down the structure, at the sieges of Ballyally Castle (County Clare), Mallow (County Cork), Rochestown (County Tipperary), and Tralee Castle (where three sows were used).[79] In the case of the great sow used at Ballyally Castle in 1641, the structure was:

35 feet long and 9 feet broad; it was made upon four wheels made of whole lumber, bound about with hoops of iron; the axle-trees whereon she ran were great round bars of iron, the beams she was built on being timber. They had cross beams within, to work with their leavers to forcer along as they pleased to guide her. The hinder part of the sow was left open for their men to go in and out at. The forepart of the sow had 4 doors, 2 in the roof, and 2 in the lower part which did hang upon great iron hooks, but were not to open till they came close to the wall of the castle, where they intended to work through the castle with their tools they had provided. The roof of the sow was built like the roof of a house with a very steep ridge; the lower part as the walls of a house. She was double planked with many great oaken planks, and driven very thick with five stroke nails, which nails cost £5, being intended for a house of correction which should have been built at Ennis. This sow was likewise covered over with two rows of hides, and two rows of sheepskins; so that no musket bullet or steel arrow could pierce it, of which trial was often made.[80]

However, we know of no case in which sows proved effective in capturing the castles.[81]

[77] F. Grose, *The antiquities of Ireland* (2 vols., London, 1791) I, pp. 83–4; Gilbert (ed.), *Contemporary history*, I, p. 82.
[78] Gilbert (ed.), *Irish confederation*, IV, frontispiece; P. Lenihan, 'Aerial photography: a window on the past', *History Ireland*, I, no. 2 (1993), pp. 9–13.
[79] T. C. Croker, 'Narratives illustrative of the contests in Ireland in 1641 and 1690', *Camden Society*, 14 (1841), pp. 16–19; Hazlett, 'History', p. 120; P. C. Power, *History of South Tipperary* (Cork, 1989), p. 66; M. Hickson (ed.), *Ireland in the seventeenth century; or, the Irish massacres of 1641* (2 vols., London, 1884), II, pp. 108, 117.
[80] Croker, 'Narratives', pp. 117–18.
[81] Gilbert (ed.), *Irish confederation*, I, p. xlv; Gilbert, *Contemporary history*, III, p. 229; Grosart (ed.), *Lismore papers*, second series, v, p. 79.

The Irish proved rather more successful in bringing their conduct of the war at sea up to continental standards. Although Randal MacDonnell, marquis of Antrim, still contemplated using galleys to convey his troops to Scotland in 1638, as Gaelic chieftains had always done, in 1645 he invested in a pair of Dunkirk frigates, the finest light warships to be found anywhere in the Western world. They did not sail alone. In July 1642 a 200-ton, eighteen-gun Dunkirk frigate brought over Owen Roe O'Neill and his regiment from Flanders, and by September the Lords Justice reported from Dublin that 'seven or eight ships more, some of them carrying twenty-four pieces of ordnance, are come . . . in aid of the rebels'.[82] Between December 1642 and February 1643 confederate agents in the Spanish Netherlands issued at least twenty letters of marque to foreign frigates willing to protect the Irish coast, and keep open the sea lanes to the continent, in return for freedom to capture all enemies of the 'Catholic cause'. By the end of 1642 the Venetian ambassador in London estimated that the confederate fleet consisted of '30 well-armed ships at sea', and for most of the 1640s the confederate navy probably numbered between forty and fifty warships.[83] About half of the crews appear to have been Irish, trained by their Flemish colleagues to the same peak of professional ferocity that in 1649 earned Wexford, one of their principal bases, the epithet of 'the Dunkirk of Ireland, and a place only famous for being infamous'.[84] The *recorded* prizes of the Irish privateers between 1642 and 1650 totalled only 250, but one informed contemporary thought that 'these privateers took over a six year period, from the parliamentary ships of all three kingdoms, 1900 vessels and 1500 captives . . . and this does not include those ships which had been sunk in various encounters'.[85] This record, if true, would have made the Irish privateers more successful than either their English or Flemish counterparts. Small wonder that, in 1649, Prince Rupert led the royal navy to southern Ireland in an attempt to join forces with the most successful fleet in his uncle's service: fortunately for Cromwell, Admiral Blake cleared them from Kinsale before they began

[82] Henry, 'Ulster exiles', pp. 57–8; HMC, *Ormonde MSS*, II, p. 191.
[83] *Calendar of state papers . . . existing in the archives . . . of Venice, 1642–3* (London, 1925), p. 211. For further details see Jane H. Ohlmeyer, 'Irish privateers during the civil war, 1642–50', *Mariner's Mirror*, 76 (May 1990), pp. 120–1.
[84] *The Irish Monthly Mercury*, issue 1 (London, 1649), p. 3. Also see Jane H. Ohlmeyer, 'The "Dunkirk of Ireland": Wexford privateers during the 1640s', *Journal of the Wexford Historical Society*, 12 (1988–9), pp. 23–4.
[85] Richard O'Ferrall and Robert O'Connell, *Commentarius Rinuccinianus . . .* ed. Revd Stanislaus Kavanagh (IMC, 6 vols., Dublin 1932–49), I, pp. 519–20, quoting Dr Walter Enos of Wexford (reference kindly communicated by Jane Ohlmeyer).

to jeopardize his life line across the Irish Sea to London (see chapter 3 above).

The 'reception' of the Military Revolution in England offers an instructive comparison. As in Ireland, few places possessed modern fortifications in 1642; moreover most of these lay on the coast, whereas most of the fighting during the Civil War took place inland. Even London only acquired full bastioned defences, initially of earth, after the war began. Few other places of strategic significance constructed a full circuit of Italian-style ramparts during the 1640s: instead most remained enclosed by outdated medieval walls, occasionally reinforced with a few 'modern' outworks, and wholly susceptible to bombardment. It is therefore strange to find that relatively few places were in fact reduced by artillery until 1645. The explanation, however, is simple: given the highly unsettled state of most of the kingdom during the early war years, with powerful detachments from both sides roaming the roads, it was extremely hazardous to convey a siege train around the country. One risked losing it (as Parliament did at Lostwithiel in 1644, forfeiting forty heavy guns to the king). Just as in Ireland, most towns were therefore taken by storm with no preliminary battery, while the few remaining strongholds suffered bombardment from only a handful of big guns at any one time.[86] Only after their victory at Naseby in June 1645 could the New Model Army move its siege train around at will, and even so its first full-dress siege, involving a full circumvallation and a main field army, did not take place until 1648 (against Colchester). Likewise many battles of the English Civil War, including the decisive engagements at Naseby and Preston (1648), involved no action by field artillery (indeed, at Preston, neither side brought any to the battle); while at other times, field guns were used effectively only to defend entrenched positions against frontal attack.

Again, as in Ireland, the warring parties in England normally controlled territory through mutually dependent systems of large and small garrisons, usually a single major fortress with a network of smaller ones, stretching in a radius of up to thirty miles, both to protect the parent stronghold from blockade and to preserve recruiting and supply grounds. The fall of the main fortification or the defeat of the regionally dominant field army normally caused the surrender of the outlying garrisons, since their military value had ended: between April 1645 and August 1646 the New Model Army forced the surrender of forty-seven

---

[86] W. G. Ross, 'Military engineering during the Great Civil War, 1642–1649', in F. G. Day (ed.), *Professional papers of the corps of royal engineers* (London, 1887: Royal Engineers Institute occasional papers), XIII, pp. 86–205.

strongholds.[87] Finally, although the English navy possessed more and better capital ships than the Confederates, it nevertheless proved incapable of keeping the ports of its Irish allies permanently open or of preventing enemy privateers from getting out. In short, Ireland's adjustment during the 1640s to the new ways of warfare pioneered on the European continent proved to be no less rapid and no less impressive than that of England. Even Protestant opponents of the Confederation like Sir Arthur Annesley and Sir William Parsons had to admit in December 1646 that '[the Irish now] have their men in a better order of war and better commanded by captains of experience and practice of warr then ever they were since the conquest and these much imboldened by late successes as well in the field as fortresses. They are abundantly stored with armes and munition'.[88] Ireland's eventual defeat and subjugation by England stemmed essentially from political, not military, factors.

---

[87] Details in the excellent study by M. E. Lewis, 'The use of ordnance in early modern warfare, with particular reference to the English Civil War 1642–9' (unpublished MA thesis, Manchester University, 1971). See also the useful review article of M. J. Braddick, 'An English military revolution?', *The Historical Journal*, 36 (1993), pp. 965–75.

[88] State of the kingdom of Ireland by Sir Arthur Annesley and Sir William Parsons, 10 December 1646 (BL, Egerton MSS 917, fo. 25v). Reference kindly communicated by Jane Ohlmeyer.

CHAPTER 5

IRELAND INDEPENDENT: CONFEDERATE FOREIGN POLICY AND INTERNATIONAL RELATIONS DURING THE MID-SEVENTEENTH CENTURY[1]

JANE OHLMEYER

THE CONSTANT passage of priests, scholars, traders and mercenaries, has always maintained strong links between Ireland and the continent, but never more than during the early modern period when the Catholic princes of Europe carefully monitored, and occasionally intervened in, Irish affairs. As relations between England and Spain deteriorated, Philip II and his son, Philip III, sent successive expeditionary forces to Ireland: in 1579 a papal force of Italians and Spaniards landed at Smerwick in order to help the Irish insurgents; in 1601 Philip III, eager to divert English attention and resources from the Netherlands, dispatched another Spanish expeditionary force to Kinsale to aid the uprising led by Hugh O'Neill. In addition the success of the Protestant Reformation in Scotland, France's traditional ally during the later decades of the sixteenth century, followed by the union of the Scottish and English crowns in 1603 forced France to consider Ireland as a possible ally and during the 1640s France jockeyed with Spain for Irish favour. However it was not until the later seventeenth century that the Bourbons replaced the Habsburgs as Catholic Ireland's principal European backer and, early in 1690, sent a substantial army to Ireland; while a century later, in 1798, a French invasion force landed in County Mayo to aid the United Irishmen. Although no army of invasion arrived from Europe during the 1640s, in few other periods have Irish politics been 'so much a part of the main stream of European history'.[2] Between 1642 and 1650, for the first and only time before 1922, Catholic Ireland pursued its own independent

---

[1] I am grateful to Toby Barnard, Nicholas Canny, Tom Connors, Geoffrey Parker, Hamish Scott, Robert Stradling and Scott Wheeler for reading an earlier draft of this chapter and for making numerous incisive and helpful comments.
[2] Donal F. Cregan, 'The confederation of Kilkenny', in Brian Farrell (ed.), *Irish parliamentary tradition* (Dublin, 1973), p. 102.

foreign policy, sending envoys abroad and receiving accredited residents at its 'sovereign seat of government', Kilkenny.

The Habsburg–Bourbon struggle for mastery dominated the political history of Europe during the first half of the seventeenth century.[3] Throughout the 1630s the three Stuart kingdoms of England, Scotland and Ireland isolated themselves effectively from this bitter conflict, but the outbreak of the Civil War ensured that the British Isles became involved in the continental struggle during the 1640s. Ireland, in particular, became an area of diplomatic contest. This chapter examines the role played by the Confederation of Kilkenny in the European conflict and assesses Ireland's position within the Catholic continental diplomatic community. Who formulated and executed confederate foreign policy during the 1640s? What motivated the Confederates and what were their aims? How, and with what success, did they pursue their diplomatic goals? And what policies were followed in Ireland by Spain, France, England and the Papacy? With whom and how did they operate while in Ireland? How successful were they in achieving their ambitions?

I – THE *CORPS DIPLOMATIQUE*

Despite the fact that foreign powers directly interfered in Irish affairs prior to 1641, Ireland, as a subordinate kingdom ruled from London, could not pursue or formulate its own foreign policy. However, after 1642, the Confederates, in violation of Charles I's rights as king of Ireland, actively engaged in international diplomacy and sought external recognition for their rebellion. Late in 1642 the first General Assembly and newly formed Supreme Council authorized a number of agents to negotiate on their behalf with foreign princes with dignity and 'not to dishonor the nation . . . by way of craving or begginge'.[4] Except for the Papacy, which, as a supranational power, only participated partially in the 'new diplomacy' common among seventeenth-century sovereign states,[5] these confederate envoys,

---

[3] Paul Kennedy, *The rise and fall of the great powers. Economic change and military conflict from 1500 to 2000* (New York, 1987), chapter 2.

[4] J. T. Gilbert (ed.), *History of the Irish confederation and the war in Ireland, 1641–53* . . . (7 vols., Dublin, 1882–91), IV, p. 94. Also see HMC, *Report on the Franciscan manuscripts preserved at the convent, Merchants' Quay, Dublin* (Dublin, 1906), p. 198. For further details of the duties of and problems faced by early modern ambassadors see Garrett Mattingly, *Renaissance diplomacy* (London, 1955; reprinted, 1965), chapters 2–4.

[5] For instance the Papacy refused to send ambassadors to Protestant capitals. For further details see Charles H. Carter, 'The ambassadors of early modern Europe: patterns of diplomatic representation in the early seventeenth century', in Charles H. Carter (ed.), *From the Renaissance to the Counter-Reformation. Essays in honor of Garrett Mattingly* (New York, 1965), pp. 269–95, especially p. 271.

accredited by a revolutionary council, posed an embarrassing set of problems for the other European monarchies. Thus initially neither the French nor the Spanish administrations welcomed them and flatly refused to grant them ambassadorial status, a rank reserved for legitimate powers like France, Spain, England or, after 1609, the Dutch Republic.

Ultimately, however, the Irish agents were admitted as residents to the leading continental, Catholic courts where, like all early modern diplomats, they gathered information, won prestige and support for their cause, negotiated agreements, settled minor disputes and attended state functions. With the principal exception of the delegates to Protestant Holland, the confederate envoys belonged to a religious order (including three Franciscans, three Jesuits, a Dominican and an Augustinian) and, although reared in Ireland, had been educated on the continent on a strict diet of Counter-Reformation theology. Well versed in Irish, Spanish, French and Latin, the diplomatic *lingua franca* of Europe until the later seventeenth century, and intimately connected to all the Catholic capitals of Europe through their religious affiliations, these clerical diplomats were ideally placed to further the confederate cause.[6]

The most diligent was the Franciscan theologian and vicar-general of the Irish regiments serving in Flanders, Hugh Bourke, who, according to the anonymous author of *An aphorismical discovery of treasonable faction*, ran 'from courte to courte . . . [and] wearied all the courts of Europe with his pretences, suites and beggaries [on behalf of the Irish cause]'.[7] Initially Bourke managed Irish affairs in the Spanish Netherlands, Holland and the Empire. Then, late in 1643, he moved to Madrid where he replaced Francis Magennis, another Franciscan, and James Talbot, an Augustinian.[8] The equally important task of securing French support fell first to Matthew O'Hartegan, a Jesuit, who enjoyed the confidence of leading French officials, Anne of Austria and Henrietta Maria of England during his

---

6 This use of clerical envoys was typical of early modern diplomacy, see Geoffrey Parker, *The Thirty Years War* (London, 1984), pp. 22–3, 67, 93–4. Interestingly Charles II used an Irish Dominican to represent his interests at the Portuguese court, see Benventura Curtin [Margaret MacCurtain], 'Dominic O'Daly: an Irish diplomat', *Studia Hibernica*, 5 (1965), pp. 98–112. I am grateful to Kevin McKenny for bringing this reference to my attention.

7 J. T. Gilbert (ed.), *A contemporary history of affairs in Ireland, from A.D. 1641 to 1652* . . . (3 vols., Irish Archaeological Society, Dublin, 1879), II, p. 142.

8 In the Spanish Netherlands he was assisted by another Franciscan, Nicholas Shee, and by Henry Plunket, a Jesuit; in Holland by Captain Robert Lambert; in Germany by Count William Gall; and in Spain by Luke Wadding, SJ, of Salamanca. The Spanish administration initially feared that Bourke favoured France and requested a replacement; nevertheless he remained in Madrid and, with Philip IV's assistance, became bishop of Kilmacduagh in 1647. He returned to Ireland with Berehaven and became 'a prime member' of Ormond's faction, Gilbert (ed.), *Contemporary history*, II, p. 143.

sojourn in Paris; then, after March 1645, to Dr Edward Tirrell, the Dominican superior of the Irish College in Paris.[9] Most influential of all was the confederate agent in Rome, Luke Wadding, the Franciscan guardian of St Isidore's College, who worked closely with Antonio Barberini, Pope Urban VIII's nephew and Cardinal Protector of Ireland, and with the papal 'committee on Irish affairs' in order to promote the Catholic cause.[10]

Thus the Confederates had at their disposal an extensive and cheap diplomatic system which stretched all over Europe. However, as O'Hartegan astutely noted, these clerical residents lacked experience in the workings of high diplomacy being 'novices in matters of state'.[11] He therefore urged the Confederates 'to depute lay gentlemen with your despatches, and give them your employments abroad . . . because a gentleman of any fashion, will never faile to gett in any courte in Christendome'.[12] Accordingly, the Supreme Council periodically deployed prominent Irishmen on diplomatic forays. For instance Geoffrey Barron, a nephew of the Franciscan Luke Wadding, travelled to Paris in search of aid in 1642 and again in 1645. In the spring of 1644 seven confederate agents (including Viscount Muskerry, Nicholas Plunket and Geoffrey Browne) discussed a possible peace treaty with Charles I at Oxford; while, later the same year, Richard Bellings, secretary of the confederate Supreme Councils, served as roving agent to the Papacy, France, Venice, Genoa and Tuscany.[13] In the spring of 1648 prestigious teams of Irish diplomats travelled to the Vatican (Nicholas French and Nicholas Plunket) and France (Viscount Muskerry, Geoffrey Browne and the marquis of Antrim) in the hope of winning foreign support for the flagging Irish war-effort.[14] Finally in 1651, in a last-ditch attempt to secure continental aid, Nicholas Plunket, Geoffrey Browne and Theobald, Viscount Taaffe entered into lengthy negotiations with the duke of Lorraine.

Even though Charles I flatly refused to acknowledge the sovereignty of the Confederation, he nevertheless, using his lord lieutenant, James Butler, marquis of Ormond, as his principal intermediary, constantly pressed the Supreme Council to favour his own interests over all others. In addition,

---

[9] O'Hartegan was recalled due to his 'indiscreet penn' and his scandalous, vain conduct, Gilbert (ed.), *Irish confederation*, I, p. xxxix; II, p. ix; IV, p. 205. Also see Thomas J. Morrissey, 'The strange letters of Mathew Hartegan, S. J., 1644–45', *Irish Theological Quarterly*, 37 (1970), pp. 159–72. I am grateful to Tom Connors for bringing this reference to my attention.

[10] Early in 1649 Wadding was accused of favouring the Irish Royalists and was discredited in Rome.

[11] HMC, *Franciscan MSS*, p. 175.   [12] Gilbert (ed.), *Irish confederation*, IV, pp. 64–5.

[13] The other agents included Donough MacCarthy, Alexander MacDonnell, Sir Robert Talbot, Dermot O'Brien and Richard Martin.

[14] Even though the Council deputed Sir Richard Blake to travel to Madrid on their behalf, it seems that he never left Ireland, Gilbert (ed.), *Irish confederation*, VII, p. 37.

Charles, who 'regarded Ireland as no more than a strategic pawn' in his
struggle against the English Parliament, sent special envoys (or, to use
Ormond's term, 'interlopers') – such as Antrim, Daniel O'Neill, the earl of
Glamorgan and George Digby – directly to Kilkenny in order to secure aid
for the royalist cause in Britain.[15]

Ireland's ambiguous constitutional position and the fact that, in the
hierarchical world of seventeenth-century international diplomacy,
Catholic Ireland clearly ranked as a third-rate power (on a par with
Catalonia or the Ukraine), meant that France and Spain not only baulked
at receiving Irish agents, but refused to send fully accredited ambassadors
to Kilkenny despite being urged by their respective agents in Ireland to do
so.[16] Instead they relied on the services of resident agents or envoys.[17] In all,
four Spanish diplomats went to Ireland during the 1640s.[18] Miguel Gallo,
the first to arrive, had laboured for the Habsburgs for twenty-five years in
Flanders, Burgundy and Germany before being briefly sent (in 1643) as a
commissioner to Ireland.[19] Early in 1644 the Confederates received
François Foissotte, a native of Burgundy and a lawyer, with previous
experience as a military commander in Franche Comté, Lorraine and
Savoy and as a minor diplomat in England, France, Italy, Flanders
and Switzerland.[20] Despite being recalled the following year, he remained

---

[15] John Lowe, 'Charles I and the confederation of Kilkenny, 1643–1649', *IHS*, 14 (March 1964),
p. 13. Also see Thomas Carte, *History of the life of James, first duke of Ormond* (second edn., 6 vols.,
Oxford, 1851), VI, p. 7. For details on Antrim see Jane H. Ohlmeyer, *Civil war and restoration in the
three Stuart kingdoms: the career of Randal MacDonnell, marquis of Antrim, 1609–1683* (Cambridge, 1993),
chapter 5; for Glamorgan see John Lowe, 'The Glamorgan mission to Ireland 1645–6', *Studia
Hibernica*, 4 (1964), pp. 155–96.

[16] For details on the distinctions between ambassadors and envoys see Carter, 'The Ambassadors
of Early Modern Europe', pp. 273–4. I am grateful to Hamish Scott and Robert Stradling for
bringing these points to my attention.

[17] An Imperial representative also appears to have resided in Ireland for a brief period in 1646,
D. Massari, 'My Irish campaign', *The Catholic Bulletin*, 6 (1916), p. 658.

[18] According to one contemporary account, they also served as translators, scribes, accountants
and military contractors and travelled from one end of the country to the other in search of
suitable soldiers and shipping, *Relación de los servicios de D. Francisco Foissotte en Borgoña, Flandes,
Inglaterra, Francia, y en ocho años y medio que asistió en Irlanda a negocios del Real servicio de V. Magestad*
([Madrid?], 1652) (Biblioteca Nacional, Madrid 2367, fos. 191–207v).

[19] Gallo then accompanied recruits raised by Foissotte back to Spain, arriving in San Sebastian
in December 1644, Robert Stradling, *The Spanish monarchy and Irish mercenaries: the Wild Geese in
Spain, 1618–88* (Dublin, 1994), p. 164. I am grateful to Dr Stradling for allowing me to see his
manuscript in advance of publication.

[20] Foissotte probably arrived late in 1643, but was not granted an interview with the Supreme
Council until February 1644. For a charming resumé of Foissotte's career as a diplomat see
Foissotte to Coloma, 23 December 1646/2 January 1647 (A[rchivio] G[eneral,] S[imancas,]
Spain], E[stad]o 2525 unfol.) and Foissotte to Rosas, 14/24 October 1644 (AGS, G[uerra]
A[ntigua] 1570 unfol.). See especially *Relacion de los servicios de D. Francisco Foissotte* which is
Foissotte's published account of his mission in Ireland. On his instructions see Gilbert (ed.), *Irish
confederation*, III, pp. 102–3.

at his post at least until the spring of 1652 and during these years dispatched *c*. 6,500 recruits to serve in the Habsburg armies.[21] Of all the Spanish envoys the most senior was Diego de la Torre, brother of a prominent government official, who had served as a secretary of state and war in Flanders before being posted to Kilkenny in August 1645 (he arrived the following March).[22] However, largely because he spent his time in Ireland quarrelling with Foissotte, de la Torre left late in 1646 having recruited only 140 men and was replaced by Dermot O'Sullivan Beare, count of Berehaven, a native Irishman brought up as a page at Philip III's court.[23] Given Ireland's geographical remoteness from the Iberian peninsula and the cumbersome nature of the Spanish Council of State, the body responsible for formulating foreign policy, this decision to send resident agents who enjoyed little power, and deferred constantly for instructions to Madrid, Saragossa, Brussels and to Ambassador Cárdenas in London, proved to be a tactical error. Undoubtedly, a high-ranking diplomat with more autonomy could have served Spain's interests more effectively in Ireland and could possibly have outmanoeuvred their Bourbon counterparts.[24]

For the French agents formed an especially professional body. Monsieur de la Monnerie – 'gentleman-in-ordinary of the chamber to the most Christian king' – arrived in Ireland early in 1644.[25] In February 1646 he was replaced by Claude Dumolin, an experienced councillor, a member of the household of Louis XIV, and an old acquaintance of Ormond, who arrived with orders 'to obtain levies and fresh recruits' and to 'stretch out a hand in the most friendly way' to the Catholic party.[26] Early in 1647 Philippe Du

---

[21] Stradling, *Spanish monarchy*, p. 164. In 1654 Foissotte became co-commander-in-chief of the Irish forces in Spain (p. 81).

[22] De la Torre actually arrived in January 1646 and appears to have remained in Ireland until late 1649. For details on his career see Consulta of the council of state, March/4 April 1645 (AGS, Eo. 2064 unfol.), Contreras to Coloma, 3/12 August 1645 (AGS, Eo. 2525 unfol.), de la Torre's instructions, 7/17 September 1645 (AGS, Tribunal Mayor de Cuentas, 2635 unfol.) and Consulta of the count of Monterey, 1/11 September 1645 (AGS, Eo. 2525 unfol.).

[23] By April 1649 Berehaven had returned to Spain. In December 1652 Philip IV nominated Juan Triquet to recruit in Ireland, but he never arrived. Also see Stradling, *Spanish monarchy*, pp. 65–9.

[24] The Spanish envoys consistently pressed Philip IV to send a higher ranking diplomat. See for example, Foissotte to Coloma, 23 December 1646/2 January 1647 and to Philip IV, 18/28 May 1648 (AGS, Eo. 2525 and Eo. 2566 unfol.).

[25] M. A. Chéruel, *Lettres du Cardinal Mazarin Pendant son Ministère* (2 vols., Paris, 1872), I, p. 605. After failing to export troops from Galway he was recalled at the end of 1644. La Monnerie returned to Ireland early in 1647 and remained there until January 1649.

[26] *Calendar of state papers . . . existing in the archives . . . of Venice, 1643–1647* (London, 1926), p. 238. Also see Gilbert (ed.), *Irish confederation*, V, pp. 351–2, VI, p. 74, VI, p. 291 and Brendan Jennings (ed.), *Wild Geese in Spanish Flanders, 1582–1700 . . .* (IMC, Dublin, 1964), p. 600.

Talon, described by one Royalist as 'a person of much consideration and employment', joined Dumolin.[27]

All the pope's representatives in Ireland were clerics. In April 1643 Urban VIII nominated the Neapolitan, Pietro Francesco Scarampi as his agent (he arrived in June). According to one papal source, Scarampi quickly 'won the hearts and affections of all classes' and, almost immediately, the Supreme Council requested that he be given the title and powers of a papal nuncio.[28] This was not to be, and instead Giovanni Battista Rinuccini, the Tuscan archbishop of Fermo, was appointed nuncio by the pro-Spanish Innocent X in 1645. The pope dispatched Rinuccini, together with 50,000 crowns (c. £1,000), to Ireland on the understanding that he remained 'impartial in regard to the conflicting interests of the French and Spaniards'[29] and that he would not meddle in Irish politics, but instead strive 'to restore and re-establish the public exercise of the Catholic religion in the island of Ireland'.[30] As a papal nuncio, or ambassador, Rinuccini was the most senior of Kilkenny's *corps diplomatique*.[31]

These diplomats, both in Ireland and abroad, faced two formidable obstacles in implementing their respective foreign policies. First, like other residents of the day, they were hopelessly underfunded. For example Foissotte, during eight years of service, never received more than 40 escudos (or £9) per month out of the 120 escudos per month he had been promised. Moreover the expenses he incurred as a result of his sojourn 'consumed the greater part of his own estates [in Burgundy], which were very considerable'.[32] In 1645 the disgruntled agent articulated his predicament to the Spanish ambassador in London in the following terms: 'It is not necessary for his majesty [Philip IV] to send millions of ducats here nor that he should declare war . . . the sort of thing one spends on a fiesta

---

[27] Thomas Carte, *The life of James duke of Ormond* . . . (3 vols., London, 1735–6), III, p. 548.

[28] Massari, 'My Irish campaign', 6 (1916), p. 222.

[29] Richard O'Ferrall and Robert O'Connell, *Commentarius Rinuccinianus, de sedis apostolicae legatione ad foederatos Hiberniae catholicos per annos 1645–9* ed. Revd Stanislaus Kavanagh (IMC, 6 vols., Dublin, 1932–9), VI, pp. 84–5.

[30] Patrick J. Corish, 'Ormond, Rinuccini and the Confederates, 1645–9', in T. W. Moody, F. X. Martin and F. J. Byrne (eds.), *A new history of Ireland*, III: *Early modern Ireland 1534–1691* (Oxford, 1978), p. 317.

[31] Much material relating to Rinuccini's stay in Ireland is contained in *Commentarius Rinuccinianus* and considerable portions of Rinuccini's correspondence (1645–9) have been translated and printed in Giuseppe Aiazza, *The embassy in Ireland of Monsignor G. B. Rinuccini* . . . , translated by Annie Hutton (Dublin, 1873). The only adequate biography of the nuncio in English is Michael J. Hynes, *The mission of Rinuccini, 1645–49* (Louvain, 1932) which is essentially a summary of the *Commentarius*.

[32] *Relación de los servicios de D. Francisco Foisotte.*

in Madrid is all one would need'.[33] His plea fell on deaf ears and, as a result, Foissotte's levies of troops for Spanish service were largely financed, at extortionate rates, by Flemish merchants and privateers living in Waterford, Wexford, Brussels or Dunkirk.[34] Similarly straitened circumstances forced the French agents to borrow cash from Waterford and Kilkenny businessmen at ridiculously high rates (around 45 per cent) during the early 1640s when coinage was particularly scarce; even in 1648 La Monnerie found himself obliged to pay 15 per cent in interest to a local merchant who lent him £2,000. The equally poverty-stricken confederate agents operating in Europe likewise received their sparse funds from Irish merchants, living in the major ports of France, Flanders and Spain, or from sympathetic clergymen.

The second obstacle which hampered the smooth running of international relations was distance. Maintaining regular communications between Kilkenny and the principal European capitals presented a serious problem to the Confederates, while foreign agents in Ireland depended on the good offices of merchants trading with, or clerics travelling to, the continent to deliver their letters. In the event a shortage of shipping and poor weather delayed many despatches; while others were intercepted by Parliament or captured by pirates and privateers. It could therefore take between three and eight months for a letter to reach Madrid, Brussels, Rome, Paris or even the royalist capital of Oxford from Kilkenny; while news and orders took up to eleven months to reach Ireland from Spain, up to six from France and up to four from England. Small wonder that Don Diego de la Torre complained to his master Philip IV that the appalling postal service constituted 'the greatest problem of my job' for it meant that he could not 'send successive accounts of what is happening and receive in good time the royal orders of your majesty'.[35]

II — FOREIGN POLICY OBJECTIVES

Like all diplomats at all times, the Irish envoys represented the interests of their political masters at the various courts and provided the Supreme Council with intelligence. They also strove to secure recognition for their rebellion from the leading continental potentates and to persuade Charles I to grant Irish Catholics lasting political autonomy, freedom of worship

---

[33] Copy of paragraphs from a letter of Foissotte to Cárdenas, 22 May/1 June 1645 (AGS, Eo. 2566 unfol.).
[34] Especially Antonio Nicholas Vanderkipp [Anton van de Zipe] and Adrian Van Haute.
[35] De la Torre to Philip IV, 8/18 February 1648 (AGS, Eo. 2566 unfol.).

and permanent tenure of their land. Their most immediate concern, however, was to provide supplies for the confederate armies for, in the words of the Supreme Council in April 1643:

> Our wants are money, arms and ammunition; these we have no way to provide for, the country being exceedingly exhausted, unless we may be assisted by those who wish well unto our cause beyond the seas.[36]

This lament demonstrates the painful awareness, almost from the outset, that in order to combat effectively the anti-Catholic coalition, financed and supplied by the English Parliament, the Confederates had to secure substantial material aid and moral support from abroad. This urgent and chronic necessity to provide for Catholic Ireland's 'wants' to a large extent determined the Confederates' foreign policy.

First and foremost they needed money which was 'the main sinew' of any war (see chapter 8 below).[37] Second, in order to defeat their enemies on the battlefield, the Confederates also required cannon, muskets (and spare parts for them), powder, shot, swords, bullets, iron, steel and armour. It was the daunting task of the Irish diplomats on the continent to secure adequate supplies of these essential items. Thus in 1644 O'Hartegan, pressured the French government to provide the Confederates with 200,000 crowns outright (c. £4,500) together with a yearly stipend, arms and ammunition, while Luke Wadding in Rome and Hugh Bourke in Brussels, and later Madrid, were equally importunate. In addition to cash, the agents implored powder manufacturers, armourers, musket makers, miners, smiths, printers and 'any other that hath relacion to the warr, to imploy themselves in this countrye where all warlicke accomodacions are soe necessarye and soe coveted'.[38] As their reward these foreign workmen were to be granted free board and lodging, exempted from paying local taxes and allowed to set their own prices for any goods they manufactured. Merchants, who agreed to ship military hardware to Ireland, received similar privileges.

Finally, and no less important, the confederate agents encouraged Irish veterans serving in Germany, France, Flanders and Spain to return home in order to train and lead the inexperienced native armies.[39] At the same time they assembled a fleet designed to keep communications open with Catholic Europe, to protect Irish merchant vessels on the high seas and to

---

[36] Gilbert (ed.), *Irish confederation*, II, p. 262.
[37] HMC, *Franciscan MSS,* p. 238.
[38] Gilbert (ed.), *Irish confederation*, II, pp. 125–6.
[39] This proved difficult since English diplomats abroad consistently tried to undermine their efforts. See for examples, Public Record Office, State Papers 77/31, fos. 188–v, 199–v, 207, 211–12, 220–1, 224–6v, 234–5, 259–v; 78/111, fos. 113, 154–5v, 186–7, 192–3v and Gilbert (ed.), *Contemporary history*, I, pp. 461, 518, 521–3.

hinder the war-effort of their enemies. Since the Confederates could not afford to buy sophisticated warships (such as Dunkirk frigates, which were 'accustomed to go whithersoever they will, caring nothing for anybody' and cost roughly £2,000 each), the Supreme Council instructed their agents in Flanders to find experienced mariners who would bring their vessels to Ireland.[40] On arrival these sailors received confederate 'letters of marque' which authorized them to act as privateers and capture at sea any enemy of the Irish cause (see chapter 4 above).[41]

Military necessity dictated the objectives not only of confederate foreign policy but also of those powers who sent agents to Ireland during the 1640s. The outbreak of the First English Civil War in August 1642 and Parliament's willingness to turn to Scotland for armed support (the Solemn League and Covenant was signed in September 1643) forced Charles I to ask, however reluctantly, the Confederates to provide troops, money and munitions.[42] Thus in the spring of 1644 Antrim, a Gaelic warlord and royalist envoy, persuaded the Supreme Council to send an expeditionary force to Scotland together with munitions to England, while, the following year, Edward Somerset, earl of Glamorgan, a Catholic magnate from Wales requested a further 10,000 confederate troops for service in Britain.

Like Charles I, Louis XIV and Philip IV craved Irish mercenaries and, during the 1640s, the ability of the Confederates to send cannon-fodder to serve in the Habsburg or Bourbon armies shaped their relations with these superpowers. The reason for this was obvious. During the early decades of the seventeenth century the Spanish Habsburgs were not only deeply involved in a protracted and bitter struggle in the Netherlands, which became particularly acute in 1645 as the French amplified their assault on Dunkirk, but also remained totally committed to the Imperial cause in Germany. After 1640 the revolt of Catalonia and Portugal undermined their already tenuous hegemony over western Europe and distracted Spain's attention and meagre resources from the vital but more distant theatres of war abroad. To top it all the demographic decline of Castile, Spain's traditional recruiting ground, further reduced the number of available soldiers. The Spanish empire clearly lacked sufficient recruits to maintain its already over-extended armies, and therefore officials in both

40 HMC, *Franciscan MSS*, p. 123.
41 *Ibid.*, p. 223 and Gilbert (ed.), *Irish confederation*, VI, p. 234. The presence of an Irish navy in European waters brought with it extra burdens for the confederate diplomats who were now expected to secure the release of confederate mariners and captured shipping and to persuade foreign powers to allow Irish privateers to sell prizes in their ports.
42 For details on the Irish troops sent to England by Inchiquin see p. 53 above and by Ormond see p. 50 above and footnote 83 below.

Brussels and Madrid eagerly sought Catholic mercenary soldiers from Ireland while at the same time trying to prevent their great rival, France, from recruiting there.[43] For France, just like Spain, was deeply involved in the German war and, in addition, was committed to send troops to Italy, to the Netherlands, and (after 1640) to the Iberian peninsula to aid the Catalan and Portuguese rebels.[44] Thus, crudely stated, the yardstick of a 'successful' foreign policy in Ireland was measured in French and Spanish eyes by the number of troops their agents succeeded in exporting for as little money as possible; and on the degree to which they could freeze their opponents out. In the words of the Spanish agent, 'even if we were to secure no further advantage than to get out some troops, or to keep out the French, I believe it would be no mean achievement: God save us from the damage that would befall our monarchy if the French ever got a foothold in Ireland'.[45]

III – INTERNATIONAL RELATIONS, 1642–1648

Although the aims and ambitions of the various protagonists involved in Irish affairs thus had much in common, the methods used by the Confederates, the Spaniards and the French to achieve them were very different. In Ireland the General Assembly and its executive body, the Supreme Council, possessed ultimate responsibility for making confederate foreign policy. During the early years of the war they tried to turn their cause into a crusade by claiming that an international Protestant conspiracy, led by English Puritans, threatened the Roman religion. If Catholic Ireland should fall, the Supreme Council reminded their agent in Flanders, 'heresy will not only prevaile but alsoe extinguish the orthodox faith [in] all the north partes of the world. The Hugonetts of France, Germany and Holland, and their correspondents, are not to be forgotten; and . . . the disunion of Catholic princes is too well known'. They added that, if only the Catholic princes would support their cause, Ireland 'might from thenceforth be a great bulwarke against all the hereticks of the Northerne partes of Europe'.[46]

---

[43] This had also been the case prior to 1641, see J. H. Elliott, 'The year of the three ambassadors', in Hugh Lloyd-Jones, Valerie Pearl and Blair Worden (eds.), *History and imagination. Essays in honour of H. R. Trevor-Roper* (London, 1981). On Spanish 'overstretch' see Stradling, *Spanish monarchy*, chapters 1 and 2.

[44] Ideally France wanted to maintain two Irish regiments see A[rchives du] M[inistère des] A[ffaires] E[trangères, Paris], Correspondance Politique Angleterre, Côte 50, fos. 70–1v.

[45] Copy of paragraphs from a letter of Foissotte to Cárdenas, 22 May/1 June 1645 (AGS, Eo. 2566 unfol.).

[46] Gilbert (ed.), *Irish confederation*, IV, pp. 93–5. Also see HMC, *Franciscan MSS*, p. 198.

Their rhetoric had little impact. While the Papacy remained keen to see Catholicism triumph in Ireland, Pope Urban VIII (and, after 1644, Innocent X), in addition to allying with Venice against the Ottoman Turks, waged a personal war against the duke of Parma in Italy and lacked the resources to launch and finance the crusade as many Irishmen at home and abroad naively hoped. As a result papal support proved at best lukewarm and limited to a few 'benedictions, exhortations and indulgences'.[47] Likewise France and Spain, afraid of offending the English Parliament, of losing the services of their Irish troops and of becoming embroiled in yet another armed struggle, initially ignored the calls for help.[48] Indeed, for a time, the governor-general of the Spanish Netherlands actually banned anyone from assisting the Irish insurgents which, according to the English ambassador, 'the Irish here take extremely to hearte, and give out that the Spaniards are more ther ennimies, then [sic] the English'.[49] However the diplomatic overtures of the English Parliament towards the French, Dutch and Portuguese, Spain's great enemies, resulted in a *rapprochement* between Ireland and Spain. By the end of 1642 the Confederates had provisionally designated Spain as their European benefactor. Richard Bellings later recorded France's reaction to this development: Cardinal Mazarin 'having understood that the king of Spain' had given money to the Irish agents in Madrid 'sought to ingratiate himself to the nation'. He added that 'the [supreme] council was not displeased that the people should take notice of the correspondence with foreign princes' and encouraged these French overtures on the grounds that they would enhance their power to secure greater aid from Philip IV.[50]

Clearly then an effective Irish foreign policy revolved around the ability of the Confederates to exploit rivalries among the continental powers to their own advantage, and they did so by offering France and Spain the use of safe ports along the Irish coast, together with Irish mercenaries. The Supreme Council reminded Philip IV in 1644 that, in return for his support, Spanish ships en route to the Low Countries 'may finde good harbors [in Ireland] where to rest and be refreshed'. In addition his armies in Flanders would be supplied with 'great store of corne, flesh and fish' and 'many companyes of men to serve him as soldiers in his warrs (there being none

---

[47] HMC, *Franciscan MSS*, p. ix.
[48] Also see Ian Roy, 'Les puissances européenes et la chute de Charles I', *Revue d'Histoire Diplomatique*, 92 (1987), pp. 92–109.
[49] Gilbert (ed.), *Contemporary history*, I, p. 523.
[50] [John Lodge (ed.),] *Desiderata curiosa Hibernica, or a select collection of state papers* (2 vols., Dublin, 1772), II, pp. 245–7.

more faithful to him)'.[51] Safe harbours along the Irish coast were certainly attractive to both the Habsburgs and the Bourbons. Foissotte for one planned 'to create little by little a colony of Flemings and Waloons' at Dungarvan and to maintain there 'two or three frigates to take advantage of whatever may occur'; while in 1648 it was rumoured both that Mazarin had offered to pay 100,000 ducats (over £20,000) for the port of Duncannon and that France had been promised possession of all of Ireland's major ports in return for substantial aid.[52]

Control of shipping would also facilitate the passage of troops. The virtues of the Irish soldier, 'Men inured to war and accustomed to hardship' according to one Spanish official, were well known.[53] The Spanish Council of State observed in 1647 that 'The Irish are foreign Catholics, neighbours affected to Spain and brave soldiers – a combination which will not easily be found in any other nation'.[54] Even the staunchly Protestant William III of Orange later paid his own tribute: 'There lives not a people more hardy . . . neither is there any will endure the miseries of warre . . . so naturally, and with such facility and courage that they do'. He added that 'the Irish are soldiers the first day of their birth'.[55]

The first Irish mercenaries, the Confederates' most effective diplomatic asset, were earmarked for foreign service in November 1642 when the confederate agent in Spain, Father James Talbot, persuaded the Madrid government to send 20,000 escudos (c. £4,500) in gold to Kilkenny in return for 2,000 troops.[56] After the conclusion of a cease-fire between the Confederates and the Royalists (September 1643), Ireland began to provide manpower for both the continental armies and those of Charles I on a far larger scale. Philip IV himself noted 'the opening that this now provides to bring out Irish troops for Flanders and Spain, before they are recruited for the service of either the king of Great Britain . . . or [the king] of France' and heartily endorsed the decision to send Foissotte from Brussels to

[51] Gilbert (ed.), *Irish confederation*, IV, p. 93.
[52] Foissotte to Rosas, 14/24 October 1644 (AGS, GA 1570 unfol.) and Foissotte to Francesco de Melo, 25 November/5 December 1644 (AGS, Eo. 2525 unfol.). On Mazarin's interests see Foissotte to Philip IV, 18/28 May 1648 (AGS, Eo. 2566 unfol.) and paper I presented by Crelly to a parliamentary committee, December 1648 (AGS, Eo. 2524, fo. 81).
[53] Jennings (ed.), *Wild Geese*, p. 390.
[54] Consulta of the council of state, 20/30 March 1647 (AGS, Eo. 2068 unfol.).
[55] Quoted by J. P. Prendergast, *The Cromwellian settlement of Ireland* (third edn., Dublin, 1922), p. 87.
[56] They were also prepared to trade their veterans to the Venetians for their struggle against the Turks. Thus in one of his dispatches early in 1648 the Venetian ambassador in France recorded how 'the Catholics there [Ireland] have considered your serenity's need of men and their own need of money, and are disposed to listen to overtures, as they consider war against the Turk and against the heretic as equally important', *Calendar of state papers . . . existing in the archives . . . of Venice, 1647–1652* (London, 1927), p. 54.

Kilkenny.[57] Cardinal Mazarin also spotted this golden opportunity to secure infantry and sent La Monnerie, together with 50,000 florins (c. £3,850), arms and munitions, to Kilkenny. Both initiatives were rewarded; early in 1644 the agents of France, as well as Spain, received permission to recruit 'a levy within this kingdom of two thousand foot with their officers'.[58] This angered Philip IV for, instead of receiving the preferential treatment that he felt Spain's past loyalty to Ireland merited, his agents now competed with both the Royalists and the Bourbons for troops. To make matters worse, two developments in the spring of 1645 allowed France to replace Spain as Ireland's leading diplomatic ally: the French blockade of Dunkirk, which hindered communications between Ireland and Spanish Flanders, and the dominant position temporarily enjoyed within the confederate Supreme Council by a party loyal to the pro-French marquis of Ormond.

Simply stated, two principal confederate groups influenced the making of Irish foreign policy at this point. The first comprised members of Old English families, many of whom were Ormond's clients ('Ormondists') and pro-French. They normally dominated the Supreme Councils and, as the 1640s progressed, showed increasing eagerness both to win French support and to conclude a peace with Charles I, even if it compromised the future safety of the Catholic religion. The group included men such as Lord Mountgarret (Ormond's great-uncle), president of the first six Supreme Councils and an admirer of France; Mountgarret's son-in-law, Richard Bellings, secretary of the Council and (according to the Spanish agent) 'very hostile to Spain and very pro-French';[59] and Viscount Muskerry, Ormond's senior brother-in-law, a supreme councillor and a French client. The lawyer Patrick Darcy, described by the Spanish agent as the most important person in the Council and 'one of Ormond's creatures and no friend of ours', allegedly received a French pension.[60]

The second group, known in contemporary diplomatic correspondence, as the 'Old Irish' faction, consisted of members of Gaelic families, predominantly from Ulster, and of clerics who remained intent on securing freedom for the Catholic religion as the price of any compromise with the

---

[57] Minute of Philip IV's letter to Melo, 30 December 1643/9 January 1644 (AGS, Eo. 2525 unfol.).

[58] Jennings (ed.), *Wild Geese*, p. 41; Gilbert (ed.), *Irish confederation*, III, pp. 102–3. It appears that in return for this concession Spain alone paid the Council 50,000 florins (roughly £3,846) see, receipt from the Supreme Council, 5 September 1644 (AGS, Eo. 2525 unfol.).

[59] Foissotte to Rosas, 14/24 October 1644 (AGS, GA 1570 unfol.). De la Torre made similar complaints about Bellings, see Consulta of the council of state, 14/24 July 1646 (AGS, Eo. 2523 unfol.).

[60] Foissotte to Melo, 25 November/5 December 1645 (AGS, Eo. 2525 unfol.).

king. It was to this party that the Spanish and papal diplomats turned for support. General Owen Roe O'Neill, the archbishops of Cashel and Tuam and the bishop of Down all received Spanish hand-outs; while Antrim and Nicholas French, the influential bishop of Ferns and Clogher tended to support the Habsburgs. This Old Irish/Spanish party enjoyed greater popularity than the French faction and one French traveller, who visited Ireland in 1644, shrewdly noted in his journal that the Irish 'love the Spaniard as their brothers, the French as their friends'.[61] This was particularly true in the privateering and merchant communities of southern Ireland. After Wexford fell to the Confederates in September 1642 the Lords Justice reported to London that 'the rebels have set up Spanish colours on their walls in defiance of the king and kingdom of England'; while a popular chant heard in the streets of Wexford during the early 1640s was 'God bless the king of Spain; For but for him we should all be slain'.[62] The extent of Spanish influence over the town of Waterford and the proficiency with which the Irish clerics in the city spoke Spanish also distressed the French envoy.

While the Old Irish/Spanish faction enjoyed considerable support in the country at large and in the General Assemblies in particular, the Francophile 'Ormondists' out-voted and out-manoeuvred them in the all-powerful Supreme Council. In fact, by 1645, matters looked so bleak to the Madrid government that it recalled Foissotte and sent a more senior diplomat, Don Diego de la Torre, to Ireland. However, much to Spain's delight, the Supreme Council refused to grant the French permission to recruit because the 'Ormondists' considered Charles I's needs to be more important. Then in the autumn of 1646, pro-Spanish Confederates, led by Rinuccini, supplanted the 'Ormondists' as the dominant party within the Supreme Council. Almost at once Colonels James Preston and Patrick Barnewall received permission to levy two regiments for Spain while France had to make do with one. The resurgence of Spanish power can be attributed partly to Ormond's failure to win continued confederate support for the royalist war-effort in Britain and his inability to prevent Rinuccini from purging his supporters from the Supreme Council, together with the fact that the Spanish envoys had subsidized the Old Irish party with modest payments throughout the autumn of 1646.[63] It also helped that

---

[61] T. Crofton Croker (ed.), *The tour of the French traveller M. de Boullaye le Gouz in Ireland, A.D. 1644* (London, 1837), p. 43.

[62] HMC, *Calendar of the manuscripts of the marquis of Ormonde*, ns (8 vols., London, 1902–20), II, pp. 185–6.

[63] See the accounts of de la Torre (AGS, Tribunal Mayor de Cuentas 4a, legajo 2635, unfol.) and Foissotte to Philip IV, 20/30 December 1646 (AGS, Eo. 2525 unfol.).

Pope Innocent X (according to Bellings) 'was believed to have been partial to the Spaniard [and] might have disposed the Irish to have an absolute dependence upon the Catholic King [Philip IV]'.[64]

Spain did not retain control for long, however, and over the summer of 1647 France slowly re-emerged as the leading foreign force in Irish affairs. On the one hand, cordial relations between Spain and Rinuccini, for a time the most powerful man in Ireland, turned sour after the capture, late in 1646, of an English ship carrying Spanish gold to pay the Army of Flanders by a frigate belonging to the nuncio.[65] On the other, the French agents proved particularly successful in penetrating the ranks of many Irish families who had traditionally supported the Habsburgs. Thus Colonel James Preston, who had served the Spanish crown for fifteen years, agreed in 1646 to send to France 500 men whom he had in fact levied for Spain, after receiving a bribe of slightly less than £300.[66] In 1648 the French also bought, for an annual pension of 600 escudos or £125, the services of his father, General Thomas Preston, a distinguished veteran of the Spanish Army of Flanders.[67] Even James Talbot, the confederate agent in Madrid, defected and from the winter of 1647 supplied the French with classified information on the activities of the Spanish agents in Ireland.[68]

Logistical problems compounded these political difficulties and further complicated international relations. In the rueful words of one agent: it became 'more difficult to find troops in Ireland, and having found them to transport them, than many people think'.[69] Occasionally the regiments which had been so laboriously levied dispersed for want of adequate shipping; and when transport ships could be located, hiring costs often proved prohibitive. For instance, during the later 1640s the master of the *St Nicholas of Waterford* charged £200 for transporting 450 soldiers to France and, between 1647 and 1648, the French agents spent over £2,500 on hiring shipping.[70] The parliamentary blockade of the Irish coast constituted

---

[64] *Desiderata curiosa*, II, p. 267.
[65] For details see Aiazza, *Embassy*, pp. 406–7, 421, 426–8, 442 and copy of the Relación sent by Miguel Routtare to the marquis of Monasterio, 30 November 1647 (AGS, Eo. 2526 unfol.).
[66] See AMAE, Correspondance Politique Angleterre, Côte 52, fos. 3–7 and Côte 55, fo. 341v.
[67] See AMAE, Correspondance Politique Angleterre, Côte 57, fos. 265–6 and de la Torre to Philip IV, 30 April/10 May 1649 (AGS Eo. 3019 unfol.).
[68] See AMAE, Correspondance Politique Angleterre, Côte 55, fos 246, 370.
[69] Foissotte to Coloma, 18/28 May 1648 (AGS, Eo. 2566 unfol.).
[70] Memoir of the money spent on Irish levies [1648] (AMAE, Correspondance Politique Angleterre Côte 57, fos. 357–60). In an effort to solve these problems the agents bought their own vessels. Thus de la Torre spent 11,000 escudos, or nearly a third of his total budget, buying and outfitting a small frigate (the *Santa Barbara*); the count of Berehaven, purchased another Dunkirker (the *Santa Theresa*); and the French agent bought a small vessel of c. 15 tons (the *Falcon*).

another headache and made it nearly impossible to export troops anywhere over the entire summer of 1644. Late in 1645 adverse weather conditions prevented nearly 600 troops destined for France from leaving Waterford, allowing the Spanish resident, Foissotte, to sabotage the entire levy.[71] A few months later the Supreme Council, fearing a parliamentary offensive in County Clare, diverted three regiments, raised by Glamorgan for service in the royalist army, to besiege Bunratty Castle.

IV – A PROTECTOR FOR IRELAND, 1648–1652

In the later 1640s the Confederates became increasingly aware of the need to prevent the English Parliament, their implacable foe, from becoming so powerful that it could invade and destroy them. To achieve this, two options lay open to them: either they could aid Charles I with all their might, in return for the best political and religious concessions they could extort, and hope for a royalist victory in Britain; or they could abandon the king altogether and seek to make Catholic Ireland, with the aid of foreign powers, impregnable to invasion from England.

In the spring of 1648, when their war-effort reached a particularly low ebb, the Confederates gave these alternatives serious consideration. Hardly surprisingly both France and Spain now vied for the privilege of becoming Ireland's 'protector' knowing full well that 'whoever protects Ireland will control it'.[72] Ideally, France wanted Charles I to triumph in all his kingdoms; but, failing that, Mazarin was prepared to welcome Ireland as a French satellite state (like Savoy) or a French protectorate (like Catalonia) and, early in 1648, the French agents in Kilkenny suggested that Louis XIV should 'not only become arbiter but absolute master of all the affairs of the Confederates'.[73] At the very least, according to the French secretary of state, Brienne, Ireland must be prevented from falling under Spanish control, which (in his view) would be worse than if it became Protestant. Indeed at this point France promised the exiled Henrietta Maria finance for an assault on England in return for possession of all the major forts and ports in Ireland, together with a supply of Catholic mercenaries.[74] For his part, Philip IV found the prospect of Bourbon domination of his Irish

[71] *Relación de los servicios de D. Francisco Foisotte.*
[72] De la Torre to Philip IV, 20/30 April 1647 (AGS, Eo. 2523 unfol.).
[73] La Monnerie to [Brienne], 31 January/9 February 1648 (BL, Harleian MSS 4551, fo. 34v). Also see Foissotte to Philip IV, 8/18 May 1648 (AGS, Eo. 2566 unfol.). On Anglo-French relations see C. V. Wedgwood, 'European Reaction to the death of Charles I' in Carter (ed.), *From the Renaissance to the Counter-Reformation*, pp. 405–9.
[74] Ohlmeyer, *Civil war and restoration*, pp. 207–9, 221.

recruiting grounds intolerable and so, through his envoys, urged the Confederates to choose Spain as their benefactor because a French 'protector' would not only refuse to restore Catholicism but would leave the reins of power in the hands of Ormond and other 'heretics'.[75]

In the event, despite the queen's prediction that her husband's continued willingness to offer the Irish 'as a sacrifice' would eventually 'force' them to 'give themselves to some foreign king',[76] the Confederates eventually opted to join forces with the Royalists and it was not until 1650, when the English Parliament had commenced the reconquest of Ireland, that the Catholic party turned again to Europe for aid. However by this point, France, crippled by the bitter civil wars known as the Fronde, proved unable to help; while Philip IV refused to jeopardize his new cordial relationship with the English Parliament (he was the first European monarch officially to recognize the Commonwealth) by treating with 'Irish rebels'. Therefore in the autumn of 1650, desperate for money and arms, the Confederates approached Charles, duke of Lorraine, an independent warlord who, after being expelled from his duchy by France in 1634, served the Habsburgs as a military contractor. After lengthy negotiations with the duke's ambassador to Ireland, Abbot Stephen de Henin, the confederate delegates promised to designate Lorraine as 'royal Protector of Ireland' and to grant him control of Galway, Limerick, Sligo and Duncannon. In return the duke offered the Catholic party £20,000 together with 'arms, shipping, ammunition and warlike provision'.[77] Even though Lorraine actually provided the Confederates with £6,000, and in July 1652 sent a pinnace to Inishbofin Island, this last-ditch attempt to involve a continental potentate in Irish affairs ended in failure and infuriated Charles II, who saw his sovereignty in Ireland being undermined.[78] The Cromwellian conquest of Ireland continued unabated.

Despite hopes that either the exiled English king or Innocent X's successor, Pope Alexander VII, would finance and lead an invasion of Ireland, and that following the outbreak of war with Parliament (in October 1655) Spain might launch an offensive against England using Ireland as its base, after 1652 Catholic Ireland ceased to be a force in

---

[75] De la Torre's reasons for not allowing the French faction to control Ireland [1648] (AGS, Eo. 2566 unfol.). It was rumoured that he promised the Confederates 100,000 escudos and fifteen frigates laden with arms and munitions if they chose Philip IV, AMAE Correspondance Politique Angleterre, Côte 57, fos. 55–62.

[76] Cited in Richard Bagwell, *Ireland under the Stuarts and during the Interregnum* (3 vols., London, 1963), II, p. 59.

[77] *Memoirs of the right honourable marquis of Clanricarde . . .* (Dublin, 1744), pp. 78–83.

[78] *Commentarius Rinuccinianus*, VI, pp. 166–72, 178.

international affairs. Like the Italian kingdoms of Naples and Sicily, which had lost their own battles for autonomy to the Habsburgs, the Westminster Parliament once again dictated Ireland's foreign policy.[79] The 'daily intelligence', received by Cromwellian officials in Dublin during the later 1650s, that the Irish planned 'to invade the Commonwealth with foreign forces' and stir up rebellion 'within our bowels', remained mere speculation.[80]

V – THE DIPLOMATIC ACHIEVEMENT

The English reconquest of Ireland tends to obscure the fact that each of the foreign powers which dealt with the Confederates during the 1640s achieved at least some of their goals. The French agents recruited in excess of 7,000 troops between 1644 and 1649 and, equally important from their perspective, prevented a further two regiments from leaving to fight for Spain. In addition, the prevalence of Francophile 'Ormondists' on the Supreme Councils allowed France to exercise considerable influence over Irish politics (especially between the spring of 1645 and the autumn of 1646 and between late 1647 and late 1649) and undermined Spain's traditional powerbase by attracting Habsburg supporters to the Bourbon camp.

By contrast, Spain, largely due to the inferior quality of its agents and limited resources, only held real political influence briefly in 1642–3 and between November 1646 and late 1647; but the support Philip IV enjoyed among the Irish populace at large and the influence his subjects wielded over the principal confederate ports partly compensated for this. As for recruiting, the Spanish agents proved less fortunate, for only c. 4,000 troops reached the Iberian peninsula and Flanders between 1644 and 1649.[81] Ironically the years after the defeat of the confederate cause represented the high point of Habsburg success in Ireland for between 1651 and 1654/5 over 18,000 soldiers (c. 3,600 per annum) left Ireland to serve in the territories controlled by Philip IV – but they did so under licence from, and in ships subsidized by, the English government. As the declared enemy of the English Parliament France was forbidden to recruit in Ireland at all.

[79] Ibid., vi, pp. 189, 195.
[80] Thomas Birch (ed.), A collection of the state papers of John Thurloe . . . (7 vols., London, 1742), v, pp. 348–9.
[81] Stradling, Spanish monarchy, p. 164. Irish troops raised by Foissotte arrived on Iberian soil in October and December 1644 (1,230 men), August 1647 (500 men) and April 1649 (1,817 men). De la Torre's recruits arrived in September 1646 (140 men); while Christopher Mayo's landed in September 1649 (350 men).

Though the Papacy failed to conclude a settlement which protected the Catholic religion on a permanent basis, between October 1641 and the Cromwellian conquest Catholics in Ireland enjoyed complete freedom of worship. As Rinuccini noted in 1647: 'despite the machinations of hell, the Catholic religion is [as] openly professed [in Ireland] . . . as in Italy'.[82] However Rinuccini's persistent meddling in Irish affairs, especially his determination to excommunicate those who adhered to the 'Ormond Peace' of 1646 and the 'Inchiquin Truce' of May 1648, wrought havoc within the Confederation and served to polarize the Catholic political factions and to undermine the confederate war-effort (see chapters 3 and 6). Intervention in confederate affairs by Charles I and his representatives in Ireland proved equally fatal for the Irish cause and did little to improve the royalist position. For, of all the powers competing for Irish manpower, Charles I proved the least successful. As the fortunes of war turned against him in England, Charles depended increasingly on immediate and substantial support from Catholic Ireland; yet, despite protracted talks, the two regiments sent to Scotland by Antrim (June 1644) represented the only confederate assistance Charles received for his British war-effort.[83] Worse still the king's evident willingness to negotiate with 'Irish rebels' and 'papists' did his image in Britain untold damage and gave substance to parliamentary propaganda reports that England was on the verge of being reduced to popery.

What then of the Confederates: how successful was the foreign policy of Ireland's first independent government of modern times? Their agent in Holland, Oliver French, paid his own tribute to the confederate successes. In 1641, he later wrote, 'we were naked men, destitute of arms, ammunition and experienced commanders'; yet within seven years 'with God's assistance we have provyded ourselves of armes and ammunition and called home our experienced commanders . . . from forraigne services, and furnished ourselves with a considerable number of frygatts and shipps of war . . . and thereby annoyed our enemies, both by sea and by land'.[84] Irish diplomatic successes were by no means limited to logistics. Despite the fact that Ireland remained a third-rate European power, the Confederates also managed to secure the respect of their enemies who, according to Oliver French, now treated them 'as a considerable party . . . and give us leave to talke upon equall termes'. Irish diplomacy also won the Catholic cause

---

[82] Aiazza, *Embassy*, p. 329.
[83] In stark contrast Ormond and the Irish Royalists dispatched during the early 1640s in excess of 20,000 troops to England and Wales, see Joyce Lee Malcolm, 'All the king's men: the impact of the crown's Irish soldiers on the English civil war', *IHS*, 22 (1979), pp. 239–64.
[84] Gilbert (ed.), *Irish confederation*, VI, pp. 233–4.

international acclaim, 'this defensive warr' as French noted 'being approved of by most of the states and potentates of Christendom'.[85] Moreover the presence of high-powered foreign dignitaries in Kilkenny made the Confederates feel part of the international community; or in the words of one Royalist 'gave notable countenance to the assembly'.[86]

However Irish diplomats failed to secure adequate funds for their cause. In the summer of 1646 de la Torre warned Philip IV 'that this council does not place any value on offers of arms and ammunition because they already have in this kingdom all they need of these. All they lack is money' (see chapter 8 below).[87] Nevertheless papal sources sent some £25,000 in cash and a further £31,000 in bills of exchange and this facilitated O'Neill's great victory at Benburb in June 1646 (see chapter 3 above). Of the 100,000 crowns (roughly £22,000) promised by France less than a third, nearly £7,300, reached the confederate treasury; while Spain contributed only £5,000, admittedly most of it in desperately needed gold coin. Though nearly £70,000 may seem considerable, it could not sustain the Catholic war-effort for a prolonged period of time and, according to Bellings, 'all foraign aids which they [the Confederates] had received were matters rather to amuse the people, and to excite them to greater contributions at home, than any real ease of the burthen they groaned under'.[88]

There can be little doubt that the European Catholic powers all wished the Irish cause well, but none could offer realistic succour. As one Spanish official wrote of international affairs in 1643:

> All the north [is] in commotion . . . England, Ireland and Scotland aflame with Civil War . . . The Ottomans tearing each other to pieces . . . China invaded by the Tartars, Ethiopia by the Turks, and the Indian kings who live scattered through the region between the Ganges and the Indus all at each other's throats.[89]

War in Italy had exhausted the papal exchequer; Venice was fighting against the Turks; internal revolts and external conflict between France and Spain swallowed up their resources. Ireland's foreign policy successes in the 1640s may well have depended upon the ability of the Confederates to manipulate these international struggles to their own advantage, but

---

[85] Gilbert (ed.), *Irish confederation*, VI, p. 234.
[86] Edward, earl of Clarendon, *The history of the rebellion* . . . , ed. W. D. Macray (6 vols., Oxford, 1988; re-issued, 1992), II, p. 491.
[87] Consulta of the council of state, 14/24 July 1646 (AGS, Eo. 2523 unfol.).
[88] Gilbert (ed.), *Irish confederation*, VI, p. 10.
[89] From the anonymous tract *Nicandro*, quoted in John H. Elliott, *The count-duke of Olivares. The statesman in an age of decline* (New Haven and London, 1986), p. 659.

ultimately perpetual war on the continent ensured that Ireland became as much a victim of the seventeenth-century 'General Crisis' as any other nation. Only massive amounts of foreign aid over a prolonged period of time, which, according to one leading early modern European scholar, served as 'an indispensable requirement for any revolt, if it were to have a chance of perpetuating itself',[90] could have prevented the English Parliament from dealing eventually with its 'Irish Problem'; and those continental subsidies were always lacking.

However Ireland's rebellion was not the only victim of the 'General Crisis'. After the outbreak of the Fronde, in 1648, Catalonia, a protectorate of France and geographically isolated from the Atlantic world, experienced similar frustrations which eventually culminated in the fall of Barcelona to Philip IV in October 1652. Similarly Mazarin lost control of the revolt of the Spanish kingdom of Naples due to a series of French diplomatic blunders.[91] Conversely foreign intervention proved a critical variable in tipping the scales of victory in favour of the Dutch, Portuguese and Ukrainian rebels. During the later decades of the sixteenth century the charismatic Dutch leader, William of Orange, laboured tirelessly to persuade France, England, Sweden and certain German and Italian princes to support his cause. And with some success: after 1573 France dispatched intermittent aid; while between 1585 and 1604 England committed troops and sent subsidies and advisers to assist the Dutch rebels, who won recognition for their cause from Spain in 1609 and during the seventeenth century enjoyed great power status.[92] Likewise the Portuguese became masters of 'survival diplomacy' and sent residents to, and received agents from, Paris, the Hague, Barcelona and even London. In June 1641, shortly after the outbreak of the rebellion, their diplomats signed a mutual aid treaty with France (a Bourbon naval force arrived in Lisbon a few months later) and concluded a ten-year truce with the Dutch. Moreover the presence of Portuguese delegates at the Westphalian peace conference in 1648 amounted to *de facto* recognition of Portugal's independence by the rest of Europe.[93] Unlike the Dutch and Portuguese revolts, the Irish rebellion ended in failure but it nevertheless enabled Catholic

[90] John H. Elliott, 'Revolution and continuity in early modern Europe', in Geoffrey Parker and Lesley M. Smith (eds.), *The general crisis of the seventeenth century* (London, 1978), p. 129.

[91] R. B. Merriman, *Six contemporaneous revolutions* (Oxford, 1938), p. 134.

[92] Geoffrey Parker, 'The Dutch revolt and the polarization of international politics', in Parker and Smith (eds.), *The general crisis of the seventeenth century*, p. 60.

[93] John H. Elliott, 'The Spanish monarchy and the kingdom of Portugal 1580–1640' in Mark Greengrass (ed.), *Conquest and coalescence: the shaping of the state in early modern Europe* (London, 1991), p. 65 and Merriman, *Six contemporaneous revolutions*, pp. 120–7, 135–6, 138–41, 151–3.

Ireland to begin the lengthy process of forging its own international identity, which was something the Confederates, despite their diplomatic immaturity, did as effectively as the Dutch after 1581 or the Portuguese after 1640.

CHAPTER 6

'POLITICAL' POEMS IN THE
MID-SEVENTEENTH-CENTURY CRISIS

MICHELLE O RIORDAN

THE OUTBREAK of the 1641 rebellion followed by a decade of civil war caused many Gaelic poets and writers to speculate upon the origins of this conflict and to apportion praise and blame accordingly.[1] In 1957 Cecile O'Rahilly edited and published five of these 'political poems' (as she labelled them). These works, perhaps because of their use of a more popular register of contemporary Gaelic vernacular, rather than the standardized literary language of formal poetry, and the seeming transparency of their style, are often understood, in so far as they address upheaval in both religious and secular affairs, to present an almost documentary account of the disintegration of Ireland in the mid-seventeenth century.[2] They have also been interpreted as partisan compositions, reflecting the aspirations and preoccupations of the 'Old Irish' (or native Gaelic Irish) side in the confederate wars.[3] Moreover this 'Old Irish' classification has been taken to be synonymous with support for the papal nuncio, Giovanni Battista Rinuccini, archbishop of Fermo who arrived in Ireland in October 1645, and with acquiescence in his censures in 1646 and 1648 against the treaties concluded between the Catholic Confederates and James Butler, marquis of Ormond and Murrough O'Brien, Lord Inchiquin. In contrast

---

[1] The extent to which poetry can be used as historical source material is a matter of some controversy. The current debate is addressed in Michelle O Riordan, *The Gaelic mind and the collapse of the Gaelic world* (Cork, 1990). See also Tadhg Ó Dúshláine, *An Eoraip agus litríocht na Gaeilge 1600–1650* (Baile Átha Cliath [Dublin], 1987) and Mícheál Mac Craith, 'Gaelic Ireland and the Renaissance', in Glanmor Williams and Robert Owen Jones (eds.), *The Celts and the Renaissance: innovation and tradition* (Cardiff, 1990), pp. 57–89.

[2] Cecile O'Rahilly (ed.), *Five seventeenth century political poems* (Dublin 1952; reprinted 1977), pp. vii–ix; and see for instance B. Ó. Cuív, 'The Irish language in the early modern period', in T. W. Moody, F. X. Martin and F. J. Byrne (eds.), *A new history of Ireland*, III: *Early modern Ireland 1534–1691* (Oxford, 1976), pp. 507–45, 541 (hereafter *NHI*).

[3] *NHI*, p. 541. See for instance Nicholas Canny, *From Reformation to Restoration: Ireland, 1534–1660* (Dublin, 1987), p. 212.

the 'Old English' (or Catholic Anglo-Irish) have been traditionally portrayed as those who defied the nuncio and, even in the face of excommunication, tried to prevent him from interfering in domestic politics.[4] However a close reading of this 'political' poetry suggests that these labels inadequately describe the complex nexus of allegiances and values held by Irish Catholics during these years. In addition it indicates that, on the one hand, divisions plagued the Catholic Confederates long before Rinuccini's arrival in Ireland; while, on the other, internecine quarrelling did not necessarily reflect the commitment – or lack of it – to the Catholic church or religion on the part of those who agreed with, or opposed, the nuncio. For example the poem 'Músgail do mhisneach, a Bhanbha', written by the poet/priest Pádraigín Haicéad in the formal style of the professional 'bardic' syllabic poetry, suggested that there was no clear exclusive association between the Old Irish and pro-nuncio position; nor was the Old Irish/pro-nuncio, Old English/anti-nuncio bias taken for granted.[5] In fact it seems that the poems were largely written with the conviction that devotion to Catholicism and recognition of Charles I's position as sovereign of Ireland were in no way incompatible.

These 'political' poems can be divided into three categories: 'An Síogaí Rómhánach' eulogized Owen Roe (Eoghan Rua) O'Neill and expressed a definite pro-nuncio bias, as did the syllabic poem 'Músgail do mhisneach, a Bhanbha' which emphatically denounced those who defied the nuncio in 1646. Then three poems – 'Aiste Dháibhí Cúndún', Seán Ó Conaill's 'Tuireamh na hÉireann' and Éamonn an Dúna's 'Mo lá leóin go deó go n-éagad' – echo, in many respects, the sentiments expressed in some prose compositions by members of the Old English clergy (discussed below) who were opposed to the nuncio. Finally 'Do chuala scéal do chéas gach ló mé', Séamus Carthún's 'Deor-chaoineadh na hÉireann', and Donnchadh Mac

---

4 I will use the terms 'Old English', 'Old Irish', 'pro-nuncio' and 'anti-nuncio' without assuming that there is any necessary homology between these two groups.
5 Among the 'political poems' of the period which will be looked at in this discussion are 'Músgail do mhisneach, a Bhanbha' [Rouse your courage, Banbha], in Máire Ní Cheallacháin, *Filíocht Phádraigín Haicéad* (Dublin, 1962) no. 36, pp. 38–43 (hereafter *Pádraigín Haicéad*); 'An Síogaí Rómhánach' [The Roman fairy], in O'Rahilly (ed.), *Political poems*, pp. 12–32; 'Do chuala scéal do chéas gach ló mé' [I heard tidings that tormented me every day], in Pádraig de Brún, Breandán Ó Buachalla and Tomás Ó Concheanainn, *Nua-dhuanaire* 1 (Dublin, 1971; reprinted 1986) pp. 31–4; 'Deor-chaoineadh na hÉireann' [The tearful lament of Ireland], in Cuthbert Mhág Craith (ed.), *Dán na mbráthar mionúr* (2 vols., Dublin 1967, 1980), 1, pp. 251–5; 'Aiste Dháibhí Cúndún' [Dáibhí Cúndún's poem] in O'Rahilly (ed.), *Political poems*, pp. 33–49; 'Tuireamh na hÉireann' [The lament of Ireland], *ibid.*, pp. 50–82; 'Mo lá leóin go deó go n-éagad' [My day of sorrow until I die], *ibid.*, pp. 83–100. No attempt will be made to provide a literary analysis of the poems, though it is understood at all times that they are literary items and must be read as such.

an Chaoilfhiaclaigh's 'Do fríth, monuar, an uain si ar Éirinn' generally lamented the distress and dislocation caused by the civil war, the Cromwellian conquest and land transfers together with the religious persecution of the 1650s.

The poems, produced in some instances by Roman Catholic clergymen, both secular and regular, stemmed from the native literary tradition and were heavily influenced by the style and content of contemporary continental compositions.[6] These vigorous compositions, largely in accentual metre, shared many common but variable features: the poet began his work with an anguished description of his personal agony at the current distress of Ireland, of her church and, above all, of her noble families; he devoted the body of the poem to a cursory survey of the history of the Gael in Ireland and of the foreigners, especially the Anglo-Norman settlers, who were absorbed into her culture; he ended the poem with a prayer, or a benign prophecy forecasting victory, or a prediction of aid to come. There is a clear geographical division among the poems – between Ulster and Munster – in respect to the area of interest indicated in the poem rather than the origin of the poet. 'An Síogaí Rómhánach' can be described as an 'Ulster' poem which championed Owen Roe O'Neill and the nuncio and clearly favoured the Old Irish.[7] Though the content of the compositions of Munster provenance gave sufficient reason to believe that the writers endorsed the aims of the confederate Catholics and regretted the hasty departure of Rinuccini for the continent in February 1649 and that they found the destruction of the country in the course of the Eleven Years War deeply distressing, they did not evince overwhelming support for the nuncio or Owen Roe.

In this chapter I will look at each poem individually, provide a brief descriptive analysis of its content and attempt to ascertain the political loyalty of the author through the association of his stated allegiances, aspirations and complaints, however vague or ambiguous, with the overtly partisan contemporaneous accounts.[8] Thus when the loyalties hinted at in the poems are compared with those declared in extant polemical prose literature, a clearer division seems to emerge linking the 'Munster' poems

---

6 Interestingly these works followed a pattern identifiable in writings of the 'baroque' period, both in prose and poetry. For instance both Catholics and Protestants made extensive use of the Bible, particularly of the dolorous passages from the Books of Job, Jeremiah, Isaiah and the Psalms, to decry the excesses of the other, see Ó Dúshláine, *An Eoraip agus litríocht na Gaeilge 1600–1650*, pp. 180–211.

7 The poet was not necessarily a native of Ulster, see O'Rahilly (ed.), *Political poems*, p. 13 n. 2.

8 Only 'Músgail do mhisneach, a Bhanbha' by Pádraigín Haicéad is in syllabic metre, see *Pádraigín Haicéad*, p. 114.

with a position close to that of Bishop French and Archdeacon John Lynch, Old English, anti-nuncio Catholic Royalists. However this approach also has its limitations. For even 'Ulster poems', such as 'An Síogaí Rómhánach', while emphatically biased in favour of Owen Roe did not carry the vehemence of *An aphorismical discovery of treasonable faction*, penned anonymously in English between 1652 and 1660, in its declared adherence to the nuncio and its robust castigation of the anti-nuncio 'faction' – though individual waverers were subjectively judged by the author who excused those who fell outside his main target, mainly Ormond and his more powerful supporters. Similarly no poem reflected the separatism and anti-Old English polemic of Conor O'Mahony's tract, *Disputatio apologetica de jure regni Hiberniae pro Catholicus Hibernis adversus haereticos Anglos* (Lisbon, 1645), though 'An Síogaí Rómhánach' did pray for the banishment of the Gaill, or foreigner, in order 'to free Ireland'.[9] Finally no poem echoed the single-minded dedication to the aspirations of the nuncio for Ireland exhibited in the *Commentarius Rinuccinianus*, compiled in Florence by Fathers O'Ferrall and O'Connell between 1661 and 1666.

In short, unlike the prose accounts, the 'political poems' discussed here emphasize those topics upon which all Catholic, Royalist noblemen and leaders, regular and secular clergy could agree and avoided contentious and divisive issues. However, at the same time, they serve to highlight the divisions inherent in Irish politics and society prior to Rinuccini's arrival and long after his departure.

I

Pádraigín Haicéad: 'Músgail do mhisneach, a Bhanbha'
[Rouse your courage, Banbha]

The accomplished poet Pádraigín Haicéad (d. 1654) was born in County Tipperary sometime around the beginning of the century.[10] His mother's family were Kearneys, related to the Butlers of Dunboyne, and his uncles included Bishop Patrick Comerford of Waterford and Philip Kearney, clerk of the Confederation. During the 1640s Haicéad, a Dominican, became increasingly embroiled in confederate politics and adhered unwaveringly to the papal nuncio, even to the point of stirring soldiers to join with Owen Roe O'Neill.

---

[9] O'Rahilly (ed.), *Political poems*, ll. 305–12, pp. 32–3.
[10] *Pádraigín Haicéad*, pp. ix–xx; and Aibhistín Valkenburg, 'Pádraigín Haicéad, O.P. 1604?–1654', *Irisleabhar Mhá Nuad* (1985) pp. 70–83.

In a preface to the poem Haicéad noted that it had been composed in response to the 'First Ormond Peace' signed in 1646 by some Confederates in defiance of Rinuccini's strictest admonitions. Thus Haicéad argued that by allying themselves with 'heretics' and by separating themselves from the devoted body of the Confederation of Kilkenny, this 'faction' placed Ireland in great danger.[11] He continued that these individuals, whom he portrayed as ungrateful children disobeying and humiliating their mother, Ireland, had incurred God's wrath, which could be appeased only by their returning to the papal nuncio's party.[12] For Haicéad only those who remained loyal to the papal party could be labelled as Ireland's worthy children and 'true family' and he condemned the anti-nuncio Confederates as secularists who put affairs of state above those of the church. While the poet acknowledged their traditional role as administrators and defenders of the royal interest in Ireland, he condemned their greed for church lands which, he argued, motivated their defiance of the nuncio.[13] Haicéad reduced the complex question of allegiance into one simple pro- or anti-nuncio equation and thereby deliberately dismissed the abstraction of the state and 'reason of state' as an unworthy rationale by which to guide the nation.[14] Though belligerent in tone, Haicéad's poem did not castigate by name opponents of the nuncio and concluded with the observation that those who had erred had not done so irrevocably.[15]

Anonymous: 'An Síogaí Rómhánach' [The Roman Fairy]

The poem known as 'An Síogaí Rómhánach', dated by O'Rahilly to between 1650 and 1653, is in accentual metre and very different in literary style and tone from Haicéad's syllabic composition. It is a lamentation by

---

[11] 'Faction' was a term in vogue in England at the time, and applied always in the pejorative sense to those who appeared to be against the *status quo*. The English Civil War gave rise to great discussion of the various factions, especially in the two partisan newspapers, *Mercurius Aulicus* (royalist) and *Mercurius Britanicus* (parliamentarian).

[12] *Pádraigín Haicéad*, ll. 149–52, p. 43.

[13] *Ibid.*, ll. 93–6, p. 41.

[14] *Ibid.*, ll. 89–92, p. 41. This rejection of profane 'realpolitik' was not confined to Roman Catholic clergy. Daniel Harcourt, a minister from the diocese of Down and Connor before the rebellion, explained the outbreak of rebellion in *A new remonstrance from Ireland* (n.d., London), p. 3, saying that the government had put 'politic ends before pious' and now had to reap the fruit of tolerating 'idolatrous Canaanites' in their midst, cited in Alan Ford, *The Protestant Reformation in Ireland, 1590–1641* (Frankfurt, 1987) p. 275. Fr Richard O'Ferrall's report to the Vatican denigrated those whose political direction was decided by secular considerations rather than by that of the well-being of the Roman Catholic church, Richard O'Ferrall and Robert O'Connell, *Commentarius Rinuccinianus . . .*, ed. Revd Stanislaus Kavanagh (IMC, 6 vols., Dublin, 1932–49), v, p. 504.

[15] *Pádraigín Haicéad*, ll. 109–12, 157–60, pp. 42–3.

a visionary woman who bemoaned the troubles of Ireland from the reign of Henry VIII to the death of Charles I. This work dealt specifically with military aspects of the Confederate Wars, and mentioned individuals who played major roles in the conflict. However the hero was undoubtedly Owen Roe O'Neill whom the poet described in traditional terms as being valorous, strong, proud, handsome and victorious in all circumstances.[16] No vituperative list of his rivals and opponents appears in this poem apart from those over whom he achieved a military victory; nor is mention made of the general's willingness to negotiate with the parliamentary commanders after the summer of 1648.[17] O'Neill's successor, the bishop of Clogher, Eimhear (Ever or Heber) MacMahon, also featured though the poet ignored his controversial appointment and instead mourned his untimely death, together with the losses of Henry Roe O'Neill, son of Owen Roe, and Colonel Hugh Maguire, who all died as a result of the bishop's ill-advised battle with Sir Charles Coote at Scariffhollis in June 1650.

The poet drew attention to the fact that Ireland's miseries largely stemmed from the people themselves; especially their lack of religious and political unity combined with their duplicity and eagerness to collaborate. In particular he singled out those clergy who, contrary to Rinuccini's instructions, adhered to the 'First Ormond Peace' and to the 'Inchiquin Truce'. He used the word 'cuaine' (the semantic range of which includes 'pack', 'brood', 'litter') to describe these reprobates and added that: 'My curse will fall on those members of the clergy / and on their company, until judgement day . . . who brought shame on Ireland / and were in opposition to the Gaelic nobles / upon whom fell the late nuncio's interdict'.[18] Interestingly this is one of the few poems (and the only one published by O'Rahilly) which actually mentions Rinuccini's censure of 1646, which placed all those who favoured the peace with the king under excommunication and suspended the faculties of all priests who accepted it, or his second excommunication order, which applied to those who accepted the truce between Lord Inchiquin and the Confederates.[19]

Despite the deaths of the Ulster leaders at Scariffhollis and the perfidy of the breakaway clergy the poet continued to hope that Aodh Buí O'Neill,

---

[16] The poem was, in this respect, quite specific and the events depicted in Owen Roe's battle-roll can be ascertained from other sources.

[17] For a list of his campaigns see O'Rahilly (ed.), *Political Poems*, ll. 147–53, p. 24; ll. 211–12, p. 27.

[18] *Ibid.*, ll. 250–6, pp. 28–9.

[19] John Lynch in his unpublished account of the bishops of Ireland, 'De praesulibus Hiberniae', completed in France *c.* 1672, noted that this excommunication was not published in the diocese of Ardfert and Aghadoe by the bishop, Dr Richard O'Connell, because of widespread popular support for the Ormond Peace, Denis O'Connor, 'Dr Richard O'Connell and the "New Religion" in Kerry, 1603–1653', *Irish Ecclesiastical Record*, 13 (May 1903), pp. 385–99, p. 397.

Owen Roe's nephew, Colonel Farrell, Hugh O'Byrne and Sir Phelim O'Neill, would lead the people to victory which, in turn, would isolate the English and cut off communications with the Scots.[20] Before long, according to the poet, the English, Calvin and Luther would be held up to ridicule and the Irish nobility, together with the Catholic Church and clergy, would be restored to their former dominant positions.[21]

Séamus Carthún's 'Deor-chaoineadh na hÉireann' [The tearful lament of Ireland] and Anonymous, 'Do chuala scéal do chéas gach ló mé' [I heard tidings that tormented me every day]

In a similar vein these two poems lamented the destruction of the country, the dispossession of her nobles and her clergy together with the general corruption of the legal system and the judiciary. In a familiar dramatic opening the poet recorded how his senses had been disabled with grief because of Ireland's troubles; no people, he argued, had suffered as much since the bondage of the Children of Israel in Egypt.[22] He begged God to help the country, because no physician could heal her wounds, many of which have been self-inflicted and included a lack of unity and trust among the Irish – especially the military leaders.[23] He appealed for salvation and prayed that Ireland would be delivered from her enemies.

This poem, ascribed to Father Séamus Carthún, OFM, is of particular interest since, from other sources, it has been suggested that the putative author was an enthusiastic anti-nuncio activist who wrote 'Deor-chaoineadh na hÉireann' while imprisoned, or under church discipline, in connection with his activities in defiance of Rinuccini.[24] The poet had incurred papal censure and excommunication by adhering to the 'Inchiquin Truce' of 1648 and by encouraging others to defy the nuncio, a scandal described in some detail in *An aphorismical discovery* and *Commentarius Rinuccinianus*.[25] However the poem itself did not refer to the excommunication and might well be regarded as either the work of a person

---

[20] O'Rahilly (ed.), *Political poems*, ll. 268–96, pp. 29–31.

[21] *Ibid.*, ll. 297–312, pp. 31–2.

[22] Mhág Craith (ed.), *Dán na mbráthar mionúr*, I, ll. 13–18, 23–5, 252. Cf. Gratianus Lucius (John Lynch), *Cambrensis Eversus* [St Malo, 1662], ed. and transl. Matthew Kelly (The Celtic Society, Dublin, 1848), III, chap. xxvii, p. 79.

[23] Mhág Craith (ed.), *Dán na mbráthar mionúr*, I, ll. 90–123, pp. 254–5; Cf. O'Rahilly (ed.), *Political poems*, ll. 365–72, p. 76.

[24] Mhág Craith (ed.), *Dán na mbráthar mionúr*, I, pp. 252–5, II, pp. 236–9. A number of Franciscans of that surname are mentioned in *An aphorismical discovery* and it seems likely that the man to whom the poem is attributed is the one of those.

[25] *Commentarius Rinuccinianus*, IV, pp. 50–4.

uncommitted on either side, or a supporter of the bishops who went against the nuncio.

Though dated to the mid-seventeenth century the anonymous 'Do chuala scéal do chéas gach ló mé' did not refer directly to the Eleven Years War as a military event, but instead described the distressed circumstances arising from it, allocating blame and approval in a predominantly religious context.[26] The poet portrayed the country as being tired and beaten, brought down by oppression and distress and dwelt upon the destruction of the church, the dispossession of native Munster lords, the use of unfair, contrived legal procedures and, finally, the exodus of Irish soldiers to continental armies.

The Munster theme is found in three other poems – 'Aiste Dháibhí Cúndún', Seán Ó Conaill's 'Tuireamh na hÉireann' and Éamonn an Dúna's 'Mo lá leóin go deó go n-éagad' – all of which favoured the Old English, whatever their attitude to the nuncio. These looked to the leadership of the local nobility, especially the O'Briens and the MacCarthys, and eloquently defended the Old English, whose virtue they catalogued, while, at the same time, denigrating the 'New English' Protestant settlers as 'rabble', as 'English-speaking bastards' or as 'English-speaking louts' who were neither educated nor of noble blood.[27]

'Aiste Dáibhí Cúndún' [Dáibhí Cúndún's poem]

This poem is of uncertain authorship despite the attribution in the title.[28] It focused on how the wars had affected the Irish social hierarchy: the kingdoms were without a king – which distressed the nobility; while the people, oppressed by war, also remained miserable.[29] The poet specifically referred to the banishment of the nobility beyond the Shannon and to the interruption of traditional, aristocratic pursuits such as hunting, spearcasting, riding, fencing, needlework and studies in liberal arts or languages.[30] He also mourned the sorry condition of the Catholic

[26] Pádraig de Brún, Breandán Ó Buachalla and Tomás Ó Concheanainn, *Nua-dhuanaire* I (Dublin, 1971; reprinted 1986), pp. 31–4, 109.
[27] They favoured Old English families, descended from the Anglo-Normans, as exemplary members of the local nobility. In this they mirrored the preoccupations of Old English apologists like Keating, Lynch and French.
[28] See Geoffrey Keating, *Foras feasa ar Éirinn: the history of Ireland*, ed. David Comyn and P. A. Dineen (4 vols., London, 1902–4), III, p. 369.
[29] O'Rahilly (ed.), *Political poems*, ll. 21–4, p. 36, and cf. Lynch, *Cambrensis Eversus*, II chap. xxv, p. 607, where Lynch outlined how each class was affected: plebians were transported; the rich were taxed; the gentry were harassed; the nobles were insulted; the rights of cities and towns were despoiled and infringed upon; and the nation was treated with contempt.
[30] O'Rahilly (ed.), *Political poems*, ll. 273–80, p. 47.

church which, in the absence of the bishops and priests, had been left a 'widow'.[31]

More specifically the poet listed some of the confederate defeats in Munster at the hands of Lord Inchiquin – the battle of Liscarroll (1642), the retaking of the Castle of Cloghlea (1643), the battle of Knocknanuss (1647) – together with royalist defeats in Leinster, namely the battle of Rathmines (August 1649) and Cromwell's excesses at Drogheda (September 1649).[32] He bemoaned the failure of the earl of Glamorgan's mission in 1645 to secure a suitable compromise between the king and the Catholic party and deeply regretted the 'insult' offered to Rinuccini, who left Ireland after the declaration of the 'Second Ormond Peace' in January 1649, believing his mission a failure.[33] The poem concluded with a prayer that God would see fit to raise some leader from among the Munster nobility, an O'Brien or a MacCarthy who 'would take responsibility at the opportune moment, who would fight this slaughter fiercely and who would banish the ravagers with scourges . . . [then] I would not have my ears battered by anyone, nor let anyone "kick my arse" without a struggle, nor would I allow any English-muttering boor to "break my chaps" without throttling the words in his throat'.[34]

Seán Ó Conaill, 'Tuireamh na hÉireann' [The lament of Ireland]

Though the precise identity of the author of 'Tuireamh na hÉireann' remains unclear, he was probably Seán Ó Conaill a native of County Kerry and a dependent of MacCarthy Mór.[35] Like the others, the poem opened with a dirge about the destruction of the country, the clergy and the people. The poet argued that the war, a direct product of the Protestant Reformation, had been lost through Catholic disunity and political myopia. He lambasted the Cromwellians for transporting civilians to the colonies and swordsmen to the continent and, above all, for banishing the Old English, whom he described as gentle, law-abiding upholders of the church and religion, who had quickly intermarried with the native Irish with the result that 'the Irish were anglicized and the English were hibernicized'.[36] The poet's account of the Nine Years War of the 1590s and the outbreak of the 1641 rebellion could be read as insinuating that he regarded these

---

[31] *Ibid.*, ll. 193–5, p. 44.
[32] *Ibid.*, ll. 230–9, p. 46.
[33] *Ibid.*, ll. 245, p. 46. Also see J. T. Gilbert (ed.), *A Contemporary history of affairs in Ireland* . . . (Irish Archaeological Society, 3 vols., Dublin, 1879), iii, pp. 72–4.
[34] O'Rahilly (ed.), *Political poems*, ll. 296–308, pp. 48–9.
[35] *Ibid.*, pp. 53–4.   [36] *Ibid.*, ll. 280, p. 72.

developments as a little precipitate or ill-judged, while being laudable in the defence of rights and religion.[37] The poet's concluding prayer begged God to forgive the sins and restore the rights of the Irish.

Éamonn an Dúna, 'Mo lá leóin go deó go n-éagad' [My day of sorrow until I die]

Éamonn an Dúna, probably a MacCarthy from County Cork, began 'Mo lá leóin go deó go n-éagad' with a lament about the miserable condition of Ireland. He believed that the war had dismembered the Irish 'body politic': the nation has lost her 'head', Charles I; her 'family', the noble and warrior classes; and her 'spouse', Owen Roe O'Neill.[38] The demise of the great native Gaelic nobles and the Old English families of Munster, whom he described as gentle, generous patrons of the poets, particularly alarmed him, as did the transportation of troops to the continent and the abduction and pressing of private individuals.[39] He decried these injustices at one point in a revealing mixture of English and Irish verse: 'Transport, transplant, mo mheabhair ar Bhéarla./ Shoot him, kill him, strip him, tear him. / A Tory, hack him, hang him, rebel, / a rogue, a thief, a priest, a papist' ['Transport, transplant' is my understanding of English. / Shoot him, kill him, etc.].[40] The poet went on to argue that the unnecessary and over-zealous application of the law, which resulted in hanging for minor offences, robbery of goods and illegal seizures, had impoverished and defeated the Irish.[41] He complained of not being allowed to toast the king at a meal or in a tavern, and of the abuse that the Catholics had suffered at the hands of disrespectful, Protestant sects, who remained ignorant of Roman customs.[42] This vigorous poem concluded with a prayer that God would restore Charles II to his throne and his brother the duke of York, as the champion of the clergy: '[I pray for] . . . your return in force without peril and coming gaily into your rightful patrimony with your king leading before you, and the duke of York a prop of the clergy'.[43]

This poem seems to reflect a clear Old English royalist position. The poet ignored internal Catholic dissension and looked to the restoration of Charles II for the resolution of the nation's trials. Significantly even though he offered no overt support for the nuncio, he hailed Owen Roe as Ireland's 'spouse', which could possibly indicate where the poet's true loyalty lay or

---

[37] *Ibid.*, ll. 321–52, pp. 74–5.
[38] *Ibid.*, ll. 401–4, p. 99.
[39] The poet gave a list of Old English surnames very similar to that in 'Tuireamh na hÉireann', *ibid.*, ll. 381–96, pp. 76–7.
[40] *Ibid.*, ll. 129–32, p. 90.   [41] *Ibid.*, ll. 50–74, p. 88.
[42] *Ibid.*, ll. 189–206, pp. 92–3.   [43] *Ibid.*, ll. 413–16, p. 100.

could be interpreted as an attempt to blend various allegiances into one harmonious strand, something which occurred in late seventeenth-century poetry.

II

Contemporary partisan prose, which either welcomed or rejected Rinuccini's influence, provides a useful contrast for, and context into which to set, the poems. Geoffrey Keating (d. 1644?), was a Tipperary-born priest educated at Bordeaux and is best known for his history of Ireland, *Foras feasa ar Éirinn*, a synthesis of Irish history from earliest times to the Anglo-Norman invasion. Written in defence of the Gaelic and Anglo-Irish against the perceived calumnies of 'New English' historians, it greatly influenced later poets and writers, especially John Lynch (*c.* 1599–*c.* 1673), archdeacon of Tuam, who endorsed Keating's version of Irish history to the extent that he translated *Foras feasa* into Latin.[44] A powerful spokesman for the anti-nuncio position Lynch's best-known work, *Cambrensis Eversus* (St Malo, 1662), was a history of Ireland from earliest times until the mid-1650s, which was self-consciously Old English, though Lynch himself eschewed the category, claiming the right to be known as Irish, without qualification. Yet he wrote *Cambrensis Eversus*, among other reasons, to vindicate the Old Irish and Old English respectively against 'slanders' of Giraldus Cambrensis, and the writings of the New English who used Giraldus' works to vilify all the Irish.[45] For instance, Lynch tried to dissociate the Old English from any involvement in fomenting the Ulster rebellion, continually emphasizing the traditionally *politique* ways of the Old English.[46] He thus distanced himself from the Northern 'commotion' which he described as 'a sedition of the common people, who, when they heard that their properties, religion and lives were doomed to destitution, were suddenly maddened into fury'. In his dedicatory epistle to Charles II he added that 'only the dregs of the people, the rabble of men of ruined fortunes or profligate character, that were hurried on for a moment by the delirious madness . . . were involved in the recent rebellion'.[47]

The 'Munster' poems (outlined above) are echoed in Lynch's descriptions of clerical deprivation, transplantations, transportations and the

---

[44] Even the Anglo-Norman surnames listed by Keating are echoed in 'Mo lá leóin go deó go n-éagad' and 'Tuireamh na hÉireann', Keating, *Foras feasa*, III, pp. 368–9.

[45] Lynch greatly admired Gaelic learning and was a friend of the renowned Gaelic scholar An Dualtach MacFirbhisigh, correspondent and friend of the equally famed scholar Roderick O'Flaherty.

[46] Lynch, *Cambrensis Eversus*, III, chap. xxvii, p. 85.   [47] *Ibid.*, I, pp. 13–15.

rapaciousness of the lowborn foreign newcomers or, in his words, 'swarms of Englishmen, collected from the barbers' shops, and highways, and taverns, and stables and hogsties of England'.[48] Like our poets, Lynch lamented the unfair and ruthless application of the law to dispossess faithful nobles, and considered the indictment of all the Irish indiscriminately in the blame attaching to those who wilfully rebelled against their king (a tiny minority, according to Lynch) to have been 'the most atrocious act of injustice recorded, so far as I am aware, in the annals of the world'.[49] Like the poets Lynch also condemned the Irish failure to unite in opposition to their common foe during the 1640s and asked 'Are not five hundred years powerful enough to make one people of the English and the Irish [i.e. Old English and Old Irish]?'[50] Even though in other works he denounced Rinuccini as the source of political disunity within the Confederation,[51] in *Cambrensis Eversus* he lauded Rinuccini's attempts to 'raise Ireland from her prostrate condition, but the evil genius of the land blasted his exertions and the fond hopes of the Irish . . . '[52] However, rather ironically, the anonymous author of *An aphorismical discovery* condemned Lynch himself as a particularly divisive force and as being among 'the most waueringe, inconstante, mutinous, irregular, illiterat, shamelesse, ungodly, and impious of all the then congregation, the scume of all religiositie, the froathe of all litterature, and the outcast of all ciuill and honorable demeanour, experto crede'.[53]

The works of Nicholas French (1604–78), bishop of Ferns, especially *The vnkinde deserter of loyal men and true frinds* (Paris, 1676), and *A narrative of the earl of Clarendon's settlement and sale of Ireland* (Louvain, 1668), display a slightly different focus of loyalty and political allegiance. Born in Wexford and educated at Louvain (where he later became president of the Irish College), he represented Wexford on the Supreme Council and, despite Rinuccini's opposition, accepted the 'Second Ormond Peace' of January 1649. However, the treatment of Catholic Royalists after the Restoration, which he regarded as unprecedented 'to this day and perhaps our posterity to the Worlds end . . . ' meant that he later regretted his pro-Ormond stance and became, as his vicious attack in *The vnkinde deserter* demonstrated, one of his

---

[48] *Ibid.*, III, chap. xxvii, p. 75.   [49] *Ibid.*,III, chap. xxvii, pp. 108–11.

[50] *Ibid.*, III, chap. xxviii, p. 161.

[51] For instance in his *Alithinologia and Alithinologiae supplementum* (St Malo?). See Patrick J. Corish, 'Two contemporary historians of the confederation of Kilkenny: John Lynch and Richard O'Ferrall', *IHS*, 8 (1953), pp. 226–7, n. 31; and Corish, 'John Callaghan and the controversies among the Irish in Paris, 1648–54', *Irish Theological Quarterly*, 21 (Jan. 1954) 32–50.

[52] Lynch, *Cambrensis Eversus*, II, chap. xxv, p. 737, and compare II, chap. xxiv, pp. 617–21.

[53] Gilbert (ed.), *Contemporary history*, III, p. 74.

most vocal critics.[54] Like Lynch and perhaps like our poet in 'Mo lá leóin go deó go n-éagad', French remained hostile to the Ulster rebellion because he viewed it as the agent of destruction and misery which ushered in an era which confirmed usurpers in unlawful possessions, held loyalty as a crime, and rewarded treason.[55] The disappointments experienced by the Catholic Royalists in Ireland after the Restoration particularly disgusted French and he must have felt as disappointed by the turn of events after 1660 as the author of 'Mo lá leóin go deó go n-éagad' who looked to the return of Charles II as Ireland's salvation. Clearly French held much in common with both pro- and anti-nuncioists and the similarities between French's polemical prose and the poetic diatribe of Seán Ó Conaill leads one to associate the unknown allegiance of the latter with the known sentiments of the former.

One of the most detailed contemporary accounts of the period, written from the point of view of a supporter of Owen Roe O'Neill by someone of both 'ancient' and 'recent Irish' blood, is *An aphorismical discovery of treasonable faction*.[56] It is a very florid account, full of classical and biblical references which abounds with personal insights and subjective comment. The author, who probably served in Ulster possibly under the command of Shane O'Hagan, clearly enjoyed royalist, pro-nuncio sympathies and contended that the country was never militarily conquered but simply strategically occupied because of the internal disputes among the Irish: 'what was won by the policie and craft of the one, and lost by the simplicitie and disunion of the other, onely the Neylls never condescended to any such bargaine'.[57] The allegiances outlined in *An aphorismical discovery*, which insist on the supremacy of the O'Neill family, especially Owen Roe, resembled those described in 'An Síogaí Romhánach'. Both accounts eulogized Owen Roe: the poet believed that 'His death is of no moment at all to me, since it is not that the foreigners killed him, but that God, who wished to deliver him, called him to heaven to be among the saints';[58] while, the author of *An aphorismical discovery* portrayed Owen Roe as having been too good for earthly trials. 'Some deeminge God in his divine clemencie, not to deale soe straight with this poore nation, as to bereaue them of this

[54] Nicholas French, *A narrative of the earl of Clarendon's settlement and sale of Ireland* (Louvain, 1668), p. 33.
[55] 'When the Presbyterians practises and Covenant began to disturb these Kingdoms, the Papists and Prelatiques in Ireland . . . joyned their hearts and hands against presbytery for the King . . . but this their design was quashed by an inconsiderate attempt by some Northern Gentlemen, which occasioned the late rebellion', French, *Settlement and sale*, p. 35.
[56] Gilbert (ed.), *Contemporary history*, I, pp. viii–xi, 9.
[57] *Ibid.*, I, pp. viii–ix, and II, pp. 26–8. Quote from I, p. 3.
[58] O'Rahilly (ed.), *Political poems*, ll. 202–4, pp. 26–7.

theire onely champion, rather the worlde beinge not worthy of soe good a masterpeece, lulled him asleepe, snatched him away to some secret corner of the world . . . to keepe him there for future better purposes'.[59] However, unlike the poet, the author of *An aphorismical discovery* outlined in minute detail his fealty to Owen Roe and blamed his successor, the bishop of Clogher, for the slaughter of the remnants of O'Neill's army at Scariffhollis, claiming that the misfortune can be attributed to the 'ill manage of one man too much given to his owne opinion'.[60] These distinct prejudices and biases are absent from most of the poems which remain deliberately vague.

Equally biased, this time in favour of Rinuccini, upon whose personal papers it was based, is *Commentarius Rinuccinianus* which affirmed the position of the extreme nuncioist party and asserted that the Old Irish adhered more consistently to Rome than the Old English. This work divided the inhabitants of Ireland into three groups, the Old Irish, the Anglo-Irish and the English. It condemned the Anglo-Irish for consistently siding with the English against the Old Irish, even when common religious concerns should have drawn them together, and argued that their temporizing and materialism sundered the Confederation and destroyed the common front which the Catholics had enjoyed against their heretical English foe. Hardly surprisingly the *Commentarius*, unlike 'An Síogaí Rómhánach', adopted a doctrinaire position as regards adherence to the nuncio, and in this is closest to Haicéad's and to the author of the *An aphorismical discovery*.

Most extreme of all, however, was a controversial text written by Father Conor Mahony (b. *c.* 1594), a County Cork Jesuit who spent his adult life in Portugal. His 130-page tract *Disputatio apologetica de jure regni Hiberniae* was a separatist document, which urged the Irish to abandon allegiance to the heretical Charles I and to chose a king from amongst their native nobility. Disgusted by it, the Supreme Council burned it in Kilkenny, and certainly none of the poems discussed here reflect its radical proposals. Though a maverick document in its time, Mahony's work could be seen as a reasonably logical expression of the many abortive plots and plans which

---

[59] Gilbert (ed.), *Contemporary history*, II, pp. 62–3.
[60] This account made much of an old Irish saint's prophecy predicting defeat for those who travelled from Monaghan to Derry to give battle. While Owen Roe's son, Henry Roe O'Neill took the prediction seriously, the bishop ignored it, with disastrous results, see Gilbert (ed.), *Contemporary history*, II, pp. 84–8. Such prophecies of defeat and victory were very common and similar claims were made for the death of Alasdair MacColla MacDonald, see David Stevenson, *Alasdair MacColla and the Highland problem in the seventeenth century* (Edinburgh, 1980) p. 219; while seer Allan Dubh Cameron of Lochiel predicted Argyll's defeat at the battle of Inverlochy, *ibid.*, p. 154.

had kept Irish exiles in Europe busy since the 'Flight of the Earls' in 1607.[61] No doubt John Lynch had Conor O'Mahony's extremist plans that the Irish elect their own king in mind when he declared: 'Yet this obtrusive king-maker, [Constantinus] Marulus [Mahony], duns his reader ... with arguments as useless for persuasion as they are absurd in principle, propounding the foolish and criminal project that the Irish would select some of their own plebeians for the crown, and depose King Charles, whose ancestors' brows have been adorned with it during several centuries'.[62]

III

The political poetry of some contemporary royalist English poets, such as Abraham Cowley (d. 1667), also displayed many of the characteristics of the Irish verses.[63] For instance they shared similar views on Cromwell's policy of transportation; 'all murdering, and all torturing', Cowley wrote, 'is more Humane and more supportable, than his selling of Christians, Englishmen, Gentlemen; his selling of them (oh monstrous! oh incredible!) to be slaves in America'.[64] The vigour, the venom, the obsession with social standing and noble blood, and the abhorrence of radical, religious sects, displayed in Cowley's poems 'The Puritan' and 'The Civil War', bear a superficial comparison, at least, with the Irish 'political poems'. He lambasted Luther, Calvin, Zwingli and several other zealots together with other baseborn men who supported the Parliamentarians, as the heroes of the 'Mechanicks' and, in 'The Civil War', agreed entirely with the Irish poets that the Cromwellian hordes remained beneath contempt.[65] His contention that even in death, the noble blood of the Royalists refused to mix with the base fluids of the Parliamentarians gelled well with contemporary royalist opinion in Ireland: '... and fate / ... sets us here a rate / Too deare a rate she sets and we must pay / One honest man for ten such slaves as they. / Streames of blacke tainted blood the field besmeare, / But pure welcolour'd Drops shine here and there. / They scorne to mix with floods of baser veines / Just as th'ignobler Moistures Oyle disdaines.' And: 'What

[61] See Tomás O Fiaich, 'Republicanism and separatism in the seventeenth century', *Léachtaí Cholm Cille II* (Maynooth, 1971), pp. 74–87.
[62] *Cambrensis Eversus*, III, p. 69.
[63] See Michelle O Riordan, 'A seventeenth-century "political poem"', in Myrtle Hill and Sarah Barber, (eds.), *Aspects of Irish studies* (Belfast, 1990), pp. 117–26.
[64] Abraham Cowley, *Essays, plays and sundry verses*, ed. A. R. Waller (Cambridge, 1906), p. 370.
[65] See, for instance, above Éamonn an Dúna's 'Mo lá leóin go deó go n-éagad' in O'Rahilly (ed.), *Political poems*, ll. 289–304, pp. 95–6.

should I here their Great ones Names reherse? / Low, wretched Names, unfit for noble Verse.'[66]

The seventeenth century was the last period in Irish history when the Gaelic literati and literary members of the Roman Catholic clergy, both Gaelic and Old English, were linked by ties of culture, blood and aspirations to the provincial and for a time, national rulers, and when their writings reflected closely aspects of the political aims of those groups. The catharsis of the collapse of Gaelic Ireland is not realized in a politically precocious way in the contemporary Gaelic 'political' poetry examined here. Clearly the poems articulate the aspirations of both the pro- and anti-nuncio parties in Ireland, but no composition adopted the extreme position of either side. Thus no poem which I have associated with the Old English denigrates Owen Roe O'Neill or the Ulster party, while no work favouring the nuncio's party called for the proclamation of a native king or allocated blame for the defeat of the Confederacy to the Old English. What they provide is a pointer to the direction in which Gaelic letters was about to proceed; the discourse of defeat taking the place of the vigour and hubris of poets' vainglorious compositions when all was yet to be played for.

[66] Abraham Cowley, *The civil war*, ed. Allan Pritchard (Toronto, 1980), Book I, ll. 273–80, p. 80 and Book III, ll. 383–4, p. 117

CHAPTER 7

STRAFFORD'S GHOST: THE BRITISH CONTEXT OF VISCOUNT LISLE'S LIEUTENANCY OF IRELAND

JOHN ADAMSON

The very same Instruments who did cooperate with th[']erle of Strafford, and wear promoted by him for bribery, are still spetially trusted and imploied.

[Viscount Valentia] to Sir Philip Perceval, 4 August 1647.[1]

AS A brittle peace was established in England and Scotland during 1646, Catholic Ireland once again confronted the threat of a renewed British offensive to reduce it from independence to foreign rule. For the first time since 1642, large-scale military operations in Ireland became a viable proposition for the two Protestant kingdoms of Britain. At the same time a question of fundamental importance was brought starkly into the light: the terms under which the Irish rebellion was to be suppressed would have a profound impact on the post-war relations between all three Stuart kingdoms. Would Ireland retain a measure of the autonomy that had been established by the Confederacy, or would it lose even its status as a dependent kingdom, declining still further to the rank of a colony?[2] For the victorious English Parliamentarians and the Covenanter Scots there was another question. How was Ireland to be pacified? By conciliation between the disparate groups of confederate Catholics, Ormondist Royalists, Ulster Scots and beleaguered Protestants still loyal to the Parliament at Westminster? Or would there be a new conquest: an act of righteous Protestant revenge for the 'massacres' of 1641? And if Ireland was to be

[1] BL, Add. MSS 46,931/B, fo. 148. I am grateful to the editor, to Professor Robert Ashton, Professor Alan Macinnes and to Dr T. C. Barnard for reading and commenting on an earlier draft of this essay. For reasons of editorial consistency, the spelling 'Perceval' has been adopted for all members of this family throughout this book; but it should be noted that the spelling found in Sir Philip's signature is 'Percivalle'.

[2] On the status of Ireland in the seventeenth century, see Patrick Kelly, 'Ireland and the Glorious Revolution: from kingdom to colony', in Robert Beddard (ed.), *The revolutions of 1688* (Oxford, 1991), pp. 163–90.

reconquered, no less fraught with distinctively British implications lay the problem of how this could be achieved. Was Scotland to assert its new-found equality with England under the Solemn League and Covenant of 1643 and the treaties between the two kingdoms (reaffirmed as recently as January 1646) by taking a major role in a joint offensive against the Irish rebels?[3] Or was the new conquest to be an exclusively English affair, reducing Ireland once again to the status of a client kingdom of England, and confirming Westminster as the centre of power within the Stuart monarchies?

This chapter considers the political processes by which those questions came to be defined, and examines the period during which many of their answers came to be determined: the years between the parliamentarian victory in England and the establishment of a new parliamentarian lord lieutenancy of Ireland in 1646, and the recrudescence of a new phase of war in all three kingdoms in 1648.

I

The Irish were now better armed and more proficient in war than at any time 'since the Conquest':[4] such was the terse assessment in December 1646 delivered to the Derby House Committee, the principal English body administering preparations for the forthcoming Irish campaign. In Leinster, the Catholic forces held almost the whole province except for Dublin and part of the Pale (which remained under the control of the marquis of Ormond); in Connacht, they were master of all but Sligo Fort and half a dozen other strongholds; and in Munster, they controlled the important garrison towns of Limerick and Waterford and almost all the province except for Cork, Kinsale and Youghal. Only in Ulster was there an extensive tract of the kingdom not yet in Confederate hands.[5] Yet for the English Parliamentarians, even this area of Protestant domination was problematic, for it was controlled by the Scots. By December 1646, there were seventeen regiments of foot (or roughly 8,000 men), 'whereof of the Scotch army entermixt with the inhabitants [there were] 3,500; and of

---

[3] C[ommons] J[ournal], IV, p. 394: on 3 January 1646 the Commons resolved that an act should be passed by the Parliaments of England and Scotland for confirmation of the Large Treaty of 1641, the treaty concerning Ireland of 6 August 1642 (for the bringing of 10,000 Scots into Ulster) and the Anglo-Scottish treaty of 29 November 1643.

[4] Bodl., Carte MSS 19, fo. 605: report on the state of Ireland by Arthur Annesley, Sir William Parsons, Sir Adam Loftus, Sir John Temple and Sir Hardresse Waller, 10 December 1646.

[5] Bodl., Carte MSS 19, fo. 604r–v.

the Old Brittish [English and Scottish settlers in Ulster], 5,000' – besides a further 850 horse.[6] By the time the English Parliament confronted the question of renewing the war in Ireland it seemed axiomatic that Scottish forces would play a major part in any forthcoming campaign.

Beyond that, however, what the English Parliament's policy should be towards Ireland remained anything but clear. Parliamentary debates on the subject revealed the same tensions over what was the appropriate way to run the war-effort that had hitherto dogged the conduct of the English conflict: should war be prosecuted to an 'absolute victory' – 'regayning the whole kingdom into [the] just subjeccon to the Crowne of England', as the aim was summarized in a report prepared by Sir John Temple and other leading Protestant counsellors;[7] or might there be room for some element of negotiation and compromise, if not with the Catholic Confederacy, then at least with the Protestant 'royalist' interest in Ireland, the party led by Charles I's nominee as lord lieutenant, the marquis of Ormond? Would the new war be an exclusively English campaign, or could there be a 'British offensive' – that is, an Anglo-Scottish war-effort – against the Catholic Confederacy: a combination of a parliamentarian army and Ormondist Protestants, in alliance with the Ulster Scots, to restore Ireland to obedience – but which stopped short of the wholesale plunder of Old English estates that the Adventurers' schemes for 'conquest' seemed to entail?[8]

In the spring of 1646 it was far from certain – perhaps far from likely – that Ireland would ever be subject to a thorough-going 'reconquest'. For all the acquisitiveness of the Adventurers, neither the original Adventurers' Ordinance of 1642, nor the so-called 'Doubling Ordinance' of 14 July 1643 (which was dismally undersubscribed), had raised more than a fraction of the actual costs of the Irish war-effort.[9] By the summer of 1645, relations between Parliament and the Adventurers were distinctly cool. When, in November 1645, William Hawkins, the London merchant and spokesman for the investors, presented their demands for the massive extension of the policy of confiscation, it is telling that the Parliament at first rejected them

---

[6] *Ibid.*, fo. 605.   [7] *Ibid.*, fo. 606.

[8] The implications of such a conquest for the land settlement in Ireland were, however, complex. Conquest opened up the way to a large military presence which was most conveniently recompensed with Irish land, and which could, in turn, compete with the Adventurers. See T. C. Barnard, *Cromwellian Ireland: English government and reform in Ireland, 1649–1660* (Oxford, 1975).

[9] K. S. Bottigheimer, *English money and Irish land: the 'Adventurers' in the Cromwellian settlement of Ireland* (Oxford, 1971), p. 85. On the so-called 'additional sea adventure to Ireland', see Robert Brenner, *Merchants and revolution: commercial change, political conflict, and London's overseas traders, 1550–1653* (Cambridge, 1993), pp. 400–10.

out of hand.[10] The Adventurers alone were in no position to stipulate the terms of a new English conquest of Ireland.

And if Ireland had to be reduced to obedience, then obedience to what? How were Ireland's colonial spoils to be shared out between the two Protestant British kingdoms? Scotland, which had made so conspicuous a contribution to the Protestant war-effort in Ulster, had an obvious claim to a share in the exploitation of Ireland. A re-assertion of an exclusive English overlordship of Ireland, such as had prevailed until 1641, not only flew in the face of all England's commitments under the Anglo-Scottish treaties, but would also entail military expenditure on a prodigious scale at the very time when opinion in England was turning firmly against further military taxation.

Within the English Parliament attitudes towards the Irish were equally divided. Here the influence of Sir John Temple has had an abiding effect on the historiography, leaving the impression that opinion at Westminster was overwhelmingly in favour of a new English conquest. The impression has been created that in 1646 MPs were united in the belief that Catholic guilt for the 'massacres' of Protestants in 1641 could only be expiated by Irish blood, and that Irish Royalists (whether Protestant or not) who had connived in Ormond's 1643 cessation with the Confederates were effectively seen as 'accessories after the fact' (also see chapters 2 and 11). Yet within the parliamentarian party, attitudes to Ormond were sharply divided. Despite his acquiescence in the 1643 cessation, he had maintained high-level contacts at Westminster – particularly with the bi-cameral interest led by the earl of Essex and Denzell Holles which, throughout the years 1643–6, had sought to promote a lenient agreement with the king. Essex was himself the half-brother of a Catholic Anglo-Irish peer, the marquis of Clanricard: a loyal Ormondist and the only leading Catholic landed magnate prepared to challenge the Confederacy. Essex held Clanricard's proxy in the English House of Lords and had attempted to use it as recently as March 1645 in a bid to prevent the adoption of Fairfax's officer-list for the New Model Army. Ormond's principal man of business in London, William Perkins,[11] was in fact one of Essex's household servants

---

[10] PRO, SP 63/261/9, pp. 55–9 (*Cal. S P Ire., 1633–47* [London, 1901], p. 418). Cf. *The state of the Irish affairs, for the honourable members of the Houses of Parliament* ([2 January] 1645[/6]), BL, E 314/7.

[11] Bodl., Carte MSS 1, fo. 171: Ormond to Perkins, 16 July 1639; NLI, Ormond MSS 2307, fo. 81: Perkins to Ormond, 29 June 1641; HMC, *Calendar of the manuscripts of the marquis of Ormond*, ns (8 vols., London, 1902–20), I, p. 112: Perkins to Ormond, 23 March 1647; House of Lords RO, M[ain] P[apers], 22 June 1648, fo. 123 (*L[ords] J[ournal]*, x, p. 341). (I owe the first three of these references to the kindness of Mr W. P. Kelly.)

and operated in the capital, under Essex's protection, on Ormond's behalf.[12]

There were of course sound political reasons for Parliamentarians maintaining links with the king's lord lieutenant. After the collapse of the royalist cause in England in the summer of 1646, there was speculation that Ormond would place Dublin under parliamentarian protection and join forces with the victors in the English Civil War to take the offensive against the Confederates. Ormond's announcement, in September 1646, that he was at last prepared to consider placing Dublin under English control initiated a protracted series of proposals and counter-proposals which did not approach resolution until April 1647. But even before these negotiations were concluded there were numerous instances of co-operation between Ormond and the English parliamentary commissioners in Belfast: in October 1646, for instance, they ordered the English fleet to relieve Ormond's garrison with urgently needed supplies of gunpowder.[13] And for all his loyalty to the king's cause, Ormond nevertheless enjoyed a high reputation at Westminster. That hard-nosed New Model Army officer, Major-General Philip Skippon, spoke warmly of him in November 1646;[14] and one officer could write to him, without undue hyperbole, in January 1647, as the negotiations for the surrender of Dublin dragged on: 'Greate Lord, had your Lo[rdshi]pp improved your oppertunitye in deliveringe of Dublin to the Parliament, noe man could ever have won the Hearts of all Honest people in England more then yow'.[15] In the spring of 1647, there was every possibility that this was an 'opportunity' which Ormond might yet exploit.

For if the English were not to ally with the marquis, there was every indication that Monro's Scottish army in Ulster would. By the end of the autumn of 1646, the Ulster Scots' sympathies were clearly inclining more to an alliance with the Ormondist cause than to maintenance of the increasingly strained alliance with the English Parliamentarians. As Ormond himself observed in October 1646, 'The Scottish officers will not refuse us [Ormond's forces at Dublin] help when they see (as I am confident they will) wee are able to preserve our selves'.[16] He did not have

---

[12] BL, Add. MSS 5497, fo. 93v: Perkins's signature to receipts for monies due to Essex, 17 April 1644. In November 1645, the House of Lords ordered that he be discharged from legal process by writ of habeas corpus, 'he being a servant of the earl of Essex'. *LJ*, VIII, p. 4.

[13] Bodl., Carte MSS 19, fo. 161: Ormond to Lord Digby (draft), 12 October 1646.

[14] *Ibid.*, fo. 402: Sir William Parsons to Ormond, 16 November 1646.

[15] Bodl., Carte MSS 20, fo. 212: [Capt?] Matthew Wood to Ormond, 29 January 1647.

[16] Bodl., Carte MSS 19, fo. 161: Ormond to Digby (draft), 12 October 1646.

to wait long for this prognosis to be proved accurate. By November 1646, Monro had offered precisely such a conjunction: 'for wee consider our selves to be soe weakned by our sending of men into Scotland, and our losse receaved in the Fields', he wrote to Ormond, 'as without the coniunction of the Brittishe in these partes wee cannot be assuired of our maintenance heir'.[17]

For the English Parliamentarians, pursuit of such an alliance with Ormond would inevitably constitute a rebuff to the Adventurers, for it effectively ruled out a 'conquest' and large-scale confiscations of Irish lands. As we have seen, the Adventurers' own bargaining position was relatively weak, and so long as the support of the Old Protestant community could be secured in reducing Ireland to obedience to English (or to Anglo-Scottish) rule, there was little motive for honouring the commitment to massive confiscations of Irish land which the Adventurers' ordinances (and, still more, the Adventurers' proposals of November 1645 for yet further confiscations) had entailed.[18] Even so prominent a war-party man as Henry Marten – someone whom D'Ewes regarded as amongst the hottest of the 'fiery spirits' – sneered at the quixotic crusading zeal of those pressing for a new conquest of Ireland. In a series of notes, dating from late 1646 or early 1647, apparently intended for a speech on the instructions to be given to the commissioners to negotiate with Ormond, Marten put the case for offering negotiations with the Ormondists: 'Upon the wholl matter, I conceive it most acceptable to God and Christ, most agreeable with common iustice, most consistent with the rules of policy, if not to graunt them almost any termes for peace, at least to hearken to their demaunds in order thereunto, which, for ought wee know, may be reasonable, or if wee think they cannot be, let [us] contrive some propositions of our own, and admitt of peace upon them.' Marten was equally astringent against those who sought to turn the war in Ireland into a religious crusade: 'Hee that would state the quarrell in Ireland upon religion and thinkes this way to make all Christendome a protestant is discended sure from those gallant ancestors that ly burryed in Palestine, whither they were carryed with a forward desire to recover the holy land, and beat the wholl world into Christianity.'[19] While we should be wary of regarding Marten as

[17] *Ibid.*, fo. 328: Monro and other Scottish officers to Ormond, 10 November 1646.
[18] PRO, SP 63/261/9, pp. 55–9 (*Cal. S P Ire., 1633–47*, p. 418). For the Old English, see Aidan Clarke, *The Old English in Ireland, 1625–42* (Ithaca and London, 1966), chapter 12; Clarke, 'Colonial identity in early seventeenth-century Ireland', in T. W. Moody (ed.), *Nationality and the pursuit of independence. Historical Studies* XI (Belfast, 1978), pp. 57–71.
[19] Brotherton Library, University of Leeds, Marten MSS Box 78, fo. 13.

representative of parliamentary opinion in general, his crisp observations serve as a corrective to the view that the English Parliament was hell-bent on a crusade against popery in Ireland, or necessarily united in its support for the policy of conquest that Cromwell was to effect from 1649.

Many questions remained open. But at least two characteristics of the forthcoming campaign seemed clear: first, the new offensive would entail a conjunction between an English expeditionary force and the British Protestant forces already in Ireland (principally, Monro's Scottish forces in the north and the Munster Protestants under Lord Inchiquin); and second, if less certainly, that there would be some form of *rapprochement* between the Westminster Parliament and Ormond – a negotiation which, at the very least, was likely to act as a brake on the colonizing designs of the Adventurers, and to offer some measure of protection to the interests of the Old English.

Yet the strategy for the campaign against Ireland which was adopted at Westminster during the winter of 1646–7 – and which was ultimately to be realized in the Cromwellian conquest of 1649–50 – gave the lie to all these expectations. It repudiated the two key elements implicit in the thinking which had been dominant hitherto, aspects which seemed so eminently practical as to be almost axiomatic: that the offensive to defeat the Confederates should be a British venture, and that Ormond, Ireland's greatest Protestant magnate, was a natural ally in any projected campaign. Instead, the group which had emerged at Westminster in control of English policy towards Ireland by the end of 1646 repudiated both these principles. It advocated an entirely English campaign to subjugate Ireland – to the exclusion of the Scots from any part in the expected victory over the rebels; it viewed any collaboration with Ormond with distinct hostility; and, still more controversially, advocated a 'scorched-earth' solution to the problem of Ireland: conquest, confiscation, and colonization. The adoption of this policy was to send a seismic shock through all three Stuart kingdoms, and to lay bare the fault-lines in the Parliament's alliances, both in Ireland and in Scotland. But before examining this policy's consequences we must first consider two other questions. Who were this policy's advocates? And what were the ideas which moved them to adopt so draconian a solution to the 'settlement' of Ireland?

II

The moment at which parliamentarian policy concerning Ireland took definite shape was January 1646, with the decision to appoint a new commander-in-chief for the projected Irish campaign and to invest him with the powers, and later with the title, of lord lieutenant.[20] Nominated to Strafford's former office, on 21 January 1646,[21] was the twenty-seven-year-old nephew of the earl of Northumberland, Philip Sidney, Viscount Lisle,[22] an officer who had served under Strafford in the war against the Scots of 1640, and was the son and heir of the second earl of Leicester – himself one of Strafford's closest allies at court during the 1630s. Moreover, Lisle, like his uncle Northumberland, was to be closely identified with the anti-Scottish party at Westminster and with the political Independents: with the interest associated in the Commons with St John, the younger Vane, and Sir John Evelyn of Wiltshire, and, more generally, with leading officers of the New Model Army. Northumberland, not eight months earlier, had played a decisive part in the creation of that army, and was one of the most active members of the Lords engaged in dealing with Irish affairs. It was to Northumberland that Lord Broghill, one of the leading commanders in Munster and soon to be one of Lisle's principal allies in Ireland, had turned in 1645, confident that the earl would 'powerfully sollicite' Parliament for military relief to be sent to the province.[23]

Lisle came to be seen not merely as a prospective commander-in-chief in Ireland, but as the emissary of a particular interest at Westminster: he was identified with the anti-Scottish interest, with the Independents, and with what the diarist Thomas Juxon called 'Ld Northumberland's partie'.[24] As Sir William Parsons reported to Ormond of politics in England: 'The 2 visible parties spoken of to support the divisions are the presbytery and the independency, and under theis denominacons yt is thought do all other lesser divisions and partialities ranke themselves, as occasion serves.'[25] The

[20] BL, Add. MSS 31,116 (Whitaker diary), p. 503: There was 'a very long debate both forenoon and afternoon whether the government of Ireland should be committed to the hands of one person', Laurence Whitaker noted in his diary for 5 January, and only 'upon the dividing of the House' was it 'resolved for one person'. The division, which evidently took place while the House was in committee of the whole, is not recorded in the Journal: *CJ*, IV, p. 397.
[21] *CJ*, IV, p. 413.
[22] Something of the intimacy between Lisle and Northumberland is suggested by the celebrations attending the baptism of Lisle's first son in January 1647, on the eve of Lisle's departure for Munster to take up his command as lord lieutenant. Lisle named his son Algernon after his uncle, Northumberland, who also stood as god-parent to the child (HMC, *Report on the manuscripts of Viscount De L'Isle*, VI [London, 1966], pp. 560–1: Leicester's diary), and Northumberland, with appropriate avuncular concern, duly paid the fees of Lady Lisle's nurse and midwife (Alnwick Castle, Northumberland acc., U. I. 6 [Lancelot Thornton acc. to 17 January 1648]: £10 to Lady Lisle's nurse and midwife).
[23] BL, Add. MSS 25,287 (Broghill letter-book, 1644–9), fo. 32v: Broghill to Northumberland, [before December 1645]. In October 1647, one of Lord Broghill's gentlemen presented Northumberland with the gift of a bay horse: Petworth House, MS 333: stable acc. of Charles Kirke, entry for 20 October 1647.
[24] Dr Williams's Library, MS 24.50 (Juxon diary), fo. 100.
[25] Bodl., Carte MSS 19, fo. 402v: Sir William Parsons to Ormond, 16 November 1646.

names of the peers signing the warrants to Lisle's deputy treasurer-at-wars, Nicholas Loftus,[26] surviving in the State Papers for the autumn of 1646, read almost as a roll-call of 'the Ld Northumberland's partie' in the House of Lords: Northumberland himself, Salisbury, Saye and Sele, Kent, Nottingham, Howard of Escrick, Denbigh and Pembroke.[27] And it is a reminder of the close links between this aristocratic faction and the army of Sir Thomas Fairfax that all but one of these peers had voted, in March 1645, in favour of the creation of the New Model Army and the de facto exclusion of Scots from the ranks of its officer-corps.[28] From the moment of Lisle's arrival in Ireland in February 1647, the recurrent charge levelled against him was that his 'conquest' of Ireland was part of a larger design to entrench a single faction as the dominant political interest within England and Ireland.

The new lord lieutenant was to enjoy the symbols, and many of the powers, of regality. In December 1646, the Committee for Irish Affairs at Derby House decreed that a sword of state was to be borne before the new lord lieutenant as an 'Ensigne of honour and Authority';[29] and in January 1647, another meeting approved the list of what the Derby House Committee designated Lisle's 'Privy Councillors for Ireland' – the first body to bear that title without the prior approval of the king.[30] Lisle was to be authorized to issue grants under the Irish great seal; and, like Strafford before him, was to wield extensive powers of patronage over appointments to military and, once Ireland was pacified, to civil offices. The aspirations of Hawkins's supporters amongst the Adventurers for a 'commander-in-chief to be appointed with very full civil and military powers', as demanded in November 1645, were now fulfilled.[31] Moreover, given that the bulk of

---

[26] PRO, SP 16/539/Part 3, fos. 217, 219, 221.

[27] PRO, SP 16/539/Part 3, fos. 252–9: warrants from 4 August to 19 October 1646. That this group of peers justified Juxon's description as a 'party' may be confirmed by the fact that, with few exceptions, they voted as a single block throughout the period 1645–7: see J. S. A. Adamson, 'The peerage in politics, 1645–49' (PhD thesis, Cambridge University, 1986), appendices.

[28] *LJ*, VII, p. 297. The one exception then was Denbigh; and even he had become, by the autumn of 1646, a close political ally of this group.

[29] PRO, SP 21/26 (Derby House Committee, mins.), p. 2.

[30] *Ibid.*, p. 5. For the meetings of Lisle's council in Ireland: BL, Add. MSS 46,931/A, fos. 160–1: Henry Whaley to the lord mayor and aldermen of London, [?] Mar. 1647; HMC, *De L'Isle*, VI, p. 566: Leicester's diary. Some members of Lisle's council were pre-war appointees as Privy Councillors for Ireland; the new men, named without royal sanction, were Arthur Annesley, Sir Gregory Norton and Richard Salway. (I am grateful to Dr T. C. Barnard for a discussion on this point.)

[31] PRO, SP 63/261/9, pp. 55–9: 11 Nov. 1645 (*Cal. S P Ire., 1633–47*, p. 418). I am unable wholly to agree with Professor Bottigheimer's conclusion that Lisle's appointment to the lieutenancy was a rebuff to the Adventurers (*English money and Irish land*, p. 97). To judge from their public

the new Irish expeditionary force was expected to be drawn from the ranks of the New Model Army, so long as Lisle remained lord lieutenant, it was under his overall command that the army expected to serve – even if generalship in the field went to the army's proven senior officers. The question of who was to be lord lieutenant of Ireland thus had implications which went far beyond the immediate military problem of the suppression of the rebellion. Once the armies in England were disbanded at the end of its civil war, the 'chief governor of Ireland' and his army would be the English Parliament's major standing army; it was likely to become the lynch-pin upon which would depend the security of the post-war Parliamentarian government in England. As William Warner had advised as early as the 1580s, 'Whoso England will subdue, with Ireland must begin.'[32]

But there was another aspect of this political configuration that is perhaps less obvious: its relation to the Straffordian interest of the late 1630s. So effectively was Strafford cast in parliamentary mythology as the archetypal villain of the Personal Rule that it is easy to overlook the fact that there were strong continuities, in both policy and personnel, between the Straffordian interest of 1639–40 and the junto which emerged in control of parliamentarian Irish policy at the end of the First English Civil War. It is easy to forget that Northumberland, one of the most influential parliamentarian figures at Westminster during the 1640s, had been among Strafford's closest political allies during the 1630s; that he had shared Strafford's deep-seated hostility to Presbyterianism and to the Scots, and had concerted plans with him in the late 1630s to employ the Irish army to quell the Covenanter revolt.[33] And in the preparations to suppress the Scottish resistance in 1640, it was Strafford who had served as the trusted lieutenant-general to Northumberland, the lord general appointed for that campaign. In electoral politics, Northumberland seems to have used his local

---

statements, the Adventurers were divided as to their intentions for the government of Ireland. One group of Adventurers clearly would have preferred the powers of chief governor to be placed in commission (*The state of the Irish affairs*, p. 21); others – and, in particular, those supporting William Hawkins – believed that overall command should be consolidated in the hands of a single person. Lisle and his principal adviser, Sir John Temple, stood for precisely the programme of thorough-going conquest that these Adventurers hoped to see pursued; indeed, Hawkins's proposals of November 1645 may have been timed to advantage Lisle's candidature for the lieutenancy.

32 William Warner, *Albions England* (1596 edn.), Bk. x, p. 242; quoted in C. Hill, *A nation of change and novelty* (London, 1990), p. 133.
33 William Knowler (ed.), *The earl of Strafforde's letters and dispatches* . . . (2 vols., London, 1739) II, p. 186. 'No foreign Enemies could threaten so much Danger to this Kingdom as doth now this beggarly Nation', Northumberland had written to Wentworth of the Scots in July 1638.

patronage to secure Strafford's secretary of state, Sir Philip Manwaring, a seat at Morpeth in the Short Parliament of April that year; and at court Strafford correspondingly supported the interests of Northumberland and of Northumberland's brother-in-law, the earl of Leicester. In February 1640, on the resignation of Sir John Coke, Strafford backed Leicester to succeed Coke as secretary of state.[34] And, as we have seen, Viscount Lisle was an intimate of this circle and had served under Strafford in the second Bishops' War.[35] Hostility to the Scots remained an abiding feature of this group into the 1640s. At the end of the war of 1642–6 in England, Lisle's ascendancy was to mark a decisive shift in English policy towards Scottish involvement in Ireland – a return to the policy of excluding Scots from exercising influence in Ireland, military or economic, which had been one of the axioms of Strafford's rule.

It was in the course of 1646, as preparations for Lisle's intended campaign proceeded at a Sisyphean pace, that the implications of Lisle's lieutenancy for the future government of Ireland were gradually revealed. This process of redefinition was itself merely one instalment in a much older controversy over the status of, and treatment appropriate to, the Irish, to which Edmund Spenser's *View of the present state of Ireland* of 1596 – that handbook for the scorched-earth solution of the Irish problem – had been the most notorious contribution.[36] From the end of 1645, Lisle and his propagandists set about redefining the English Parliament's war-aims in Ireland in a distinctively Spenserian form. His circle during the 1640s contained two of the most influential contemporary exponents of this draconian approach to the government of Ireland: William Hawkins, the Adventurers' spokesman who had first proposed the massive extension of confiscations of Irish land in November 1645; and Sir John Temple, whose account of the Irish 'rebellion' appeared in April 1646, at the beginning of Lisle's term of office as lord lieutenant.[37] Both men were long-standing Sidney retainers: Hawkins serving as solicitor to Lisle's father, the earl

---

[34] C. V. Wedgwood, *Thomas Wentworth, first earl of Strafford, 1593–1641: a revaluation* (London, 1961), p. 274.

[35] For Strafford's residence at Leicester House, see Strafford's letters to Sir George Radcliffe, 2, 19 May, 11 June 1640: T. D. Whitaker (ed.), *The life and original correspondence of Sir George Radcliffe* (London, 1810), pp. 199–201; Hull RO, BRL (Hull corporation corr.) p. 299: Strafford to Hull corporation, 15 July 1640.

[36] Brendan Bradshaw, 'Robe and sword in the conquest of Ireland', in Claire Cross, David Loades, and J. J. Scarisbrick (eds.), *Law and government under the Tudors* (Cambridge, 1988), p. 162. Edmund Spenser, *View of the present state of Ireland*, ed. W. L. Renwick (Oxford, 1970); for the dating, *ibid.*, p. 172.

[37] Sir John Temple, *The Irish rebellion . . .* ([27 April] 1646), BL, E 508. For its influence, see Nicholas Canny, *Kingdom and colony: Ireland in the Atlantic world, 1560–1800* (Baltimore, 1988), pp. 137–8; J. A. Froude, *The English in Ireland in the eighteenth century* (3 vols., London, 1872–4).

of Leicester, and Temple (the Irish master of the rolls) as an occasional
lobbyist for, and long-standing friend and adviser to, the Sidney family.[38]
Temple, who was to be appointed to Lisle's privy council in January 1647,[39]
exercised a powerful influence over the new lord lieutenant and was to be
the principal public apologist for the values and objectives which underlay
his projected campaign.

Temple's history of the revolt, the *Irish rebellion*, is perhaps the most
unambiguous statement of the ideology of Lisle's circle.[40] It was acquired
by the London bookseller, George Thomason, on 27 April 1646, less than
a fortnight after Lisle's patent as lord lieutenant of Ireland had passed
the English great seal; and it was probably not mere chance that the
appearance of Temple's account of the 'massacres' of 1641 coincided so
neatly with Lisle's formal appointment to the lieutenancy.[41] In stressing not
merely the crime of rebellion, but the unparalleled iniquity of the
'massacre', Temple's polemic sought to sanction a sweeping new conquest.
Ireland was to be treated as a *tabula rasa* on which the conqueror could write.
a new political order at will.[42] Of the rebels in 1641, Temple claimed:
'Nothing lesse then a generall extirpation [of the English] will now serve
their turne; they must have restitution of all the Lands to the proper
Natives, whom they take to be the ancient proprietors and onely true
owners, most unjustly despoiled . . . '[43] Temple justified a new conquest of
Ireland by attributing to the Catholic rebels of 1641 a political programme
which, in fact, was a mirror image of his own design.

But Temple was not only concerned with the prospect of a new conquest,
but also with the political problem of how, and by whom, it was to be
achieved. What should the new lord lieutenant's attitude be towards the
Old English, and, still more importantly, towards Ormond? The real
villains of Temple's *History*, as Nicholas Canny has pointed out, were the
Catholic Old English landowners of the Pale: 'the Irish of Ulster had merely
been pawns who had been enlisted to put the strength of the government to
the test'; thus, in Temple's view, it should become a fixed principle of
government that no Catholic should ever own land in Ireland again.[44]
Temple, however, went further: his attacks were not merely generally

[38] The son of the provost of Trinity College, Dublin, his family had been in the service of Sir Philip
Sidney in the 1580s. *DNB*, 'Sir John Temple'.
[39] PRO, SP 21/26 (Derby House Committee, mins.), p. 5.
[40] On Temple also see chapters 2, 8 and 11.
[41] For Thomason's copy, BL, E 508.
[42] Cf. Walter Love, 'Civil war in Ireland: appearances in three centuries of historical writing',
Emory University Quarterly, 22 (1966), p. 65.
[43] Temple, *The Irish rebellion*, p. 79.   [44] Canny, *Kingdom and colony*, p. 63.

against the Irish and the Catholic Old English, but against even the Old Protestants. And if the anti-Ormondist implications of Temple's argument were more implicit than explicit in the *Irish rebellion*, they were trumpeted loudly five months later in the second major contribution to the 1646 debate on the future of Ireland – a work which also appears to have emanated from within this Lisle–Temple circle – Adam Meredith's *Ormonds curtain drawn*, a violent assault on the personality and policies of the king's lord lieutenant. Its author was the son of Temple's ally on the former Irish Privy Council, Sir Robert Meredith, with whom Temple had opposed Ormond's 1643 cessation; and it was Temple himself who supplied Meredith with compromising information concerning Ormond's friends, and who made 'alteracons' to Meredith's draft while it was in press.[45]

Publication of this onslaught on Ormond's alleged perfidy seems to have been intended to coincide with the renewed parliamentary debate on Irish policy in the autumn of 1646 – deliberations which were to result, on 12 October, in the establishment of a new Committee for Irish Affairs at Derby House which was gradually to acquire command over almost all

---

[45] *Ormonds curtain drawn: in a short discourse concerning Ireland* [5 October 1646]. At first sight, Meredith's authorship (at least of the principal draft) seems to be established conclusively by his admission to this effect to Sir Philip Perceval, early in 1647 (HMC, *Report on the manuscripts of the earl of Egmont*, 1 [London, 1905], pp. 353–4, 356). Yet Meredith also made it clear that his original draft was altered by a second party before printing: a person 'whom [Meredith] confessed', wrote Perceval, 'had made theise alteracons contrary to truth and to his [Meredith's] intencon' (BL, Add. MSS 46,931/A, fo. 16). That Temple was the person most likely to have made these alterations is established by two pieces of evidence. The first is the annotation on Thomason's copy (BL, E 513/14) which bears a note beneath the title, in Thomason's hand, 'By Sr John Temple, but not Finished: S: Gellibrand', identifying Temple as the author (at least of the final recension) and Samuel Gellibrand (who was a friend of Thomason's) as the printer. Gellibrand already knew Sir John Temple, as he had recently acted for him as the printer of his *Irish rebellion*, and it is likely that it was Gellibrand who provided Thomason with the information associating Temple with the production of *Ormonds curtain drawn*. Despite Meredith's avowal that *he* was the author of the work, further information from the papers of Sir Philip Perceval indicates that Thomason's ascription of the book to Sir John Temple may at least be half true. In a speech drafted in July 1647 for delivery to the House of Commons, Perceval pointed out that the accusations against him of malfeasance as commissary of victuals in Ireland came from a petition (by the baker, Thomas Hill) which Temple had not only presented to the Commons, but which he had also improperly procured to be referred to himself for consideration. The accusations contained in this petition, Perceval complained, 'were printed as truths, with my name in the margent [i.e. the marginalia in *Ormonds curtain drawn*, p. 32], I will not say by whom, but the author of it [Meredith] did point at that member of this House who gave him the papers and certificates of those unworthy persons for yt', a reference which clearly identifies Temple as Meredith's supplier, since it was to Temple that the papers incriminating Perceval had been referred (BL, Add. MSS 46,931/B, fo. 99v; calendared in HMC, *Egmont*, 1, p. 426). The most likely hypothesis is that Meredith was acting as the stalking horse for Temple (and, through him, for Lord Lisle). It is revealing that at the time Perceval was most exercised about *Ormonds curtain drawn*, he went to protest to neither Meredith or Temple, but to Lord Lisle, evidently holding him responsible for the 'misinformations' which were being circulated against him (HMC, *Egmont*, 1, p. 354: 15 January 1647).

aspects of Parliament's Irish policy.[46] For the next six months, until the end of March 1647, this was a body which was to be dominated by Lisle's allies and friends: in January 1647 it was to approve Temple's appointment to Lisle's new Council. Clearly modelled on the form of Spenser's *Short view* of 1596, *Ormonds curtain drawn* forcefully puts the case against any English collaboration with Ormond or, for that matter, with any other of the Irish (whether Gaelic or Old English). The argument unfolds in a series of exchanges between, in turn, Civilis, an English 'person of reputation'; Marcus, an *ingénu* who rehearses that efforts to reform the Irish had hitherto been 'by the preaching of the Word, and not by drawing of the Sword';[47] and the principal interlocutor, Decius, 'an Irish gentleman' and admirer of Lord Lisle, who might well be Temple's *alter ego*.[48] Although Civilis puts a strongly authoritarian case for English rule over Ireland ('The Irish, according to my observation, are a people not to be ruled but with a rod of iron: *Aut serviunt humiliter, aut superbe dominantur*'),[49] it is Decius (speaking for Temple?) who puts a still more extreme argument for excluding the Old English, whether or not they had converted to Protestantism, from the future government of Ireland. The very worst of the Irish, Meredith argues, were the Protestant Old English who had enjoyed the 'benefits' of English civility: 'none [are] more eager followers of [the Irish's] barbarous customes, then such as . . . were bred up with all possible care in our Schooles and Universityes, and in the Protestant Religion' – a direct reference to Ormond, the only major member of the Old English to have been brought up a Protestant in England.[50]

This well-timed restatement of the Spenserian position was clearly intended to influence the contemporaneous formulation of policy in Parliament.[51] Strictures against the Old English and the Protestantized Irish had a specific political objective: to pre-empt any deal between Parliament and Ormond, who, notwithstanding the eclipse of the royalist cause in the autumn of 1646, remained the major Protestant power-broker in Ireland, with an influential body of support at Westminster. From this perspective, Ormond was the arch-villain: 'the cheife instrument of all the misery that at this day the Protestants of that Kingdome groane under, and

---

[46] *CJ*, IV, p. 690. Bodl., Carte MSS 19, fo. 145: Ormond's copy of the order setting up the Derby House Committee.

[47] *Ormonds curtain drawn*, p. 5.

[48] *Ibid.*, sig. A (for Decius), pp. 26–7 (for his admiration of Lisle).

[49] *Ibid.*, p. 6.

[50] *Ormonds curtain drawn*, pp. 16–17; BL, Sloane MSS 4819, fo. 337.

[51] On Spenser, cf. the remarks of Brendan Bradshaw, in 'Sword, word, and strategy in the reformation in Ireland', *The Historical Journal*, 21 (1978), pp. 475–502, esp. at p. 490.

the most faithfull servant to the Irish that ever they had, wherein I must say, he has done but what his blood and nature required of him, his Family having long since degenerated into *Irish*'.[52] Ormond's followers were, by implication, as corrupt as their leader; and among those singled out for particular obloquy was Sir Philip Perceval, denounced for his role as a wartime profiteer (while commissary for the victuals in Ireland) and for his part, as Ormond's secretary, in the negotiations for the cessation with the Confederate Catholics in 1643.[53] As we shall see, Perceval, who was elected to the English House of Commons early in 1647, was to become one of the key figures in the campaign against Lisle's lieutenancy and the political influence of the Independents.[54]

By the autumn of 1646 the ideology of Lisle's circle at Westminster had been expounded with brutal clarity. The lord lieutenant and his adherents were to rule over a nation which they manifestly despised. England's major failing in its dealing with Ireland, they maintained, was not that it had been too severe in Ireland, but that it had been too nice. That, at least, was an error they were determined not to repeat.

III

But if the Spenserian ideology of Lisle's circle threatened Ireland with a new conquest, the implications for Scotland of the ascendancy of Lisle's party at Westminster were scarcely less grave. For just as Lisle's party repudiated any alliance with Ormond or with Protestants who had colluded in the cessation of 1643, so too they scorned any alliance with the Scots. To contemporaries, this reversal of policy was a startling volte-face. Before January 1647, all proposals for the reduction of Ireland had hitherto treated

---

[52] *Ormonds curtain drawn*, p. 15.
[53] *Ibid.*, p. 32; for the MS: BL, Sloane MSS 4816 (Collections relating to Ireland), fos. 343v–44. In a revealing anecdote, Richard FitzGerald, a parliamentarian agent in Herefordshire, recounted to Sir Philip Perceval a conversation that had taken place between Sir William Parsons (the master of the wards in Ireland) and Sir Adam Loftus (Lisle's treasurer-at-wars) concerning the political reliability of (the Protestant) Lord Inchiquin: 'noe blemish was alleaged to be in him – with a conclusion[:] yet hee is Ir[ish]'. BL, Add. MSS 46,931/A, fo. 249; (only briefly calendared in HMC, *Egmont*, I, p. 411).
[54] It seems likely that the unfinished treatise by Henry Parker, *The Irish massacre. Or a true narrative of the unparallell'd cruelties exercised in Ireland* ([after September 1646?] BL, E 353/15), was begun with a view to providing further ammunition to this campaign. The nephew of Viscount Saye and Sele (one of Lisle's supporters in the Derby House Committee), Parker allied himself with the political Independents during 1646, having earlier been in the service of the earl of Essex. For his writings on Ireland, see Norah Carlin, 'Extreme or mainstream?: the English Independents and the Cromwellian reconquest of Ireland, 1649–51', in Brendan Bradshaw, Andrew Hadfield and Willy Maley (eds.), *Representing Ireland: literature and the origins of conflict, 1534–1660* (Cambridge, 1993), pp. 212–13.

it as axiomatic that it would be undertaken by an Anglo-Scottish campaign. Indeed, the Scots had been the dominant partner in the Irish war-effort since the outbreak of hostilities in England in 1642. By February 1645, it was 'now manifest', as Charles I wrote to Ormond, 'that the English rebelles have (as far as in them lyes), given the comand of Irland to the Scots'.[55] Notwithstanding Monro's defeat at Benburb in June 1646 and the withdrawal of part of his army back to Scotland later in that year, Ulster remained the obvious Protestant-held bridgehead in Ireland for any new onslaught against the Confederates. Conduct of the war in Ireland as a joint Anglo-Scottish campaign also had a symbolic significance: as a manifestation of the 'brotherly union' of the two kingdoms which had supposedly been created by treaty and by the Solemn League and Covenant of 1643. Brotherly amity was now in acutely short supply.

For the beginning of Lisle's term of office had marked a decisive break with that policy. His was to be a campaign to re-establish an exclusive *English* overlordship of Ireland: the significance of the sword of state carried before the English lord lieutenant as an 'Ensigne of honour and Authority' was unlikely to have been lost in Edinburgh.[56] And on 12 March 1647, the Derby House Committee declared that it 'should be signified to the Councell of Scotland [viz. the Committee of Estates], or. to the Lord Chancellor there, that the two Houses of Parliam[en]t will not pay the Scottish Army now in Ireland any longer, And that it is the intention of the Parliam[en]t of England *to carry on the warre in Ireland with there owne forces*'.[57] The Scots were to play no further part.[58]

In Edinburgh, such moves appeared not merely to break the spirit of the treaties concluded since 1641; they represented a menacing change in the whole tenor of English policy towards Scotland. It scarcely inspired confidence in Scotland that Northumberland, the general who had presided over the preparations for the war against the Scots in 1640, now exercised such influence in the conduct of policy at Westminster; or that his nephew, who had also fought against them in that war, was now lord lieutenant of Ireland. Northumberland had made no secret of his contempt for that 'beggarly nation';[59] and the chief suspicion in Edinburgh was that an English army which threatened to vanquish, not merely Munster, but all of Ireland, might in turn be used against Scotland – as,

[55] Thomas Carte, *History of the life of James, first duke of Ormond* (6 vols., Oxford, 1851), v, p. 13: Charles I to Ormond, 27 February 1645.
[56] PRO, SP 21/26 (Derby House Committee, mins.), p. 2.
[57] *Ibid.*, p. 27 (12 March 1647); my emphasis.
[58] Cf. S[cottish] R[ecord] O[ffice], PA 11/5 (Committee of Estates, reg.), fos. 3, 11, 18v, 28v–29.
[59] Knowler (ed.), *The earl of Strafforde's letters*, II, p. 186.

indeed, was to happen in 1650 and 1651. Such misgivings seemed to be corroborated by the decision of Lisle's political backers to abandon the joint Anglo-Scottish war-effort and to embark on a reconquest of Ireland without Scottish military aid. The fact that Lisle's reconquest should begin in the relatively insecurely held bridgehead of Munster, rather than in Ulster, where there was a far stronger (if largely Scots) Protestant military presence, underlines the extent to which the character of Lisle's campaign was determined as much by ideological as by military considerations.

Thus the implications for Scotland of political developments in England during the winter of 1646–7 were ominous. They raised once again the abiding fear, as Baillie had put it in 1637 when Strafford was at the height of his power, that 'our poor country [should be] made an English province'.[60] Scotland's autonomy, precariously secured by the wars with England in 1639 and 1640, and confirmed by the treaty of London in 1641, could once again be called into question by Ireland's reduction to the status of an English fiefdom, and by the presence of an English army of occupation within striking distance of Scotland's west coast. Should 'the Independents' in England, and Lisle's supposedly closely related interest in Ireland, entrench themselves in power in 1647, Scotland would be confronted by an Independent-dominated junto at Westminster almost as hostile to the Scottish Kirk as had been the government of Charles I. The possibility of a future 'encirclement' of Scotland – its reduction to the status of a suzerain to the régime at Westminster – was then a real and plausible fear: the recurrent apprehension, as the Scots' commissioners in London had put it in 1640, that Scotland would become 'a conquered province, as Ireland, under subjection to England'.[61]

In Ireland, even before Lisle's arrival in Munster in February 1647, the character of his government-in-waiting was already causing widespread alarm – among Ormondist Royalists and, not least, among the Munster Protestants who were to be the first to come under the new lord lieutenant's rule. That Ormond should loathe all that the new parliamentarian régime stood for was only to be expected. To him, the English Parliament was bent on reducing all to its subjection: 'The severe, if not barbarous, dealings [of the English Parliament] with those [in England] that held out, is a signe to mee of the slavery they would bring them under, and all others that are not

---

[60] Quoted in Allan I. Macinnes, *Charles I and the making of the Covenanting movement, 1625–41* (Edinburgh, 1991), p. ii.
[61] Quoted, *ibid.*, p. 195. I am grateful to Professor Macinnes for a discussion of these points.

[– like the Parliamentarians –] halfe protestants and the other halfe knaves'.[62] But the fear that the new lord lieutenant's arrival portended the future 'enslavement' of Ireland was apprehended no less keenly by Murrough O'Brien, Lord Inchiquin, the English Parliament's appointee as lord president of Munster. 'There appears but very little difference betweene the effecte of his Lo[rdshi]ps [Lisle's] access and those wee might expect from being subdued by the Rebells', Inchiquin wrote of the lord lieutenant's arrival in February 1647: it had more 'the semblaunce rather of a Conquest then of releif'.[63] As a Gael and as one who had collaborated with Ormond in the cessation of 1643, Inchiquin was deeply distrusted by Lisle.[64] Relations between the two were further strained by the rivalry in' Munster between the Gaelic O'Briens and the Protestant Boyles, whose leading member, Roger Boyle, Lord Broghill (the son of the first earl of Cork), had attached himself firmly to Lisle's coat-tails and was exercising a dominant influence in counsel.[65] As Inchiquin complained in a letter to the earl of Warwick, Lisle was 'solely guided by my lo: of Broghill and his faction'.[66] And Broghill, of course, had his own localist reasons for siding with Lisle against Inchiquin, whom he regarded as suspect, as Old Irish, and as an obstacle, owning as he did most of the fertile lands bordering on the Boyles' in the barony of Imokilly.[67]

From the moment of Lisle's arrival in the province, his régime made no secret of the fact that its ambition was the consolidation and extension of the New English interest in Ireland – the cause of English colonists who had settled in Ireland since the beginning of the Jacobean plantations. Inchiquin's administration was censured by the new lord lieutenant as inefficient, indulgent, and lax. Preliminary enquiries were said to have revealed corrupt muster lists, military forces far under their paper strength, and extensive grants of 'protections' against confiscation or sequestration of property to Papists and royalist sympathizers that had cheated the Irish treasury of its due. Grants of protection were promptly banned; officials were censured; the tax burden on English settlers was lightened while that on the native population increased. Henceforth, fiscal matters were to be

---

[62] Bodl., Carte MSS 19, fo. 161: Ormond to Digby [draft], 12 October 1646.
[63] BL, Add. MSS 46,931/A fo. 76: Inchiquin to [Thomas Pigott], 5 March 1647.
[64] HMC, *Egmont*, I, pp. 376–8.
[65] BL, Add. MSS 46,931/A, fo. 76: Inchiquin to [Thomas Pigott], 5 March 1647. For the rivalry between Inchiquin and Broghill: BL, Add. MSS 46,930, fo. 136: John Davies to Perceval, 28 November 1646.
[66] BL, Add. MSS 46,931/A, fo. 101: Inchiquin to Warwick, 14 March 1647.
[67] J. A. Murphy, 'The politics of the Munster Protestants, 1641–1649', *Journal of the Cork Historical and Archaeological Society*, 76 (1971), pp. 1–20. I am grateful to Dr T. C. Barnard for a discussion of this point.

vetted by 'a Committee of Accompts, as in England' – a body of professional auditors responsible for scrutinizing accounts and reporting to the lord lieutenant and his Council (as in England it did to Parliament). Ireland was to be subject to the authoritarian rule of the lord lieutenant and his Council: Irish practice was to conform to that of England.[68]

Lisle's distrust of all things Irish was made brusquely evident. Irish Protestant forces that had hitherto served Parliament under Inchiquin were now regarded as politically suspect. Across Munster, in the key County Waterford strongholds of Tallow, Moyallo and Lismore, Irish garrisons and their officers were removed and replaced by English forces under the lord lieutenant's direct command. In the garrison towns, the new military presence could hardly be missed. The Irish grey-coats were sent to out-garrisons, one of Inchiquin's officers later complained, and the English 'Redd Cottes possessed them selfes in all our holdes' (Lisle's red-coats were, of course, wearing the uniform of the New Model Army). Even the Old Protestants were objects of suspicion to the lord lieutenant's henchmen, for whom, 'in theire Oppinnion, any old prodistant was worse then a papest . . .'[69]

The revelation of the character of Lisle's régime, emerging gradually between October 1646 and March 1647, also appears to have acted as a major check on Ormond's readiness to deliver up Dublin to its Parliamentarian governor-designate (and the lord lieutenant's brother), Colonel Algernon Sidney. Having made overtures towards the English Parliament for the delivery of the capital in September 1646, Ormond began to backtrack during the months between October and the following March – the period during which Lisle's supporters effectively controlled the Derby House Committee.[70] It was only at the end of March 1647, by which stage Lisle's reappointment was beginning to look increasingly unlikely, that Ormond took definitive steps to entrust Dublin to a parliamentarian governor, culminating in July with his surrender of his sword of state to parliamentary commissioners. One observer succinctly summarized the view of Lisle from Ormond's Dublin: the 'Lo: Lieuten: [Lisle was] heere hated amongst the Irish most of anie man liveing'.[71] To Ormond,

[68] BL, Add. MSS 46,931/A, fo. 160: Henry Whaley to the lord mayor and aldermen of London, read in the Aldermanic Court, 23 March 1647 (HMC, *Egmont*, I, pp. 366–7). *Ibid.*, fo. 152: order of the Irish council, [29 March 1647].

[69] BL, Add. MSS 46,931/A, fo. 186: [Capt?] John Hodder to Sir Philip Perceval, 21 April 1647 (HMC, *Egmont*, I, p. 391).

[70] *Cal. S P Ire. 1633–47*, p. 543: parliamentary commissioners in Dublin to Viscount Lisle, 23 November 1646.

[71] BL, Add. MSS 46,931/A, fo. 165: Cosny Molloy to Perceval, 5 April 1647.

Lisle's 'Independency' was as obnoxious as Rinuccini's Tridentine clericalism.[72]

In the spring of 1647, of course, the threatened 'conquest' was still in the future. Lisle still waited upon the arrival of the detachments of the New Model Army that were expected to form the core of his fighting force. But no one was in any doubt that a re-conquest was Lisle's eventual aim, nor that that conquest would, at very least, call into question the political position (and, almost certainly, the land tenures) of the Irish and Old English, Protestant and Catholic alike.

IV

The English Parliament's abandonment of its commitment to an Anglo-Scottish campaign in Ireland and Lisle's first contentious attempts to impose his authority on Munster inevitably had a profound effect north of the Tweed, contributing to a growing perception that the 'junto' now dominant at Westminster was betraying the Covenant and threatening to reassert an English hegemony – that is to say, an overwhelming political and military dominance – within the British Isles. In the Scottish Parliament of November 1646–March 1647 (whose meeting ran almost contemporaneously with this decisive shift in English policy towards Ireland), resistance to the threat of a reascendant English dominance was to produce a striking volte-face in Scottish politics. Central to the leadership of this resistance was James Hamilton, first duke of Hamilton, the highly anglicized Scottish magnate and one-time master of the horse to Charles I, whose own Irish ambitions (and especially his plans for participation in the plantation of Connacht and County Londonderry) had been steadfastly opposed by Strafford in the 1630s.[73] Hamilton served as the rallying point for a diffuse alliance of moderate Covenanters and erstwhile Royalists that was to emerge, at the end of the Parliament in March 1647, as the most powerful interest on the Scottish Committee of Estates.

Relations between the two kingdoms were increasingly soured by the Scots' refusal to relinquish their military strongholds in Ulster and, in particular, by their insistence that Belfast should remain a Scottish garrison

---

[72] On the progress of the negotiations see Bodl., Carte MSS 20, fo. 513: Ormond's copy of the Derby House Committee warrant of 22 March 1647; BL, Add. MSS 46,931/B, fo. 18: Arthur Annesley to Perceval, 9 June 1647. There is the possibility that Annesley, the son of Lisle's critic, Viscount Valentia, and himself a supporter of Inchiquin, encouraged Ormond to delay the surrender of Dublin until Lisle's commission had been terminated.

[73] M. Perceval-Maxwell, 'Ireland and Scotland, 1638 to 1648', in John Morrill (ed.), *The Scottish national covenant in its British context* (Edinburgh, 1990), p. 195.

town to which English forces were denied access. When Lisle's red-coats were sent to claim the town, the English commissioners complained to the Scottish Parliament in February 1647 that they were refused harbour and 'exposed to such extremities, that many of them are scattered and lost, and the rest much endangered, to the great prejudice of the kingdom of England'.[74] In Ulster, there was the growing threat that tensions over the custody of Belfast would result in military confrontation between England and Scotland.

The apprehensions of Hamilton and his correspondents during this period bear a marked similarity, and are voiced in an almost identical rhetoric, to those of Inchiquin and Ormond in Ireland. Where Inchiquin discerned in Lisle's lieutenancy 'a designe resolved upon long before [his] arrivall' to engross office-holding into the hands of a small, religiously heterodox clique,[75] Hamilton similarly regarded political events in England as leading towards the re-establishment not merely of English dominance within the British Isles, but of a narrowly based oligarchic régime, dominated by the political 'Independents'. Reports, current in the autumn of 1646, that the Independents' backstairs diplomacy, conducted through Wat Stewart,[76] had brought the king to the brink of an agreement filled Hamilton with foreboding.[77] Three political objectives were therefore imperative: first, the maintenance of the Scottish military presence in Ulster; second, the restoration of the king on conditions which permitted him personal executive authority in each of his three kingdoms – on such terms, in other words, that 'monarchie' could serve as a buttress for Scottish autonomy; and third, the maintenance of a Scottish army capable of intervening in England to ensure that the king was not reduced to the status of a cipher for an English parliamentarian clique. (Settle peace without the 'Kings intrest' being maintained, Hamilton had declared, and 'some of us shall not onely want power, but wish to be out of the world'.)[78] As in Ireland, where Inchiquin complained that 'My Lo[rd] Lt: [Lisle] hath nothing in designe or accon but plotts how to place and displace such as are,

[74] *LJ*, IX, p. 101: English parliamentary commissioners at Edinburgh to the Parliament of Scotland, 27 February 1647. Cf. the instructions of the English parliamentary commissioners at Belfast to Lieutenant-Colonel Owen O'Conelly (their agent to the Parliament in Scotland), 15 December 1646. Significantly, the English parliamentary commissioners in Ireland recommended that O'Conelly make his approaches to Lord Warriston and to Hamilton's principal opponent in the 1646–7 Parliament, the marquis of Argyll: *Cal. S P Ire. 1633–47*, p. 561.

[75] BL, Add. MSS 46,931/A, fo. 76.

[76] SRO, Hamilton MS G[ifts and] D[eposits] 406/1/2044: [Lauderdale] to Hamilton, 28 November [1646].

[77] *Ibid.*, 406/1/2102: Hamilton to [Sir Robert Moray], 21 November 1646.

[78] *Ibid.*, 406/1/2103: Hamilton to [Sir Robert Moray], 24 November 1646.

or are not, independents',[79] so Sir Robert Moray wrote to Hamilton of the English Independents: these were men who sought to be invested with 'the whole power of the State and [over the] kings persone, by Offices and charges'.[80]

Such language registers a common perception of a 'British threat': for here 'Independency' and 'the Independents' are catchphrases that denote far more than simply preferences for church government. From the pens of men such as Inchiquin and Hamilton, 'Independency' designated what might be termed an imperial design within the Stuart kingdoms, the re-establishment of England as the dominant nation within the British Isles. From such a perspective, the character of the new English ascendancy was clear: a narrowly based junto ruling in the name of a puppet king; with Ireland governed by an English viceroy, backed by an army of occupation. In this sense, 'Independency' threatened Scottish autonomy (just as it threatened to exclude Scotland from the exploitation of Ireland), no less in the late 1640s than had the pretensions of Charles I's 'imperial crown' during the late 1630s. The earl of Lauderdale, resident as Scottish commissioner to London in the summer of 1647 and one of the shrewdest observers of contemporary politics, was to put the problem to Hamilton most succinctly: '[It] is to be Considered . . . if Scotland can be in security when England is conquered by the Independents'.[81]

This perception that government at Westminster was once again coming under the domination of a clique which threatened Scotland's (and Ireland's) security, produced a reaction in Edinburgh as fierce as anything yet witnessed in Dublin or Munster. The Scottish Parliament proved almost unanimous in its commitment to maintaining a military presence in Ireland. Against repeated English requests and in direct contravention of the treaties, they refused to hand over Belfast to the English Parliament's commissioners. By the end of the Scottish Parliament in March 1647, there had been a major realignment in Scottish politics: a drift towards a new form of royalism in which the interests of Scottish autonomy had come to be identified with the preservation of the monarch against his becoming the puppet of an English Independent clique. The extent of this drift towards what might be termed a 'nationalist royalism' was evidenced not only by Hamilton's majority on the new Committee of Estates, elected on 20 March 1647, but by the inclusion within its number of such figures as Traquair

---

[79] BL, Add. MSS 46,931/A, fo. 138: Inchiquin to Perceval, 29 March 1647 (HMC, *Egmont*, I, p. 380).
[80] SRO, Hamilton MS GD 406/1/2067/1: Sir Robert Moray to Hamilton, 14 November 1646.
[81] *Ibid.*, 406/1/10808.

and Roxburghe, the Royalist arch-incendiaries of 1641. The Scottish 'revolution' seemed about to turn full circle.

V

Thus by the end of March 1647, Lisle's fledgling régime faced a reaction in all three kingdoms. From Munster, Inchiquin was galvanizing a vigorous campaign against the lord lieutenant through his lobbyists at Westminster. In Ulster, the Scottish army was reported to have declared for the king.[82] And in Edinburgh there had been a sea-change in Covenanter politics: with Hamilton in the ascendant, there was once again the possibility that Scotland might intervene in England, for a third time that decade, should the king of Scots be reduced to the status of a prisoner of an English Independent régime. The political convictions that were eventually to produce the Engagement of December 1647 and Hamilton's invasion of England the following summer had already crystallized during the last weeks of that Scottish parliamentary session.

The effect of this convergence of interests was drastically to undermine Lisle's powerbase at Westminster: the political Independents and 'Northumberland's party'. From early in that spring of 1647, Inchiquin, seconded at London by Sir Philip Perceval, had led a vigorous campaign to obstruct Lisle's authority in Munster and to galvanize opposition to the new lord lieutenant at Westminster. Since his appointment as lord president of Munster in January 1645, Inchiquin had established an effective alliance with Lisle's enemies at Westminster: with such men as the earls of Warwick and Suffolk, and Lord Willoughby of Parham in the Lords; Sir Philip Stapilton, Sir John Clotworthy and Denzell Holles in the Commons.[83] To this receptive audience, Lisle's campaign was represented by Inchiquin as a concerted strategy to bring the government of Ireland under the tutelage of the political 'Independents'. Their 'immoderate severity and harshness towards us', Inchiquin wrote of Lisle and his party on 5 March 1647, 'wee observe to proceed from a designe resolved upon long before their arrivall in this Kingdome, where it was preconcluded that o[u]r not adhereing to

---

[82] Bodl., Carte MSS 19, fo. 629: [Lord] Lambart [of Cavan] to Ormond, 15 December 1646.
[83] BL, Add. MSS 46,930, fo. 35: Inchiquin to Perceval, 8 September 1646. See also, Add. MSS 46,930, fo. 79: Perceval to Inchiquin, 18 October 1646; Add. MSS 46,931/A, fos. 188–9v: Inchiquin to Perceval, 22 April 1647. As early as September 1646, Inchiquin was writing to Perceval asking him to represent 'my humble service unto Sr Phillip Stapleton and Mr Hollis' (see letter of 8 September 1646, above); and Warwick was enlisted by Inchiquin to defend his reputation against possible attacks from within the Derby House Committee (Add. MSS 46,931/A, fo. 101: Inchiquin to Warwick, 14 March 1647; cf. HMC, *Egmont*, 1, p. 374).

the independent party' should mean that they would be treated with even worse severity than the Catholic rebels.[84] 'Independency', Inchiquin insisted in his despatches to parliamentary allies at Westminster, was the hallmark of Lisle's régime; and this stress on the religious heterodoxy of Lisle's government seems to have been contrived as much with an eye to what the Scottish commissioners would report back to Edinburgh as it was to what might blacken Lisle's reputation amongst the Presbyterian interest in England. The doctrine preached by the lord lieutenant's chaplains in Ireland, Inchiquin claimed, was 'strong and Direct independancy, and the Governm[en]t prescribed and pursued by the Parliam[en]t [was] both inveighed against and decryed publiquely in the Pullpitt'.[85]

Lisle's strategy of reconquest was not merely vulnerable to such lobbying from Ireland. Its Achilles' heel was the terms of Lisle's patent of appointment as lord lieutenant. Initially granted for a year, it required renewal before 15 April 1647; and although Lisle seems to have taken his renewal in office for granted, the balance of factional power in the Commons had changed markedly since his first appointment. The party which had been the prevailing interest in the Commons when Lisle was appointed in April 1646 no longer enjoyed anything more than an uncertain influence in the lower House twelve months later.[86] To rally support for Lisle's continuance in command, his backers turned to their natural constituency: the Protestant settlers in Ireland and their would-be successors in Irish colonization, the London Adventurers within the City government. On 23 March 1647, before the lord mayor and the court of aldermen, a letter was read from Henry Whaley (an Adventurer to the tune of £1,200),[87] making the case for retaining Lisle and sending further reinforcements of horse and foot (essential 'before a perfect Conquest can be expected'). And at the same time, Sir Adam Loftus, the vice-treasurer of Ireland and Lisle's treasurer-at-wars, had been dispatched from Munster to lobby for the lord lieutenant with members of the two Houses at Westminster.[88] 'I find [Loftus] so p[er]verse and willfull', wrote one of Inchiquin's partisans, 'that

[84] BL, Add. MSS 46,931/A, fo. 76: Inchiquin to [Thomas Pigott], 5 March 1647.
[85] *Ibid.*, fo. 99v: enclosure in Inchiquin's letter to Perceval, 13 March 1647; for the Scottish commissioner Hew Kennedy, see also, [Perceval] to Sir William Stewart, 9 March 1647: *ibid.*, fo. 80.
[86] The fact that Lisle left to take up his command with only two months of his tenure of office yet to run was itself testimony to his expectation that renewal was probable, if not certain. Perceval seems to have made enquiries to establish the exact terms and date of expiry of the commission: Bodl., Carte MSS 206 (Carte's listing of the Perceval correspondence), fo. 66.
[87] Bottigheimer, *English money and Irish land*, appendix A, p. 212.
[88] BL, Add. MSS 46,931/A, fo. 113: Colonel Thomas Pigott to Perceval, 19 March 1647 (HMC, *Egmont*, I, p. 376). For Loftus as vice-treasurer, see *Cal. S P Ire. 1633–47*, p. 748.

malice cannot invent more then he dare act to hurt anie hee has a prejudice to.'[89]

But Lisle's adversaries were just as adept at spinning malice of their own. In the month leading up to the vote on renewal, Inchiquin, Perceval and their English and Scottish allies concerted a campaign against the new lord lieutenant in the lobbies of Westminster with an intensity not seen since the prosecution of Strafford in 1641. Inchiquin had dispatched to London the MP and officer in his army, Colonel William Jephson, with the intention of pre-empting Loftus's representations on Lisle's behalf.[90] And by mid-March 1647, Inchiquin was already moving steadily, and with surprising effectiveness, towards securing Lisle's dismissal and averting Temple's policy of 'conquest'.[91]

By the last week of March 1647, it was clear that Lisle's allies were losing control of the Derby House Committee. Its sittings abruptly ceased on 26 March and remained suspended for more than a week while the battle for control of the Irish campaign was fought out on the floor of the two Houses.[92] Led in the Commons by those whom Inchiquin termed 'Stapilton and Hollis and those of the presbyterian p[ar]tie',[93] and in the Lords by Warwick and the youthful third earl of Suffolk, this anti-Lisle party at Westminster embarked on a design which had two main elements: first, to dismiss Lisle from the lord lieutenancy and to dismantle his office; second, to neutralize what was believed to be Lisle's political powerbase (and that of the bi-cameral interest which had supported him), the New Model Army, by restructuring its senior officer-corps. Fairfax and Cromwell (its present general and lieutenant-general) were to be prevented from holding senior commands in Ireland; those sections of the army which refused to serve abroad were to be disbanded. 'My Lord Lisle and all men that favour Independency will be outed', predicted one anxious admirer of the New Model, fearing the 'ruin' of the army.[94]

The first part of his prediction, at least, proved all too accurate. The rout

[89] BL, Add. MSS 46,931/A, fo. 172: Colonel T[homas] P[igott] to [Perceval], 9 April 1647 (HMC, *Egmont,*1, p. 388).
[90] BL, Add. MSS 46,931/A, fos. 101, 113 (HMC, *Egmont*, 1, pp. 374, 376). For an earlier instance of Jephson making representations at Westminster on Inchiquin's behalf, see Inchiquin to Jephson, 17 July 1644: *A letter from the Right Honourable the Lord Inchiquin* (London, 1644), pp. 6–7.
[91] BL, Add. MSS 46,931/A, fo. 113 (HMC, *Egmont*, 1, p. 376).
[92] PRO, SP 21/26 (Derby House Committee, mins.), p. 33 (26 March 1647). They were not resumed until 7 April: *ibid.*, p. 34.
[93] For Inchiquin seeing this group as his political allies, see: BL, Add. MSS 46,931/A, fo. 190v: holograph memorandum by Inchiquin, [*c.* April 1647] (HMC, *Egmont*, 1, p. 394).
[94] HMC, *Ormond*, II (1899), p. 60: [–] Mosse to William Roe, [April, before 20th] 1647 (possibly from John Mosse, secretary to the commissioners of the English Parliament at Edinburgh: see *LJ*, IX, pp. 101–2).

of what Juxon had termed 'Northumberland's partie' began in the last days of March 1647 and continued over the following week. Lisle was dismissed as lord lieutenant and his office vested in a commission. His council was *ipso facto* disbanded. Other prominent members of the Lisle–Northumberland interest also lost their commands. Algernon Sidney, the intended successor of Ormond as governor of Dublin, was replaced by the career soldier, Colonel Michael Jones – a man with local connections, and thought ill-disposed to the Independents.[95] And on 7 April, three weeks after the election of the new Scottish Committee of Estates, the membership of the Derby House Committee was radically restructured to give a clear majority to the pro-Scottish party led by Warwick, Stapilton and Holles – the very group which had engineered the dismissal of Viscount Lisle. Not only was the active membership of the Derby House Committee virtually transformed; so too were the sources of advice on Irish policy. Where Lisle's men, and especially Temple, had exercised a major influence at Derby House up to the end of March, Lisle's dismissal spelt the end of their power and the triumph of Inchiquin's Irish lobby at Westminster. It was now Inchiquin's major-general, William Jephson – the officer he had dispatched to London to lobby against the lord lieutenant – who put forward to the Derby House Committee a new series of proposals for the management of the war in Ireland.[96] Like the Derby House Committee, control of the war in Ireland was now under new and very different management.

The new commanders for the Irish campaign shared none of the Lisle–Temple group's knee-jerk hostility to the Old English. Skippon, the distinguished but valetudinarian New Model Army officer who was appointed as commander-in-chief, was believed to be well disposed to Ormond and Inchiquin. He had recommended Ormond to the mayor of Bristol in November 1646;[97] and Inchiquin's agents regarded him as a man with whom they could do business. 'I have a great interest in M[ajor] G[eneral] Skippon', one of Inchiquin's friends, Thomas Pigott, boasted to Sir Philip Perceval a few days after Lisle's fall, 'which I will improve to [Inchiquin's] advantage'.[98] The new lieutenant-general of horse, Edward Massie, was virtually a crypto-Royalist and, towards Ormond and Inchiquin, likely to be more accommodating still.[99]

---

[95] *LJ*, IX, p. 133.　　[96] BL, Add. MSS 46,931/A, fo. 169 (HMC, *Egmont*, I, pp. 387–8).
[97] Bodl., Carte MSS 19, fo. 402: Sir William Parsons to Ormond, 16 November 1646.
[98] BL, Add. MSS 46,931/A, fo. 172: Pigott to Perceval, 9 April 1647 (HMC, *Egmont*, I, p. 388).
[99] Massie's relations with Skippon are difficult to establish, but he was on sufficiently close terms to have proposed him for freedom of the Leathersellers' Company in January 1646. W. H. Black, *The history and antiquity of the Worshipful Company of Leathersellers* (London, 1871), p. 101. (I owe this reference to Miss Frances Kelly.)

Now dominated by Inchiquin's allies, the Derby House Committee continued to prepare for a campaign against the Confederates; but gone was the hostility to the Old English and to the Protestant Irish which had been the hallmark of Lisle's régime. There was once again the possibility that a *rapprochement* with Ormond would bring his moderating influence to bear on the formulation of English policy towards Ireland. The strategy of conquest which had been adumbrated so forcefully by Temple had, it seemed, been permanently shelved; and when, in April 1647, a new loan was raised to fund the campaign (now to be commanded by Skippon), it was conspicuous that there was no attempt to provide security for the loan in Irish land.[100] Irish interests had proved themselves adroit at exploiting factional divisions in England and able to affect, in turn, the outcome of deliberations at Westminster. Inchiquin clearly recognized as much. He had resorted, with dazzling effectiveness, to what was in effect the age-old stratagem of weakening an unpopular viceroy by appealing over his head to Whitehall.

VI

Had this coup succeeded permanently in ousting the likes of Lisle and Temple from the control of Irish affairs, there is little doubt that the changed circumstances at Westminster would have held out a very different course for the future of Ireland. But the days during which Inchiquin's supporters at Westminster could recommend their friends for plum appointments in Ireland were to be short-lived. With the April 1647 coup at Derby House, relations between the parliamentary executive and the New Model Army deteriorated rapidly; and after the tense stand-off over the summer between the junto at Derby House and the army, and the botched attempt by the Presbyterians in July to effect an unconditional restoration of the king, Fairfax's red-coats intervened directly in politics, marching on London on 6 August to restore order and return the peers and members of the Commons who had declared their solidarity with the army to their places in the two Houses at Westminster.[101]

For Ireland, the effect of the army's intervention in August 1647 was to restore to power those whose policies Ormond and Inchiquin had found so repugnant during Lisle's ascendancy up to March 1647. In the public declaration approving of the army's march on London, dated 4 August, Lisle's name, following precedence, heads the list of Commons

---

[100] *LJ*, IX, pp. 148–9.
[101] John Rushworth, *Historical collections*, part IV (1701), II, p. 756.

signatories.[102] In the aftermath of the army's march on London, Inchiquin's supporters were scattered: Holles had scurried off into exile, Stapilton died within days of his arrival at Calais, and the bossy peers who had been intruded into the membership of the Derby House Committee in the *putsch* of April 1647 were either flown or under arrest. Lord Willoughby of Parham, whom Perceval had regarded as one of Inchiquin's loyal supporters, had had enough and soon after deserted to the king.[103] Inchiquin's opponents were once again in the ascendant, and the prosecution of charges against him for the misgovernment of Munster was renewed in the English Parliament – an augury of worse things to come.[104] It was hardly surprising that by the spring of 1648 Inchiquin, too, was on the verge of defecting to the king.

Developments in London at the beginning of August 1647 thus appeared to augur nothing less than the restoration of the 'Independent Junto' at Whitehall. Although there was no attempt to restore the office of lord lieutenant after the army's march on London, Temple and (from November) Lisle were once again attending the deliberations of the powerful Committee for Irish Affairs at Derby House, and were among those steering Parliament's Irish policy back towards the objective of the total conquest which they had espoused before the fracas at Derby House in April had thrown them off course.[105]

In the British context, however, the change of personnel at Westminster raised a far larger problem. The return to power of Lisle's backers in the autumn of 1647 – Northumberland's party in the Lords, the supporters of Lisle and Temple in the Commons – raised once again the threat which had been felt all too keenly in Ireland (and also in Scotland) during the preparations for Lisle's original campaign: that with England 'conquered by the Independents' (as Lauderdale had put it),[106] there was the threat of a new English hegemony within the British Isles. And as always when the status of Ireland and Scotland were perceived to be threatened by the supposed ambitions of a régime at Westminster, as Dr Wormald has put it, there was a 'British Problem'.[107]

Of course at one level Lisle's lieutenancy was an obvious fiasco. He

---

[102] *Ibid.*, p. 755.

[103] BL, Add. MSS 46,931/A, fo. 173v: [Perceval to Inchiquin], 13 April 1647. Willoughby is probably also the 'L[ord] W' referred to in *ibid.*, fo. 81: [Perceval to Inchiquin], 9 March 1647.

[104] HMC, *Egmont*, I, pp. 462–3: Jephson to Perceval, 12 September 1647.

[105] PRO, SP 21/26 (Derby House Committee, mins.), pp. 99, 101, 104, 108, 110, 113, 117.

[106] SRO, Hamilton MSS GD 406/1/10808.

[107] Jenny Wormald, 'The creation of Britain: multiple kingdoms or core and colonies?', *Transactions, Royal Historical Society*, sixth series, 2 (1992), pp. 175–94, especially at p. 192.

conquered not an inch of Irish ground, and his administration proved divisive in Munster and Westminster alike. Yet his lieutenancy also clearly defines a watershed in Anglo-Irish relations, a moment at which a 'junto' at Westminster once again sought to assert that England, in Edmund Waller's phrase, was 'The seat of Empire' – an *imperium Anglicanum* – within the British Isles.[108] The decision to pursue an exclusively English conquest of Ireland was the practical assertion of just such an English *imperium*. It inevitably created apprehensions in Edinburgh that Scotland would be excluded from the colonial exploitation of Ireland; and that, in the event of a successful English conquest of Ireland, Scotland would once again be vulnerable to an English military presence on both sides of the Irish Sea. Except for the brief ascendancy of the Holles–Stapilton interest between April and July 1647, when men sympathetic to Inchiquin and Ormond dominated the executive at Whitehall, developments in Westminster were perceived to threaten, directly or potentially, the security of Ireland and Scotland almost continuously from the end of 1646 until the tensions between the three kingdoms erupted into a second phase of 'British civil war', in the spring of 1648. In turn, the change at Westminster was the catalyst for a major realignment of political groupings in Ireland, and throughout each of the other Stuart kingdoms. Before the threat that Ireland and Scotland would once again be reduced to the state of 'English provinces' – indeed, that Ireland would suffer a far worse fate than any that had befallen it hitherto – Charles I could represent himself as the one effective legal bulwark against a return to English dominance. With Charles as king of Scotland and Ireland, his adherents could hold out the king's restoration as the most effective means of preserving the jurisdictional autonomy of Scotland, and preventing the wholesale spoliation of the Old English in Ireland by a new wave of English Parliamentarian *conquistadors*.

By the spring of 1647, the 'Covenanter' Hamilton, the 'Royalist' Ormond, and the 'Parliamentarian' Inchiquin were each on convergent trajectories – trajectories which were to intersect in common resistance to the English parliamentarian régime in 1648.[109] To the other kingdoms of

---

108 Edmund Waller, *A panegyric to my Lord Protector* (1655), quoted in David Armitage, 'The Cromwellian Protectorate and the languages of empire', *The Historical Journal*, 35 (1992), p. 531.

109 Developments in Scotland seem to have been closely followed by Ormond, who remained in France until September 1648, and by Inchiquin in Ireland; it is suggestive that a copy of Charles I's letter to the queen relating the promises he had received from the Hamiltons (as a result of which 'my Game will be farre from desperate') survives amongst Perceval's papers: a copy of a document sent on to Inchiquin? BL, Add. MSS 46,930, fo. 152v: Charles I to Henrietta Maria, 12 December 1646.

Britain, the return to power of the 'Independent junto' in the autumn of 1647 had raised Strafford's ghost: the spectre of a resurgent English dominance within the British Isles. In turn, this threat provoked a British reaction no less violent than that of 1638–41. Although the similarities may not be pressed too far, there is a sense in which the objectives of Lisle and his adherents were viewed as being similar in effect to Strafford's imperial designs for the subordination of Ireland (and Scotland) to the dominance of Whitehall. To Viscount Valentia, who had served as a member of Lisle's council, those continuities were nowhere more obvious than in the personnel of the régime. 'So long as S[i]r John Temple his motions may be credited and they who support him', wrote Valentia in August 1647, just as 'Independency' seemed poised once again to regain control of the Irish campaign, 'I looke for no good for Ireland; for I knowe how he and his confederates came to their places; and they who must buy must sell: if I am not deceived, S[i]r J[ohn] T[emple] would be another Radcliffe'. Valentia was ready, he declared, to appear at the bar of the Parliament, in the words of the epigraph to this essay, to 'evidence it plainely that the very same Instruments who did cooperate with th[']erle of Strafford, and wear promoted by him for bribery, are still spetially trusted and imploied'.[110] To this extent, the 'Independents' were more than the promoters of an 'imperial design' for English mastery within the British Isles; they were Strafford's heirs.

In Ireland, as in Scotland, by galvanizing an alliance between erstwhile parliamentarian moderates and constitutional Royalists – between the likes of Inchiquin and Ormond in Ireland and Monro and Hamilton in Scotland – this reaction provided Charles I with the means to fight a second civil war. By the beginning of 1648, Inchiquin no longer held out any hope that the threat posed by Independency could be averted (as it had been in April 1647) by the play of faction at Westminster. In February 1648, he began negotiations with Viscount Taaffe and the Confederates – talks which led to his repudiation of the English Parliament and his declaration for Ormond and for the king.[111] By June 1648, even the Scottish Committee of Estates, still nominally loyal to the Covenant, was prepared to make common cause with Inchiquin. Notwithstanding his alliance with the Confederates, they were 'very sensible of the great extremities the Lord

[110] BL, Add. MSS 46,931/B, fo. 149: [first Viscount Valentia] to Perceval, 4 August 1647 (partly printed in HMC, *Egmont*, I, pp. 441–2). For Valentia's support for Inchiquin, HMC, *De L'Isle*, VI, p. 566: Leicester's diary (8 April 1647).
[111] James Tuchet, third earl of Castlehaven, *Memoirs; or, his review of the civil wars in Ireland* (London, 1815), p. 105.

Inchiquin hath been reduced to by the malice of the Independent party in England'.[112] The governor of Dublin, Colonel Michael Jones, reported this convergence of Scottish and Irish anti-parliamentarian interests to Speaker Lenthall in July 1648, even as Hamilton's army was entering England: 'Ormonde and Inchiquine are confederate, as with the Irish, soe with the now ryseing party in Scotland, and with some Scotts in Ulster, and that there have letters lately arrived in Mounster sent from Scotland by an expresse, which have bin comunicated by Inchiquine to the Rebells' Councell at Kilkenny'.[113] The Celtic kingdoms were to make common cause in the suppression of the junto at Westminster – a crusade which, Ormond argued, transcended divisions of nationality or religion.[114]

Thus within each of the three kingdoms there had been a redefinition of the royalist cause. The objective which now united Inchiquin, Ormond and Confederate Catholics with Hamilton in Scotland, was, in Professor Perceval-Maxwell's phrase, 'internal political autonomy, the link between the three kingdoms being provided by the king and the king alone'.[115] It was also a moment which revealed Charles I's skills as political chameleon at their finest: by 1642, as Professor Russell has argued, the breaker of the Petition of Right had cast himself effectively as the champion of the rule of law;[116] by 1648, the would-be *imperator* of the 1630s had re-cast himself no less effectively as the one bulwark which stood between the other kingdoms and the resurgent tyranny of Westminster.

For Charles I, it was a perilous strategy: in making his own person the hedge against both the draconian reconquest of Ireland feared by Inchiquin and Ormond, and the military encirclement of Scotland apprehended by Hamilton, he acquired the resources with which to fight the Second Civil War. In the event of military failure, however, he made his own execution an almost ineluctable necessity. So ironically, in 1648, it was Charles I, the would-be guarantor of the autonomy of all three Stuart kingdoms, who now stood in the way of England's imperial dominion within the British Isles. And with apt symmetry, when Hamilton's army had been routed at Preston, and Irish forces (as in 1640) had once again failed to materialize, it was another old Straffordian, John Cooke – veteran of Strafford's

---

[112] HMC, *Report on the MSS of the duke of Portland*, 1 (London, 1891), p. 469: Committee of Estates to Inchiquin, 28 June 1648.
[113] *Ibid.*, pp. 485–6.
[114] Carte, *Ormond*, v, p. 23.
[115] Perceval-Maxwell, 'Ireland and Scotland, 1638 to 1648', p. 207.
[116] Conrad Russell, *The causes of the English civil war* (Oxford, 1990), chapter 6.

entourage in the 1630s and author of a letter of encouragement and advice to the beleaguered ex-lord lieutenant as he awaited his trial for treason in 1641[117] – who now stepped forward to conduct the prosecution of the king.

---

[117] C. H. Firth (ed.), 'Papers relating to Thomas Wentworth', *Camden Miscellany*, IX (London, 1895), pp. 14–20; Wilfrid Prest, *The rise of the barristers: a social history of the English bar, 1590–1640* (Oxford, 1986), p. 282; Barnard, *Cromwellian Ireland*, pp. 266–75.

CHAPTER 8

THE IRISH ECONOMY AT WAR, 1641–1652

RAYMOND GILLESPIE

THE TRADITIONAL interpretation of seventeenth-century Irish economic history juxtaposes phases of construction, characterized by colonization, and periods of destruction caused by almost inevitable rebellion consequent on that colonization. Thus the years between 1603 and 1641 and again between 1660 and 1688 were viewed as periods of prosperity, which the wars of 1641 to 1653 and 1689 to 1692 largely negated. This simplistic stop–go model of the Irish economy, articulated in 1919 by George O'Brien (later professor of economics at University College, Dublin) and based on qualitative evidence culled from the complaints of central government about the lack of supply for the army and the devastation it caused, was shared by many late seventeenth-century observers.[1] Sir William Petty, for example, devoted a chapter of his *Political Anatomy of Ireland* (1672) to the economic costs of the Irish Civil Wars.[2] He suggested that 616,000 people had perished in the conflict (37,000 of whom were allegedly massacred during the early months of the rebellion) and, by estimating the productive capacity of each of these persons and by valuing their property, he calculated that the Irish economy lost roughly £10 million. By including the outlay in maintaining the army, combined with destruction of grain and livestock, he concluded that, over a period of ten years, the strife absorbed a total of £32,255,000. In other words, his estimate of the value of people, stock and land in Ireland was reduced from £13.5 million before the war to £5.2 million after it. Petty's was not the only assessment of the damage caused by a decade of warfare. In 1689, during the Jacobite crisis, when fears of fresh rebellions and massacres abounded, one pamphleteer purported to show that the wealth of Ireland had fallen from £17 million in 1641 to just over £2 million in 1653. After the Williamite war another

---

[1] George O'Brien, *The economic history of Ireland in the seventeenth century* (Dublin, 1919), pp. 100–15.
[2] C. H. Hull (ed.), *The economic writings of Sir William Petty* (2 vols., Cambridge, 1899), I, pp. 149–54.

commentator, George Storey, fixed the costs of the conflict of the 1640s at £34,480,000.[3] The apparent precision of these estimates is, of course, spurious. Calculating wartime losses at a moment of crisis like the 1690s reflected the artful use of the new science of political economy for propaganda purposes; it was designed to create the same alarmist effect as the reprinting in 1679 of Sir John Temple's *History of the rebellion*, which told of the atrocities committed by the rebels in 1641 and 1642. The estimates of the cost of the rebellion also warned England, in the language of the political economist, of the dangers, indeed impossibility, of trusting or dealing with the Catholic Irish. When the threat to Protestant Ireland receded in the late 1690s the estimates of the cost of the Confederate Wars of the 1640s fell accordingly; by 1698 they had shrunk to only £1 million.[4]

The lack of reliable economic data for the 1640s helps account for the credulity accorded to these widely varying estimates. Most of the country lay under the control of the Confederation of Kilkenny, whose archive was largely destroyed, while the bureaucracy of the Dublin government ground to a virtual halt. The Court of Exchequer, for instance, effectively stopped giving decrees in 1644, as did Chancery.[5] Payments of customs were not recorded. This applied not only in Ireland but in England where the absence of port books for most of the 1640s makes it impossible to measure export changes with Ireland's largest pre-1641 trading partner.

Even if these staple sources for the economic history of the 1640s had survived they would probably be of limited value since the war was highly regional and its effects are most apparent through local experiences. A case in point is the extent of property destruction. Using the Civil Survey of the 1650s it is possible, in some cases, to measure the original distribution and scale of property loss. In County Wexford, for example, damage to property was greatest in the north of the county; of the twenty-one castles and twenty-six mills in the three northern baronies seventeen and twenty-two respectively were in ruins. In the four southern baronies of sixty-eight castles and twenty-seven mills only eleven and three respectively were destroyed.[6] In Kildare the contrast between the northeast of the county, which was in the front line of much of the military action, and the rest of the county was equally striking. Civil Survey estimates of the value of buildings in northeast Kildare show a drop from almost £126,000 in 1640

[3] *State of the papist and protestant proprietors in the kingdom of Ireland* (London, 1689), p. 8; George Storey, *A continuation of the impartial history of the war of Ireland* (London, 1693), p. 361.
[4] *A discourse concerning Ireland and the different interests thereof* (London, 1698), p. 10.
[5] National Archives, Dublin, RC 6/2 12/1–2.
[6] R. C. Simington (ed.), *The civil survey*, IX: *Wexford* (IMC, Dublin, 1953).

to £4,350 in 1654.[7] Some devastation, such as that at Maynooth, was spectacular; the castle fell in value from £3,000 in 1640 to £500 in 1654. However property valuations do not provide a comprehensive measure of economic dislocation as a result of war. County Meath, for instance showed almost no evidence of losses recorded in the Civil Survey, except around Kells which lay on the route of armies marching to Ulster. Similarly the inventories of the goods of those to be transplanted to Connacht in 1653–4 show Meath to be rich in livestock and grain. Yet Meath paid the price of peace. In a request for an abatement of the assessment in 1656 it was alleged that people had flocked into the county from surrounding areas during the 1640s, exhausting the land through continual tillage.[8] Thus Meath's problems were different from, if no less severe than, those regions which saw direct military activity.

The varied economic consequences of war can only partially be explained by the military crisis. Ireland in the 1640s was not uniformly commercialized, with areas of the country, especially the north and west, less developed than the east and south.[9] This meant that commercial difficulties, caused by the conflict, immediately crippled the towns of the south and east, while more rural areas in the north and west, which depended for survival on cattle rather than grain and were less tied to a market economy, proved more resilient to the ravages of warfare.

I

In the late months of 1641 the Irish economy was in poor shape. The political problems of 1639–41, combined with harvest failures, produced economic instability which contributed to the rising of the Ulster Irish on 22 October. The customs yield in 1640/41 could have been as much as 35 per cent lower than the 1637/8 level and only a third of the subsidy granted in the parliament of 1640 had been paid by July 1641.[10] Such fiscal difficulties were not unusual in pre-war Ireland which, lacking a mint, depended for its money supply on a surplus in the balance of trade, the export element of which was heavily dominated by unprocessed

[7] R. C. Simington (ed.), *The civil survey*, VIII: *Kildare* (IMC, Dublin, 1952).
[8] W. H. Hardinge, 'On the circumstances attending the outbreak of the civil war in Ireland', *Transactions, Royal Irish Academy*, 24 (1866), p. 415; TCD, MS 844, fo. 172.
[9] On the question generally, Raymond Gillespie, *The transformation of the Irish economy, 1550–1700* (Dundalk, 1991), pp. 24–9.
[10] Raymond Gillespie, 'The end of an era: Ulster and the outbreak of the 1641 rising', in Ciaran Brady and Raymond Gillespie (eds.), *Natives and newcomers: the making of Irish colonial society 1534–1641* (Dublin, 1986), pp. 204–8.

agricultural products.[11] A natural disaster or a political upheaval which retarded trade quickly produced monetary problems since the volume of coin in the economy fell and fixed payments, such as rent, could not be made. If such circumstances lasted for any length of time markets would crash and a commercial crisis would result. This is precisely what happened in the late months of 1641 and early 1642 when an already dire situation was exacerbated by a collapse of confidence created by the fear and instability generated by the unexpected nature of the rising, suspicions of a nationwide Catholic conspiracy, rumours of massacres, and of the king's alleged involvement in the insurrection.

This military and economic instability immediately affected the towns, where trade, already depressed, ground almost to a halt. Thus admissions to freedom in towns during 1642 were significantly lower than the previous year: Belfast granted freedom to only two men in 1642 (against nineteen in 1641) while Dublin's admissions fell from seventy-one to fourteen. In the case of Dublin the reduction was greatest among those who had served apprenticeships, from twenty-two in 1641 to three in 1642, suggesting that those qualified had either left the city or decided not to set up their craft there. Dublin merchants, normally the largest group admitted to freedom in any year, were most affected and none were inducted between 1641 and 1647.[12] The uncertain economic climate in towns also manifested itself in other forms. In Dublin the number of marriages in both the inner city parish of St John and of St Michan, outside the walls, fell sharply between 1641 and 1642. In 1639 the ratio of marriages in St John's to cess payers in the parish was 0.06:1, by 1643 it had dropped to 0.02:1.[13] Further disruption took place as refugees poured into urban areas. The mayor of Waterford complained in December 1641 that 'The thronging of strangers into this cittie dayly makes us fear . . . we may be driven to great extreamitie and danger of starving'.[14] During late 1641 and early 1642 the situation in Dublin deteriorated and the city experienced dreadful food shortages, together with dramatic increases in food prices. Hardly surprisingly, deaths among the refugees occurred regularly; while fears abounded that these strangers would bring disease into the city or betray it to the enemy. The

[11] For this type of crisis see Raymond Gillespie, 'Meal and money: the harvest crisis of 1621–4', in E. M. Crawford (ed.), *Famine: the Irish experience* (Edinburgh, 1989), pp. 75–95.

[12] J. T. Gilbert (ed.), *Calendar of the ancient records of Dublin* (19 vols., Dublin, 1889–1944), III; R. M. Young (ed.), *The town book of the corporation of Belfast* (Belfast, 1896), pp. 249–51.

[13] James Mills (ed.), *The register of St John the Evangelist, Dublin, 1619–99* (Dublin, 1906); H. F. Berry (ed.), *The register of the church of S. Michan, Dublin, 1636–65* (Dublin, 1907). For the St John's cess see NLI, MS 1618, fos. 21, 36, 43, 50, 58, 64, 74, 81, 85.

[14] J. T. Gilbert (ed.), *History of the Irish confederation and the war in Ireland* (7 vols., Dublin, 1882–91), II, p. 8.

population of Dublin, in particular, became highly mobile. Of the cess payers in the parish of St John in 1643 only about a third had been there in 1640; whereas of those in the parish in 1640 over 80 per cent were included in the 1638 cess. By contrast the population of Belfast remained somewhat more stable with about half of those in the 1642 cess being cessed in 1640.[15] Towns became key military targets. For instance the Munster insurgents hoped to starve Cork, which had 'no magasin of provisions and fedd but on the weekly market', into submission.[16] The vulnerability of urban areas was clearly shown at the siege of Drogheda (November 1641 to March 1642) when the Catholic army sealed off the town on the landward side and by a boom across the river Boyne. Food prices quickly soared until the siege was lifted and 'the market at very cheap rates was abundantly furnished'.[17] Blockades by sea were strategically possible, especially by parliamentary shipping in the later stages of the conflict. However, even in the early weeks of the war, fishing boats frustrated Dublin's trade by blocking the harbour.[18]

Paradoxically towns could also be threatened by those seeking to protect them. In their desperation to thwart a lengthy siege, by depriving their assailants of supplies and by hoarding provisions within the walls, townsmen inadvertently prevented grain being resown for the next harvest and thus jeopardized their own survival. Nevertheless, the Dublin government took this risk and, in November 1641, ordered that all crops within ten miles of the capital be brought into the city and sold, or burnt.[19] The devastation caused by this, together with 'rebel' action, proved considerable with the counties around Dublin showing the highest losses per deponent in the depositions taken in early 1642.[20] However, it seems that the administration miscalculated the military capabilities of the insurgents, together with the severity and length of the war, with the result that grain prices, fixed in December, proved to be too high and had to be lowered in January 1642.[21] In March Ormond, on campaign in North Leinster, was told to stop burning corn and hay and by June it became apparent that the grain shortage was such that there would be no seed for the next harvest and so

15 NLI, MS 1618, fos. 50, 58, 64, 74, Young (ed.), *Town book*, pp. 19–20, 21–2, 25–7, 35–6.
16 Gilbert (ed.), *Irish confederation*, I, p. 73.
17 *Ibid.*, 50, 52.
18 HMC, *Calendar of the manuscripts of the marquis of Ormonde*, ns (8 vols., London, 1902–20), II, pp. 39, 47, 68–9.
19 R. R. Steele (ed.), *Tudor and Stuart proclamations* (2 vols., Oxford, 1910), II pt. I, nos. 355, 360, 364; Gilbert (ed.), *Irish confederation*, I, p. 249.
20 HMC, *Eighth report* (London, 1881), app. I, p. 573a provides a summary of the deposition evidence.
21 Steele (ed.), *Tudor and Stuart*, II pt. I, no. 370.

'likely to cause much famine next year'. A series of proclamations in early 1643 attempted to avert this calamity by promising protection to anyone prepared to plough and sow in the Dublin area and by encouraging fishermen to import grain.[22] Dublin may have been more severely affected than many cities by the war, but the nature of the upheaval meant that all urban centres suffered.

In rural areas the impact of war was patchy. In Munster, where little military activity occurred, the fear of the rising by itself generated economic problems. As one of Sir Philip Perceval's Cork tenants wrote in November 1641 'but now as the times are, none will buy but all ready to sell, for we live in great fear'. Another tenant was forced to borrow money to pay his rent since those who owed him money would not pay being 'struck with a mighty fear'. By December Perceval's brother-in-law wrote that 'trade is quite dead and if I offered your stock for sale I should not get a quarter its value and no money either but must trust rascals who would never pay'.[23] Fortunately most Munster landlords had been able to collect their autumn rents before the outbreak of the rebellion. On the Boyle estates, which were widely scattered throughout the province, collectors managed to gather £3,393 in the final quarter of 1641 which compared favourably with an average rent collection of £3,564 in the last quarter of the years 1635–8. However by the first quarter of 1642 rent collectors on the estate only accounted for £16, against an average of £1,937 in the same quarter for 1635–8.[24] The story was similar elsewhere. The president of Munster told Sir Philip Perceval in December 1641 'there can be no thought of receiving rents here and we must look about for some other way of subsistence till God send more quiet times'.[25]

Elsewhere landlords proved even less fortunate. Ulster had been hit more severely than other parts of the country by the recession of the late 1630s because of the greater political instability and heavy quartering of Wentworth's 'New Army' there. As a result the province's share of the Irish customs had fallen from 12.3 per cent in 1632/3 to 6.5 per cent in 1640/1 and there had been complaints that some rents were not received in 1640/1.[26] Moreover the rising had begun in Ulster in late October, before the autumn rent was due, and hence estate balances were at a particularly low ebb. To make matters worse, the outbreak of rebellion now required

[22] *Ibid.*, nos. 377, 379, 381.
[23] HMC, *Report on the manuscripts of the earl of Egmont* (2 vols., London, 1905–9), I, pp. 148, 151, 154.
[24] NLI, MS 6894; MS 6900.
[25] HMC, *Egmont*, I, pp. 156–7.
[26] Gillespie, 'End of an era', pp. 206–7; Jane Ohlmeyer, *Civil war and restoration in the three Stuart kingdoms: The career of Randal MacDonnell, marquis of Antrim, 1609–83* (Cambridge, 1993), p. 76.

landlords to shoulder greater expenditure than normal (see chapter 11 below). Ulster proprietors had to raise and pay for forces for their protection much earlier and to a much greater extent than those in other parts of the island. In Leinster, for instance, the army comprised almost entirely the Irish standing army, funded by the Exchequer, together with some reinforcements from England; while in Munster landowners raised 1,400 men and 340 horse for their protection. Ulster landlords, by contrast, raised and paid, mainly from their own resources, 8,500 foot and 740 horse under royal commissions dating from late 1641 to early 1642.[27]

II

By the beginning of 1642 the rebellion had spread throughout Ireland. The effect was to deliver a massive shock to an economy already in the throes of a commercial crisis and it was the middle of the year before the economy stabilized, albeit at a much lower level of activity than it had displayed in 1641. On the Boyle estate in Munster, for example, rent receipts quickened noticeably after May 1642 and arrears of rent began to come in for the first time since December 1641. The annual rent receipts for 1642 and 1643 are close, £329 and £307 respectively, which suggests that this may be the level of rental income appropriate to wartime, representing about a tenth of 1630s quarterly levels.[28] In Belfast and Dublin admissions to freedom increased in 1643 over the 1642 levels indicating some recovery; while in Dublin the share of admissions of apprenticeship had returned to its pre-war level.[29]

This partial improvement cannot be attributed simply to adjustment to new realities. Other factors were also at work. The harvest of 1642 seems to have been very good locally. The Lords Justice noted that in areas little affected by war there had been a bountiful crop: 'Longford, Louth, Westmeath and Meath are abundantly plentifull in cattell, corne and graine and indeed are granaries and stores whereout the province of Ulster to be furnished with corne and cattell'.[30] In addition to the abundant harvest, both the Confederates and the Dublin administration began to deal with the currency problem. The collapse of trade in 1641 and 1642 had left the Irish economy without enough coin to function effectively. This placed a premium on specie in Ireland which was valued at a premium above

---

[27] HMC, *The manuscripts of the marquis of Ormonde*, os (2 vols., London, 1895–9), I, pp. 123–7; Gilbert (ed.), *Irish confederation*, III, pp. 24–6.
[28] NLI, MS 6900.
[29] Sources as in n. 12.
[30] James Hogan (ed.), *Letters and papers relating to the Irish rebellion* (IMC, Dublin, 1936), p. 99.

its metal content. The London government exploited this situation by providing £20,000 for suppression of the rising in Spanish reales, which traded at 10 per cent above their intrinsic value. Such an overvalued currency increased prices and further depressed commerce because merchants would find that 'we have no commodity to trade with them and that this mony going there at so high a rate they must of necessity be loosers 10 in the 100 which we conceive must in time starve our army'.[31] The answer to both this dilemma and the problem of the short-term funding of the army was to strike an Irish coinage. Two coinages were issued in 1642 and one in 1643, struck on plate called in by proclamation. Trinity College, Dublin provided £2 7s 6d worth of silver in 1642 and £54 18s 3d in 1643. By February 1643 £1,200 worth of plate had been surrendered.[32] In terms of financing the army this was not significant but by providing temporary stability for limited trade it made some impact. The Confederation also struck £4,000 worth of coin in 1642. Even though this infringed upon the royal prerogative, something which the Confederates had vowed not to do, they claimed that it was necessary for maintaining His Majesty's service 'not otherwise presuming the power'.[33]

A second factor promoting stability was the movement of the economy on to a more war-based footing. Some regions of the country clearly adapted more rapidly than others. Assessments for the maintenance of the confederate army suggest that counties in the southeast, such as Wexford and Kilkenny, were able to bear a higher share of the cost than others.[34] Kilkenny probably profited from the location of the confederate capital there; while Wexford seems to have benefited from privateering under the auspices of the Confederation. Between December 1642 and February 1643 the Confederation issued at least twenty letters of marque to captains of foreign shipping prepared to act as a confederate navy in return for freedom to rove the seas for plunder. By the mid-1640s the number of ships had increased considerably as had the sphere of operations. It is difficult to measure the economic effect of this on the ports from which they operated but it was clearly considerable. One ship brought prizes to Wexford worth £1,500 and in 1648/9 another brought in prizes worth £8,000.[35]

---

[31] *Ibid.*, p. 137; HMC, *Egmont MSS*, I, p. 304; Thomas Carte, *History of the life of James, first duke of Ormond* (second edn., 6 vols., Oxford, 1851), II, p. 27.

[32] Douglas Bennet, *The silver collection of Trinity College, Dublin* (Dublin, 1991), app. 2; James Simon, *An essay towards an historical account of Irish coins* (Dublin, 1810), pp. 46–8; HMC, *Ormonde*, ns, II, pp. 234–5.

[33] Gilbert (ed.), *Irish confederation*, I, p. 115; Carte, *Ormond*, II, p. 360.

[34] *Cal. S P Ire., 1633–47*, p. 403.

[35] Jane Ohlmeyer, 'Irish privateers during the civil war', *Mariner's Mirror*, 76 (May, 1990), pp. 119–33.

Enterprises such as this proved lucrative, if sporadic, and by 1644 Ormond considered the possibility of issuing letters of marque on behalf of the Dublin government.[36]

In addition, the presence of the army was not entirely destructive and locally they provided some economic stimulus. Soldiers had to be fed and housed, often at considerable profit to suppliers. The residents of Derry, according to one group of officers, exploited the army for 'so great is the covetousness of the people in the town having since the troubles exacted such extreme rates for chambers and lodgings that a house formerly set at a rate of £8 or £10 per annum now by partitioning off rooms to yield 30 or 40 pounds per annum'.[37] Many soldiers, who were also craftsmen, exercised their skills if the opportunity presented itself. At Naas, for example, in May 1642 officers set to work men who were weavers, tanners and spinners employing them at sixpence a day and using local materials.[38] Such initiatives, together with the good harvest, the partial stabilization of the currency and the orders of both the Confederation and the Dublin government that markets were not to be impeded helped in a large measure to stabilize the concurrent crises of late 1641.[39]

Despite this, levels of economic activity remained too low to support the demands being made on it. As the confederate Supreme Council noted in 1643 'although the people contribute cheerfully what they have, yet the stock of money now in the kingdom answers not their desires'.[40] On the civil side there were two administrations to be supported in Ireland, that of the Confederation as well as the Dublin government. One observer complained, of the expenses associated with the Confederation's bureaucracy, that there was

> a world of clerks and attorneys, a set number of commissioners in every county, receivers and applotters. The exchequer was full with daily taxations, customs, monopoly, enemy lands or custodians, excise and many others of that kind, came daily to the exchequer which was a world of money, but the most part, or rather all, was spent in daily wages of the Supreme Council, judges, clerks, and other mechanical men and little or nothing went to the military.

Some took this argument further, alleging in 1647 that 'it is evident that the bad government of the Catholics is the real cause why money is not to be

---

[36] Carte, *Ormond*, VI, p. 53.   [37] HMC, *Ormonde*, os, I, p. 72.
[38] *A true relation of the state of Ireland* (London, 1642), pp. 3-4.
[39] *Cal. S P Ire., 1633-47*, p. 363; Benignus Millett, 'Calendar of volume 1 of the Scritture riferite nei congressi, Irlanda in Propaganda archives', *Collectanea Hibernica*, 6-7 (1963-4), pp. 54-5; Gilbert (ed.), *Irish confederation*, II, pp. 82-3.
[40] Gilbert (ed.), *Irish confederation*, II, p. 205.

found; I am even told that there are many commissaries whose accounts have never been examined'.[41]

What the army itself cost is difficult to estimate, but it was large and shortage of funds ensured that payments to troops remained nearly always in arrears. In 1642, for instance, the annual charge of Ormond's force totalled £607,452, or more than seven times the income of Ireland in 1640.[42] In the absence of regular pay, the armies had to be fed and armed. The provisions for Ormond's forces in Leinster, comprising fifteen regiments of foot, twenty-two troops of horse of dragoons, for one week in 1643 amounted to 49,248 pounds of butter, 49,649 pounds of cheese, 447 barrels of wheat and rye, 367 barrels of peas and 356 barrels of oats.[43] The logistics of assembling and transporting such quantities were daunting and involved the requisitioning of horses, which were in increasingly short supply being 'destroyed between the enemy and us' (also see chapter 3 above).[44]

Since supplying troops posed problems for all sides during the war, armies often had no alternative but to forage for cattle and other goods or to capture enemy markets.[45] This had a dramatic impact on the local population and the arrival of a large military force, whether friendly or otherwise, invariably caused problems. The Leinster economy, for example, could not adequately sustain and supply the forces stationed there; while the presence in Dublin of over 4,000 foot soldiers in 1644, or over 10 per cent of the peacetime population, proved disastrous.[46] However, when military units remained small, damage to the local economy could be minimized. For instance in Ulster, where confederate forces were divided into manageable units each with its own cattle and herdsmen, the economy responded with a marked shift away from grain to livestock rearing which helped to alleviate supply problems.[47] In 1646 the 'abundant supply, especially of animals and all kinds of eatables which were sold at an absurdly low price' at a fair in Cavan took one papal official totally by surprise.[48]

[41] J. T. Gilbert (ed.), *A contemporary history of affairs in Ireland* (Irish Archaeological Society, 3 vols., Dublin, 1879), I, pp. 52, 78; Guiseppe Aiazza, *The embassy in Ireland of Monsignor G. B. Rinuccini, archbishop of Fermo* . . . translated by Annie Hutton (Dublin, 1873), p. 353.

[42] *Cal. S P Ire., 1633–47*, p. 396; *Cal. S P Ire., 1647–60*, p. 335.

[43] HMC, *Ormonde*, ns, II, p. 327.

[44] *Ibid.*, I, p. 251.

[45] *Cal. S P Ire., 1633–47*, p. 435.

[46] HMC, *Ormonde*, os, I, pp. 158–9.

[47] Jerrold Casway, *Owen Roe O'Neill and the struggle for Catholic Ireland* (Philadelphia, 1984), pp. 78, 79, 84, 86–7; Charles McNeill (ed.), *The Tanner letters: documents of Irish affairs . . . extracted from . . . the Bodleian Library, Oxford* (IMC, Dublin, 1943), p. 243.

[48] Dionysius Massari, 'My Irish campaign', *The Catholic Bulletin*, 7 (1917), p. 249.

By the end of 1642 new factors appeared which worsened the economic situation in Ireland. Most important, the outbreak of the First English Civil War in August 1642 eliminated the possibility of receiving sufficient external help for an economy already hard pressed to meet the demands on it. The English conflict also disrupted Ireland's main export market. As one Cork landowner complained in September 1642 'by reason of the great troubles in England I cannot sell my wool nor get any of my debts . . . I killed a hundred fat oxen at Doneraile, Mallow and Youghal that would have yielded me £700 in England'.[49] The collapse of English trade, partly as a result of the hostilities there and partly because the king controlled few maritime centres with which Irish confederate towns could trade, is clearly shown in a surviving Waterford port book. In the early part of the seventeenth century the ports of southwest England, especially Bristol, had been one of the main destinations for the trade of southeast Ireland but by 1643/4 of the 1,236 tons of shipping (or twenty-two vessels) which left Waterford only 135 tons (or three vessels) were destined for England. The remainder were bound for ports in France (such as Nantes, Bordeaux and St Malo), Flanders (Dunkirk), Spain (Bilbao) or Germany (Hamburg). Imports into the city came from the same sources.[50] By spring 1642 the Dublin government also bought grain in France and by September looked to Amsterdam for supplies.[51] Catholic merchants dominated most of this continental traffic but since the parliamentary navy, which Richard Bellings described in 1646 as 'absolute masters of the sea', targeted confederate ports and shipping, overseas trade remained dangerous and sporadic.[52]

III

The economic disruption caused by the onset of hostilities in England convinced many in Ireland of the need to conclude a cease-fire. Whereas the harvest of 1642 had been bountiful, that of 1643 proved disastrous. This, together with the collapse of trade in late 1642, reduced the revenue available to the Dublin government significantly and led to the introduction of a new book of rates for customs and excise.[53] By early 1643 government officials had resorted to seizing merchants' goods (promising payment in

[49] HMC, *Egmont*, I, p. 181.
[50] Bodl., Carte MSS 6, fo. 506. I am grateful to Jane Ohlmeyer for drawing my attention to this.
[51] HMC, *Ormonde*, ns, II, pp. 159, 190.
[52] Gilbert (ed.), *Irish confederation*, VI, pp. 1–2.
[53] HMC, *Ormonde*, ns, II, p. 299; Steele (ed.), *Tudor and Stuart*, II, pt. I, no. 382.

London) and to trading these in England for supplies with which to relieve
Dublin. However, these measures devastated the capital's merchant
community and forced Protestant leaders to sign, in September 1643, a one-
year cessation of arms. The agreement contained a number of significant
economic provisions and, in addition to providing for freedom of supply, it
allowed for 'free passage, intercourse, commerce and traffic during the said
cessation'.[54] The Confederates also agreed to pay Ormond £30,800, half
in cash and half in cattle, which prevented bankruptcy in the Dublin
exchequer.[55] The immediate effect of the truce was to reduce military
expenditure, which fell from £50,520 a month in 1642 to £28,863 by 1645.[56]
However even these charges were substantial and the government tried to
enhance the pace of recovery by issuing a series of proclamations in 1644
and 1645 which allowed all imported goods to be free of customs and
promoted the export of available commodities, mainly hides and fish. It
also encouraged farmers near Dublin to reoccupy their lands and tried to
inject coinage into the economy in order to provide funds for trade.[57] The
process of calling in plate, begun in 1642, continued until 1647 and at least
some of the newly minted coin seems to have been directed at encouraging
overseas commerce.[58] Certainly the gold coinage, issued by Ormond in
1646, was intended for high value payments incurred by large volume
trade.[59] In Munster Inchiquin struck coins in 1643 and, the following year,
asked for a 'publique order or proclamation . . . for making currant
the moneys lately stamped by his Majesties authoritye in Corcke . . . for the
furtherance of the publique traffique and commerce'.[60]

Despite these measures the economy remained stuck at a low level of
activity during the middle decades of the 1640s. On the Boyle estate the
temporary truce barely affected rent receipts and those for the final quarter
of 1643 were very close to those of the last quarter of 1642, while income

[54] *The grounds and matters inducing his Majesty to agree to a cessation of arms* (Oxford, 1643), sig, A2v;
   Gilbert (ed.), *Irish confederation*, II, pp. 306–7, 350–8.
[55] R. Scrope and T. Monkhouse (eds.), *State papers collected by Edward, earl of Clarendon* (3 vols.,
   Oxford, 1767–86), II, p. 156.
[56] *Cal. S P Ire., 1633–47*, pp. 369, 420.
[57] Steele (ed.), *Tudor and Stuart*, II pt. I, nos. 399, 403, 406, 408, 410, 433a; HMC, *Egmont*, I, p. 185;
   BL, Egerton MSS 917, fo. 22.
[58] The value of the plate surrendered by Trinity College, Dublin rose from £54 18s 3d in 1643 to
   £77 18s 7d in 1644 and to £180 11s 8d in 1646 before falling back to £59 11s 3d in 1647, Bennet,
   Silver collection, app. 2.
[59] Bodl., Carte MSS 154, fo. 221, MSS 164, fo. 360; William O'Sullivan, 'The only gold coinage
   issued in Ireland (1646)', *British Numismatic Journal*, 33 (1964), pp. 141–50.
[60] Gilbert (ed.), *Irish confederation*, IV, pp. 109–10; BL, Add. MSS 25, 287, fo. 34v. There were
   further issues in Cork during 1645 and in 1646 the Munster Presidency Council struck farthings
   in copper at a rate of twenty-two shillings in farthings for twenty shillings sterling.

from rents and arrears in 1644 remained identical to that of 1642. A similar picture emerges from an examination of the evidence of trade. The port books for Barnstaple, Minehead and Dartmouth for 1646/7 suggest that exports from the Munster ports were still dramatically below their 1635/6 level. Imports of wool, a staple of the Irish trade, had fallen from 20,721 cwt in 1635/6 to 1,012 cwt in 1646/7. Barrelled beef over the same period dropped from 1,244 barrels to 602 barrels and the timber trade almost ceased. Only hide imports rose from 3,172 cwt in 1635/6 to 6,628 cwt in 1646/7, suggesting an increased slaughtering of cattle to provide food in Ireland.[61] However economic improvement varied enormously. A report of December 1647 on the state of the country noted that Leinster and Munster had made some recovery, while in Ulster, where military activity by Robert Monro's forces had continued despite the various cessations, five of the nine counties were waste and of six counties in Connacht four were devastated.[62]

Even if there had been a significant upturn in the Irish economy during the mid-1640s there remained the problem of how that could be channelled into a renewed war-effort. A lack of resources and access to internal lines of communication – the Confederation controlled most of the country, with the exception of north Leinster and the area of Munster around Cork – hampered the efforts of the Dublin administration[63] (see map 1). From the confederate standpoint enhancement of their economic position through increased taxation gave rise to a constitutional problem. The General Assembly proclaimed that it was not a parliament and baulked at levying new taxation. As the confederate Supreme Council admitted in June 1644:

> we confess plenty of provision for maintaining the army may be had within our quarters and although the imposicions be heavy yet there is money in the country to answer the occasion. But the people have not given us that power over them which may be exercised without yielding an accompt of our actions and a reason for any next tax.[64]

All in all the experience of the cessation had proved disillusioning to all signatories and the economic recession continued unchecked.

The failure of all sides to improve the domestic economy meant that they

---

[61] For 1636/7 see PRO, E[xchequer] 190/1088; E190/950/1; E190/949/10. For 1646/7 see, PRO, E190/1089/11; E190/952/3; E190/952/4. The trade of Dublin and Cork was also largely in hides, Gilbert (ed.), *Irish confederation*, II, pp. 263–4; HMC, *Ormonde*, ns, II, p. 268.

[62] BL, Egerton MSS 917, fos. 25–6.

[63] T. W. Moody, F. X. Martin and F. J. Byrne (eds.), *A new history of Ireland*, III: *Early modern Ireland* (Oxford, 1976), p. 310.

[64] Gilbert (ed.), *Irish confederation*, III, p. 196.

looked elsewhere for relief. The Confederates turned to Europe, seeking subventions from the major powers there. They had little success, raising only £70,000 (or enough to pay their army for three months) mainly from the Papacy (see chapter 5 above).[65] The failure of the Irish economy to regenerate sufficiently to produce supplies, together with the king's inability to provide them, led to disillusionment among some royalist army commanders who turned to Parliament for assistance, or, as Ormond so delicately put it, sold 'their faith for meale'.[66]

There are other explanations for the failure of the Irish economy to expand more than it did during the years after 1643. In some cases local circumstances were responsible. The city of Cork, for example, declined after the cessation while nearby Kinsale and Youghal prospered in 1644 and 1645 with admission to freedom well up to pre-war levels. This rise of Youghal and Kinsale, at the expense of Cork, largely stemmed from the expulsion of Catholics, many of whom were Old English merchants, from the city by Inchiquin in 1644. This disrupted Cork's trade while stimulating that of its local competitors.[67] There were, however, more general factors at work in retarding economic progress. To begin with, the cessation did not provide adequate security to encourage economic recovery and development. As a result of the haphazard division of the country between the various combatants in 1643 it was not entirely clear who was in ultimate control in some regions. For example, in Galway the earl of Clanricard continually contested the confederate right to billet troops on his patrimony.[68] In Ulster a lengthy, disruptive dispute over the respective rights to corn and cattle, between the Irish soldiers, who returned to farming, and the Protestant settlers prevented the return of stability to the province.[69] Banditry exacerbated an already volatile situation and, according to Richard Bellings, some 'seeing with what impunity . . . men got rich by rapine . . . they began stealing and petty robberies to exercise what they thought a thriving trade'. Certainly, shortly after the conclusion of the cessation, soldiers at Newcastle near Dublin illegally charged tolls on

[65] Carte, *Ormond*, VI, p. 53.
[66] *Ibid.*, 102; M. Perceval-Maxwell, 'The adoption of the Solemn League and Covenant by the Scots in Ulster', *Scotia*, 2 (1978), pp. 1–18; J. A. Murphy, 'The politics of the Munster protestants, 1641–1649', *Journal of the Cork Historical and Archaeological Society*, 76 (1971), pp. 1–20.
[67] HMC, *Egmont*, 1, p. 291; Richard Caulfield (ed.), *The council book of the corporation of Youghal* (Guildford, 1878), pp. 249–84; J. A. Murphy, 'The expulsion of the Irish from Cork in 1644', *Journal of the Cork Historical and Archaeological Society*, 69 (1964), pp. 123–31.
[68] John Lowe (ed.), *Letter-book of the earl of Clanricarde, 1643–1647* (IMC, Dublin, 1983), pp. 7–8, 44–5, 52–6.
[69] [Edmund Hogan (ed.),] *The history of the warr in Ireland* (Dublin, 1873), p. 35; Casway, *Owen Roe O'Neill*, pp. 93–6.

the road and seized cattle for their own profit, while gangs of freebooters roamed through Connacht.[70]

Hardly surprisingly, landlords were not prepared to take the initiative in promoting economic change as they had done in peacetime. However, when one individual began to invest others often followed. As John Davis wrote from Belfast in early 1647 'I have put five ploughs upon my own land which makes people believe I have reasons unknown for doing it and has occasioned a hundred ploughs more to be going than there were when I came thither'.[71] Despite this landlords and tenants were unwilling to be tied down by leases of even moderate length which might have encouraged tenants to remain on their property. In Munster Sir Philip Perceval granted six-month leases to his tenants in 1646, while in 1649 out of 103 leases made by the countess of Cork over a third were for one year only and almost all the remainder for three years.[72] In Ulster a similar state of affairs prevailed on the Savage estate in County Down and by the 1650s almost half of the tenants held their land 'at pleasure'. Most of these were recent arrivals, only a third had been there five years previously.[73] This situation was aggravated, on the one hand, by the low population in relation to land, and hence easy availability of leases due to lack of demand, and, on the other, by the fact that many tenants showed no commitment to their holdings, knowing that an advantageous lease could always be acquired elsewhere in the country. Such attitudes promoted instability and the picture of the wartime Irish landscape was a desolate one. As Michael Jones described Wicklow in 1647 'they saw not the face of either man, woman or child of any of the country they being all fled'.[74]

Where economic security could be provided the transformation in the economic position of a region was dramatic. The return of peace to England after May 1646 once again opened select English markets to Irish trade, while Ormond's surrender of Dublin to Colonel Michael Jones in June 1647, thus lifting the parliamentary naval blockade there, transformed the local economy. Fifty-three men gained the freedom of the city in 1647 and a further 118 in 1648, as opposed to an average of only twenty-two per annum in the previous five years. Over half of the admissions in 1647 and 1648 were by 'special grace' indicating that these were new migrants into

[70] Gilbert (ed.), *Irish confederation*, I, p. 42; Lowe (ed.), *Letter-book*, p. 145; Steele (ed.), *Tudor and Stuart*, II pt. I, no. 443a. By 1647 the parliamentary commissioners were still trying to stamp out this type of activity.
[71] HMC, *Egmont*, I, p. 353.
[72] NLI, MS 6143; HMC, *Egmont*, I, p. 289.
[73] Raymond Gillespie, *Colonial Ulster: the settlement of East Ulster, 1600–1641* (Cork, 1985), p. 60.
[74] HMC, *Egmont*, I, p. 476.

Dublin availing of the temporary stability there. Of those initiated by 'special grace', eight in 1647 and twelve in 1648 (about 40 per cent in each case) were merchants. Similarly workers in the building trade were admitted to freedom suggesting sufficient optimism to begin rebuilding the city.[75] Other indications of confidence also appeared in Dublin. For instance, the marriage rate in the parish of St John rose from 0.006 marriages per cess payer in 1646 to 0.12 marriages per cess payer by 1649;[76] while the high population mobility, which had characterized the city in the early 1640s, began to fall so that the turnover of names between February 1647 and July 1649 dropped to about 44 per cent.[77]

IV

Political events in the late 1640s ensured that any stability created in 1647 and 1648 remained limited. The declaration of the 'First Ormond Peace' in the summer of 1646 had shattered the tenuous unity of the Confederation, which now fell under the control of the papal nuncio, Rinuccini. Moreover, the outbreak of the Second Civil War in England, followed by the execution of the king in January 1649, changed the nature of the conflict in Ireland from a civil war with localized adherence to the English Parliament or the king, to an extension of the British war. After May 1648 the Irish Royalists joined with Inchiquin and the Confederates in an attempt to create an army capable of defeating parliamentary forces in Ireland and of invading Britain in the king's name (see chapter 6 above). The economic consequences of this action were considerable. While supply for the Irish Royalists from England had always been scant, it did bridge some of the gap between their needs and the inadequate indigenous resources. However the declaration for the king by this combined force meant that they could expect no assistance from England, now controlled by Parliament, at a time when they needed that help most.

To make matters worse, the nature of the war in the late 1640s proved to be more extensive and violent than anything experienced hitherto. The Cromwellian army in 1649 used heavy artillery to an extent not previously seen in the war (see chapter 4 above).[78] As evidence from the Civil Survey illustrates, the English offensive left many towns in ruins: in New Ross 43 per cent of the tenements in the town were waste; while in Killamallock and

---

[75] Sources as n. 12.   [76] Sources as n. 13.
[77] Dublin City Archives, City Hall, Dublin, MR/15.
[78] James Burke, 'The New Model Army and the problem of siege warfare', *IHS*, 27 (1990–1), pp. 1–29.

Kilkenny 26 per cent and 14 per cent of tenements respectively were destroyed.[79] Areas which had been previously little affected by the war were also drawn into the conflict. Inchiquin's 1647 offensive left Tipperary, which had supplied much of Munster with grain, so devastated that the area had not recovered by 1651.[80] It was hardly surprising therefore that, in May 1648, Inchiquin complained 'I have expended all I have, or could borrow or force in my own quarters yet divers of my men have dyed of hunger after they lived a while upon catts and doggs as many have done'.[81] By 1649 the effects of Owen Roe O'Neill's campaigns and those of the parliamentarian Michael Jones had wasted the country so much that it could barely support the royalist force in camp let alone on campaign.[82]

More serious still, famine now threatened to consume the entire country. In 1648 one commentator lamented that there occurred 'so great a dearth of corn that Ireland had not seene in or memorie, and so cruel a famine, which hath already killed thousands of the poorer sort'.[83] By 1650 only a belt of land from Carlow through Kilkenny to Limerick had sufficient surplus of grain or cattle to spare for the royalist army. Indeed by 1651 grain prices in Ireland were higher than in England which represents a disaster of considerable magnitude given the monetary deflation in the Irish economy during the 1640s which meant that grain, though scarce, cost less in Ireland than England.[84]

Above all what characterized the years after 1646 was a growth of war weariness and a dramatic undermining of any remaining confidence that the Irish economy could recover. The earl of Clanricard had detected the beginnings of this process as early as 1645, noting that the inhabitants of Connacht had grown 'weary and suspicious of them [the Confederates] for the disposal of their monies'. In the same year Rinuccini discovered that merchants had become nervous about lending, especially on security such as future tax yields.[85] By 1647 the Confederation expressed disillusionment noting 'our exchequer emptie and altogether hopeless to get in moneys from a country so totally exhausted and so lamentable ruined; our expectation of great sums and helps beyond the seas being turned into wind and smoake and despayre'; 'the common people' according to another

---

[79] Simington (ed.), *The civil survey*, IX: *Wexford*, pp. 233–55; *The civil survey*, IV: *Limerick* (IMC, Dublin, 1938), pp. 155–95; *The civil survey*, VI: *Waterford* (IMC, Dublin, 1942), pp. 499–549.

[80] McNeill (ed.), *Tanner letters*, pp. 268, 361; HMC, *Egmont*, I, p. 397.

[81] Carte, *Ormond*, VI, p. 550.

[82] *Ibid.*, 599; Ian Gentles, *The New Model Army in England, Ireland and Scotland, 1645–1653* (Oxford, 1992), p. 375.

[83] Gilbert (ed.), *Irish confederation*, VI, pp. 270–1.

[84] HMC, *Ormonde*, ns, I, pp. 140–2; Gentles, *New Model Army*, pp. 384–5.

[85] Lowe (ed.), *Letter-book*, p. 131; Aiazza, *Embassy in Ireland*, p. 139.

account 'desperate, reviling and cursing those they conceive the causers of their present miseries'. In the course of the year the situation worsened. Rinuccini's report on the state of the country in 1647 stressed shortages of money, increases in disunion and the general devastation of the country, which served 'to alienate friend and exasperate enemies'.[86] Borrowing, which had previously bridged the gap between income and expenditure, became almost impossible because, apart from enormous interest rates as a result of a scarcity of lenders and funds, there was no confidence that debts would be honoured. Galway corporation refused to lend Clanricard £1,000 in 1647, since his previous loans had not been repaid. Trying to mortgage his own lands also proved futile.[87]

The impact of this new phase of the war is also seen in the more general economic position. Trade fell to an even lower level than before. Dublin's customs, which at the beginning of the 1630s had yielded almost £5,000 a year, had fallen to less than £1,400 by 1644/5 and by 1647 probably did not exceed £600.[88] As a partly extant port book illustrates, during the early months of 1649, cattle and wool exports between Dublin and Chester ground to a halt. Only the hide trade, at a twelfth of its 1639 level, and the sheepskin trade, at less than a quarter of its 1639 level, continued operating.[89] Rents suffered a similar decline. Lady Perceval's estate in Cork, set for £800 in 1648, yielded only £450 and that after 'much trouble'. The value of land had also fallen sharply so that in Cork by 1648 Colonel Barry could complain to Sir John Perceval 'It is in my opinion a hard case that land should so extremely fall in the value and the money should rise ... that I owe you more than my estate and my neck are worth'.[90]

In addition to the military and economic dislocation a further, and in the long-term more devastating, disaster struck. In July 1649, at a time when malignant dysentery or virulent typhus had already reached epidemic proportions, bubonic plague appeared in Galway, probably brought by rats on a ship from Europe. One estimate of early 1650 suggested that nearly 20,000 died in Galway alone, including some of the confederate leaders.[91]

[86] Gilbert (ed.), *Irish confederation*, VI, pp. 81–2; HMC, *Egmont*, I, p. 477; Aiazza, *Embassy in Ireland*, p. 359. This movement seems to parallel the war weariness in England in the mid-1640s which resulted in the club movement, see Joyce Lee Malcolm, *Caesar's due: loyalty and King Charles, 1642–6* (London, 1983), pp. 212–26.
[87] Lowe (ed.), *Letter-book*, pp. 221, 378, 387, 400; *A famous victory obtained by the British forces in the kingdom of Ireland* (London, 1647), p. 4.
[88] HMC, *Ormonde*, ns, I, pp. 89–90, 115.
[89] Donald Woodward, 'The overseas trade of Chester, 1600–50', *Transactions of the historic society of Lancashire and Cheshire*, 122 (1970), pp. 40–2; *The present condition of Dublin in Ireland* (London, 1649).
[90] HMC, *Egmont*, I, pp. 417, 486, 490.
[91] J. F. D. Shrewsbury, *A history of the bubonic plague in the British Isles* (Cambridge, 1971), pp. 433–5; McNeill (ed.), *Tanner letters*, p. 325; Gentles, *New Model Army*, pp. 373, 375.

In 1649 it reached Dublin. The number of burials in St John's parish during the summer months, which suggest bubonic plague, soared in both 1649 and 1650. At its height Sir William Petty suggested that the pestilence killed 1,300 a week in the capital.[92] There was no abatement of the periodic visitations of the disease until 1652. The arrival of plague, combined with a war of considerable ferocity, caused total collapse in the Irish economy and it was not until the late 1650s that any signs of improvement can be detected.

V

There can be little doubt that the 1640s represent the greatest series of crises which the Irish economy faced in the seventeenth century. Only isolated details of how individual areas fared over the whole period appear to have survived. For instance, the rents of the countess of Huntington's lands in Fermanagh and Tyrone had not recovered to the 1641 half yearly value of £381 by 1670 when they stood at £358. She appears to have received nothing at all from the property in the 1640s and less than a third of the pre-war income in the 1650s. Similarly the earl of Thomond's annual rental, which in the 1620s stood at just over £3,800, had dropped to £1,359 by 1646. In 1659/60 it had recovered to only £1,947 and it was the 1680s before it regained the early seventeenth-century value. In Munster the experience on Sir Philip Perceval's lands was similar. A survey of the estate in 1677 records that the rents payable were still a long way short of the 1641 level (by between 10 and 20 per cent).[93]

It would be wrong to present the 1640s as a period of unmitigated economic disaster. As with most wars there was a wide diversity of experience. Some landlords, already heavily indebted in the 1630s, felt the trauma of war quickly. Ormond, for example, was financially embarrassed before the conflict and having leased his estate for long periods at low rents he proved unable to respond to war conditions. Moreover, his lands lay in the area of some of the heaviest fighting and remained under the control of the Confederates for much of the 1640s. His rental income seems to have ceased by 1642 at a time of heavy personal military expenditure and he complained that his debts were 'many and great and that the interest

[92] Hull (ed.), *Economic writings of Sir William Petty*, 1, p. 151.
[93] For the Countess of Huntington, Huntington Library, San Marino, HAM 76. I am grateful to Jane Ohlmeyer for these figures. For Thomond see West Sussex Record Office, Chichester, Petworth House Archives, 9.B.27 (1626/7), 6.C.1 (1646), 6.B.4 (1654–60). Thomond's own estimate of his rental at about £7,000 per annum in the early 1640s seems grossly inflated, Hogan (ed.), *Letters and papers*, pp. 200–3. For Perceval, BL, Add. MSS 47,113.

growing thereupon will in a short tyme exceed the debts'.[94] The earl of Antrim, also heavily indebted before the war, survived with more success. He was more fortunate than Ormond since his estates saw relatively little military action. One way of measuring how the war affected the productive capacity of the earl's estates is to consider the value of tithes during the 1640s. Comparison of the yield of tithes in Ulster between 1640 and the mid-1650s shows that while Counties Armagh and Down experienced a fall of 30 and 32 per cent respectively the County Antrim tithes fell by only a quarter, suggesting that Antrim's lands were less affected than other parts of Ulster.[95] The earl also became involved in privateering schemes which provided him with additional income and he had access to revenue from his wife's estate.

Some actually benefited from the fighting. In Cork the Southwell family reckoned themselves to be worth £150 a year in 1641 but by 1664 Robert Southwell enjoyed £1,014 largely through the opportunities presented by the war for trade and victualling armies. For newcomers, such as Sir William Petty, there would be equally lucrative openings. As Inchiquin appreciated as early as 1644 'there is noe doubt (if God make us vanquishers) but deserving men will have estates conferred on them in the end of this as it was in the end of the last warres . . . of Ireland'.[96] Studies of areas as diverse as Counties Mayo and Louth indicate that in the redistribution under the Cromwellian and Restoration regimes many pre-1641 landlords benefited but to do this they were required to play a complicated political game and to survive the heavy burdens of taxation of the 1650s. Only the most wily succeeded (see chapters 9 and 11 below).[97]

From an economic perspective the crises of the 1640s and the difficulties of the early 1650s fundamentally reconfigured the Irish economy. The interruption of agriculture and the collapse of trade made it possible to rebuild the economic system anew in the late seventeenth century. It is clear, for example, that even before the passage of the Cattle Acts in 1665

[94] Carte, *Ormond*, v, p. 358.
[95] Representative Church Body Library, Dublin, GS 2/7/3/27; T. G. F. Patterson (ed.), 'Cromwellian inquisitions as to parishes in County Armagh in 1657', *Ulster Journal of Archaeology*, third series, 2 (1939), pp. 212–49.
[96] Carte, *Ormond*, vi, p. 172; T. C. Barnard, 'The political, material and mental culture of the Cork settlers, c. 1650–1700', in P. O'Flanagan and C. Buttimer (eds.), *Cork: history and society* (Dublin, 1993), p. 339.
[97] For examples, Raymond Gillespie, 'Landed society and the Interregnum in Ireland and Scotland', in R. Mitchison and P. Roebuck (eds.), *Economy and society in Scotland and Ireland, 1500–1939* (Edinburgh, 1988), pp. 38–47; Gillespie, 'Lords and commons in seventeenth-century Mayo', in R. Gillespie and G. Moran (eds.), *'A various country': essays in Mayo history, 1500–1900* (Westport, 1987), pp. 54–6; Harold O'Sullivan, 'Land ownership changes in the county of Louth in the seventeenth century' (unpublished PhD thesis, TCD, 1992).

Irish trade was moving away from live cattle towards barrelled beef and butter which became the foundation of prosperity in late seventeenth-century Ireland.[98] That shift was only possible because older patterns of economic activity had been broken by war. Similarly the restructuring of landownership in some parts of the country as a result of the war of the 1640s saw the emergence of large consolidated estates which could be more effectively managed than before.

While the 1640s proved a ruinous decade in Irish economic life, as George O'Brien maintained, the pattern of disruption was more complex than it appears at first sight. Military action certainly curtailed Irish economic activity but it was not the only, nor even the principal, inter-ruption. The nature of the Irish war of the 1640s was not that of a large-scale destructive war. The set-piece battle, for example, played little part. The most traumatic influence on economic life in the early stages of the conflict was a series of commercial crises whose effect remained highly regionalized. The nature of those disasters reflected structural problems in the Irish economy, particularly the dependence on a favourable balance of trade to control the money supply. Similar difficulties had occurred in the 1620s and 1630s but they had been of short duration and were followed by a period of rapid recovery. The failure of the economy to regenerate during the cessation, because of the situation in England, as well as Irish circumstances, made the dislocation of the 1640s different from what went before and proved especially detrimental by undermining confidence and trade. The military situation, especially after 1647, exacerbated the recession further; while the outbreak of plague in 1649 made it catastrophic. It was the combination of a series of calamities, economic, military and natural which had such a deadly effect on the Irish economy. This complexity makes the 1640s unique. The crisis of the 1690s was neither so severe nor so complicated.

[98] For a general view of this change see Gillespie, *Transformation*, pp. 41–8.

CHAPTER 9

THE SEVENTEENTH-CENTURY LAND SETTLEMENT IN IRELAND: TOWARDS A STATISTICAL INTERPRETATION

KEVIN MCKENNY

THE ENGLISH and French Revolutions of the seventeenth and eighteenth centuries, frequently regarded as social movements, failed to transform to any degree the landed class of those countries. However, this was not the case in seventeenth-century Ireland where an immense transfer in the ownership of property occurred. Using an extensive computerized profile of land holding in West Ulster (Counties Donegal, Tyrone and Londonderry) as a pilot study, this chapter re-examines this rare revolution in land tenure and asks who gained most from it: the Protestants who lived in Ireland before 1641; the soldiers and adventurers who came to Ireland as a consequence of the civil wars of the 1640s; or predatory speculators who took advantage of the unsettled situation to acquire vast estates?[1] In addition it considers whether property was lost simply on account of religion, race, or by a landholder's failure to adjust to the new economic order which had taken root in Ireland during the early seventeenth century.

I

This revolution in landholding has attracted much scholarly attention. In 1691 Sir William Petty, who was responsible for surveying Irish land in the later 1650s, hypothesized that Catholics emerged at the Restoration with

---

[1] I intend to compile a computer profile for the whole of Ireland. A database computer program will allow one to treat a very large body of people (those who held land at the onset of the revolution, and those who received land as a consequence of it), from diverse backgrounds and situations and attempt various measurements and generalizations. Both biographical and numerical information, assembled in a series of coded fields will, among other things, enable proficient identification and analysis of land settlement and revolutionary patterns on an island-wide, county, barony and parish level.

less than a third (2,280,000 acres) of the 'good land of Ireland'.[2] Statistically speaking Petty remained the accepted authority until early this century when W. F. T. Butler challenged his conclusions and suggested that Catholics retained only one seventh of Ireland's profitable land (1,110,000 acres).[3] Writing in the 1950s J. G. Simms, in a study of the Williamite land settlement (1689–1703), questioned Butler's findings and concluded that the Protestant share of Irish land increased from the 41 per cent which they held in 1641 to a massive 78 per cent by 1688.[4]

These studies, however, tend to overemphasize the sectarian nature of the land transfer and fail to examine the social and economic consequences of this upheaval on Irish society and omit any discussion, whether in cultural, political or economic terms, of the people involved. Recently Raymond Gillespie drew attention to the danger of identifying religious affiliation as the salient characteristic for explaining these tenurial upheavals. As the examples of Counties Antrim and Galway, areas which apparently remained strongly Catholic throughout the seventeenth century, demonstrate, the holdings of a few key Catholic magnates (in these instances the earls of Clanricard and Antrim) can distort any general conclusions.[5] Gillespie also convincingly argued that the Cromwellian, Restoration and even Williamite confiscations did not serve as the principal mechanism for change. Instead, for him the

> ability to evolve and implement survival strategies in the face of religious and political change depended on more than simply religious belief. Rather it was determined by a whole set of attitudes to land, including knowledge of law, access to capital, economic ideas, and political manoeuvring.[6]

In other words, the mere fact that one was a Catholic did not necessarily imply automatic confiscation of land. For instance, the close relationship

---

[2] Petty did not signify what the Catholic share of the land was in 1641. Instead, he indicated that 5,200,000 acres (69.3 per cent) of the good land was held by 'papists and sequestered Protestants'. This is often overlooked in enumerating the amount of acres held by Catholics in 1641, see *The political anatomy of Ireland* (London, 1691), pp. 15–16.

[3] W. F. T. Butler, *Confiscations in Irish history* (London, 1977 edition), p. 202. The principal authority for Butler's estimate was a report presented to the English Parliament in 1699 by a Forfeiture Inquiry Committee. This report, along with nine books of the commissioner's research, are in the library of Trinity College Dublin (TCD, MS N1.3). The commissioner's findings and a description of these books are given in HMC, *House of Lords MSS*, ns (London, 1908), IV, pp. 7–39.

[4] J.G. Simms, *The Williamite confiscation in Ireland, 1690–1703* (London, 1956). Simms' grounds for refuting Butler's statistics are laid out in his 'Historical revision: land owned by Catholics in Ireland in 1688', *IHS*, 7 (1950), pp. 179–90.

[5] Raymond Gillespie, 'A question of survival: the O'Farrells of Longford in the seventeenth century', in Raymond Gillespie and Gerard Moran (eds.), *Longford: essays in county history* (Dublin, 1991), p. 14.

[6] Gillespie, 'A question of survival', p. 14.

between Charles II and the Old English Catholic magnate, Theobald Taaffe, first earl of Carlingford, meant that after 1660 the earl both recovered his own lands in Ireland and those of his relatives. A letter from Taaffe to his land agent in County Louth reveals the extent of the king's favour.

> I have little to add to what I then wrote but I am sure if there be anything wanting in the King's letters, its my own fault, for I could insert what words I pleased, it being his intention I should not be disturbed in anything I possess; yet if any new thing be necessary send me in writing what it is and I believe I shall obtain it.[7]

Armed with such royal patronage, Taaffe was able to amass quite a sizeable estate in Leinster and around his ancestral home at Ballymote in Sligo.

Only a systematic study of the enormous mass of available qualitative and quantitative source material will expose the extent of Catholic 'survival' during these years. The most valuable of these are the Books of Survey and Distribution, the 'Civil Survey', the Down Survey maps and Terriers, and the so-called 1659 'Census', all of which were compiled, to varying degrees, in order to facilitate the process of confiscation, settlement and taxation during the 1650s and 1660s. The Books of Survey and Distribution, which resemble ledgers, are laid out in a series of columns and record information relating to land tenures in 1640 and in the post-1660 period. They are accounting exercises *par excellence* and are, in themselves, one of the most revolutionary items to appear from the upheavals of the period.[8] Aside from being the earliest catalogue of landholders in 1641 (survey side) and after 1660 (distribution side), they provide a very comprehensive list of seventeenth-century Irish place names and, more importantly, graphically depict the destruction of the old Gaelic order, especially in relation to land tenures. While these Gaelic, sometimes parochial, land units had been accepted as the basis for earlier plantations, including the plantation of Ulster, they were, during the Cromwellian period, reduced to a simple fraction: the plantation

---

[7] Theobald Taaffe to John Bellew, 20 December 1661 (Bellew–Carlingford Papers in the possession of Bellew Family of Barmeath, County Meath). A transcript of part of this collection is in the NA and in Harold O'Sullivan 'Land ownership changes in the county of Louth in the seventeenth century' (unpublished PhD thesis, TCD, 1992).

[8] Only three sets, out of the five originally compiled, survive: the 'Quit Rent', 'Taylor' and 'Annesley' sets. For an elaborate introduction to these and the differences between them, see the introduction in Robert C. Simington (ed.), *Books of survey and distribution*, II: *Mayo* (IMC, Dublin, 1956); Geraldine Talon, 'Books of survey and distribution, County Westmeath: a comparative survey', *Analecta Hibernica*, 28 (1978), pp. 105–15.

)ut of this evolved the townland, which became the standard unit used to distribute forfeited land and is the key to reconstructing the entire pattern of landholdership in Ireland during this period.[10] However the number of discrepancies and errors in the Books of Survey make them difficult to interpret. In the case of West Ulster, for example, the survey column, contrary to popular perceptions, contains the names of 1641 landowners together with lessees, freeholders and even, in some instances, tenants, while it omits many people who were freeholders, or who might have held the land in fee farm or fee simple, or, in certain cases, actual owners. For example, in the barony of Tirhugh, County Donegal, James McGrath, Irish Catholic, was listed the 'owner' of 19,748 profitable and 1,425 unprofitable acres, which appears from the format of the Book of Survey to have been forfeited to the Bishop of Rapho. Complimentary sources (described below), indicate, however, that McGrath did not actually own this land but rather leased it from the church who retained possession of it after the Restoration. Moreover McGrath's holding only amounted to 310 acres profitable and 190 unprofitable, and not the 21,173 acres total, listed in the Book of Survey.[11] Errors like this tend to create the illusion that Catholics held a lot more land in 1641 than was actually the case. In this instance the 21,173 acres incorrectly attributed to McGrath constitutes a 13 per cent increase in Catholic landholdership in County Donegal over what was in fact held by them. Consequently, when one comes to total the amount of land lost by Catholics in Donegal, one would incorrectly arrive at a figure 13 per cent greater than the actual Catholic loss. Similarly in Counties Kildare, Down, Cork, Louth and Meath, it appears that the Catholic portion of land has been artificially enhanced (while the Protestant share was decreased) for the

---

9 These land units – polls, tates, ballyboes, quarters and ballybetaghs – were extremely complex as they dealt not only with methods of landholding, but also with the relationships between various members of the Gaelic septs. For further details see P. J. Duffy, 'The territorial organization of Gaelic landownership and its transformation in County Monaghan, 1591–1641', *Irish Geography*, 14 (1981), pp. 1–26; Duffy, 'Patterns of landownership in Gaelic Monaghan in the late sixteenth century', *Clogher Record*, 10 (1981), pp. 304–22; Liam Price, 'The place-names of the books of survey and distribution and other records of the Cromwellian settlement', *Journal, Royal Society of Antiquities of Ireland*, 81 (1951), pp. 89–106.

10 The importance of the townland in the development of the geography of Ireland is explored in T. S. McErlean, 'The Irish townland system of landscape organization', in T. Reeves-Smyth and F. Hammond (eds.), *Landscape archaeology in Ireland* (Oxford, 1983), pp. 315–40.

11 R. C. Simington (ed.), *The civil survey, A.D. 1654–56, Counties of Donegal, Londonderry and Tyrone* (IMC, 10 vols., Dublin, 1931–62), III, p. 65. This source, along with the Down Survey maps, helps explain the large discrepancy in the Books of Survey. The three quarters of land called Culled, Pettigoe and Coolemore, which are in the parish of Carne (often called Tarmonmagrath), barony of Tirhugh, County Donegal, were not distinguished and separated from the rest of the parish which lies in the barony of Lurg, County Fermanagh.

pre-1641 period. Consequently a sectarian study of the land revolution, based on the Books of Survey and Distribution alone, would have more Catholic 'landowners' losing land to Protestant outsiders than was actually the case.

Clearly then the survey side of these ledgers does not reflect accurately the land holding pattern in pre-war Ireland. Other sources, such as the Civil Survey, which like the Domesday Book was based on inquisitions taken from knowledgeable native inhabitants and describes in great detail the townlands, parishes and baronies prior to the Cromwellian land upheavals, help redress these deficiencies. While the Civil Survey and earlier Gross Survey were based on rough approximations of confiscated land, the Down Survey, drawn up by William Petty, was effected by exact measurement and mapping[12] and is especially important in identifying settlement patterns in mid-seventeenth-century Ireland. The later super-imposition of the Down Survey maps on the nineteenth-century Ordinance Survey maps demonstrates how the settlements of the 1640s eventually became buried under landlord demesnes – perhaps the most enduring legacy of the Cromwellian period in Ireland.

A final source worth noting is the so-called 'Census' (actually a poll-tax return dating from 1660), assembled and compiled by Séamus Pender.[13] Arranged by county, barony, parish and townland (in urban areas, by city and street) this provides a partial listing of adults, along with their religious and, in many cases, ethnic origins. There is much speculation as to its usefulness but once its limitations are recognized and accounted for (by perhaps avoiding absolute totals and instead concentrating on inter-parish or inter-baronial comparisons), this particular source furnishes critical insights into the ethnic diversity of the Irish population, albeit in an often crude form.[14]

[12] The logistics of surveying land in seventeenth-century Ireland can be seen in Henry Osborne, *A more exact way to delineate the plot of any spacious parcel of land, as baronies, parishes, and townlands, as also of rivers, harbors and loughs, &c. than is yet in practice. Also a method or form of keeping the Field book, and how to cast up the superficial content of a plot most exactly* (Dublin, 1654). The value and origins of this particular pamphlet is explored by K. T. Hoppen, *The common scientist in the seventeenth century: a study of the Dublin Philosophical Society, 1683–1708* (London, 1970), pp 10–15. The tricks of the seventeenth-century surveyor's trade are definitively discussed in J. H. Andrews, *Plantation acres: an historical study of the Irish land surveyor and his maps* (Omagh, 1985), pp. 297–332.
[13] Séamus Pender, *A census of Ireland c. 1659. With supplementary material from the poll money ordinances, 1660–1661* (IMC, Dublin, 1939).
[14] William Smyth, 'Society and settlement in seventeenth-century Ireland: the evidence of the "1659 Census"', in William J. Smyth and Kevin Whelan (eds.), *Common ground: essays in the historical geography of Ireland presented to T. Jones Hughes* (Cork, 1988), pp. 57, 61, 66, 71, 74, 78.

II

In order to determine the impact of the Cromwellian settlement on West Ulster it is first necessary to sketch briefly the pattern of land-holding there on the eve of the 1641 rebellion. Counties Donegal, Tyrone and London-derry, totalling 432,435 plantation acres, had been extensively settled by large numbers of people from England and the lowlands of Scotland during and after the Ulster plantation.[15] Within a short space of time an élite planter society emerged which was responsible for unleashing a new economic order.[16] The need to adapt to this more market- and money-oriented economy, which threatened the traditional values of many Gaelic septs, led to an, as yet unmeasured, turnover of land in various parts of the island.[17]

In particular the early decades of the seventeenth century witnessed an

---

[15] Philip Robinson, *The plantation of Ulster: British settlement in an Irish landscape, 1600–1670* (Dublin, 1984); Michael Perceval-Maxwell, *The Scottish migration to Ulster in the reign of James I* (London, 1973). These deal with an official migration to Ireland, while a largely unofficial migration is explored in Raymond Gillespie, *Colonial Ulster: The settlement of East Ulster, 1600–1641* (Cork, 1985).

[16] Raymond Gillespie saw the new market economy of settlers as 'ruled by the "invisible hand" of impersonal market forces'. The use of land, for example, was traded for a price (rent), negotiated between landlord and tenant guided by the laws of supply and demand. All surplus products were redistributed through the market for a price, which was then used to pay for other goods including the initial use of the land. However the native model took the form of a barter economy where goods and services were supplied to the lord in return for protection and other such incentives. 'Lords and commons in seventeenth century Mayo', in Raymond Gillespie and Gerard Moran (eds.), *'A various country': essays in Mayo history, 1500–1900* (Mayo, 1987), p. 45. Gaelic Irish literature resonates with indignation for the destruction of the society that sustained them. T. J. Dunne, 'The Gaelic response to conquest and colonization: the evidence of the poetry', *Studia Hibernica*, 20 (1980), pp. 7–30; Michelle O Riordan, *The Gaelic mind and the collapse of the Gaelic world* (Cork, 1990); Bernadette Cunningham, 'Native culture and political change in Ireland, 1580–1640', in Ciaran Brady and Raymond Gillespie (eds.), *Natives and newcomers: essays on the making of Irish colonial society, 1534–1641* (Dublin, 1986), pp. 148–70. This latter source is especially valuable as a counter to the genre of inferring national identity formation from the writings of these bards, established by Brendan Bradshaw, 'Native reaction to the westward enterprise: a case study in Gaelic ideology', in K. R. Andrews, N. P. Canny, P. E. H. Hair (eds.), *The westward enterprise: English activities in Ireland, the Atlantic and America, 1480–1650* (Liverpool, 1978), pp. 66–80. Bradshaw fails to consider that these bards might have been reacting to the establishment of the new economic order as opposed to resistance to the 'foreigner'.

[17] This type of unofficial land acquisition, and consequent loss, must be measured and incorporated within the existing historiography. Some inroads into this problem have already been made. For instance see William J. Smyth, 'Property, patronage and population. Reconstructing the human geography of mid-seventeenth century County Tipperary', in William Nolan and Thomas G. McGrath (eds.), *Tipperary: history and society. Interdisciplinary essays on the history of an Irish county* (Dublin, 1985); Smyth, 'Land values, landownership and population patterns in County Tipperary from 1641–1660 and 1841–50. Some comparisons', in L. M. Cullen and François Furet (eds.), *Ireland and France, 17th–20th centuries: towards a comparative study of rural history* (Paris, 1980), pp. 60–84.

inordinate amount of estate consolidation, as planters and a minority of natives sought to create more viable holdings. Among other things tables 9.1 and 9.2, which relate to landholdership and not ownership, represent the sum of individual land acquisitions or land losses during this period. From these one can adduce that 216 (50 per cent) Protestants from England comprised the largest ethnic group of landholders in the three counties under review and that they held 234,816 acres, or 54 per cent of the total area. Protestants from Scotland totalling 119, or 28 per cent of the total number of landholders, holding 23 per cent, or 99,513 acres, formed the second largest ethnic group. In addition eight Irish Protestants (of either Gaelic Irish or Old English descent), one Dutch Protestant (Wilbrant Olpherts, who held a sizeable estate of 1,166 acres in the barony of Killmacrenan, County Donegal),[18] and a total of ten Protestants whose ethnic origin cannot be determined with any degree of accuracy held land.

In order to determine whether the Cromwellian confiscations and subsequent Restoration settlement discriminated more on the basis of race than religion, the Catholics of the area are divided into three separate ethnic groups: Scottish Catholics, Old English Catholics and Gaelic Catholics.[19] Of the sixty-six Catholics accounted for, only two of these, George Dowdall and Henry Hovendine who between them held a mere 681 acres, were Old English.[20] Six Catholics from Scotland, who controlled a little more than 3 per cent (14,991 acres in the barony of Strabane) of the total area, included four members of the Hamilton family, Robert Algeo

---

[18] It is not certain when this particular family settled in the area. They perhaps belong to the group of Dutch engineers who Chichester reported had settled in Derry during the early stages of the plantation. The Olpherts soon ingratiated themselves with planter society and owned a number of houses in Derry. Wilbrant became mayor of the city in 1633-4 and later distinguished himself defending the city against the Jacobites in 1689, BL, Add. MSS 4756, fo. 117; 'Rent roll of Derry, 15 May 1628', in T.W. Moody, J.G. Simms (eds.), *The bishopric of Derry and the Irish Society of London, 1602–1705* (IMC, 2 vols., Dublin, 1968), i, p. 59; 'List of civil officials of Derry and Coleraine, 1613–41', in T. W. Moody, *The Londonderry plantation, 1609–41. The City of London and the plantation in Ulster* (Belfast, 1939), p. 449; George Hill, *An historical account of the plantation in Ulster at the commencement of the seventeenth century, 1608–20* (Belfast, 1873; reprint Shannon, 1980), pp. 182–3. For a general introduction to the Dutch influence in Ireland see Rolf Loeber, 'English and Irish sources for the history of Dutch economic activity in Ireland, 1600–89', *Irish Economic and Social History*, 8 (1981), pp. 70–85.

[19] This important question was raised by Karl Bottigheimer who posited: 'Were the Connaught transplanters and the Celtic Irish synonymous? . . . Was race more important than religion in the Cromwellian and restoration settlements?': 'The Restoration land settlement in Ireland: a structural view', *IHS*, 18 (1972), p. 21.

[20] The Hovendines became so intimate with the O'Neills that their Old English ethnicity was all but eliminated. Henry was the stepfather of Sir Phelim O'Neill, through his marriage to the widow of Sir Henry Oge O'Neill and was one of the few Old English who took part in the 'Flight of the Earls'. Exile did not appeal to Hovendine, however, and he successfully petitioned to return to Ulster sometime in the 1630s, Hill, *Plantation in Ulster*, pp. 32, 40, 248.

Table 9.1.[a] *The ethno-religious pattern of landholders in West Ulster, 1641, by county*[b]

Ethnicity	County Donegal no.[c]	%	County Londonderry no.	%	County Tyrone no.	%	West Ulster Totals no.	%
EP	71	40	78	77	67	45	216	50[d]
SP	69	39	5	5	45	30	119	28
RC	23	13	13	13	22	5	58	14
OE	0	—	0	—	2	1	2	—
IP	3	2	3	3	2	1	8	1
SC	0	—	0	—	6	4	6	—
DP	1	—	0	—	0	—	1	—
UP	7	4	1	1	2	1	10	2
OT	5	3	1	1	2	1	8	1
County totals	179	100	101	100	148	100	428	100

[a] These tables were constructed by categorizing and aggregating landholders by their ethno-religious origins. This was facilitated by extracting data from three separate fields in the database.
[b] The codes used for the ethno-religious denominations in the tables are as follows:
EP English Protestant
DP Dutch Protestant
SP Scottish Protestant
SC Scottish Catholic
RC Roman Catholic (Gaelic)
OE Old English (Catholics)
IP Irish Protestants (of either Gaelic, or Old English descent)
UP Unknown Protestant – used when it is known that the subject is a Protestant but whose ethnic origin could not be determined
OT Other, used for church, school or college land.
[c] It is important to remember that landholders and not landowners are what we are dealing with here. To that end, landholders include all those in the respective areas who either owned the land, held it in freehold, by fee farm, fee simple, or leased it from the church, the London Companies or from other individuals. The only landholders excluded are those who were 'mere' tenants.
[d] All percentages are to the nearest whole and are computed as portions of each of the respective counties. For example, the 71 English Protestants in County Donegal, comprised 40 per cent of the 179 landholders in that county in 1641. The West Ulster total percentages are portions of the entire number of holders in the area. Percentages of less than 1 per cent are not recorded.

and David Marghee – the latter two holding their land in fee farm from James Hamilton, baron of Strabane. The remaining fifty-eight Catholics, all of Gaelic Irish descent, had remained in Ireland after the 'Flight of the Earls' in 1607, and obtained grants in the baronies set aside for 'servitors' – soldiers and crown officials involved in the establishment of Ireland in the opening decades of the seventeenth century. These Gaelic Irish held 47,710 acres (11 per cent of the total area) and comprised the third largest ethnic group (see table 9.3).

As table 9.3 illustrates, the early seventeenth-century plantation, which, for security reasons, confined the native Irish to those baronies which were

Table 9.2. *The ethno-religious pattern of landholdership in West Ulster, 1641, by county*[a]

Ethnicity	County Donegal		County Londonderry		County Tyrone		West Ulster Totals	
	acres	%	acres	%	acres	%	acres	%
EP	64,149	39	107,845	82	62,822	45	234,816	54[b]
SP	63,349	39	843	1	35,321	25	99,513	23
RC	16,193	10	15,431	12	16,086	12	47,710	11
OE	0	—	0	—	681	—	681	—
IP	360	—	274	—	519	—	1,153	—
SC	0	—	0	—	14,991	11	14,991	3
DP	1,166	1	0	—	0	—	1,166	—
UP	5,443	3	72	—	242	—	5,757	2
OT	12,132	7	6,526	5	7,990	6	26,648	6
County totals	162,792	100	130,991	100	138,652	100	432,435	100

[a] For a listing of the codes used see table 9.1. All acreage figures include both unprofitable and profitable which the respective landholders held in their possession in 1641 according to the Books of Survey.

[b] All percentages are to the nearest whole and are computed from the total acres held by the respective ethno-religious groups by county and by West Ulster. For example, the 107,845 acres held by the English Protestants in County Londonderry, comprised 82 per cent of the total area (130,991 acres) of that county. Similarly the 234,816 acres held by English Protestants in West Ulster constituted 54 per cent of the total area of West Ulster (432,435 acres).

allocated to the 'servitors', determined the distribution of Gaelic Catholic landholdership.[21] After 1603 the English government, determined that the power structures of the major Gaelic families should be weakened, deliberately reduced many minor Gaelic families to tenant level in order to diminish the power of the chieftain (the epitomization of the 'old order') by undermining his economic and political power over his followers. To that end the state allotted a one or two ballyboe freehold to Catholics in certain specified areas, while the leaders of respective septs received much larger grants which they, in turn, subdivided among lesser families. Thus in West Ulster the Mac Sweenys held all their land in the barony of Killmacrenan, County Donegal, the O'Neills and O'Hagans primarily in Dungannon Barony, County Tyrone, and the O'Cahans in three of Londonderry's four baronies.[22] As table 9.3 indicates this policy of segregation proved, with a single exception, successful, as neither Gaelic Irish nor Old English

[21] T. W. Moody, 'The treatment of the native population under the scheme for the plantation of Ulster', *IHS*, 1 (1938–9), pp. 58–63.
[22] There was also a remarkable continuity between the distribution of these septs in 1641 and that portrayed by Kenneth Nicholls for 1534. D. B. Quinn and K. W. Nicholls, 'Ireland in 1534', T. W. Moody, F. X. Martin and F. J. Byrne (eds.), *A new history of Ireland, III: Early modern Ireland, 1534–1691* (Oxford, 1976), pp. 1–38.

Catholics held any property (freehold or otherwise) in any area not specifically set aside for them in the original Ulster plantation.[23] Similarly, in the 1606 division of Monaghan, 60 per cent of the land was divided among twelve major Gaelic families and no less than three hundred of their followers, who were elevated from their subservient status to that of freeholders.[24]

Confiscations and plantation aside, significant amounts of land also changed hands prior to the outbreak of the war. To begin with some Protestant newcomers mortgaged their farms to British merchants and land speculators who had established themselves in Derry or Coleraine,[25] while others, who had received their holdings during the plantation, sold out before 1641.[26] Catholic landholders, especially the native Irish, suffered even greater financial hardships. While the Gaelic system which predominated in West Ulster was perhaps more varied and complex in its manifestation than that exercised in other parts of Ireland, the new economic order everywhere, especially the imposition of its more individualized and commercial concepts of landholdership, represented a change which the backward-looking Gael, who had traditionally received loyalty – rather than rent – from his lands, had problems adapting to.[27] Mortgage foreclosure and escheatment became particular burdens for native landholders. For instance Sir Phelim O'Neill, one of the leaders of

---

[23] The only exception to this was that James McGrath leased lands from the church in the barony of Tirhugh, Simington (ed.), *Civil survey*, III, p. 65.

[24] P. J. Duffy, 'The evolution of estate properties in South Ulster, 1600-1900', Smyth and Whelan (eds.), *Common ground*, p. 91. Of these 300 freeholders, no less than 124 were from the principal sept of the area – the MacMahons.

[25] The problems of the British planters are discussed in R. Hunter, 'The English undertakers in the plantation of Ulster, 1610-41', *Breifne*, 4 (1973), pp. 471-99; W. H. Crawford, 'Landlord-tenant relations in Ulster, 1609-1820', *Irish Economic and Social History*, 2 (1975), pp. 5-21; P. Roebuck, 'The making of an Ulster great estate: the Chichesters, barons of Belfast and viscounts of Carrickfergus, 1599-1648', *Proceedings, Royal Irish Academy*, 79, section C, (1979), pp. 1-25. For other areas of Ulster, see Gillespie, *Colonial Ulster*, pp. 138, 195; Gillespie, *Settlement and survival on an Ulster estate. The Brownlow lease book, 1667-1711* (Belfast, 1988); Jane H. Ohlmeyer, *Civil war and restoration in the three Stuart kingdoms: the career of Randal MacDonnell, marquis of Antrim, 1609-1683* (Cambridge, 1993), pp. 66-7.

[26] This fact has been adduced by comparing the 1641 landholdership patterns established from the database, with the appendices given in Robinson, *Plantation of Ulster*, pp. 195-227 and from the 'grants and grantees' listed in Hill, *Plantation in Ulster*, pp. 259-353. While Robinson only recorded grantees names with the total acreage they received, Hill identified the town-lands, quarters or ballyboes where each of the grantees received land. Tracing the movement patterns of each of these individual land units creates the aggregate of British (and other) land movement between the original plantation and 1641.

[27] Gaelic customs and traditions were more enduring in Ulster than elsewhere as it was the last part of Ireland brought out of its Gaelic insularity, C. Thomas Cairney, *Clans and families of Ireland and Scotland: an ethnography of the Gael, A.D. 500-1750* (Jefferson, North Carolina, 1989); T. H. Mullin and J. E. Mullan, *The Ulster clans, O'Mullan, O'Kane and O'Mellan* (Belfast, 1966). Also see footnote 16 above.

Table 9.3. *West Ulster landholdership of the major Gaelic septs, 1641*

Sept name[a]	No. of individuals	Acres held	Baronies[b]
Mac Sweeny	17	10,043	Killmacrenan
O'Boyle	1	4,317	Killmacrenan
O'Cahan	7	7,216	Coleraine, Kennaght, Terkerin
O'Donnell	3	994	Dungannon, Killmacrenan
O'Hagan	4	783	Dungannon
O'Mullan	4	737	Kennaght, Dungannon, Terkerin
O'Neill	10	12,358	Clogher, Dungannon, Loghinsholin
O'Quinn	5	1,701	Dungannon, Terkerin
Others	14	10,345	Coleraine, Kennaght, Enishowen,[c] Dungannon, Killmacrenan, Tirhugh
Totals	65	48,494[d]	

[a] Some of the members of these septs had converted to Protestantism by 1641 but they are included here as it is the intention of this particular table to ascertain sept landholdership, regardless of their supposed religion.
[b] The baronies of Killmacrenan, Enishowen and Tirhugh are in County Donegal; Coleraine, Kennaght, Terkerin and Loghinsholin are in County Londonderry and Dungannon and Clogher are in County Tyrone.
[c] These fourteen included the marquis of Antrim, James and Patrick McHenry, Manus Magilligan, Randall and Hugh McDonnell, Johnikin O'Divin, Toby Sheile, Hugh O'Dungan, Turlagh O'Gallagher, Shane McDevitt, Daniel McLoughlin, Richard O'Doherty, and James McGrath.
[d] Of this total of 48,494 acres, 784 of these were held by Gaelic Irish Protestants. James, Mary and Donel Mac Sweeny held 360 acres; Brian O'Neill held 150 acres; James O'Quinn held 34; and Daniel and Tomlin O'Mullin held 240 acres.

the 1641 rebellion, borrowed extensively, some of it on the very eve of the insurrection, using his estates as collateral. This caused major problems in the 1650s and 1660s when his property was being disposed of, as his creditors had first to be satisfied before his acres could be settled on a local 'younger son' of an established planter family.[28] Likewise, debts encumbered the patrimony of Randal MacDonnell, second earl of Antrim[29] and the Hamiltons, Catholics from Scotland, who had mortgaged their estates to their British neighbours in the decade before 1641.[30] This was also the case elsewhere. In County Wexford, for example, 124 native

[28] Simington (ed.), *Civil survey*, III, pp. 284–5. A local officer, Captain William Hamilton eventually received this estate at the Restoration, 'Abstracts of grants of land and other hereditaments under the acts of Settlement and Explanation, A.D. 1666–1684', *Record Commission Ireland, Report 15* (Dublin, 1821–5), pp. 107–8.
[29] Ironically they helped him to retain his property through the revolutionary period since his creditors assumed it was in their best interests to ensure that Antrim was restored to his estates, see Ohlmeyer, *Civil war and restoration*, pp. 65–8.
[30] For example, all of their land in the parish of Ardstragh (Strabane barony), was mortgaged to John Dixon of London, through his attorney, Robert Lawson, for £900, Simington (ed.), *Civil survey*, III, p. 384.

Irishmen received patents for land but, by 1640, that number was reduced by about two-thirds, due, in the main to mortgage foreclosure. Similarly in Counties Cavan and Monaghan, large planter estates quickly absorbed the Gaelic freeholds.[31]

Even though bankruptcy troubled many members of the Gaelic Irish community, others became very adept at retaining their lands by adopting progressive economic policies. The O'Cahans, for example, reorganized and rationalized their property, selling off extensive tracts of their land, while simultaneously attracting many non-Gaelic tenants into the estate they retained.[32] Antrim exhibited similar survivalist strategies, going so far as to engage one of Ireland's foremost Catholic lawyers, Patrick Darcy, 'in order to draw up new leases that would put his estates on a nice stable footing'.[33] In short, the observable pattern of landholdership in West Ulster on the eve of the rebellion in 1641 was one of both consolidation and decay.

III

The infrastructure of the so-called 'Cromwellian' land settlement rested on 'An Act for the speedy and effectual reducing of the rebels in His Majesty's Kingdom of Ireland' (commonly called the Adventurers' Act), which had been passed by the English Parliament in March 1642 and offered for sale millions of acres of land belonging to Irish 'rebels' in order to raise the capital needed to suppress the rebellion.[34] In addition to using the confiscated property as collateral with which to repay those Adventurers, who had or who were about to advance money for the purpose of financing the parliamentary war-effort, Parliament enacted the 'Doubling Ordinance'

[31] Henry Goff, 'English conquest of an Irish barony. The changing patterns of land ownership in the barony of Scarawalsh, 1540–1640', in Kevin Whelan and William Nolan (eds.), *Wexford: history and society. Interdisciplinary essays on the history of an Irish county* (Dublin, 1987), pp. 122–49; Duffy, 'Evolution of estate properties', p. 96; Mary O'Dowd, 'Gaelic economy and society', in Brady and Gillespie (eds.), *Natives and newcomers*, pp. 120–47; O'Dowd, *Power, politics and land: early modern Sligo, 1568–1688* (Belfast, 1991).

[32] For example, Shane O'Cahan let all his lands in Feaughanvale Parish, barony of Terkerin, County Londonderry, to British tenants, Simington (ed.), *Civil survey*, III, pp. 239–40. Jane Ohlmeyer has demonstrated, in relation to land holdings, that there was a 'high degree of mutual interdependence between Catholics and Protestants', *Civil war and restoration*, p. 40. Others of the O'Cahan sept were not so survivalist-minded as they were implicated in a plot against the government in 1615 and subsequently forfeited both life and estate. Raymond Gillespie, *Conspiracy: Ulster plots and plotters in 1615* (Belfast, 1987); Mullin, *Ulster clans*, pp. 121–30.

[33] Ohlmeyer, *Civil war and restoration*, pp. 25–6, 36; Gillespie, *Colonial Ulster*, pp. 90–101, 130–8.

[34] Statutes of the Realm 16 Car. i, c. 33. The origins and the act itself is definitively examined by Karl Bottigheimer, *English money and Irish land: the 'Adventurers' in the Cromwellian settlement of Ireland* (Oxford, 1971), pp. 30–53.

(July 1643) whereby all its soldiers who had served in Ireland were to receive compensation in Irish lands for their arrears of pay.[35]

When the Parliamentarians emerged victorious in 1652 they set about implementing their policy which took the form of an 'Act for the Settling of Ireland'.[36] This crucial ordinance, along with the Adventurers' Act of 1642, created the legal base for the land confiscation and settlement which was to follow. It categorized the people of Ireland, both Protestant and Catholic, according to their involvement in the rebellion and, perhaps more importantly, according to their loyalty to the king, or disloyalty to the Parliament (a 'crime' which most of the British – especially Scottish – settlers of West Ulster were charged with). This ordinance went on to declare five categories of people exempt from pardon for life and estate, while other clauses identified those who had fought against the Parliament, or who could not prove 'constant good affection' towards the parliamentary cause.[37] Samuel Rawson Gardiner estimated that, as a result of this legislation, nearly 80,000 people risked loosing both their lives and estates.[38] More recently Karl Bottigheimer, identifying the objects of this ordinance, concluded;

> The very distinction in the act of 1652 between the 'inferior sort and others
> ... of the higher rank and quality', with more specific promise of clemency
> for the former, suggests that the act was 'land-minded', and that it was more
> concerned to establish the guilt of those who had something to confiscate
> than those who had not.[39]

---

[35] This ordinance allowed soldiers to convert their arrears into land at the same rate as the Adventurers. Parliament later altered its policy and *obliged* soldiers to receive Irish land in lieu of pay, Bottigheimer, *English money*, p. 119. Land was also used to pay soldiers in England. This practice differed from Ireland, however, because 'In England the soldier's debenture was a promise to pay a certain sum of money for which the land was merely a security. In Ireland the soldier's debenture expressly stated that the sum was to be paid in land', see C. H. Firth, *Cromwell's army: A history of the English soldier during the civil wars, the commonwealth and the protectorate* (London, 1962), p. 202; Bottigheimer, *English money*, p. 117; H. J. Habakkuk, 'The parliamentary army and the crown lands', *Welsh History Review*, 3 (1967), pp. 403–26; and Ian Gentles, 'The sales of crown lands during the English Revolution, 1649–1660' *Economic History Review*, 26 (1973), pp. 615–35.

[36] C. H. Firth and R. S. Rait (eds.), *Acts and ordinances of the Interregnum* (3 vols., London, 1911), II, pp. 598–603.

[37] Among the West Ulster landholders excepted from pardon were Sir Phelim O'Neill, Hugh O'Neill, Turlagh O'Donnell, Turlagh O'Neill, Mulmurry Mac Sweeny, Manus O'Cahan, Brian and Turlagh O'Quinn. In addition to these Catholics were the Protestants, Sir Robert Stewart and John Bramhall, bishop of Derry, John T. Gilbert (ed.), *A contemporary history of affairs in Ireland from A.D. 1641 to 1652* (Irish Archaeology Society, 3 vols., Dublin, 1879–80), III, pp. 341–6.

[38] Samuel Rawson Gardiner, 'The transplantation to Connaught', *English Historical Review*, 14 (1899), pp. 700–34.

[39] Bottigheimer, *English money*, p. 128; W. F. T. Butler, saw it as the most extraordinary document ever produced by any body of legislation, *Confiscations*, p. 21.

How, then, did this legislation affect the landholdership patterns in West Ulster?[40] To begin with, the act did not distinguish between Catholic and Protestant but rather between Royalist and Parliamentarian and since many of the British planters in West Ulster had supported the king and his exiled son throughout the 1640s their lands were now confiscated by Parliament.[41] However Oliver Cromwell later relented and, in September 1654, allowed these and other Protestant colonists whose lands had been confiscated for their royalism to compound for their delinquency by the payment of a composition fine of twice the annual value of the estates.[42] Even though the history of this composition remains to be written,[43] it appears that in West Ulster the majority of those who paid their fines were Scottish, while others, including those protected by the 'Dublin Articles' (an agreement entered into by Ormond and the Parliament in 1647, whereby Irish Protestants would not incur any penalty for their previous royalist proclivities), had their compositions set aside.[44]

Catholic landholders in West Ulster proved less fortunate. On the one hand, the Commonwealth transported thousands of Catholic soldiers to continental Europe and many civilians to the West Indies or the

[40] Other ordinances enacted to accommodate the settlement are discussed in Bottigheimer, *English money*, pp. 115–42. The forfeited land in County Donegal was reserved for the Munster Protestant army (who had arrears of pay due before June 1649), while Londonderry and Tyrone were reserved for soldiers who had served in Ireland after Cromwell's arrival.

[41] The jurors assembled to facilitate the creation of the Civil Survey outlined these royalist proclivities. For example, 'Andrew Hamilton esquire, British Protestant, a besieger of Derry'; 'John Stewart, British Protestant, by information at Duke Hamilton's Engagement'; 'Lieutenant Colonel Robert Stewart who was in arms against the state in 1649'; 'Sir George Hamilton a besieger of Dublin with the Marquess of Ormonde'; 'George Cunningham, which George was at Worcester fight', Simington (ed.), *Civil survey*, III, pp. 24, 31, 42, 251, 396.

[42] 'An ordinance for admitting Protestants in Ireland to compound', Firth and Rait (eds.), *Acts and ordinances*, II, pp. 1015–16; 'Orders for composition', Robert Dunlop (ed.), *Ireland under the Commonwealth* (2 vols., Manchester, 1913), II, pp. 444–5. For details on the threatened transplantation of Scottish settlers see *ibid.*, II, pp. 292–4, 329–34, 338–9, 351–4, 360–1, 578–85; James Seaton Reid, *History of the Presbyterian church in Ireland* (3 vols., London, 1853), II, pp. 177–82, 471–4; Robert M. Young (ed.), *Historical notices of old Belfast and its vicinity. A selection from the manuscripts collected by Pinkerton for his intended history of Belfast, with additional documents, letters and ballads* (Belfast, 1896), pp. 73–108. *Mercurius Politicus* (16–23 June 1653), pp. 2520–3.

[43] For an English parallel see C. B. Phillips, 'The royalist composition papers and the landed income of the gentry: a note of warning from Cumbria', *Northern History*, 13 (1977), pp. 161–74; J. T. Cliffe, 'The royalist composition papers and the landed income of the gentry: a rejoinder', *Northern History*, 14 (1978), pp. 164–92.

[44] *Several papers of the treaty between . . . Ormonde . . . for the king . . . and . . . commissioners authorized by the Parliament of England on the other part. With the commissioners instructions concerning the Lord of Ormonde, the instructions concerning the Protestants of Ireland and composition of delinquents . . .* (Dublin, 1646), BL, Thomason Tract, E378(4); Council to the Lord Protector, Dublin, 1 April 1654, T. Birch (ed.), *A collection of the state papers of John Thurloe . . .* (7 vols., London, 1742), IV, p. 668. For example, the state waived the composition fine of Sir Alexander Stewart, who died fighting for the king at Dunbar, Dunlop (ed.), *Commonwealth*, II, p. 592.

colonies;[45] and, on the other, it ordered native landholders to transplant themselves to Connacht. Thus many of the Mac Sweenys from County Donegal served with distinction in continental armies;[46] while Turlagh O'Neill and Richard O'Cahan, originally from Dungannon and Kennaght baronies respectively received lands in Connacht (O'Cahan quickly sold his to a local merchant).[47] However, as table 9.4 indicates, not all Gaelic Catholics lost their estates.

Five Catholics of Gaelic Irish descent, one Old English, and a total of six Catholics from Scotland managed to retain all or part of their original land. Even though Henry Hovendine was restored in the 1660s to only part (292 acres) of his pre-war property in the barony of Dungannon, he received a grant of 570 acres in the same barony (see table 9.5) which had previously belonged to Turlagh O'Neill and Randal MacDonnell. Hovendine, therefore, emerged at the Restoration with a larger estate (862 acres) than that which he held (593 acres) in 1641. Similarly Antrim was restored to only a part of his original estate in County Londonderry, but he too was compensated out of other Catholic lands in the area. The remaining four Catholics of Gaelic Irish descent – Shane McDevitt, Daniel McLaughlin, Richard O'Doherty and Patrick O'Hagan – also managed to hold on to their small freeholds after 1660.[48]

---

[45] A balanced view of this civilian transportation is in Hilary Beckles, 'A riotous and unruly lot: Irish indentured servants and freemen in the English West Indies, 1644–1713', *William and Mary Quarterly*, 47 (1990), pp. 503–22; '"Black men in white skins": The formation of a white proletariat in West Indian slave society', *The Journal of Imperial and Commonwealth History*, 15 (1986), pp. 5–21. The nationalist genre of 'slave hunts' can be seen in Joseph Williams, *Whence the black Irish of Jamaica* (London, 1932); J. P. Prendergast, *The Cromwellian settlement of Ireland* (Dublin, 1922 edition). The military transportation has not yet received attention save that of George Sumner Steadman, 'The Cromwellian transportation of the Irish' (unpublished PhD thesis, Yale University, 1897).

[46] Originally from Scotland, this particular sept arrived in Ireland in the early sixteenth century as gallowglasses (mercenaries), Gerard A. Hayes-McCoy, *Scots mercenary forces in Ireland, 1565–1603* (Dublin, 1937), pp. 24–7. They left for the continent in the early 1650s where they and their descendants continued their militarist tradition by distinguished military service. Marquis MacSwiney, 'Notes on the formation of the first two Irish regiments in the service of Spain in the eighteenth century', *Journal, Royal Society of Antiquities of Ireland*, 57 (1927), pp. 7–20; J. C. O'Callaghan, *History of the Irish brigades in the service of France* (Glasgow, 1870).

[47] O'Neill obtained 400 acres in the barony of Costello, County Mayo while O'Cahan received 600 acres in the barony of Gallen (also County Mayo), R. C. Simington (ed.), *The transplantation to Connaught, 1654–58* (IMC, Shannon, 1970), pp. 199, 208; *Books of survey and distribution*, II: *Mayo*, pp. 149–59; 'List of transplanted Irish, 1655–59', HMC, *The manuscripts of the marquis of Ormonde*, os (2 vols., London, 1895–9), II, pp. 114–76.

[48] Hamilton and Antrim appeared before the Court of Claims of 1663 in order to be restored to their 1641 land holdings, 'Index to the decrees of innocence in the Chief Rembrancer's Office' (National Archives Dublin, Ferguson Manuscripts, p. 29). Ohlmeyer, *Civil war and restoration*, pp. 261–4; L. J. Arnold, 'The Irish Court of Claims of 1663', *IHS*, 24 (1985), pp. 417–30; Geraldine Talon (ed.), *The Court of Claims 1663, submissions and evidence* (IMC, forthcoming).

However of the fifty-eight Gaelic Catholic landholders in 1641, only five actually retained their property, reducing the area which they held in 1641 (41,710 acres) to 12,204 acres by the end of the Restoration period. The fact that all Catholics from Scotland retained their land, and one of the original two Old English Catholic landholders expanded his holdings suggests that race was perhaps more important than religion in determining confiscation or restoration. Or, perhaps those who survived, especially the Gaelic Catholics, did so because they had the good fortune of having a 'friend' at court. Others resorted to other stratagems. In some instances Gaelic Irish landholders attempted to retain their property by a timely conversion to Protestantism. These individuals then asserted that much of the land occupied by other members of their sept was mortgaged to them and that, as Protestants, they should be allowed to retain it. For example, James Mac Sweeny attempted to convince the authorities of this but they refused to believe him when he failed to produce the 'deeds of writing of the said mortgage', which Mac Sweeny (falsely) claimed had been burnt. While he was unsuccessful in saving the lands of his sept he was, however, allowed to retain his own 180-acre freehold in the barony of Killmacrenan, County Donegal.[49]

Of those whose land was confiscated in West Ulster, little is known save that only two of them managed to receive some compensation for their losses in the province of Connacht. The state then doled out 41,290 confiscated acres to twenty-five new grantees; four Catholics and twenty-one Protestants (see table 9.5). Of the Protestants, eighteen had letters patent passed for this land in the 1660s: no less than thirteen of them belonged to established planter families domiciled in Ulster prior to 1641; while of the remaining five it is only certain that one of them, Thomas Morris, of Fleetwood's regiment, came to Ireland after that date.[50] Counties Tyrone and Londonderry (containing 15,929 and 9,722 forfeited acres respectively), were originally granted to soldiers who had accompanied Cromwell to Ireland in 1649. None of this group retained any land in Londonderry after the Restoration. Instead local merchants and landholders, domiciled there prior to 1641, laid claim to this land with 443 acres passing to Catholics and 9,279 to Protestants (see table 9.5). A similar pattern is observable in County Tyrone where 12,581, or 79 per cent, of the forfeited acres fell to local planter families. Of the remaining 2,702 acres it

[49] Simington (ed.), *Civil survey*, III, p. 104.
[50] C. H. Firth and Godfrey Davies, *The regimental history of Cromwell's army* (2 vols., Oxford, 1940, reprinted 1991), II, pp. 647–9. There is insufficient evidence to identify the remaining four, but they could well have held land elsewhere in Ireland before 1641.

Table 9.4. *Catholics who retained or recovered land in West Ulster, post-1660*

Name			1641 Holding	1660s Holding[a]	Barony/County
Algeo, Robert		SC	152	152	Strabane, Tyrone
Antrim, Randal	ERL	RC	6,656	5,663	Coleraine, L'derry
Hamilton, Claude	LRD	SC	166	166	Strabane, Tyrone
Hamilton, George	SIR	SC	7,764	7,764	Strabane, Tyrone
Hamilton, James	ESQ	SC	3,495	3,495	Strabane, Tyrone
Hamilton, James	LRD	SC	3,294	3,294	Strabane, Tyrone
Hovendine, Henry		RC	593	292	Dungannon, Tyrone
Marghee, David		SC	120	120	Strabane, Tyrone
McDevitt, Shane		RC	60	60	Enishowen, Donegal
McLaughlin, Daniel		RC	40	40	Enishowen, Donegal
O'Doherty, Richard		RC	60	60	Enishowen, Donegal
O'Hagan, Patrick		RC	95	95	Dungannon, Tyrone

[a] The 1660s holdings are given here only as a portion of original estates which were held in 1641. For example, Robert Algeo held the same estate – 152 acres – in the 1660s as he did in 1641. Henry Hovendine, however, only held 292 of his original estate of 593 acres.

is only certain that 783 of them passed to a soldier, Thomas Morris, from Fleetwood's regiment.[51]

The 15,639 confiscated acres in Donegal were belatedly granted to the regiments of the Protestant Munster army who had turned to Parliament in 1649. However, unfortunately for this group, the Restoration overtook their disbandment and Charles II, remembering their untimely desertion to Cromwell, refused to include them in the land settlement. Instead, he awarded these acres to pre-war Irish Protestants (known as '1649 Officers') who had adhered to the royalist standard after the death of Charles I in January 1649.[52] Thereby all of the confiscated land in Donegal passed to six Protestants from this group: two of them, Sir John Stephens and Sir Hans Hamilton, held their land in trust for other '49 Officers; further acres were awarded to Paul Brasier and Sir John Ponsonby in satisfaction of debentures which they had purchased from others; while Colonel Carey

---

[51] A further 1,283 acres were disposed of to Catholics, and the remaining 1,282 to persons whose planter status in 1641 cannot be determined.

[52] The Restoration settlement in respect of these 1649 Officers is quite complicated as it involved all of the lands granted them being set up along the lines of a property company, whereby all the real estate and assets within this '49 Security, as it was termed, were sold, leased or let and the monies received, used to satisfy the pay arrears owed to this group. The '49 Security was still in operation as late as 1703. For further details see Kevin McKenny, 'A seventeenth-century "real estate company". The 1649 Officers and the Irish land settlements, 1641–1681' (unpublished MA thesis, NUI, Maynooth, 1989); McKenny, 'Charles II's Irish cavaliers: The 1649 Officers and the restoration land settlement', *IHS*, 28 (1993), pp. 409–25.

Dillon and William Cunningham received their portions in satisfaction of outstanding arrears of pay.

IV

During the seventeenth century Ireland was transformed from a tribal kingdom into a recognizably 'modern' state. The forces of change which facilitated this were not all compressed into the decade between 1649–59, but were also at work during the early and later decades of the century. However the upheavals of the 1650s significantly aided this process of renewal by accelerating the destruction of the 'old order' and making Ireland more receptive to mercantilist ideas. In other words, what the 'Cromwellian' upheavals laid to rest, was not so much Catholic landholding patterns, but rather the last vestiges of Gaelic tradition and custom which prevented many from modernizing. In 1654 Sir Edward Hyde, later earl of Clarendon, speculated on the impact a decade of war had had on Ireland:

> We are at a dead calm for all manner of intelligence. Cromwell, no doubt is very busy . . . and they doubt not to plant that kingdom without opposition. And truly, if we can get it again, we shall find difficulties removed which a virtuous prince and more quiet times could never have compassed.[53]

Since Cromwell had, as Hyde noted, 'removed' the remaining constraints of the feudal past, after 1660 it became increasingly viable for landowners, both Protestant and Catholic, to develop and consolidate their estates.

In the final analysis, however, 'Old Protestants' who had settled in Ireland prior to the rebellion's outbreak in 1641 benefited most from these upheavals because they found themselves ideally placed during the 1650s to purchase both land and debentures from English soldiers, eager to hurry home (also see chapter 11 below).[54] In fact the failure of Cromwellian policy in Ireland, which aimed to colonize large numbers of people on numerous small estates, can be partly attributed to this sale of debentures because it ensured that fewer people settled on very large holdings. For instance, of the 41,290 acres disposed of in West Ulster, it is certain that 37,499 acres, or 91 per cent, of this came into the possession of pre-1641

---

[53] Sir Edward Hyde to Mr Betius, 29 May 1654 (Bodl., Clarendon State Papers, III, fo. 244).
[54] By the mid-1650s an open market came into existence which exclusively sold these debentures. In an attempt to control the process, debenture brokers were prohibited from purchasing them at less than eight shillings in the pound. However as Petty, himself an active debenture purchaser, alluded to, debentures were sold on the open market for as low as four and five shillings in the pound, *Political anatomy*, p. 26.

Table 9.5. *Recipients of confiscated land in West Ulster, post-1660*

Name	Title	Religion	Planter status[a]	Acres	Baronies
01 Antrim Randall	Marq	C	Y	368	Coleraine
02 Beresford Tristram		P	Y	1,734	Kennaght
03 Brasier Paul		P	Y	415	Coleraine
03 Brasier Paul		P	Y	4,338	Killmacrenan
04 Carey Edward	Cpt.	P	Y	1,130	Kennaght, Terkerin
05 Cooke Ann	Lady	P	Y	1,408	Kennaght
06 Coote Thomas		P	Y	609	Dungannon
07 Cunningham William		P	Y	1,911	Killmacrenan
08 Dillon Carey	Col	P	Y	166	Killmacrenan[b]
09 Edwards Hugh		P	Y	1,638	Kennaght
09 Edwards Hugh		P	Y	1,536	Dungannon
10 Forrestall Luke		P	X	488	Dungannon
11 Hamilton George	Sir	C	Y	713	Dungannon
12 Hamilton Hans	Sir	P	Y	2,145	Killmacrenan
12 Hamilton Hans	Sir	P	Y	1,241	Dungannon
13 Hamilton William	Cpt.	P	Y	6,971	Dungannon
14 Hill Samuel		P	Y	324	Coleraine
14 Hill Samuel		P	Y	2,224	Dungannon
15 Hogan Hugh		P	X	92	Dungannon
16 Hovendine Henry		C	Y	570	Dungannon
17 May Edmund		P	X	127	Dungannon
18 McClanaghan Andrew		P	X	575	Dungannon
19 Morris Thomas		P	N	783	Dungannon
20 Ponsonby John	Sir	P	Y	2,671	Killmacrenan
21 Rowley Hugh		P	Y	110	Coleraine
22 Rowley John	Sir	P	Y	2,357	Coleraine, Terkerin[c]
23 Stephens John	Sir	P	Y	4,408	Killmacrenan
24 Thompkins Alex		P	Y	163	Terkerin
25 York James	Duke	C	N	75	Loghinsholin
Total				41,290	

[a] This column is used to identify those were settled in Ireland prior to 1641. Y indicates pre-1641 settler status; N indicates that they had come over since that time; and X indicates that this information is not known one way or the other.
[b] These 166 acres originally belonged to Thomas Dutton, English Protestant and John Cunningham, Scottish Protestant.
[c] Seven of these acres originally belonged to Simon Hillman who was an English Protestant.

(mainly local), settlers whom it was not originally intended for. Thus the legislation implemented in the Cromwellian and Restoration period to facilitate a lasting settlement in Ireland became a blueprint for a house which was never built. Moreover the fact that there were some willing to purchase and, more importantly, many eager to sell debentures and land, ushered in a period of predatory speculation, which alone was responsible for that scramble for land so characteristic of the years after the Restoration. This allowed many Protestants, together with a considerable number of

Catholics, to emerge with their original property intact or with considerably enhanced estates.

Taken in isolation, the 1650s appear as an era when land was won, and lost, primarily on account of religion and, to a lesser extent, for royalist proclivities. However, when looked at in the context of the overall revolution in land tenure in seventeenth-century Ireland, it seems that the acquisition or loss of property cannot be attributed solely to one's religion, but to a variety of survival strategies and complex politicking in both Dublin and London.

CHAPTER 10

RADICAL RELIGION IN IRELAND, 1641–1660

PHIL KILROY

THE ESTABLISHED church in Ireland viewed the rebellion of 1641 as both a judgement and a scourge of God. Members were filled with foreboding that the work of the Reformation was about to be overthrown.[1] Although the established church had struggled for survival since its foundation, it had succeeded in developing a distinctive theology suited to the peculiar situation in Ireland and to the theological background of its ministers. Founded by statute in 1560, the church had tried to assert itself without the active support of secular legislators and despite the fact that the rights of lay patronage and lay control of property hampered its internal administration.[2] After 1633 Lord Deputy Thomas Wentworth recognized these inherent weaknesses and planned to improve the church: to overhaul its financial basis; to re-examine the observance of church discipline, especially with regards to plurality, non-residence and the education of ministers; and, most significantly, to establish doctrinal uniformity with the Church of England.[3]

The rebellion of 1641 and the ensuing decade of warfare not only

---

[1] The extent of these fears is reflected in the legislation enacted in 1662: An Act for keeping and celebrating the Twenty-Third of October as an anniversary Thanksgiving in this Kingdom (14 & 15 Charles II). Sermons on deliverance from the dangers of the 1641 rebellion became a regular feature of church life until the end of the eighteenth century. For further details see T. C. Barnard, 'Crises of identity among Irish Protestants 1641–1685', *Past and Present* (May, 1990), pp. 50–8; Jacqueline R. Hill, 'Popery and protestantism, civil and religious liberty: the disputed lessons of Irish history 1690–1812', *Past and Present*, 118 (1988), pp. 100–1, 111–12; Royce MacGillivray, 'Edmund Borlase, historian of the Irish rebellion', *Studia Hibernica*, 9 (1969), pp. 86–9; Phil Kilroy, 'Protestantism in Ulster, 1610–1641', in Brian Mac Cuarta (ed.), *Ulster 1641* (Belfast, 1993), pp. 25–36.

[2] Aidan Clarke, 'Varieties of uniformity: The first century of the Church of Ireland', in W. D. Sheils and Diane Wood (eds.), *The churches, Ireland and the Irish. Studies in church history*, xxv (Oxford, 1989); Alan Ford, *The Protestant Reformation in Ireland, 1590–1641* (Frankfurt, 1985).

[3] R. B. Knox, *James Ussher, archbishop of Armagh* (Cardiff, 1967), pp. 44–53; Clarke, 'Varieties of uniformity', pp. 120–1.

interrupted this process of reform but threatened the very existence of the established church. The clergy responded in varying ways to the turmoil: the archbishop of Armagh, James Ussher, had left Ireland before the outbreak of the insurrection and never returned, while John Bramhall, bishop of Derry, quit the country shortly after the war began, fearing for his life.[4] The absence of the two leading figures in the established church left bishops and ministers to cope on their own: some, such as William Goldbourne, bishop of Kildare, quietly carried on very much as before;[5] others, such as Dr Henry Jones, dean of Kilmore and later bishop of Clogher, positively accepted the new régime, seeing it as the best means for promoting Protestantism in Ireland, and in this context accepted employment as official preachers (or in Jones's case as scout-master-general); while some left the ministry altogether and joined forces with the army.[6]

Despite the outbreak of war in all three kingdoms, the Long Parliament continued to hope that the established church could be reformed and passed legislation in 1642 and 1643 which reserved land for new churches and provided for the reorganization of parishes.[7] However it was not until parliamentary forces took control of Dublin in June 1647 that effective change occurred and the Directory of Worship, based on Presbyterian church order and discipline, superseded the Book of Common Prayer and the traditional ceremonies of the church. This signalled a radical transformation which the clergy, then resident in Dublin, tried to resist, stating that they could not accept modifications in religious matters unless authorized to do so by the king. They argued that the Directory was alien to their tradition and contrary to the Reformation, as established in both

---

[4] C. R. Elrington, *The whole works of the Most Reverend James Ussher . . . with a life of the author and an account of his writings* (16 vols., Dublin, 1847), I, p. 207; Knox, *James Ussher*, pp. 54, 76; John Bramhall, *Works of John Bramhall . . .* , ed. John Vesey (Dublin, 1676), preface; Hugh Kearney, *Strafford in Ireland 1633–41: a study in absolutism* (Manchester, 1959 edition), pp. 113–26, 211; Henry McAdoo, *John Bramhall and Anglicanism, 1663–1963* (Dublin, 1964), pp. 12–13.

[5] St John D. Seymour, *Adventures and experiences of a seventeenth century clergyman . . .* (Dublin, 1909), pp. 4–8, 16–20. Goldbourne was ordained bishop of Kildare in 1644, W. Monck Mason, *The history and antiquities of the collegiate and cathedral church of St Patrick near Dublin* (Dublin, 1810). In 1647 Ormond appointed Edward Parry bishop of Killaloe, St John D. Seymour, *The puritans in Ireland 1647–1661* (Oxford, 1921).

[6] Prominent among those who acted as ministers were Essex Digby and Ambrose Jones, who were appointed bishops at the Restoration; Dr John Lesley, bishop of Raphoe, received a stipend for preaching in Derry. For Jones see Seymour, *The puritans in Ireland*, pp. 7–10, 25–6, 53–6, 116–17 cf. the appendix, pp. 1–22 where Seymour estimated that of the 385 ministers, officially recognised during the Interregnum, 167 were former members of the established church. Also see St. John D. Seymour, 'Faithful Teate', *Journal, Royal Society of the Antiquaries of Ireland*, sixth series, 10 (1920), pp. 39–45; Barnard, 'Crises of identity among Irish Protestants', pp. 56–8.

England and Ireland, and asked to be allowed to continue their ministry 'till such time as further order be taken by a convocation of the clergy and an Act of Parliament in this kingdom'.[8]

This was a vain request and the Directory was enforced first in Dublin and, after 1649, throughout the rest of the country. In addition the Long Parliament planned to introduce into Ireland a Presbyterian system of church government, based on *The form of church government to be used in the church of England and Ireland*, which had been instituted in England in August 1648. It stated that the Directory should be used for worship and that church government should be by congregational, classical, provincial and national assemblies. The *form of church government* also laid down rules and procedures for ordination, for disciplinary procedures and for the role lay people were to play in the church.[9] Ironically, however, this settlement, which was essentially Presbyterian in tone and content, was never implemented in Ireland and so throughout the Interregnum no formal, legal basis existed for the ecclesiastical changes which took place there.

However the political situation favoured Scottish Presbyterians in Ulster. In the early years of the Ulster plantation Scottish Presbyterian ministers had been accepted by the established church, with some accommodation granted to their theological position, particularly regarding ordination.[10] However the 1634 Convocation, convened by Wentworth, radically altered their status and forced Scottish Presbyterian ministers either to conform or be ejected from their livings.[11] To make matters worse, after May 1639 and the outbreak of the Bishops' Wars in Scotland, Wentworth required all Ulster Scots to take an oath (known as the 'black oath') of loyalty and allegiance to the king.[12] However the following year, shortly after

---

[7] T. C. Barnard, *Cromwellian Ireland. English government and reform in Ireland 1649–1660* (Oxford, 1975), p. 95.

[8] E. Borlase, *The history of the execrable Irish rebellion* (London, 1680), appendix, pp. 97–8. Also see Seymour, *The puritans in Ireland*, pp. 1–7.

[9] *The form of church government to be used in the church of England and Ireland, 29 August 1648*; BL, Stowe MSS 155, fo. 80.

[10] John Livingstone, *A brief historical relation of the life of Mr. John Livingstone . . .*, ed. Thomas McCrie (Edinburgh, 1848), pp. 58–9; Patrick Adair, *A true narrative of the rise and progress of the Presbyterian church in Ireland (1623–1670)*, with introduction and notes by W. D. Killen (Belfast, 1866), pp. xiv–xv, 10–11; J. S. Reid, *History of the Presbyterian church in Ireland* (3 vols., Belfast, 1867), I, pp. 116–18; Marilyn Westerkamp, *Triumph of the laity, Scots–Irish piety and the Great Awakening, 1625–1760* (Oxford, 1988), pp. 20–3; Knox, *James Ussher*, pp. 174–7; David Stevenson, *Scottish covenanters and Irish confederates: Scottish–Irish relations in the mid-seventeenth century* (Belfast, 1981), pp. 12–13.

[11] Reid, *History of the Presbyterian church*, I, appendix iv, pp. 523–42.

[12] Adair, *A true narrative*, pp. 95–101; Stevenson, *Scottish covenanters*, pp. 18–19, 21–2, 32; Westerkamp, *Triumph of the laity*, pp. 36, 38.

Wentworth fell from power, Ulster Presbyterians sent a petition to Parliament which totally rejected the established church as reformed by the 1634 Convocation.[13] The old days of comprehension were over; the position of the Ulster Scots had become radicalized.

The war accelerated this process and in 1642 five Scottish Presbyterian ministers, who had accompanied the Scottish army sent to Ulster, organized the soldiers into congregations and sessions, and thereby established the first formal Presbytery in Ireland.[14] In addition, those congregations which had lost ministers in the aftermath of the 1634 Convocation asked the Scottish General Assembly for clergy to come and preach and even reside among them with the result that Presbyterian congregations mushroomed throughout the province.[15] By 1653 there were twenty-four Presbyterian ministers in Ulster; in 1654 the first Presbytery divided into three Presbyteries; and by 1659 there were five in all, with nearly eighty ministers.[16] Thus between 1641 and 1649 Scottish Presbyterians in Ulster grew in strength and, like their counterparts in Scotland, hoped that a Presbyterian form of church order and government would be established either by Parliament (a Solemn League and Covenant to that effect was signed in September 1643) or by the king (in December 1648 Charles I promised to introduce Presbyterianism into England for three years). In this context they were shocked to learn of Charles I's execution and, in February 1649, the Belfast Presbytery wrote to the 'sectarian party' in England, denouncing its actions.[17] The tone and content of the *Representation* underlined the strong position the Scottish Presbyterians felt they held in Ulster. However their views were not well received in England, and the Independents, furious at criticism from the Belfast Presbytery, instructed John Milton to write a reply in which he berated 'these pretended brethren' who, he argued, had no right to preach 'beyond the

---

13 *The humble petition of the Protestant inhabitants of the county of Antrim, Down and Tyrone etc. part of the province of Ulster concerning bishops to the Westminster Parliament* (London, 1641).

14 Edward M. Furgol, 'The military and ministers as agents of Presbyterian imperialism in England and Ireland 1640–48', in J. Dwyer, R. S. Mason, A. Murdoch (eds.), *New perspectives on the politics and culture of early modern Scotland* (Edinburgh, 1982), pp. 95–115.

15 *Acts of the General Assemblies of the Church of Scotland, 1638–49* (Edinburgh, 1691), pp. 138, 159, 190, 214 and index; Livingstone, *A brief historical relation*, pp. 37–8.

16 Minutes of the Antrim meeting, 1654–8 (PRONI, D 1759/ 1A/1); the Templepatrick session book, 1646–1743 (PRONI, CR4/12/B/1), partly published by W. T. Latimer, 'The old session book of Templepatrick Presbyterian church, County Antrim', *Journal, Royal Society of the Antiquaries of Ireland*, 25 (1895) and 31 (1901); Adair, *A true narrative*, pp. 204–24; Reid, *History of the Presbyterian church*, II, p. 205; Westerkamp, *Triumph of the laity*, pp. 47–51; Stevenson, *Scottish covenanters*, pp. 290–1.

17 *A necessary representation of the present evils and eminent dangers to religion, laws and liberties arising from the late and present practices of the sectarian party in England . . . By the Presbytery of Belfast February 15 1649* (n.p., 1649), pp. 42–3.

diocese of Patrick or Columba'.[18] He accused them of being worse than bishops and on a par with Rome, claiming 'absolute and independing jurisdiction, as from like advantage and occasion . . . the Pope has for many ages done'.[19] He waspishly added that these 'most grave and reverend Carmelites' had denied their own founder, John Knox, who had advocated the need to depose and kill unworthy sovereigns.[20]

Not all Scottish Presbyterian ministers sided with the Belfast Presbytery. For example, both Jeremy Ker, who came from Scotland in 1645/6 and ministered at Ballymoney in County Antrim, and Jeremy O'Quinn refused to read the *Representation* to their congregations and appealed to the General Assembly in Scotland for support.[21] This solved little, for the Presbyterians in Scotland were similarly divided between those who adhered to the king and accepted royal authority in religious affairs (the 'Resolutioners') and those who rejected this as contrary to the Covenant in all its purity (the 'Remonstrants'). This issue became even more divisive in January 1651 when Charles II was crowned at Scone and solemnly promised to keep the Covenant.[22]

Since this awkward alliance between some of the Scottish Presbyterians and the exiled Stuart king also threatened the stability of all three kingdoms, the Independent governor of Carrickfergus, Colonel Venables, tried in vain to win over the Scottish Presbyterian ministers to the new régime.[23] When every effort to force the clergy to take the Engagement, or an oath of loyalty to the Commonwealth, failed and the danger from Scotland increased, the government proposed in May 1653 to transplant these ministers, together with leading Presbyterian families, to Munster. As it turned out this proved unnecessary and Fleetwood and, later, Henry Cromwell negotiated a compromise settlement with the Scottish Presbyterian ministers, whereby they would receive maintenance from the government in return for their support.[24]

While problems with the Dublin government were gradually solved, divisions within Scottish Presbyterianism in Ulster continued to grow. In an

---

[18] *Observations upon the articles of peace with the Irish rebels on the letter of Ormonde to Col. Jones and the representation of the Presbytery at Belfast* (n.p., [1649]), pp. 54–5.

[19] *Ibid.*, pp. 55–6.

[20] *Ibid.*, pp. 63–5.

[21] *News from Ireland* (London, 1650). Adair, *A true narrative*, p. 124.

[22] M. Perceval-Maxwell, 'The adoption of the Solemn League and Covenant by the Scots in Ulster', *Scotia: American–Canadian Journal of Scottish Studies*, 2 (1978), pp. 3–18; J. C. Beckett, *Confrontations in Irish history* (London, 1972), pp. 26–46; Peter Brooke, *Ulster Presbyterianism* (Dublin, 1987), pp. 29–42.

[23] Adair, *A true narrative*, pp. 178–91; Seymour, *The puritans in Ireland*, pp. 70–6; Barnard, *Cromwellian Ireland*, pp. 122–4.

[24] Stevenson, *Scottish covenanters* , pp. 285–91; Seymour, *The puritans in Ireland*, pp. 95–103.

attempt to promote harmony the Act of Bangor, passed in 1654, forbade ministers, who came to Ireland, to bring in or even speak of the religious divisions in Scotland and prevented congregations from sending to Scotland for ministers without first consulting the Presbytery, which would only recommend candidates approved by both the 'Resolutioners' and 'Remonstrants'.[25] However the strong tradition of dissent within Scottish Presbyterianism, the theological, cultural and social contacts between Presbyterians in Ulster and Scotland, combined with the fact that both countries were as geographically proximate as the shores of a lake, ultimately doomed this legislation to failure.

While Scottish Presbyterianism took deeper root in Ireland, several new, disparate groups, introduced into the country by Cromwellian soldiers, emerged on the religious scene; English Presbyterians, Independents, Baptists and Quakers. Even though *The form of church government* (discussed above) was not legally enacted in Ireland, some Church of Ireland clergymen, such as Edward Worth, adopted its general thrust after the abolition of the Book of Common Prayer in June 1647.[26] English ministers, sympathetic to this Presbyterian form of church government enacted by Parliament, joined them and both groups worked together in order to strengthen their discipline and organization, to promote unity and to restrain other groups, especially the Baptists and the Quakers. To this end a group of ministers in Cork, who attributed the confusion and ineffectiveness of religion in Ireland to non-ordination, insisted that magistrates should only receive ministers legally ordained and that all should 'seek ordination from our brethren, the Scots in Ulster . . . or from our brethren in England'.[27] Though essential, this proved difficult to achieve, for journeys were long and expensive and certificates from such a distance could easily be forged.[28] In addition, the Cork ministers, especially their leader Edward Worth, wanted to establish closer links with the London Presbyterians and to create an all-encompassing body which

---

[25] Adair, *A true narrative*, pp. 208–18; Brooke, *Ulster Presbyterianism*, pp. 41–2.
[26] Bodl., Carte MSS 21, fos. 155, 176; Seymour, *The puritans in Ireland*, p. 227. For details on Worth see footnote 29 below.
[27] *The agreement and resolution of several associated ministers in the county of Cork for the ordaining of ministers* (Cork, 1657). Quakers at this time queried the ordination and ministries of Independent and Presbyterian ministers, [James Sicklemore], *To all the inhabitants of Youghal who are under the teachings of James Wood* (n.p., c. 1657/8). Wood was a newly ordained Independent minister at Youghal. Though he stayed in Ireland after the Restoration he does not appear to have conformed; but he ministered in Tipperary and was master of the Erasmus Smith school there, Barnard, *Cromwellian Ireland*, p. 192n. and in 1680 he published *Shepardy spiritualised*. Sicklemore was a ship captain, and lived at Youghal, F[riends] L[ibrary] L[ondon], *Biographies of Quakers;* BL, Lansdowne MSS 821, fo. 127.
[28] *Agreement and resolution*, p. 17.

aspired to be a national church.[29] Throughout the 1650s Worth exercised great influence in Irish ecclesiastical affairs and worked closely with ministers such as Joseph Eyres of Cork,[30] Samuel Ladyman of Clonmel,[31] Claudius Gilbert of Limerick,[32] and Daniel Burston of Waterford,[33] who sympathized with the Presbyterian tradition and were determined to forge a national church government.

Many Cromwellian soldiers were also Independents and by 1651 two congregations had been established in Dublin, one in the parish of St Nicholas within the walls and the other in Christ Church. Samuel Winter, minister at St Nicholas, came to Ireland as chaplain to the parliamentary

[29] BL, Lansdowne MSS 823, fo. 57. Worth was born in Cork and ordained in June 1641; he became dean of Cork in 1645; by 1650 he was acting as minister in Cork, with Joseph Eyres and John Murcot; in 1655 he became minister at Waterford but returned to Cork in 1658. In 1660 he resumed his office as dean of Cork and became bishop of Killaloe in 1661. For further details see John Power, 'Waterford clerical authors, from the work of Rev. Thomas Gimlette', in *Irish Literary Enquirer*, no. 3 (16 December 1865), p. 28; Barnard, *Cromwellian Ireland*, pp. 117–22, 126–32; P. Dwyer, *The diocese of Killaloe from the reformation to the close of the 18th century* (Dublin, 1878), pp. 317–43.

[30] Joseph Eyres was born in County Cork and educated at Trinity College Dublin with Worth: G. D. Burtchaell and T. U. Sadleir (eds.) *Alumni Dublinienses* (London, 1924), pp. 5, 354, 895; BL, Lansdowne MSS 823, fo. 91. He wrote *The church sleeper awakened* (Cork and London, 1659) which gives a good picture of the strengthening power of the association in Cork. Eyres belonged to a London classis and represented the Cork Association in London in 1658; Barnard, *Cromwellian Ireland*, p. 121.

[31] Henry Cotton, *Fasti Ecclesiae Hibernicae . . .* (6 vols., Dublin, 1845–78), I, p. 347; BL, Lansdowne MSS 823, fo. 51. Ladyman conformed at the Restoration and was appointed to the diocese of Cashel (Bodl., Carte MSS 221, fo. 130; Bodl., Carte MSS 160, fo. 6). Barnard, *Cromwellian Ireland*, p. 140.

[32] Gilbert was appointed to Limerick in 1652, at a salary of £150 per annum, soon raised to £200. In 1654, with eighteen laymen of the city, he wrote to Oliver Cromwell 'from the church of Christ at Limerick', asking for 'an able godly painful ministry', St J. D. Seymour, 'A puritan minister in Limerick', *Journal of North Munster Archaeological Society*, 4 (1919), p. 3ff.; Thomas Birch (ed.), *A collection of the state papers of John Thurloe . . .* (7 vols., London, 1742), II, p. 118 [hereafter Birch (ed.), *Thurloe state papers*]. Gilbert conformed at the Restoration and ministered in Belfast. In 1682 he published *A preservative against the change of religion, or a just and true idea of the Roman Catholic religion opposed to the flattering portraitures made thereof and particular to that of my lord of Condom. Translated out of the original by Claudius Gilbert, B. D. and minister of Belfast.* (London, 1683). He also contributed to Richard Baxter's *The certainty of the world's spirits* (London, 1691) pp. 214ff., 247ff.; Gilbert served as prebendary of Armagh in 1666, Cotton, *Fasti*, IV, p. 51, V, p. 208. Gilbert remained on good terms with English Presbyterians and was particularly friendly with the chaplains to the countess of Donegall who tended to be English Presbyterians.

[33] Burston conformed after the Restoration, Power, *Waterford clerical authors*, p. 28; J. Coleman, 'Some early Waterford clerical authors', in *Journal of the Waterford Archaeological Society*, 6 (1900), p. 178; Burston wrote *The evangelist evangelising* (Dublin, 1662) which was approved by Convocation in March 1663, TCD, MS 1038, fo. 76v; Cotton, *Fasti*, I, pp. 140, 156, 174. Burston was minister at Tallow in 1655 and was probably a member of the Cork Association. In his book (pp. 23, 31, 272), Burston admitted receiving 'presbyterial imposition of hands' which he rejected later on in favour of episcopal ordination. He became dean of Waterford in 1670.

commissioners.[34] He was appointed Provost of Trinity College Dublin in 1652 and held that position until 1660. His congregation tended to attract civilians and his covenant practice for admission of new members was modelled on that of New England. Charge of Christ Church fell to John Rogers, who had been sent to Ireland in 1650. He drew Cromwellian army officers to his services and required a declaration of conversion and faith, either through the medium of dreams, inner experiences or sermons heard which confirmed their conviction of election.[35]

The Independent church at St Nicholas had a strong leader in Winter and he was joined in 1654 by Samuel Mather who came to Ireland to attend Henry Cromwell.[36] Born in England but educated in New England, Mather was ordained in St Nicholas' church in 1656 by Winter, Timothy Taylor of Carrickfergus and Thomas Jenner of Drogheda.[37]

[34] [John Weaver], *The life and death of . . . Dr Samuel Winter* (London, 1671); William Urwick, *Independency in Dublin of the olden time* (Dublin, 1862); Urwick, *The early history of Trinity College, Dublin, 1591–1660* (London, 1892); Unitarian Church Dublin, New Row Baptismal Register, 1653–1737; St John D. Seymour, *Samuel Winter* (Dublin, 1941); James Armstrong, 'An appendix containing some account of the Presbyterian congregations in Dublin', in *Sermon: a discourse on Presbyterian ordination* (Dublin, 1829), pp. 78–80; *The register of Provost Winter, 1654–57*, ed. H. J. Lawlor (Exeter/London, 1907); R. L. Greaves and Robert Zaller, *Biographical dictionary of British radicals in the 17th century* (3 vols., Harvester, 1982–4), III, p. 333.

[35] W. Urwick, *Independency in Dublin in the olden time* (Dublin, 1862), pp. 10–11; Rogers published the 'Covenant of the church in Dublin'. John Rogers, *Ohel or Beth-shemish* (London, 1653), book II, chapter 7, pp. 459–61: 'The Covenant of the Church in Dublin collected out of the word of Christ according to the order of the Gospel'. This was a format for the admission of adult members and did not envisage then the question of admitting children to the church. For Rogers see Edward Rogers, *Life and opinion of a fifth monarchy man* (London, 1867), pp. 27–37, 57–74; P. G. Rogers, The *fifth monarchy men* (London, 1966), pp. 20–7, 34–5, 43–55, 54–7, 63–7.

[36] Mather was born in Lancashire in 1625; his family went to New England in 1634 and Mather graduated from Harvard in 1643. He returned to England and ministered in Oxford, Leith and then came to Dublin in 1654, Greaves and Zaller, *Biographical dictionary*, II, p. 228; *DNB*; R[epresentative] C[hurch] B[ody]; Seymour MSS, p. 41; Bodl., Carte MSS 45, fo. 277; Armstrong, 'An appendix', p. 79; Urwick, *Independency in Dublin*, pp. 16, 23; Armstrong, *Early history of Trinity College*, p. 77; Barnard, *Cromwellian Ireland*, p. 149; A. G. Matthews, *Calamy revised* (Oxford, 1934), p. 344; Cotton Mather, *Magnalia Christi Americana* (2 vols., Hartford, 1853), II, p. 39ff.; Unitarian Church Dublin, New Row Baptismal Register, fos. 1–3.

[37] Taylor was a Presbyterian and became an Independent. He was chaplain to Venables and occupied the former rector's residence in Carrickfergus. He was one of the examiners for ministers appointed in 1655 and from 1668 to 1681 he ministered in New Row, Dublin, Armstrong, 'An appendix', p. 80; Anthony Wood, *Athenae Oxonienses*, ed. P. Bliss (4 vols., London, 1813–20), II, pp. A1, 682; Reid, *History of the Presbyterian church*, II, p. 213, notes 20–2; Bodl., Carte MSS 221, fo. 79; BL, Lansdowne MSS 823, fos. 73, 780; Birch (ed.), *Thurloe state papers*, IV, p. 287; Seymour, *The puritans in Ireland*, pp. 24, 57, 72–5, 91–2, 97, 100, 126, 138, 192. Thomas Jenner was educated at Christ College, Cambridge and was minister of Horstead and Coltshall in Norfolk before going to New England. From there he went to Ireland, first to Drogheda and later to Carlow, BL, Lansdowne MSS 821, fo. 200. In 1670 he wrote a tract against the Quakers in Ireland, *Quakerism anatomised and confuted* (n.p., 1670); G. F. Nutall, *Visible saints*, (Oxford, 1957), pp. 30–1.

He was made a senior fellow of Trinity College, Dublin and co-pastor with Winter in St Nicholas' parish, though he preached every six weeks in Christ Church.[38] Including Winter, Mather and Rogers roughly thirty Independent ministers served in Ireland during the 1650s, largely in garrison towns such as Cork, Limerick and Waterford.[39] However Henry Cromwell's determination during the later 1650s to forge a conservative religious settlement (discussed below) meant that, by 1659, the Independents had lost a great deal of their political power and influence to the Presbyterians and ceased to be a major force in Irish affairs.

The demise of the Independents can also be partly attributed to the growth of the Baptists and the Quakers. Three factors explain the rapid ascendancy of the Baptists in Ireland: first, they enjoyed powerful and influential converts in the Cromwellian army; second, Deputy Fleetwood and his council allowed the Protestant sects a great deal of religious freedom which enabled the Baptists in particular to thrive; finally, desperate for ministers, the Westminster Parliament unwittingly added to their numbers by sending controversial Baptists, who had been denied positions in England and New England, to serve in Ireland.[40] The Dublin government later bitterly regretted this decision because these clergy quickly became a focus for the army officers' discontent with the Protectorate.[41] Indeed by 1655 Thomas Harrison, an Independent minister who had come to Ireland as Henry Cromwell's chaplain,[42] asserted that Baptists governed twelve of the towns and cities in Ireland and had ten lieutenant colonels, three or four majors, twenty captains and twenty-three

---

[38] Mather was also a commissioner for the approbation of ministers in Cork in August 1655, Seymour, *The puritans in Ireland*, p. 91.

[39] Seymour lists thirty-one Independent ministers; however some of them were closer to English Presbyterians. Religious boundaries and affiliations were very fluid at this time, Seymour, *The puritans in Ireland*, pp. 206–24.

[40] Barnard, *Cromwellian Ireland*, p. 100; Seymour *The puritans in Ireland*, p. 60ff. Certainly ministers were in demand, BL, Egerton MSS 1762, fos. 149v, 150v,168; Birch (ed.), *Thurloe state papers*, II, pp. 117–18.

[41] 20 January 1658, by the lord deputy and council (TCD, printed books, press A7, 1); K. L. Carroll, 'Quakerism and the Cromwellian Army in Ireland', *Journal of the Friends Historical Society*, 54, no. 3 (1978), p. 136.

[42] BL, Lansdowne MSS 821, fos. 155, 164, 170, 174, 212, 218, 332; Armstrong, 'An appendix', pp. 83–4; Thomas Harrison, *Topica Sacra* (Kirkbride, 1712), dedicated to Henry Cromwell; Edmund Calamy, *An account of the ministers, lecturers, masters and fellows of colleges and schoolmasters who were ejected or silenced after the restoration 1660* (n.p., 1713), p. 121; Urwick, *Early history of Trinity College*, p. 81; Urwick, *Independency in Dublin*, p. 18; Harrison preached in New England, England and Ireland.

[43] Birch (ed.), *Thurloe state papers*, IV, p. 91. For the development of Baptists, especially in the army see Barnard, *Cromwellian Ireland*, pp. 100–6.

officers.[43] Certainly by 1653 there were Baptist clergy in most of the garrison towns in Ireland.[44]

Like the Scottish Presbyterians, the Baptists were divided into two groups; 'Particular' or 'Calvinistic' Baptists (who believed that Christ died only for the elect), and 'General' or 'Arminian' Baptists (who held that Christ died for all).[45] Particularly influential in Ireland was Thomas Patient, a 'Particular' Baptist who had formerly belonged to the Church of England and who had been converted to the Baptist way while in New England.[46] He had to leave there on account of his radical beliefs and on returning to London he worked closely with the prominent English Baptist, William Kiffin.[47] He arrived in Ireland in 1650 and after preaching in both Kilkenny and Waterford managed to win over to his side the governors of both cities, Daniel Axtell and Richard Lawrence respectively.[48]

Though few in number, Baptist ministers entered into controversy with the other Protestant sects, especially the Independents. For instance, Patient's congregation in Waterford challenged the open communion

---

[44] BL, Add. MSS 19,833, civil list of soldiers, judges, ministers, schoolmasters, pensioners, 1654, fo. 12; Seymour, *The puritans in Ireland*, pp. 86–7, 206–24; H. D. Gribbon, 'Some lesser known sources of Irish Baptist history', *Irish Baptist Historical Society Journal*, 6 (1973–4), pp. 61–2.

[45] For definitions of the General (Arminian) Baptists and the Particular (Calvinistic) Baptists, see B. R. White, *The English Baptists of the 17th century* (London, 1985), pp. 7–9. For recent work on the Baptists in England during this period see J. F. McGregor, 'The Baptists: fount of all heresy', in J. F. McGregor and Barry Reay (eds.), *Radical religion in the English revolution* (Oxford, 1986), pp. 23–63; for Ireland see Kevin Herlihy, 'The Irish Baptists, 1650–1780' (unpublished PhD thesis, TCD, 1992), chapter 2.

[46] Thomas Patient, *The doctrine of Baptism and the distinction of the Covenants or a plain treatise, wherein the four essentials of Baptism . . . are diligently handled. By Thomas Patient, a labourer in the Church of Christ at Dublin* (London, 1654); National Archives, Dublin, M. 2817, notes relating to the 'ministers of the Gospel' appointed by the Commonwealth Government to minister throughout Ireland. Abstracted by the Revd St John D. Seymour from the original documents (since burnt) in the Public Record Office Dublin, pp. 21, 25, 82, 84; B. R. White, *The English Baptists of the 17th century*, pp. 58, 71–2, 128; White, 'Thomas Patient in England and Ireland', *Irish Baptist Historical Journal*, 11 (1969–70), pp. 36–48; Barnard, *Cromwellian Ireland*, pp. 101–2, 138, 146; Seymour, *The puritans in Ireland*, pp. 24, 33–5, 59–60, 86–88, 124–7, 141.

[47] Kiffin (1616–1701), became a Baptist in *c.* 1642 and remained a central figure among the Particular Baptists from 1644 until his death. He was well known for his opposition to open membership, to the Fifth Monarchy and to state payments of Baptist ministers, White, *The English Baptists*, pp. 70–84, 128–30, 135–8.

[48] For Axtell see Griffith Williams, 'A small part of the great wickedness . . . of the Assistants of the great Antichrist . . . in . . . Ossory', in *Four treatises* (London, 1667), pp. 3–4; Seymour, *The puritans in Ireland*, p. 86; Barnard, *Cromwellian Ireland*, pp. 66, 101, 103n, 105, 108; W. G. Neely, *Kilkenny. An urban history, 1391–1843* (Belfast, 1989), pp. 95, 97, 98, 117. For Lawrence see Ann Fowke, *A memoir of mistress Ann Fowke (née Geale) . . . with some recollections of her family, A.D. 1642–1774* (Dublin, 1892), pp. 24–5; Barnard, *Cromwellian Ireland*, pp. 53, 66n, 101, 103n, 146, 147n. Lawrence wrote several works including *The interest of England in the Irish transplantation stated* (London, 1655) and *England's great interest in the well planting of Ireland with English people discussed* (Dublin, 1656).

practised in Dublin by John Rogers' flock, finding them 'guilty of their sin of disobedience'.[49] As a result of the ensuing argument Rogers' congregation was dissolved, while Patient became one of the preachers at Christ Church and the first Baptist meeting house in Ireland opened in Swift's Alley, Dublin. In 1654 Thomas Patient published a work on adult baptism which provoked a response from Edward Warren, an Independent member of the army.[50] In another altercation in 1656 the Independent, Samuel Winter, penned a tract against the Baptists which argued firmly for infant baptism and refuted the teaching of Christopher Blackwood, a convinced Baptist and prolific writer from Kent, who had come to Kilkenny in 1653.[51] Recognizing him as 'the oracle of the Anabaptists in Ireland', four Independent ministers invited Blackwood to worship with them during a visit to Kilkenny in 1655. He grudgingly agreed to join them for a day of prayer providing a Baptist could speak last, the singing of psalms be discontinued, 'bitterness of terms' be avoided, all titles given people be kept simple and Baptists should not be withheld promotion on account of their beliefs.[52] In short Blackwood refused to compromise his firmly held beliefs or to be bullied by the Independents. The Baptists also deliberated with the Presbyterians. For example in Cork the English Presbyterians, Edward Worth and John Murcot, debated publicly in 1653 with the Baptist Dr John Harding on the issue of adult baptism.[53] In 1656 Claudius Gilbert, the English Presbyterian minister at Limerick, wrote a tract 'in answer to some fallacious queries scattered about the city of Limerick by a nameless author, about the 15th December 1656' which lamented the presence of

---

[49] Seymour, *The puritans in Ireland*, pp. 22–4.
[50] See footnote 46 above. E. W. A member of the Army in Ireland, *Caleb's inheritance in Canaan by grace not works. An answer to a book entitled The Doctrine of Baptism and the distinction of the Covenants, lately published by Thomas Patient* (London, 1656) [Signed Edward Warren at the end, p. 116]; Birch (ed.), *Thurloe state papers*, IV, pp. 314–15.
[51] Samuel Winter, *The summe of diverse sermons. Preached in Dublin before Lord Deputy Fleetwood, wherein the doctrine of infant-baptism is asserted* (Dublin, 1656); at one time Winter's wife was drawn to the Baptists, Weaver, *The life of . . . Dr Samuel Winter* , p. 43. Blackwood wrote the following: *The storming of Antichrist* (London, 1644); *Apostolical Baptism* (London, 1645); *A treatise concerning denial of Christ* (London, 1648); *A soul-searching catechism* (London, 1653); *A treatise concerning repentance* (London, 1653); *Four treatises* (London, 1653); *Some pious treatises* (London, 1654), dedicated to Lady Fleetwood. For Baptists in Kilkenny see *A memoir of Mistress Ann Fowke*, pp. 7–18.
[52] Birch (ed.), *Thurloe state papers*, IV, p. 90; Seymour, *The puritans in Ireland*, pp. 124–5.
[53] [Edward Worth], *Scripture evidence for baptising the infants of Covenanters. Produced at Cork in two sermons, one preached April the 7th, the other June the 2nd, 1653* [Cork, 1653] (Copy in Guinness Peat Association, Bolton Library, Cashel); *The several works of Mr. John Murcot . . . lately of a church of Christ at Dublin. Published by Mr Winter, Mr Chambers, Mr Eaton, Mr Carryl, and Mr Manton* (London, 1657), pp. 14, 19–20. Seymour, *The puritans in Ireland*, pp. 54, 66, 67, 113; Carroll, 'Quakerism and the Cromwellian army', p. 140; Barnard, *Cromwellian Ireland*, p. 149; National Archives, MS 2817, Notes relating to the 'ministers of the Gospel', pp. 26, 67, 74, 107.

Baptists in Ireland generally and the divisions they had brought into the country.[54]

On the one hand, such clashes reflected the differing theological stances of each group. The Baptist position was very different from that of the three other traditions in Ireland since it focused on the theology of the Covenant and was, in a sense, the logical outcome of both predestination and covenant teaching. As such it appealed to many, especially the soldiers in Ireland, during this uncertain period, for it fed the conviction of being the elect of God not just in a religious but also a political sense. On the other, these public debates proved damaging, especially to the Baptists and further exposed their weaknesses.[55] Thus colleagues in England warned the more zealous Irish Baptists in Ireland to act more cautiously, to exercise restraint and, above all, to recognize the Protectorate (established in December 1653).[56] That they chose not to do so ultimately led to their loss of power. For at the end of the day the government could not accommodate a sect which, according to one contemporary, believed that they were 'the Saints which must judge the earth'; nor could it allow them 'to tread all others under their feet and to get up the fifth-monarchy to rule the world', as some feared they might.[57]

The arrival of the Quakers in Ireland after 1655 further complicated the religious scene and destabilized domestic politics.[58] While members of

[54] Claudius Gilbert, *The Libertine schooled* (London, 1657). Gilbert recognised that these queries were based on Blackwood's *The storming of Antichrist* and simply circulated by the Baptist minister, James Knight, and reminded readers that the Baptists had been refuted by both Winter and Worth.

[55] For instance, as early as 1653 Zachery Crofton warned both the Independents and the Baptists of the dangers posed by these debates and mutual excommunications, see his *Bethshemesh clouded or some animadversions on the Rabbinical Talmud of Rabbi John Rogers* (London, 1653), p. 156. Crofton was born in Dublin and he dedicated this work to one of the elders of Winters' church, Daniel Hutchinson, alderman of the city of Dublin. Crofton belonged to the English Presbyterian tradition.

[56] White, *English Baptists*, p. 83; Seymour, *The puritans in Ireland*, pp. 84–5. In June 1653 the Baptists in Waterford had written to their colleagues in London asking for greater contact with other Baptist congregations in England, Scotland and Wales, and for some ministers to visit them in Ireland, B. R. White, 'The organisation of the Particular Baptists, 1644–1660', *Journal of Ecclesiastical History*, 17 (1966), pp. 220–1.

[57] Reuban Easthorp to Henry Cromwell, 11 June 1657 (BL, Lansdowne MSS 822, fo. 86).

[58] William Edmundson (d. 1712) considered to be the founder of Quakerism in Ireland, came to Lurgan in 1653 and the following year became a Quaker, *Journal of the life of William Edmundson* (Dublin, 1715); Joseph Besse, *A collection of the sufferings of the people called Quakers* (2 vols., London, 1753). For a recent discussion of the Quakers during the Civil War period see Barry Reay, *The Quakers and the English revolution* (London, 1985); Reay, 'Quakerism and society', in McGregor and Reay (eds.), *Radical religion*, pp. 141–64; Alan Cole, 'The Quakers and the English revolution', in T. Aston (ed.), *Crisis in Europe 1560–1660*, p. 358. Also, Richard T. Vann and David Eversley, *Friends in life and death. The British and Irish Quakers in the demographic transition* (Cambridge, 1992).

the Presbyterian and Independent churches held some beliefs in common, the Quakers had moved beyond and outside the traditional frame of reference which made them a threat to both the state and all other religious groups. To make matters worse the Quakers enjoyed considerable support in the army, encouraged women to travel and preach throughout the country, were very outspoken and openly critical of all religious sectors in Ireland.[59] Since theirs was a very personalized religion, based on an inner experience of God, Quakers felt duty bound to chastise all those who held power and authority in the country. Edmund Burrough and Francis Howgill,[60] who came to Ireland in 1655, were among the more influential Quaker leaders who implored the nation to 'Cease from all your idle worship . . . Cease from all your idol shepherds and priests of Baal . . . Cease from them and wait upon the Lord . . . '[61] More particularly they exhorted judges in Ireland to do their duty, otherwise 'God will cast you out of the seat of judgement as he has done the power of kings and bishops before you', cursed the city of Dublin and even admonished Henry Cromwell.[62] The Quakers challenged ministers throughout Ireland to public debates where 'queries' (or theological questions) which questioned the fundamentals of Christian religion – the sacraments, church organization and place of worship, the doctrine taught by scripture and particularly the doctrine of predestination – were circulated.[63] They also criticized outward behaviour and dress and condemned the Baptists in particular in this respect.[64]

Nevertheless Quaker influence increased rapidly and by early 1656 Henry Cromwell considered that 'Our most considerable enemy now in our view are the Quakers'.[65] In an attempt to curb their growth he ordered

[59] Carroll, 'The Quakers and the Cromwellian army', pp. 142–3, 151–2; Phil Kilroy, 'Women and the Reformation in seventeenth-century Ireland', in Margaret MacCurtain and Mary O'Dowd (eds.), *Women in early modern Ireland* (Dublin, 1991), pp. 180–8. For Quaker women in England at this period see Christine Trevett, *Women and Quakerism in the 17th century* (York, 1991) and Keith Thomas, 'Women and the Civil War sects', *Past and Present*, 13 (1958), pp. 42–62.

[60] Edmund Burrough, *The memorable works of a son of thunder and consolation* (London, 1672). For Francis Howgill see Maurice J. Wigham, *The Irish Quakers* (Dublin, 1992), pp. 16, 20, 22 and biography in FLL.

[61] *The visitation of the rebellious nation of Ireland* (London, 1655), p. 8.

[62] *Ibid.*, p. 19. Barbara Blagdon also visited Dublin at this time and asked to speak to Cromwell, Besse, *A Collection of the sufferings*, II, p. 458.

[63] *The visitation of the rebellious nation*, p. 29; F. Howgill, *Some queries to you all who say you are ministers of Christ in Dublin and to the rest in Ireland, to be answered by you or by your upholders. From us who in scorn by your generation are called Quakers.* FLL, Swarthmore MSS, V, p. 10; Trans. VII, p. 49.

[64] George Fox, William Morris, John Perrot, *Several warnings to the baptised people* (n.p., 1659).

[65] Birch (ed.), *Thurloe state papers*, IV, p. 508; also pp. 672, 698. Quakers were active in Cork, Waterford, Kinsale and Galway in 1656, RCB, Seymour MSS, fo. 334 and BL, Lansdowne MSS 823, fo. 86. Colonel Phayre, governor of Cork, was a Quaker of some influence, though he later became a Muggletonian.

that Quakers be ejected from the army and arrested if they resisted paying tithes, preached or disturbed ministers and people. As it happened, the Quakers did not represent a political threat, but the fear that they could be ensured they suffered fierce persecution, including imprisonment, beatings, disruption of their meetings, severe fines, and confiscation of their goods.[66]

Despite this, Quakers continued to be active throughout the country and even grew in considerable strength especially in Limerick despite the efforts of Henry Ingoldsby, governor of the city, to stem their progress.[67] A succession of prominent Quakers, among them Edmund Burrough, John Howgill, Edward Cooke, James Sicklemore, Barbara Blagdon and John Perrott visited the city and debated with conservative clerics such as Claudius Gilbert. Like everyone else Gilbert saw the Quakers as a threat to the stability of the country and in *The libertine schooled* argued against giving them toleration. He associated Quakerism with 'popery and paganism' and condemned the manner in which Quakers spoke, acted, prayed and behaved, considering them to be 'melancholically mad' and reminiscent of the Anabaptists in sixteenth century Germany.[68] Samuel Ladyman, a minister of the English Presbyterian tradition, concurred with Gilbert's conclusions finding the Quaker insistence on freedom of conscience particularly odious. He insisted that conscience needed laws, for on its own it was arbitrary and uncertain; even scripture could be abused by conscience and he reminded his audience that John of Leyden claimed it was conscience that allowed him to have fifteen wives at one time.[69]

With such religious divergences Quakers and Baptists in particular clashed constantly. They exchanged and debated 'queries' and also held 'public and great contests with the [B]aptists and head of the beast'.[70] In 1657 Edmund Burrough wrote a tract specifically against the Baptists, complaining about their treatment of the Quakers in Dublin, Kilkenny, Cork, Waterford and Limerick.[71] Two years later William Morris

[66] *A narrative of the cruel and unjust sufferings of the people of God in the nation of Ireland called Quakers* (London 1659); Besse, *A collection of the sufferings.*
[67] J. M. Douglas, 'Early Quakerism in Ireland', *JFHS*, 48, 1 (1956), pp. 3–32; John Rutty, *A history of the rise and progress of the people called Quakers in Ireland , 1653–1700* (Dublin, 1751); Besse, *A collection of the sufferings*, II, pp. 457–68.
[68] Gilbert, *The libertine schooled*, pp. 18–19, 25, 55. This work was written in response to a series of queries which had been distributed in the city, based on Christopher Blackwood's *The storming of Antichrist;* Samuel Winter and Edward Worth refuted this work. The author of the queries had also pleaded for toleration of Quakers in Limerick.
[69] *The dangerous rule or a sermon preached at Clonmel in the province of Munster in Ireland, 3 August 1657, before the reverend judges of that circuit* (London, 1658), pp. 28, 33, 57, 68–71, 78.
[70] Francis Howgill to George Fox and James Naylor, 18 February 1656 (FLL, Barclay MSS, no. 61, p. 69); Richard Waller to Margaret Fell, 10 August 1657 (*ibid.*, no. 57, p. 64).
[71] Edmund Burrough, *To you who are called Anabaptists in the nation of Ireland* (1657).

addressed 'All you particular Baptists in Ireland' and berated them for their worldly behaviour and mode of dress, as well as their treatment of the Quakers.[72]

Such tensions not only polarized the several Protestant radical groups in Ireland but contributed to the general air of instability, which alarmed the Dublin administration. For his part, Lord Deputy Henry Cromwell sought to steer a way through this uncertainty and ferment by deliberately creating a moderate religious party. In an attempt to move away from the more radical influence first of the Baptists and Quakers, and later of the Independents, and towards an organized and centralized church, he cultivated both the Cork Association, under the leadership of Edward Worth, and the Scottish Presbyterians in Ulster. In January 1658 he issued a proclamation against ejected English and Scottish ministers who had come to Ireland and tried to prevent further unwanted and divisive elements entering the country in order to broaden the basis of the Protestant consensus.[73]

Cromwell also summoned ministers to Dublin to discuss their differences and to reach some agreement on religious matters which would allow them to live and act in harmony. This convention, which met in April 1658 and hoped to heal the religious divisions within the Protestant community, faced a daunting agenda which included such contentious issues as the maintenance of ministers; the use of the sacraments; church discipline and the suppression of heresy; the cultivation of regular Sabbath observance and the education of laymen in basic church doctrine; and the problem of converting the native, Catholic Irish population.[74] English and Scottish Presbyterian influences at the convention proved decisive and it quickly neutralized the power of the Independents. As a result, tithes were re-introduced which was viewed as a major victory for the Cork Association and for the Scottish Presbyterians. Hardly surprisingly Edward Cooke, a Quaker, took a dim view of these developments: 'The committee of old priests sitting at Dublin challenge the 10th part of our goods . . . [and] set

---

[72] George Fox, William Morris, John Perrott, *Several warnings to the baptised people*, pp. 3–4; White, 'The organisation of the Particular Baptists', pp. 222–3. Morris had been a Baptist and a captain in the army in Ireland; he was converted by William Edmundson and in 1659 wrote to Parliament asking that the Quakers be freed from prison and harassment and exempted from tithes, *To the supreme authority . . . the Commons in Parliament assembled* (London, 1659); FLL, biographies of Quakers; the names of Friends deceased . . . in Ireland (FLD, YMFI, fo. 2v); Besse, *A collection of the sufferings*, II, p. 446.

[73] Barnard, *Cromwellian Ireland*, pp. 117–22; N. H. Keeble and G. F. Nutall (eds.), *Calendar of the correspondence of Richard Baxter* (2 vols., Oxford, 1991), I, pp. 186, 188, 201.

[74] The humble address of the ministers by authority assembled out of the several provinces of Ireland (BL, Lansdowne MSS 1228, fo. 14); Urwick, *Independency in Dublin*, p. 25.

themselves to roost in the old mass houses up and down the nation'.[75] In spite of Quaker reservations, Worth went to England to present the findings of the convention to the English Presbyterians. He received their full approval for the work and told Henry Cromwell that those he met thought they could 'close with the congregational brethren on the terms humbly presented to your excellency by the Dublin Convention'.[76]

During the convention it became evident that the Independents in particular had lost a great deal of power and influence in the religious sphere since Henry Cromwell had effectively replaced Fleetwood in 1655.[77] In response to this they reorganized themselves in the autumn of 1659 and defined their form of church order and discipline in some detail.[78] They opposed popery and prelacy in particular 'as it is cried up by some in these days under the specious disguise of moderated, regulated or primitive episcopacy'. This was an obvious rejection of Worth and the association of ministers in Cork. In what was a tacit admission that their power and influence had waned, all were advised to keep church affairs confidential and members were instructed to have no involvement in civil and commonwealth affairs.[79] However, Henry Cromwell's departure from Ireland in June 1659, combined with an increasingly volatile political situation in England (see chapter 12 below) cut short the work of the 1658 convention. Nevertheless, as the days of the Interregnum drew to a close, and new political realities dawned, English and Scottish Presbyterians hoped that the General Convention, held in Dublin in March 1660, would establish a new church order which excluded Independents, Baptists and Quakers and they specifically recommended 'that none be permitted to gather churches (as they call them) out of our parochial congregations or to exercise acts pertaining to church government in any of their private

[75] FLL, Edward Cooke, *A paper from Quakers shewing the wickedness of the young priests lately come over into Ireland and how the evil justices of the peace set up the old mass houses for them. And also the taking away of goods out of people's houses that cannot for conscience sake pay for mending of old mass houses* (n.p., c. 1658); for Cooke, see *A narrative of the cruel and unjust sufferings*, p. 1; Edward Worth, *The servant doing and the Lord blessing* (Dublin, 1659), p. 30. Lord Chief Justice Pepys advocated tithes and fixed ministries.

[76] Worth to Henry Cromwell, 20 July 1658 (BL, Lansdowne MSS 823, fo. 79). In June 1658 Henry Cromwell wrote to his father in support of Worth; significantly he omitted to say that both were working against the Independents, Birch (ed.), *Thurloe state papers*, VII, p. 162.

[77] Barnard, *Cromwellian Ireland*, pp. 112–17; Reid, *History of the Presbyterian church*, II, pp. 560–2. See the signatures to the 1658 Address of the ministers to Henry Cromwell (BL, Lansdowne MSS 1228, fo. 14). In this address it is evident that both Samuel Winter and Edward Wale were reluctant signatories; they indicated this by signing separately from the body of ministers and with a heading 'For the substance of the matter I subscribe to the premises'.

[78] *The agreement and resolution of the ministers of Christ associated within the city of Dublin and province of Leinster* (Dublin 1659), p. 2.

[79] *Ibid*, pp. 3–8, 9–12.

meetings'.[80] However the re-establishment of the Church of Ireland quickly thwarted Presbyterian dreams and forced many ministers, especially from the Cork Association, to conform. Edward Worth resumed his office as dean of Cork and in 1661 became bishop of Killaloe; Samuel Ladyman was appointed to the diocese of Cashel; Daniel Burston later became dean of Waterford; while Claudius Gilbert moved from Limerick to Armagh where he served as prebendary.[81] Those who refused to conform, especially the Scottish Presbyterians, the Independents, the Quakers and the Baptists, were excluded from the new religious establishment in Ireland.[82]

With the restoration of the Church of Ireland the wheel had come full circle. There is no doubt that for some established church ministers life quietly reverted to the pre-1641 positions; some, most notably the ubiquitous Henry Jones, once again bishop of Clogher, had indeed survived the vicissitudes of the 1640s and 1650s with their ecclesiastical power in tact.[83] However with the introduction of the Independents, the English Presbyterians, the Baptists and the Quakers, and the re-establishment of the Scottish Presbyterians, old religious paradigms had changed radically. It took the established church over a century to grasp that several distinct, dissenting influences had taken root in Ireland, and that they could not conform to the Restoration church settlement.

---

[80] Samuel Coxe, *Two sermons preached at Christchurch Dublin beginning the general convention of Ireland* (Dublin, 1660), pp. 7, 25–6. Also see James Maguire, 'The Dublin Convention, the protestant community and the emergence of an ecclesiastical settlement in 1660', in Art Cosgrove and J. I. Maguire (eds.), *Parliament and community* (Belfast, 1983); R. L. Greaves, *Deliver us from evil* (Oxford, 1986), pp. 43–5.

[81] See footnotes 29, 31, 32 and 33 above for details.

[82] Adair, *A true narrative*, pp. 241–52, 268–9; William Montgomery, *The Montgomery manuscripts, 1660–1706*, ed. George Hill (Belfast, 1869), pp. 236–7, n. 79; Thomas Morrice, *A collection of the state letters of Roger Boyle first earl of Orrery* (Dublin, 1743), p. 22; Bodl., Carte MSS 45, fos. 77, 298–9; MSS 31, fo. 381; Bodl., Clarendon MSS 80, fo. 380; HMC, *Report of the manuscripts of the late Reginald Rawdon Hastings* (London, 1947), IV, pp. 104, 109–10.

[83] F. R. Bolton, *The Caroline tradition of the Church of Ireland* (London, 1958), pp. 30–3; Seymour, *The puritans in Ireland*, pp. 54, 198–9. The restoration settlement is discussed in Phil Kilroy, *Protestant dissent and controversy in Ireland* (Cork, 1994).

CHAPTER 11

THE PROTESTANT INTEREST, 1641–1660

T. C. BARNARD

A SOUTHWESTERLY wind whipped around a knot of grandees huddled on the strand at Youghal in January 1654. The earl of Cork, Protestant Ireland's richest resident, and his younger brother, Lord Broghill, Protestant Ireland's most subtle politician, had come for a day's racing along the firm sands. Their sport was marred when a relation of Cork's steward, William Gostelo, expounded his visions. Galleons, crowns, Prince of Wales' feathers and oak trees in the sky could be stomached. But the prophet's latest fancy, vouchsafed in a dream – that Cork would marry his daughter to the exiled Charles II – could only gratify Cork's enemies who suspected him still of royalism, on the reasonable basis that he had earlier fought for Charles I in England.[1]

In 1657, with Gostelo now in Bruges to impart God's purposes to the cavaliers, the earl caused his arms to be set above the gateway to his seat at Lismore, twenty miles up river from Youghal. This heraldic blazon crowned the rebuilding of the castle, 'by the barbarousness of the Irish rebels pulled down' during the 1640s.[2] In addition it proclaimed to all comers that Cork after a spell of straitened continental exile, lorded it over the locality. Furthermore it signalled Cork's own grudging recognition of Ireland's new rulers because, in 1658, the impetuous but personable Henry Cromwell, now governor of Ireland, abandoned the sectarian spats of

---

[1] T. C. Barnard, 'Land and the limits of loyalty: the second earl of Cork and first earl of Burlington (1612–1698)', in T. C. Barnard and J. Clark (eds.), *Lord Burlington: architecture, art and life* (London, 1994); W. Gostelo, *Charls Stuart and Oliver Cromwell United* (London, 1655), pp. 1–60, 69–125, 192–200. Since Gostelo's chronology is confused, the month is conjectural. For other races: Chatsworth, Derbyshire, Lismore MSS, diary of the second earl of Cork, 10 March 1654/5.

[2] Chatsworth, Cork's diary, 17 August 1652, 4 and 29 August 1653; NLI, MS 6256, 28 September 1657; W. Gostelo, *The coming of God in mercy* (London, 1658); Thomas Birch (ed.), *A collection of the state papers of John Thurloe* (7 vols., London, 1742), v, pp. 672–5 (hereafter, Birch (ed.), *Thurloe state papers*).

Dublin and ambled out into the countryside. Cork responded to this customary viceregal progress with an equal traditionalism: he rode out with three hundred associates and tenants to greet Henry Cromwell at the bounds of the territory in Counties Waterford and Cork which the earl treated as his principality.[3] This entourage paraded the power which made Cork a welcome ally and dangerous adversary of any Irish régime. The survival of such local influence as Cork's, and Henry Cromwell's deference towards it, form an important theme in Cromwellian Ireland: the gradual transformation of a semi-feudal host into both a formidable political interest and the raw material of a Protestant militia, an element in the making of a 'Protestant ascendancy' over Ireland. Yet, within two years the Cromwellian order had vanished. In November 1659, Cork took ship for London, where, as he knew, Ireland's future would be settled. In his absence, his agent reported from Lismore that, early in January 1660, 'precepts' had arrived, 'for choosing of two members for each county and one for each town', to assemble in Dublin on 24 January as a 'convention'. This unprecedented gathering, born of the 'highest necessity imaginable', constituted Ireland's first exclusively Protestant assembly.[4]

These episodes introduce one of the several strategies adopted during the Interregnum by the survivors from the pre-war Protestant community.[5] This essay, as well as describing the varied responses, will argue that the need of the Protestants settled in Ireland before 1649 – known to contemporaries as the 'Old Protestants' – to outwit enemies fostered both the sense and organization of a cohesive Protestant interest, so that the Confederate Wars and their aftermath mark a vital stage in a process of political maturation. The idea of the 'English' or 'Protestant interest' in Ireland was used to enlist support among English and Protestants outside, and to unite squabbling settlers within, Ireland. But spokesmen slipped inconsistently between the terms 'English' and 'Protestant', and so showed how far they disagreed as to whether the wars were primarily religious or racial, and whether ethnicity or confession better defined the protagonists. It would seem that the looser and more inclusive notion of the 'English' of Ireland sustained those, headed by Ormond and Clanricard, who adhered

---

[3] Chatsworth, Cork's diary, 2, 3 and 5 August 1658; Lismore MSS 30/12; NLI, MS 6256, 7 August 1658 and MS 6259, T. Stanley's letter, now forming part of the binding; Barnard, 'Land and the limits of loyalty'.

[4] Chatsworth, Cork's diary, 2 December 1659; Lismore MSS 31/69; Bodl., Carte MSS 44, fo. 665.

[5] T. C. Barnard, 'Planters and policies in Cromwellian Ireland', Past and Present, 61 (1973), pp. 31–69; Barnard, 'Crises of identity among Irish Protestants, 1641–1685', ibid., 127 (1990), pp. 39–83.

steadfastly to the Stuarts, and may even prefigure the outlook of the Irish Tories after 1690. In contrast, those who preferred Protestantism as the guide to political probity welcomed the Cromwellians, but mistrusted the Stuarts, as defenders of the Protestant interest in Ireland.

I

Irish Protestant survival during the Interregnum depended on regaining lands, offices and military commands, once more collecting rents, fees and perquisites, and recovering the money owed since the 1640s. Most combatants exaggerated what they had spent and lost. But, since neither the Dublin nor London government regularly remitted much cash, the burden of financing the fighting fell on, and soon impoverished, local notables. Thus, William Parsons, besieged in his midland stronghold of Birr, spent over £300 on the garrison between late November 1641 and the following January. Similarly, at Comber in County Down, Viscount Montgomery of the Ards formed his tenants into a regiment. In Sligo, it has been noted, a few settlers created defensive units, but others, ill prepared, huddled in their castles and hoped the storm would pass them by.[6] Such caution, akin to the neutralism essayed by numerous English landowners in and after 1642, probably reflected the thin scatter of Protestants in so many districts. In a centre of concentrated Protestant settlement, such as at Lismore and Youghal, we can trace, almost day by day, how the first earl of Cork raided his reserves. By New Year's Day of 1642, he was paying thirty-four soldiers a daily wage of sixpence, and by 16 January he had enlisted a full complement of one hundred. Even a Maecenas like Cork, whose annual income probably totalled £18,000 p.a., could not subsidize indefinitely the local war-effort to the tune of £20 each week, and soon he had the pay of these soldiers transferred – at least nominally – to the military establishment.[7]

While Protestant settlers like Cork, Montgomery and Parsons, took the defence of their estates upon themselves, they and their friends campaigned in England both for assistance and for a policy which would 'root out the

---

[6] Birr Castle, County Offaly, Parsons MSS, A/1/92; TCD, MS 844, fos. 183–4; R. Gillespie, *Colonial Ulster: The settlement of East Ulster, 1600–1641* (Cork, 1985), pp. 154–5; M. O'Dowd, *Power, politics, and land: early modern Sligo* (Belfast, 1991), pp. 121–2, 127–8.
[7] NLI, MS 6900; BL, Egerton MSS 80, fos. 25, 31–3, 37, 39; *The earle of Corkes victorie and Tyrones overthrow* (London, 1641[2]); A. B. Grosart (ed.), *The Lismore papers* (10 vols., London 1886), first series, v, pp. 199–233; HMC, *Calendar of the manuscripts of the marquis of Ormonde*, ns (8 vols., London, 1902–20), II, pp. 114, 143; *A letter of the earle of Corke to the state of Dublin* (London, 1642).

popish part of the natives out of the kingdom'.[8] Neither spending nor lobbying could stop Protestant Ireland from being overrun by the insurgents after 1642. Refugees and emissaries, soliciting help from Charles I, the Scottish Covenanters or the English Parliament, kicked their heels at these different headquarters, where they soon became familiar (and irksome) presences.

The need first to enlist English or Scottish aid, and then, after it had eventually arrived, to limit the influence of these interlopers, preoccupied the Irish Protestants' leaders throughout much of the 1640s and 1650s. When the reports of an uprising in Ulster in October 1641 originally convulsed London, motley 'lords and gentlemen of Ireland' already on hand, guided English MPs to their response.[9] As the 1640s – and the Irish war – dragged on, and after the Dublin Parliament and the king's court at Oxford had dispersed, suitors for Ireland congregated around the Long Parliament. Those best placed to influence policy belonged to the handful of Irish landowners, like John Clotworthy, William Jephson, John Temple and Arthur Annesley, who sat at Westminster, and those Irish office-holders and landowners who had plumped early for the parliamentarian side. The English Parliament's Irish policy waited on events in Scotland and England, on the availability of men and money, and on the shifting political configurations at Westminster, so that Irish spokesmen, for all their assiduity, achieved little before 1647.[10]

The Irish Protestant lobbyists, however, were working concurrently on several levels: the social, eleemosynary and ideological, as well as the political.[11] Successes lay outside the cramped committee rooms of Whitehall. In particular, fluent apologists twisted the older concept of the 'English of Ireland' into the emotive notion of the Protestant interest by dilating on the religious motivation behind the war. Early accounts of the alleged atrocities emphasized Protestant clergymen as victims, and bibles and churches as targets for ritualized desecration. A grizzly legend of the Irish Protestants' sufferings, endured simply because they were the English and Protestants of Ireland, was skilfully fabricated. The most powerful contributions to the genre, Temple's *Irish rebellion* (1646) and Boate's *Irelands*

[8] BL, Egerton MSS 80, fos. 31–3; *A true relation of the miserable estate Ireland now standeth in* (London, 1642).

[9] J. Nalson (ed.), *An impartial collection* (2 vols., London, 1683), II, p. 769.

[10] K. S. Bottigheimer, *English money and Irish land: The 'Adventurers' in the Cromwellian settlement of Ireland* (Oxford, 1971), pp. 30–53, 76–114; J. A. Murphy, 'Inchiquin's change of religion', *Journal, Cork Historical and Archaeological Society*, 72 (1967), pp. 59–67; Murphy, 'The politics of the Munster protestants, 1641–1649', *ibid.*, 76 (1971), pp. 1–20.

[11] Bodl., Rawlinson MSS A. 258; *Cal. S P Ire., 1647–1660*, pp. 733, 767; HMC, *Ormonde*, ns, II, pp. 343–4; [A. Meredith], *Ormonds curtain drawn* (London, 1646).

naturall history (1652), entrenched durable images of Irish barbarism and Protestant fortitude, and popularized the belief in ineradicable and inevitable animosities both between English and Irish, and Protestants and Catholics.[12]

Thus, in the 1640s, the misfortunes of war exposed many Protestants to that fate more often endured by Irish Catholics: exile. A few, whom we must regard as the truly Anglo-Irish, still owned land in England. But even the wealthy saw English rents dwindle; so too, the adept, already conversant with English politics, were disorientated by the switch-back of the 1640s. Most refugees, then, though once prosperous and powerful in Ireland, eked out a shabby existence, cut off by penury from influencing affairs. The grim atmosphere, not any spirit of Calvinist self-abnegation, caused the master of the Irish court of wards, Sir William Parsons, to ask to be buried without expense or ceremony in London, 'my present destitute condition not permitting it'. Parsons died unsure whether certain of his trustees were alive or dead in Ireland, and bequeathed remote estates in the hope that 'there shall be such a quietness in Ireland by the blessing of God'. Similarly, the bishop of Elphin, Henry Tilson, deprived of his Irish revenues, when he came to provide for his children in 1648, had only the rent of a house in Rochdale to divide between the five of them.[13]

Debts weakened Irish Protestants, immediately and in the longer term. Pinched circumstances may also have sharpened their querulousness. But the scale of the financial difficulties, together with their effects on political attitudes, remain mysterious.[14] Unlike the combatants in England and

---

[12] Barnard, 'Crises of identity', pp. 49–58; Barnard, 'The uses of 23 October 1641 and Irish Protestant celebrations', *English Historical Review*, 106 (1991), pp. 889–920; Barnard, 'The Hartlib circle and the cult and culture of improvement in Ireland', in M. Greengrass, M. P. Leslie and T. Raylor (eds.), *Samuel Hartlib and universal reformation: studies in intellectual communication* (Cambridge, 1994); Barnard, '1641: a bibliographical essay', in B. MacCuarta (ed.), *Ulster 1641* (Belfast, 1993); A. Clarke, 'The 1641 depositions', in P. Fox (ed.), *Treasures of the library, Trinity College, Dublin* (Dublin, 1986), pp. 111–22; P. Loupès, 'Le jardin irlandais des supplices: la grande rebellion de 1641 vue à travers les pamphlets anglais', in L. Bergeron and L. Cullen (eds.), *Culture et pratiques politiques en France et en Irlande XVIe–XVIIIe siècles* (Paris, 1991), pp. 41–61; W. Love, 'Civil war in Ireland: appearances in three centuries of historical writing', *Emory University Quarterly*, 22 (1966), pp. 57–72.

[13] PRO, PROB 11/215/33; PROB 11/244/84; Bottigheimer, *English money and Irish land*, pp. 76–114; E. MacLysaght (ed.), 'Commonwealth state accounts, Ireland, 1650–1656', *Analecta Hibernica*, 15 (1944), p. 280; C. Webster, 'New light on the invisible college', *Transactions, Royal Historical Society*, fifth series, 24 (1974), pp. 19–42.

[14] Gillespie, *Colonial Ulster*, pp. 138, 195; Gillespie, 'Landed society and the Interregnum in Ireland and Scotland', in P. Roebuck and R. Mitchison (eds.), *Economy and society in Scotland and Ireland 1500–1939* (Edinburgh, 1988), pp. 38–41; Jane H. Ohlmeyer, *Civil war and restoration in the three Stuart kingdoms: the career of Randal MacDonnell, marquis of Antrim, 1609–1683* (Cambridge,

Scotland, in Ireland Parliamentarians as well as Royalists were impoverished by their activism. English landowners were ruined only when wartime penalties were combined with earlier fecklessness or later mismanagement.[15] In Ireland, by contrast, the lower average income of peers and gentlemen, the primitive credit facilities, the sequestration of English estates belonging to Irish Royalists like Lord Cork, the scale and duration of the destruction and the slowness of recovery often left an awkward legacy of debt. Even a reasonably lucky squire in County Armagh, in 1659 enjoyed an income from rents of only 63 per cent of its level in 1635, and as late as 1677 it remained more than 12 per cent below its value forty years earlier.[16] Beneficiaries from Cromwellian largesse, families such as the Boyles, Cootes, and Parsons, by the end of the century faced mounting debts. Despite the later contribution of fresh warfare, or natural and contrived disasters, it is likely that some mighty houses were undermined by the chronic debility caused by debts contracted during the civil wars.[17] Ormond, for example, entrusted with Ireland's defence in the 1640s, but with little money to achieve it, raised cash by leasing lands for ninety-nine years in return for immediate fines. This strategy, coupled with his long exclusion from the profits of his property, aggravated the troubles which, by 1688, had swollen his debts to £155,000, and which, by the 1690s, threatened to overwhelm his heir.[18]

Some, led by Lord Cork, who drew 80 per cent of his notional income from Ireland, caressed the new governors and, thanks to orders first from

1993), p. 67; P. Roebuck, 'Landlord indebtedness in Ulster in the seventeenth and eighteenth centuries', in J. M. Goldstrom and L. A. Clarkson (eds.), *Irish population, economy and society* (Oxford, 1981), pp. 135–54; Roebuck, 'The making of an Ulster great estate: the Chichesters . . .', *Proceedings, Royal Irish Academy*, 79, section C (1979), pp. 1–25; Roebuck, 'Rent movement, proprietorial incomes and agricultural development 1730–1830', in P. Roebuck (ed.), *Plantation to partition: essays in Ulster history in honour of J. L. McCracken* (Belfast,1981), p. 96.

15 B. G. Blackwood, *The Lancashire gentry and the Great Rebellion, 1640–1660* (Manchester, 1978), pp. 111–58; C. Clay, 'Landlords and estate management in England', in J. Thirsk (ed.), *The agrarian history of England and Wales* v, part II (Cambridge, 1985), pp. 145–62; H. J. Habbakuk, 'Landowners and the civil war', *Economic History Review*, second series, 18 (1965), pp. 130–51; P. G. Holiday, 'Land sales and repurchases in Yorkshire after the civil wars 1650–1670', *Northern History*, 5 (1970), pp. 67–92; J. Thirsk, 'The sale of the royalist lands during the Interregnum', *Economic History Review*, second series, 5 (1953), pp. 188–205.

16 R. Gillespie (ed.), *Settlement and survival on an Ulster estate: the Brownlow leasebook 1667–1711* (Belfast, 1988), p. lix.

17 Birr Castle, MS A/1/147; Dublin Municipal Archives, C1/5/4/3, pp. 7–8; T.C. Barnard, 'The political, material and mental culture of the Cork settlers, 1650–1700', in P. O'Flanagan and C. G. Buttimer (eds.), *Cork: history and society* (Dublin, 1993), pp. 316–22; Barnard, 'Land and the limits of loyalty'; HMC, *Ormonde*, ns, VI, pp. 83, 86.

18 Bodl., Carte MSS 69, fo. 467; T. P. Power, 'Land, politics and society in eighteenth-century Tipperary' (unpublished PhD thesis, TCD, 1987), I, pp. 86–7.

Dublin and then from London, recovered estates.[19] But these fiats did not entirely reassure the supplicants. Even after 1654, when most Protestants in Munster regained their property in return for paying fines, other pre-war planters remained outside this generosity, or were liable to penalties under the 1657 Act of Attainder.[20] In addition Connacht landowners, including Coote and King, discovered that parts of their holdings had been assigned to the transplanted Irish Catholics.[21] Cork himself, as an English as well as Irish proprietor, struggled hard to escape the decimation tax (against which his brother, Broghill, inveighed in Parliament).[22] These uncertainties reminded Irish Protestants of what they had long known: that their welfare rested with the English government. In consequence the Old Protestants, utilizing skills and links acquired in the 1640s, cultivated or criticized successive régimes. A fresh crisis came late in 1659, when an unstable Dublin administration, stuffed with radicals and sectaries, seemed to apportion taxes and commands so as to victimize the Old Protestants. The latter seized Ireland's government and army, while some of their absent leaders schemed in England to construct a more congenial government (see chapter 12 below).

An obsession with land did not result in a common Old Protestant stance. Uncertainties over titles and tenure were hardly new: the anxieties of the Interregnum renewed those earlier aroused by commissions of enquiry in the 1620s and 1630s. Established or re-established settlers, familiar with, and adroit at defeating, threats of deprivation, behaved as if immovable: they restocked, rebuilt and improved, and, when possible, added to their holdings in a market awash with lands to be had on alluring terms.[23] But land alone seldom sufficed to buoy up the flotsam and jetsam of the Irish Protestant squirearchy. Cash was needed: it tended to come from English remittances, military pay, the fees from office or legal practice, clerical stipends or the profits from government contracts. The gulf, always there, widened, between those merely seated on broad acres and those with additional resources to exploit them.[24] In the Interregnum, as in the past, a

---

[19] Chatsworth, Cork's diary, 30 August 1651, 1 November 1651, 5 and 7 January 1651[2], 6 October 1652, 5 February 1652[3]; Lismore MSS 28/22, 26, 31, 36, 39; T. C. Barnard, 'Irish images of Cromwell', in R. C. Richardson (ed.), *Images of Cromwell: essays by and for Roger Howell* (Manchester, 1993), pp. 189–90; Barnard, 'Land and the limits of loyalty'; R. T. Dunlop (ed.), *Ireland under the Commonwealth* (2 vols., Manchester, 1913), I, pp. 116, 125–6.

[20] C. H. Firth and R. S. Rait (eds.), *Acts and ordinances of the Interregnum 1642–1660* (3 vols., London, 1911), II, pp. 1109, 1132.

[21] NLI, MS 16,974, p. 64; O'Dowd, *Sligo*, pp. 132–3.

[22] Bodl., Carte MSS 255, fo. 118; Chatsworth, Bolton Abbey MSS 278, pp. 20–2; J. T. Rutt (ed.), *Diary of Thomas Burton, esq.* (4 vols., London, 1828), I, pp. 312–13.

[23] Chatsworth, Cork's diary, 8 November 1654; Lismore MSS 30/2, 6, 13, 14, 36, 41.

[24] Gillespie, 'Landed society and the Interregnum', pp. 44–5.

cornucopia spilled its plenty of appointments, patents and grants, but the ability to feast depended on favour. Those who now courted the Cromwellian régime, eager to reoccupy posts procured before 1641, often found that the best had been bagged by newcomers. Yet, between 1655 and 1659, in the closets and committees outside Henry Cromwell's council in Dublin, there again worked members of the tightly interlocking official dynasties of pre-war Ireland – Davies, King, Loftus, Lowther, Meredith, Temple and Ussher.[25] These collaborators, usually familiar as exiles with London since the 1640s, thrived, and drew further apart, both in attitudes and circumstances, from the unrelenting Royalists. The latter, subject to the severest losses and penalties, were denied those *douceurs* which might have eased their plight.[26]

II

Lord Cork personified those Irish Protestants who, either reluctantly or with alacrity, accommodated themselves to the Cromwellian order. Less familiar are the Royalists. Testy English Commonwealthsmen and radicals contended that virtually all the Old Protestants, including collaborators, remained covert Royalists, and had duped the gullible Henry Cromwell into supposing otherwise. Such a view, of collective dissimulation, seemed to be confirmed in 1660 when the quislings strove to hide how they had ridden in state to church, dined, caballed and hunted with Lord Deputy Cromwell. This deliberate obfuscation, and the profession of a secret steadfastness to the Stuarts, shamelessly practised by Broghill, Coote, Dr Henry Jones, Sir Theophilus Jones and Sir John King, makes it hard, but not impossible, to exhume those who had never swerved from the king.

Between 1649 and 1660 many Irish Protestants – like their English equivalents – were deterred from working for Charles II's return because success was unlikely. Ireland in the 1650s might lack Thurloe's intelligence system, but Dr Henry Jones earned his keep as scout-master-general by

<hr/>

[25] Chatsworth, Cork's diary, 24, 27, 28 and 30 April 1657; BL, Lansdowne MSS 823, fo. 83; PRO, PROB 11/215/33; PROB 11/231/85; T. C. Barnard, *Cromwellian Ireland: English government and reform in Ireland 1649–1660* (Oxford, 1975), pp. 208–11; Barnard, 'Lawyers and the law in later seventeenth-century Ireland', *IHS*, 29 (1993), pp. 272–4; HMC, *Report on the manuscripts of the earl of Egmont* (2 vols., London, 1905–9), I, p. 600; Birch (ed.), *Thurloe state papers*, VI, p. 71; VII, pp. 455, 606, 624–5.

[26] BL, Lansdowne MSS 822, fo. 198; H. T. Crofton, *Crofton memoirs* (York, 1911), pp. 101–5; G. Hill (ed.), *The Montgomery manuscripts (1603–1706)* (Belfast, 1869), pp. 205–6; T. K. Lowry (ed.), *The Hamilton manuscripts* (Belfast, 1867), p. 66.

reporting – and magnifying – the sinister.[27] When invasions were rumoured, as in 1656, known malcontents were easily taken. Thus, Montgomery of the Ards, a fervent Royalist who relieved his despondency at the sorry turn in the king's affairs by taking to the bottle, was placed under house arrest.[28] Similarly, Sir Maurice Eustace, an ageing lawyer notorious for his royalism, had his study sealed, his papers impounded and was interrogated by Cromwellian officials.[29]

A further obstacle to any royalist rising in Ireland was the fact that, notwithstanding Ormond's and Clanricard's efforts to unite all Ireland behind its sovereign, allegiances were now shaped by confession.[30] The news from Catholic Europe, where, throughout the 1650s, Charles II and his courtiers lounged and fornicated, emphasized how the Irish Catholics were fêted. The few Irish Protestants who had opted to join their exiled monarch included oddities, like John Bramhall, Strafford's unpopular patriarch, or Daniel O'Neill, without strong links within Protestant society but with all too many in the papist camp.[31] Protestants at home in Ireland, no matter how much they hankered after Charles Stuart, blenched at the prospect of his return in the baggage train of a Spanish army and with a retinue of Irish Catholic companions. Any royalist invasion could only renew war over land, religion and power. Already, with the new congruence between politics, race and confession, the Stuart cause attracted uprooted Catholics more than Irish Protestants, and so prefigured the character of Irish Jacobitism after 1691.

Adamantine loyalty to the Stuarts is best represented by Ormond. Ormond, an orphan, had been wrenched from his Catholic family, the Butlers, and, thanks to early quarantine in the household of Archbishop Abbott in England, resisted throughout his long life the twin infections of

---

27 TCD, MS 844, fos. 179–82; Birch (ed.), *Thurloe state papers*, VI, p. 378. Cf. Bodl. Carte MSS 31, fo. 346.
28 Hill (ed.), *The Montgomery manuscripts*, pp. 195–225; MacLysaght (ed.), 'Commonwealth state accounts', pp. 273, 288.
29 Chatsworth, Cork's diary, 14 November 1656; Lismore MSS 30/87; Jennings transcripts from the commonwealth records, formerly in Christian Brothers' School, North Richmond St, Dublin, notebook c. 20 October 1656, 16 January 1656[7]; NLI, 2322/295, 2323/51,385, 8643/8, T. Page to G. Lane, 23 June 1665; TCD, Mun P/1/376; BL, Lansdowne MSS 821, fo. 3; Bodl. Carte MSS 41, fo. 70; Rawlinson MSS A 63, fo. 185; F. W. X. Fincham (ed.), 'Letters concerning Sir Maurice Eustace, Lord Chancellor of Ireland', *English Historical Review*, 30 (1920), p. 255; HMC, *Ormonde*, ns, I, p. 326; Meredith, *Ormonds curtain drawn*, p. 21.
30 A. Clarke, 'Colonial identity in early seventeenth-century Ireland', in T.W. Moody (ed.), *Nationality and the pursuit of national independence. Historical Studies* XI (Belfast, 1978), pp. 57–71.
31 D. F. Cregan, 'An Irish cavalier: Daniel O'Neill', *Studia Hibernica*, 3 (1963), pp. 60–100; 4 (1965), pp. 104–33; 5 (1965), pp. 42–76.

rebellion and popery.[32] Ormond, like Cork, an habitué of the Caroline court, instinctively sided with his sovereign when the civil wars broke out. This devotion soon confronted Ormond with the conundrum of how to serve a fickle king, preserve his own Irish inheritance (which surpassed Cork's in extent and value), protect his extensive and mainly Catholic affinity, while upholding the English interest in Ireland. His choices – twice to treat with the Confederates, to render Dublin to the English Parliament and then, in 1649, to ally with some Catholic opponents to rescue the Stuarts – excited Protestant and Catholic, English and Irish, contumely. This man, stiff in his honour, was henceforward reviled for duplicity. Yet there hung about him an engaging air of bravado. In London during 1647, waiting to collect what he was owed by Parliament, he diverted himself, not only by visiting the king at Hampton Court, but by sitting for portraits from Hoskins and Lely, and by stocking up with the latest play scripts. A boyish taste for adventure enlivened the tedium of foreign exile in the 1650s, but imperilled the Irish fortune which his wife was patiently seeking to retrieve.[33]

Lady Ormond was left to plead the interests of the Butlers, of whom she – a considerable heiress in her own right – was one. The Cromwells, father and son, loved a lord, and Lady Ormond played to their snobbishness. Tirelessly she shuttled backwards and forwards from Dunmore to Dublin and over to London; she secured testimonials from clients and admirers, who advertised how she had relieved indigent Protestants in the 1640s; she traded on the good nature of other Anglo-Irish magnificoes, particularly the Boyles, who were embarrassed to see this eminent house reduced to want, and who may have calculated that the vagaries of fate might soon restore the Butlers to their old station.[34] Lady Ormond contentedly recorded her social success with Henry Cromwell. Yet, while it might recall happier days to see the lord deputy hunt across her husband's well-stocked deer park, what she and her children needed urgently was cash. Debts beset them: in 1659, she reckoned that interest payments consumed an annual £550 of the £2,000 which the state allowed her from her own inheritance.[35]

[32] Victoria and Albert Museum, London, Ormond MSS, ii, fos. 23v–4; T. Carte, *History of the life of James, first duke of Ormond* (second edn., 6 vols., Oxford, 1851); J.C. Beckett, *The cavalier duke: a life of James, first duke of Ormond* (Belfast, 1990).

[33] Bodl., Carte MSS 30, fos. 342v, 344–4v; Carte, *Ormond*, iii, pp. 330–41; J. Lowe, 'The Glamorgan mission to Ireland, 1645–6', *Studia Hibernica*, 4 (1964), pp. 155–96.

[34] Chatsworth, Cork's diary, 17 October 1654, 20 June 1655, 17 January 1657[8]; NLI, MS 2323/51; 2484, fos. 226, 238; 2499–2501; BL, Lansdowne MSS 823, fos. 322, 324; Bodl., Carte MSS 30, fos. 357–79; Clarendon State Papers, 65, fo. 238; HMC, *Ormonde*, ns, i, pp. 178, 224–5, 247, 266, 324–6; ii, pp. 367–74.

[35] NLI, MS 2484, fo 238; 2323/313; 2324/83; Bodl., Carte MSS 30, fo. 370; 213, fos. 254, 273v.

Those impervious to Lady Ormond's wiles warned of the continuing disaffection of the Butlers. And, indeed, in 1655, the English government clapped Ormond's young heir into the Tower.[36] However, an Ormondist party in waiting, composed of kinsmen and auxiliaries from the 1640s and underpinned with the creeds of divine right monarchy and Protestant episcopacy, emerged only in 1659. Then it expanded to embrace more, frightened now by Ireland's sudden descent into military rule. Henry Cromwell's radical successors summoned Lady Ormond to a fresh inquisition. She was met on her way into Dublin by sixty coaches filled with well-wishers. Tradesmen shut their shops while the case was heard, and, after the favourable verdict was announced, the festivities in the taverns lasted late into the night. The reporter of these stories may have been whistling to cheer the dejected Ormondists, for, while the demonstrations spoke of the unpopularity of the radicals in Dublin – a theme which would recur during the coming months – the Ormonds' friends waited until the Cromwellian collaborators had first ejected the English puppets, fallen out among themselves and then turned towards Charles II, before showing their hands.[37]

Few Irish royalists were as conspicuous as Ormond, and this impedes the reconstruction of their attitudes. One who shared Ormond's outlook was Sir George Lane, heir of Tulske in County Roscommon and Ormond's devoted secretary. Lane also resembled his local patron, Clanricard, in deriving from his own powerful sense of Englishness a fealty to the English monarch. The Lanes prided themselves on long service since Elizabeth's reign on behalf of the English crown in Ireland. Their loyalty was highly personalized, centred on the monarch and his Irish deputies. A lively awareness of the English interest, of which the Lanes regarded themselves as part, embraced Catholics if of Old English ancestry and loyal.[38] By 1649 Ormond and Clanricard grounded their politics on such thinking. For the Lanes, this inclusive view was seconded by marriage into families such as the Burkes, Farrells and Fitzgeralds. In their district, the Lanes, when in favour shielded their Catholic relations and dependants in much the same

---

[36] NLI, MS 2321/417; 2322/103, 231, 389; 2484, fo. 240v; Bodl., Carte MSS 69, fo. 544v; W. C. Abbott (ed.), *The writings and speeches of Oliver Cromwell* (4 vols., Cambridge, Mass., 1947), IV, p. 589.

[37] NLI, MS 8642/12; 8646/1; Bodl., Clarendon State Papers, 65, fo. 238v.

[38] NLI, MS 8642/8, 9, 11, letters of C. Ferrall to G. Lane; 8643/1, R. Lane to G. Lane, 29 October 1661, Charles II to R. Lane, 10 March 1660[1], 1 and 22 August 1662; G. Lane to A. Molyneux, 26 October 1667; 8644/2, relationship of Lane to Clanricarde; 8644/4, paper on descent of the Lanes; Kent Archive Office, Maidstone, U.269, C.312; M. Ó Duigeannáin, 'Three seventeenth-century Connacht documents', *Journal of the Galway Archaeological Society*, 17 (1936), pp. 147–52.

way as, on a grander scale, Ormond and Clanricard did theirs. While the son was accumulating obligations and connections in exile, the father, Sir Richard, having slighted Tulske on Clanricard's orders, mouldered in the midlands, unreconciled to the usurpers. He kept the company of the like-minded, notably 'my dear friend, Captain Edward Crofton, with whom and [with] my gossip, Mr Richard Crofton, I eat most of my bread'.[39] These were attachments which reached back into previous generations and which would be fortified by marriage in the next. They suggested affective ties, tightened by shared fighting and privations, rather different in quality from the glancing social contacts maintained by so many of the Old Protestant élite, which could as easily flare into quarrels as flower into friendship. With Sir George Lane again in high favour in 1660, his father aimed to settle old scores with neighbours, such as the Cootes and St Georges, whom he despised for their accommodations with Cromwell. Lane, in addition, posted to his son a long shopping-list, of sons-in-law and cousins – Nangles, Brabazons and Farrells alongside Croftons, Longs and Gardiners – and of the local posts – clerkships and seats in the Connacht council, clerk of the peace and collector of royal rents and taxes – which would fittingly reward these sufferers.[40]

The Lanes, with their feeling for a wide kinship group, might unconsciously echo the values of Gaelic Ireland, but it was a concern common to most clientage systems, and hardly distinguished the Lanes from the Butlers on the one hand or from the Boyles on the other. More noteworthy was the extent to which the Lanes cherished ties accumulated over three generations, and discounted religion as a reliable guide to worth. Nevertheless, the contrast between the uncompromising, like the Lanes, and the Old Protestants who rallied to the Cromwellians is not absolute. The Boyles, for example, happily intermarried with families of Old English and even Old Irish stock. However, these matches, with the Barrys, Fitzgeralds and O'Briens, may have differed from the Lanes' unions, since the Boyles aimed at, even if they did not always succeed in,

---

[39] NLI, MS 8642/5, deposition of 7 July 1655; Crofton, *Crofton memoirs*, pp. 101–5; John Lowe (ed.), *The letter-book of the earl of Clanricarde 1643–47* (IMC, Dublin, 1983), pp. 186–9, 280. The Croftons were not entirely shut out of public life: J. Meehan, 'Catalogue of the high sheriffs of the county of Leitrim', *Journal, Royal Society of Antiquaries of Ireland*, 38 (1909 for 1908), p. 386.

[40] NLI, MS 8642/12, letter of R. Lane to G. Lane, received 8 August 1660; 8643/1, R. Lane to G. Lane, [?] May 1661 and 29 October 1661; 8643/8, G. Lane to T. Page, 27 June 1665; 8643/9, J. Temple to G. Lane, 13 October 1666; 8643/2, C. Ferrall to G. Lane, 2 March 1670[1]; W. Spike to G. Lane, 29 June 1670; R. Gillespie, 'A question of survival: the O'Farrells of Longford in the seventeenth century', in R. Gillespie and G. Moran (eds.), *Longford: essays in county history* (Dublin, 1991), pp. 13–26.

assimilating the partners to their own distinctive Protestant religion and culture.[41]

Easy social relations across the religious gulf, supposedly common before 1641, were a first casualty of the rebellion. The châtelaine of Birr, Lady Parsons, for example, was reminded that her Catholic neighbours 'much honour, esteem and love you, and in that degree, that one would think you are of their blood and flesh'. War brutally ruptured these relationships, so 'that those who were a little while since loving friends are now burning, killing and destroying one another'. Many, including the heir to Birr, explained the horrifying change as arising from religious passion, and vowed henceforward to trust only Protestants.[42] Ormond and Lane, and one may suggest other Irish Protestants who followed them, resisted the reflexive equation of popery with treachery, and accepted all who aligned unquestionably behind the rightful ruler.

Between the unspotted royalism of Ormond or Lane and the Irish adherents of the Cromwellians lay numerous variants and compromises. In Ulster, for example, the easy passages to Scotland and Presbyterian hopes in Charles II, assisted the survival of Stuart loyalties.[43] Two, suspected throughout the Interregnum of desiring Charles II's restoration, were Mark Trevor and Sir Arthur Forbes. Trevor, indeed, typified those Old Protestant cadets who discovered their forte in fighting. Once embarked on this exhilarating career, he was reluctant to quit it, and in 1649 joined Ormond's vainglorious coalition to save the Stuarts. His subsequent contortions baffled former comrades, but, through his charm, Trevor ingratiated himself with Henry Cromwell, whom he urged, in 1659, to defy those who had destroyed the Protectorate and to declare for Charles II. Trevor, indeed, boasted that he could conjure an army of 20,000 from Ulster. But Henry Cromwell would not be suborned, and Trevor reverted to waiting and watching.[44]

Sir Arthur Forbes, like Trevor, had soldiered in the Stuarts' other

[41] Barnard, 'Land and the limits of loyalty'; N. P. Canny, *The upstart earl: a study in the social and mental world of Richard Boyle, first earl of Cork* (Cambridge, 1982), pp. 51–64; P. J. S. Little, 'Family and faction: the Irish nobility and the English court, 1632–1642' (unpublished M Litt thesis, TCD, 1992), pp. 183–222.

[42] PRO, PROB 11/231/85; TCD, MS 814, fos. 77, 82, 90–98v; T. L. Cooke, *The early history of the town of Birr, of Parsonstown* (Dublin, 1875), p. 55.

[43] Barnard, *Cromwellian Ireland*, pp. 122–6; *A declaration by the presbytery of Bangor* (n.p., 1649); P. Kilroy, 'Protestant dissent and controversy in Ireland, 1660–1711' (unpublished PhD thesis, TCD, 1991), pp. 9–10.

[44] Bodl., Carte MSS 30, fos. 559, 572–3; 213, fo. 256; Clarendon State Papers, 60, fos. 535–6; 61, fo. 262v; 65, fo. 238v; 71, fos. 156, 295v–6; H. O'Sullivan, 'The Trevors of Rosetrevor: a British colonial family in seventeenth-century Ireland' (unpublished M Litt thesis, TCD, 1985), pp. 81–163.

kingdoms. His strong Scottish links and his Presbyterianism kept him staunch for Charles II. Nevertheless, he disarmed the suspicions of Henry Cromwell and Monck with plausible words. Only in the summer of 1659, after Henry Cromwell's removal, did he discuss with Vere Essex Cromwell, Daniel Monroe, Henry Hamilton and Trevor, how to profit from the spreading confusion.[45] As a result of these intrigues, he was briefly imprisoned. Once free again, Forbes worked through, as well as being manipulated, in his turn by, Sir Charles Coote, an old colleague. Later, Forbes and Coote depicted their efforts, which included Forbes's dispatch as Coote's messenger to the king, as the key to the Restoration in Ireland. Such boasts, while not complete inventions, spoke more of the jockeying for the prime positions in later Stuart Ireland than of scrupulous accuracy. Whatever their subsequent loyalties, Forbes and Trevor, and Coote more wholeheartedly, had embraced the Cromwellians, and hesitated to appear for Charles II until a more general movement among the Old Protestants made his return inevitable.[46]

The Cootes illustrate both the opportunities and the dangers encountered by the Old Protestants between 1641 and 1660. Leaders of an affinity that stretched through Queen's County, Roscommon, Galway, Sligo and Leitrim, the elder and younger Sir Charles Coote had soon drawn ahead of their neighbours thanks to prowess on the battlefield. But modest resources, tenuous and uncertain links with the Cromwellian conquerors and even the remoteness of their estates from Dublin held back the younger Sir Charles from the pre-eminence of which he dreamed.[47] He, together with his sons, brothers and local connections (notably the St Georges, Gores and Coles) lost much when the Irish army was remodelled in the summer of 1659. These purges, indeed, impelled Coote to act: both to reverse the changes and then to oust their authors from the Irish government. Nevertheless, in intervening boldly, he still kept close to other, similarly outraged Old Protestants and, moreover, fitted his actions to what he knew of Scottish and English events.[48] Later he would insist upon his

[45] BL, Lansdowne MSS 822, fo. 294; Bodl., Carte MSS 31, fo. 606; John Forbes, *Memoirs of the earls of Granard*, ed. G. A. H. Forbes (London, 1868), pp. 35–6.
[46] Christian Brothers' School, Dublin, Jennings MSS, notebook *c.* 11 August 1659; Bodl., Carte MSS 30, fos. 559, 572–3; 31, fo. 606; Forbes, *Memoirs of the earls of Granard*, pp. 202–8; S. W. Singer (ed.), *Correspondence of Henry Hyde, earl of Clarendon* (2 vols., London, 1828), I, p. 220.
[47] BL, Add. MSS 19,843, fos. 129, 132; Lansdowne MSS 823, fo. 271; Dr Williams's Library, London, Baxter MSS, 3, fo 39; HMC, *Ormonde*, ns, II, p. 125; J. Lodge, *The peerage of Ireland* (Dublin, 1789), II, pp. 63–77; F. Teate, *The souldiers commission, charge and reward* (London, 1658).
[48] NLI, MS 8646/1, letter of T. Page; TCD, MS 844, fos. 192–4; J. Bridges, *A perfect narrative* (London, 1660), pp. 3–4; *A declaration of Sir Charls Coot* (London, 1659[60]); *A declaration of the major general and council of officers in Ireland . . . 9 January 1659[60]* (London, 1659[60]); C. H. Firth (ed.), *Memoirs of Edmund Ludlow* (2 vols., Oxford, 1894), II, pp. 188–9, 230–1; O'Dowd, *Sligo*, pp. 137–8.

precocity in approaching the exiled monarch. But, at the earliest, he had moved only in March 1660.[49] Thereby he might have edged momentarily ahead of the pack, but he had hardly outstripped it. As late as 13 April 1660, he publicly deferred to the decisions of the English Council of State and Parliament.[50] Neither he, nor any of his lieutenants, was deputed by the Irish Convention in April and May 1660 to repair to England; instead his neighbour and rival, Sir John King, was sent, and it would be King rather than a Coote who was rewarded with a share of the Connacht presidency.[51]

Coote's behaviour, often occluded, contradictory and fumbling, like that of so many other Old Protestants who remained in or returned to Cromwellian Ireland, hints at the erratic interplay of opportunism, principle, ambition and older feuds. We may suspect that some Old Protestants stuck to the Stuarts because their local rivals had welcomed the revolution after 1649, and such animosities complicated and enlivened Irish politics after 1660, when shifts and stratagems of the Interregnum themselves added an extra dynamic.

III

The varied calculations and complex of relationships of those helmsmen who steered Protestant Ireland through the reefs of the 1650s on to the rocks of the Restoration return us appropriately to the two most adroit Old Protestant pilots: Broghill and Annesley. In discussing this pair, one can either follow the logic of Broghill's own assertion that the Protestants 'acted all as one body',[52] and stress their similarities of background, tactics and ultimate end of making Ireland unequivocally English and Protestant; or their differences, and so, by implication, the fissures and factionalism which weakened the Irish Protestant interest. Both need their place. Annesley and

---

[49] Commission of Charles II to Coote, 17 March 1660, new style (Staffordshire County Record Office, Bradford MSS, D 1287/P/616).
[50] Bodl., Clarendon State Papers, 71, fo. 156; *An account of the chief occurrences of Ireland . . . 15–22 February* [1659[60]] (Dublin, 1660), pp. 1–2, 37–8; *A declaration of the General Convention of Ireland with the late proceedings there* (London, 1660), p. 7; HMC, *Leyborne–Popham MSS*, I, p. 179; Firth (ed.), *Memoirs of Ludlow*, II, pp. 196, n. 1, 199, 209; *A new declaration and engagement of the army and forces of Ireland . . . 13 April 1660* (London, 1660), in Bodl., Carte MSS 71, fo. 379.
[51] Chatsworth, Cork's diary, 2 and 7 February 1658[9]; NLI, MS 11,959, p. 23; PRO, PROB 11/265/222; Bodl., Carte MSS 44, fo. 664; 214, fo. 238; Barnard, *Cromwellian Ireland*, pp. 24, 147n, 199, 215, 225, 290n; *Londons Intelligencer*, 4, 18–25 May 1660 (London, 1660), pp. 28, 30; A. Woolrych, *Commonwealth to protectorate* (Oxford, 1982), p. 179.
[52] [R. Boyle], earl of Orrery, *The Irish colours displayed* (London, 1662), p. 15.

Broghill alternated between co-operation and ill concealed rivalry until their friendship spectacularly exploded in 1672.[53]

A busy Irish Protestant lobby had worked in London throughout the 1640s. Since so much that concerned Ireland was still decided there, the activity continued, focused on the successive Councils of State and, after 1653, on Cromwell as protector. Parliament, too – from 1653 afforced by Irish representatives – attracted Irish Protestant attention; elections in 1654, 1656 and 1659, and then in 1660 (for the Convention) and in 1661 (for the Dublin Parliament) required meetings, and so added to those opportunities, already offered by the regular assizes, sessions and grand juries, and by *ad hoc* inquisitions, to nourish and organize a sense of their shared anxieties as Irish Protestants. Broghill, sensitive to, and able to connect, the several worlds of the barony, county and province, Dublin, Westminster and Whitehall, slid easily into the leadership of the Old Protestants.[54]

The febrile Broghill chased many will-o'-the-wisps, the most alluring of which – creating a Cromwellian party from the fractious Scottish Presbyterian clergy, erecting a Cromwellian monarchy, entrenching an Irish Protestant militia and winning for himself the Irish viceroyalty – eluded him. Often excoriated for a pliancy tantamount to apostasy, he exhibited great courage – political as well as physical – in expressing robust opinions. In the Parliament of 1656–7 he had hoped to show his own, and the Irish Protestants', high value to the Cromwellian régime by devising a fresh constitution – the 'Humble Petition and Advice' – and delivering a solid block of votes to approve it. Dejected when Oliver Cromwell declined the kingship, Broghill returned to Ireland, where he readily insinuated himself as the *eminence grise* behind the impressionable Henry Cromwell.[55] From this partnership soon emerged a radical scheme to replace the standing forces in Ireland with a militia. Since his arrival in Dublin in 1655, Henry Cromwell had been reviewing ways to retrench, and winnow out troublesome radical officers. The projected militia might include Ireland in the system of major-generals recently erected in England and Wales.[56] As

[53] BL, Add. MSS 40,860, fos. 29v, 32v; Petworth House, West Sussex, Orrery MSS, general series, 22, Anglesey to Orrery, 21 May 1672 and 23 July 1672; Orrery to Anglesey, 28 November 1672.
[54] Chatsworth, Cork's diary, 13 April 1658, 14 July 1658, 6 January 1658[9]; BL, Lansdowne MSS 823, fo. 37; T. C. Barnard, 'Lord Broghill, Vincent Gookin and the Cork elections of 1659', *English Historical Review*, 88 (1973), pp. 352–65; *Cal. S P Ire., 1647–60*, pp. 623, 655, 660–1; *A Declaration of the General Convention of Ireland*, p. 7.
[55] Chatsworth, Cork's diary, 1 and 9 September 1657, 26 October 1657, 26 January 1657[8], 18 May 1659; Lismore MSS 28/69; Barnard, 'Planters and policies', pp. 59–60; K. M. Lynch, *Roger Boyle, first earl of Orrery* (Knoxville, 1965), pp. 86–91.
[56] Dunlop (ed.), *Ireland under the Commonwealth*, II, pp. 551–2.

234 IRELAND FROM INDEPENDENCE TO OCCUPATION

envisaged by Henry Cromwell, it would be manned by the disbanded soldiers who were now settling their new holdings, would extend the social and military organization of the early seventeenth-century plantations of Munster and Ulster, and vindicate the thinking behind the massive transfers of land since 1642. In 1656, as war with Spain exposed Ireland to possible invasion, Henry Cromwell pressed ahead with the design. He toured the south and west, and consulted 'several of the most considerable and considering persons inhabiting in the respective counties of Munster'.[57] Lord Cork, that old cavalier, was one who 'had much conference in my lord's closet with him' over the matter. Other Old Protestants – Sir Hardress Waller, Mark Trevor and John King – some impeccably Cromwellian, others unabashed Royalists, were heeded.[58] Henry Cromwell not only drafted lists of regiments and officers, he had the new forces mustered in some counties. His father, however, worried about the Old Protestant complexion of this militia, vetoed the scheme.[59] In doing so, the Protector, characteristically, sought to slow his son's advancement of the Old Protestants, and also to dodge the problems which so destabilized and would soon destroy the Protectorate: the power and costs of the army.

By 1657, the original English army of over 30,000 which had reconquered Ireland had been reduced to about 9,000.[60] The soldiers' wages, still beyond the island's ability to pay, slipped further into arrears: by early 1660 they had been unpaid for sixteen months. Meanwhile civilians, especially the Old Protestants, complained of exorbitant and inequitable taxes.[61] After Henry Cromwell had resigned in 1659, the composition and uses of the army in Ireland were bitterly contested, and eventually provoked an Old Protestant coup. From December 1659 the Council of Officers in Dublin, now dominated by Coote, King, Jones and (for a time) Waller, in conjunction with Broghill in Munster and with Monck, assumed authority over the country, summoned the Convention to Dublin, and, later in the spring of 1660, while it sat, concerted matters with its members, many of whom were now military commanders. Furthermore, the Council

---

[57] *Ibid.*, p. 614; Birch (ed.), *Thurloe state papers*, v, pp. 422–3, 453, 477, 493, 586; vi, pp. 142–3, 568–9, 657, 658, 660–2, 680–1.

[58] Chatsworth, Cork's diary, 23 September 1656.

[59] TCD, MS 844, fo. 171v; Abbott (ed.), *Writings of Cromwell*, iv, p. 385; Dunlop (ed.), *Ireland under the Commonwealth*, ii, p. 622; Birch (ed.), *Thurloe state papers*, v, pp. 504, 586.

[60] Bowood House, Wiltshire, Petty Papers, box F/14; Dunlop (ed.), *Ireland under the Commonwealth*, i, p. 116.

[61] BL, Add. MSS 32,471, fo. 83v; Bridges, *Perfect narrative*, p. 14; *Cal. S P Ire., 1647–60*, pp. 638–9; *ibid., 1660–2*, p. 192; *Irelands fidelity to the parliament of England* (London, 1660), pp. 3–6; Birch (ed.), *Thurloe state papers*, vi, p. 658.

of Officers had reinstated Old Protestant officers displaced in 1659; early in 1660 the county militias were formally reinstated.[62] This essential question of who protected Ireland, and how these defences were to be organized and financed, linked the experiences of the Old Protestants before and during the 1640s with the experiments of the Interregnum and 1660s. Economy and developments in England may have inclined the young Cromwell to the idea of an Irish militia. But, since his admiration of Broghill is so well attested (he confided in Cork that he had taken the Dublin posting only because Broghill had promised his help), we may suppose that Broghill, even if he had not planted the notion in Henry Cromwell's mind, stealthily guided the latter towards creating an Irish militia. In 1658 Broghill sent for his copy of Machiavelli. Too much should not be read into this: it was *The Prince* not the *Discourses*; and at the same time he diverted himself with Grotius, Cowley's poems and Ussher's *Annals*.[63] Even so, Machiavelli, the passionate believer that citizens man their own armies and that political degeneracy could be traced to the employment of mercenaries, was an obvious intellectual source. Repeatedly Broghill urged the value of a militia: in the constitution of 1657 through which he aimed to stabilize the British state; in Munster, under the terms of the commissions which he received first from Henry Cromwell, then in 1660 from the English Council of State, and finally as lord president of the province and major-general of the Irish army.[64]

In addition, local circumstances inclined Broghill, and other Old Protestants, to the militia. The undertakers in the recent Irish plantations, when not themselves disbanded soldiers, were required to maintain on their lands specific numbers of men trained and armed to fight. During the peaceful 1620s and 1630s, these obligations, seemingly obsolete, fell into desuetude.[65] However the wars of the 1640s proved the need and value of

[62] TCD, MS 844, fo. 187v; Bodl., Carte MSS 30, fo. 573; *Account of the chief occurrences*, pp. 8, 10; Bridges, *Perfect narrative*, pp. 4, 10; *Cal. S P Ire., 1663–5*, p. 379; *Declaration of the major general and council of officers*; Dunlop (ed.), *Ireland under the Commonwealth*, II, pp. 701, 709–10; J. T. Gilbert (ed.), *Calendar of the ancient records of Dublin in possession of the municipal corporation* (17 vols., Dublin, 1889–1916), IV, pp. 162, 172.
[63] Chatsworth, Cork's diary, 2 December 1656; Petworth House, West Sussex, Orrery MSS, general series, 15, note of T. Brodrick, 21 May 1658.
[64] Houghton Library, Harvard University, Orrery MSS, MS 218 22F, letter of E. Worth to Broghill, late 1659/early 1660; BL, Egerton MSS 2542, fo. 334; Birch (ed.), *Thurloe state papers*, VII, p. 575.
[65] Gillespie, *Colonial Ulster*, p. 82; G. Hill, *An historical account of the plantation in Ulster* (Belfast, 1877), pp. 82, 450–540; M. MacCarthy-Morrogh, *The Munster plantation: English migration to southern Ireland, 1583–1641* (Oxford, 1986), pp. 147–8, 174–5, 250–1; T. O. Ranger, 'The career of Richard Boyle, first earl of Cork, in Ireland, 1588–1643' (unpublished D Phil thesis, Oxford, 1959), pp. 386–401.

such arrangements, because, only where the military provisions of the plantation articles had been obeyed, notably in parts of Munster and Ulster, were the rebels contained. Thus, despite the sorry showing of the Old Protestants during the 1640s – saved only by massive Scottish and English reinforcements – the military functions of the plantations were not discredited. Old Protestants insisted that, notwithstanding the humiliations of the 1640s, they could and should defend Ireland. Broghill himself, thanks to long campaigning, converted an abstract grasp of siege craft and tactics into renown as a general.

After 1660, Broghill, advanced now to earl of Orrery, obsessively championed the Irish Protestant militia. This *idée fixe* testified to his own apprehensions about foreign invasion and domestic subversion, his rivalry with more casual Irish viceroys and his skill at identifying and inflaming Old Protestant worries. In the 1670s, the Irish lord lieutenant, Essex, candidly confessed how Orrery, by pleading for the mustering of the militia, was regarded 'as the great champion of the Protestant interest'.[66] Bearing arms – at once a duty and a right – when denied excited Irish Protestant disquiet, which Orrery expertly, and not always disinterestedly, orchestrated. In 1659, the displacement of Old Protestant officers by suspect Englishmen produced a coup; in the 1660s and 1670s the lack of enthusiasm exhibited by Ormond and Essex estranged many Protestants within Ireland; then, in the 1680s, first the Tory reaction and next the catholicizing schemes of James II and Tyrconnell, with Protestant veterans cashiered and disarmed, and Catholics mustered, obliged terrified Protestants to band together in defiance of the government. The Protestant nation under arms, first clearly postulated by Orrery in the 1650s and 1660s, came into being.[67] (See conclusion below.)

---

[66] Bodl., Add. MSS C. 34, fos. 142–3, 147v–48v, 149, 159v, 164v, 171v, 188; Clarendon State Papers 84, fos. 168v, 173v, 222; Victoria and Albert Museum, Orrery MSS I, fos. 38v, 67, 69v, II, fos. 39, 41, 45v, 46, 55, 59, 63, 65, 67; NLI, MS 2481, fo. 64; Petworth, Orrery MSS, general series, 28, letter of 14 December 1669; L. Irwin, 'The earl of Orrery and the military problems of Restoration Munster', *Irish Sword*, 13 (1977–9), pp. 10–18; S. P. Johnston, 'On a manuscript description of the city and county of Cork . . . by Sir Richard Cox', *Journal, Royal Society of Antiquaries of Ireland*, 32 (1902), p. 354; C. Smith, *The ancient and present state of the county and city of Cork* (second edn., Dublin, 1774), I, pp. 58–9; *Seasonable advice to Protestants* (Cork, 1745), pp. 6, 30–1. Cf. Orrery, *Irish colours displayed*, p. 15.

[67] NLI, MS 8644/5; T.C. Barnard, 'Athlone, 1685; Limerick, 1710; religious riots or charivaris?', *Studia Hibernica*, 27 (1993); J. Childs, *The army, James II and the glorious revolution* (Manchester, 1980), pp. 56–82; R. Loeber and H. Murtagh (eds.), 'The reorganization of the Irish militia in 1678–81: documents from Birr castle', *Irish Sword* (forthcoming). I am most grateful to Dr Rolf Loeber for allowing me to see a transcript of this document before its publication. J. Miller, 'The earl of Tyrconnell and James II's Irish policy', *The Historical Journal*, 20 (1977), pp. 817–19; W. G. Wood-Martin, *History of Sligo* (3 vols., Dublin, 1889), II, pp. 101–5.

IV

Defence fostered co-operation among Irish Protestants; it also bred a new exclusiveness, trusting only Protestants with arms, and so further separated those, headed by Orrery, who used religion as the surest touchstone of reliability, and those who followed Ormond in believing that Englishness – an imprecise term for a bundle of attitudes in which loyalty to the English sovereign was paramount – should qualify office-holders, landowners and soldiers in Ireland. Tussles over who manned the Irish army raised the equally divisive question of who controlled it and, as a result, the need to define Ireland's constitutional relationship with England. Simultaneously, in 1659, political instability and economic distress encouraged Irish Protestants to scrutinize the inconveniences as well as the benefits of the intimate tie with England. In the spring of 1659, most Irish representatives pleaded to remain in the British Parliament and described themselves (accurately) as 'the English of Ireland' with no 'Irish teague' among them. Since they belonged to an exclusively Protestant assembly, they scarcely needed to labour their Protestantism.[68]

At this juncture, however, Annesley broke ranks, dissented from the prevalent unionism, and pleaded for 'the ancient constitution', which should include the Dublin Parliament's as well as the king's return.[69] Annesley, playing his own devious game, wrestled with Broghill for the captaincy of the Old Protestant interest. Though so alike in background, preconceptions and ambitions, their careers had diverged sharply. Annesley, owner of Welsh and Irish lands, was immediately hailed as an Irish expert when he was recruited to the Long Parliament, because his eyes did not glaze as the mantras of Irish place-names were intoned in despatches and because he knew the locales and protagonists. Disliking the turn of events, he was secluded from the Long Parliament in 1648. One of several able conservatives tempted back to Ireland in the 1650s, he begged Henry Cromwell's favour. The latter, though he admired Annesley's parts, had nothing to bestow. Instead the corporation of Dublin elected Annesley to sit at Westminster, where he was an undoubted star in 1659. Yet, more tenuously connected with the Irish provinces than Broghill, he did not enjoy uncritical admiration, and indeed, when, in the summer of 1659, he set up

---

[68] Rutt (ed.), *Diary of Thomas Burton*, IV, pp. 114, 169, 225-7, 237-43; Barnard, 'Planters and policies', pp. 63-5. A bill for the union of England and Ireland was prepared for enacting by this Parliament: BL, Lansdowne MSS 823, fo. 297v; Stowe MSS 185, fo. 139.

[69] BL, Lansdowne MSS 823, fos. 216, 229, 239, 251, 287; [A. Annesley], *Englands confusion* (London, 1659), especially pp. 20-1; D. Hirst, 'Concord and discord in Richard Cromwell's House of Commons', *English Historical Review*, 103 (1988), pp. 342, 345-6, 356.

as agent in London of the Irish Protestants, some brusquely repudiated him.[70]

During the unfolding crisis of 1659 to 1660, Broghill worked in Ireland while Annesley busied himself in London. Despite differences in tactics and their personal rivalries, each retained the Old Protestants' habit of obeying England. This instinct was encapsulated in the Old Testament apothegm, much repeated at the time, that the Irish Protestants were linked to the English as 'bone of their bone, flesh of their flesh'. The text from Genesis, in which Eve's creation is recounted, so far from asserting Irish independence, found in Eve's subjection to Adam an exact analogy for Ireland's close but subservient relationship with England.[71] Even so, some initiatives of the Irish Protestants, notably the summoning of the Convention in Dublin (scheduled to open on 24 January 1660, it was postponed until 27 February),[72] excited suspicions, at the time – and since – that, under cover of the confusion in England, they were bidding for Ireland's independence.[73] Certainly, the assembly, though in combination with fresh Old Protestant commanders and the commissioners lately appointed by England, sanctioned taxes and reorganized the army. Irish Protestant leaders, faced with a constitutional vacuum in the British Isles, improvised; but, in doing so, they paced themselves carefully against their associates in Scotland, London and the king's court, with all of whom they were in touch. They were further inhibited from deviating too sharply by fears that the Catholic primate, O'Reilly, back in Dublin, might turn any strife to the irredentist Catholics' advantage.[74] The Convention deliberately publicized how its members all descanted harmoniously on the theme, 'that the benefit of Ireland is chiefly contained in a subordination to the

---

[70] Chatsworth, Lismore MSS 31/44, 44*, 46, 47, 50; Cork's diary, 8 February 1657[8], 7 December 1658; TCD, Mun. P/1/470, 38; Gilbert (ed.), *Calendar of the ancient records of Dublin*, IV, p. 152; Fincham (ed.), 'Letters concerning Sir Maurice Eustace', p. 252; Birch (ed.), *Thurloe state papers*, VI, p. 777.

[71] Chatsworth, Lismore MSS 31/44*; A. Clarke, *The Old English in Ireland, 1625–1641* (Ithaca and London, 1966), p. 136; *Declaration of Coot*, p. 7; *The Declaration of the army in Ireland declaring their resolution for a free Parliament* (London, 1660), p. 5; Birch (ed.), *Thurloe state papers*, VII, p. 819. The text is from Genesis, 2:3.

[72] For these dates: Chatsworth, Lismore MSS 31/69; R. Caulfield (ed.), *The council book of the corporation of Kinsale* (Guilford, 1879), p. 52; *Declaration of the General Convention*, p. 8; *A letter from Sir Hardress Waller . . . to Lieutenant General Ludlow* (London, 1660), p. 13.

[73] BL, Add. MSS 32,471, fos. 82v–83; *Account of the chief occurrences*, p. 40; Bridges, *Perfect narrative*, p. 14; *Londons Intelligencer*, 4, p. 30; *A perfect diurnal*, 20, 15 March 1659[60], p. 158; E. W[arren], *A reply to the answer of Lieutenant General Ludlow* (London, 1660), pp. 15–17.

[74] Bodl., Carte MSS 30, fo. 559; Pearse Street Public Library, Dublin, Gilbert MSS 219, p. 339; *Account of the chief occurences*, p. 36; T. Ó Fiaich, 'Edmund O'Reilly, archbishop of Armagh, 1657–1669', in *Father Luke Wadding*, ed. the Franciscan Fathers (Dublin, 1957), pp. 192–5.

authority of the Parliament now sitting in England'.[75] Yet, for all that Broghill, Coote and their friends cajoled and bullied, the 137 representatives included too many novices to be highly disciplined and occasionally ran ahead of their Fabian guides.[76] Truculent members, incited by fiery Royalists like Forbes and Trevor, outside the Convention but handily in the capital, smarting from English interference since 1641, questioned this connection.[77]

A few extravagant speeches, known in odd fragments, mix hearsay, wishful thinking, misinformation and rhetorical windiness, and have been taken as heralding the dawn of Irish Protestant 'colonial nationalism'.[78] The significance of the Convention does not lie in this mistaken proposition, but in being the first entirely Protestant assembly to claim to represent Ireland. The interest it occasioned is revealed by the local publication of its proceedings in a mercury to inform a literate audience agog for news.[79] In the hectic sequence which ended in Charles II's return, the Convention, despite what some of its members later asserted, played a minimal part. It stood by, useful to authorize taxes and prepare for a conventional Parliament in Dublin, while the three kingdoms were settled elsewhere. Knowing this, those Old and New Protestants who could rushed to London; others, like Broghill, fretted at their enforced stay in Dublin, remote from the action, and decamped *en masse* for England when the Convention adjourned on 28 May.[80]

The crisis which had enveloped Irish Protestants after 1641 obliged them to muse upon their position; they tracked restlessly and inconsistently between cosmic or providential and mechanistic explanations, and between a definition of their distinctiveness as a matter of Englishness or

---

[75] *Declaration of the General Convention*, p. 10.
[76] Most of its members are listed in *Account of the chief occurrences*, pp. 37–8, to which I first drew attention in *Cromwellian Ireland*, p. 24, n. 38.
[77] Bodl., Clarendon State Papers, 71, fo. 156; Carte MSS 30, fos. 559, 572; BL, Add. MSS 45,850, fo. 20v; NLI, MS 32, fo. 14; Petworth, Orrery MSS, general series, 28, J. Sharp to Broghill, 28 and 30 March 1660; E. MacLysaght (ed.), *Calendar of the Orrery papers* (Dublin, 1941), pp. 7–8; Birch (ed.), *Thurloe state papers*, VII, pp. 817–20, 859, 908, 911.
[78] Barnard, 'Planters and policies', pp. 65–7; A. Clarke, 'Colonial constitutional attitudes in Ireland, 1640–1660', *Proceedings, Royal Irish Academy*, 90, section C (1990), pp. 372–5; J. I. Maguire, 'The Dublin Convention, the Protestant community and the emergence of an ecclesiastical settlement in 1660', in A. Cosgrove and J. I. Maguire (eds.), *Parliament and community. Historical Studies*, XIV (Belfast, 1983), pp. 121–46; F. O'Donoghue, 'Parliament in Ireland under Charles II' (unpublished MA thesis, University College Dublin, 1970), chapter 1.
[79] *Account of the chief occurrences*.
[80] Cambridgeshire County Record Office, Huntingdon, Acc. 731 dd Bush, no. 145; PRO, SP 63/303, 43, 45; Bodl., Clarendon State Papers, 71, fo. 295; *Londons Intelligencer*, 4, p. 30; Hill (ed.), *Montgomery manuscripts*, pp. 225–6; C. J. Stranks, *The life and writings of Jeremy Taylor* (London, 1952), pp. 199–201; Birch (ed.), *Thurloe state papers*, VII, p. 912.

Protestantism. Tart observers were surprised that a sense of Irishness had not been fostered. For most Protestants, however, Irishness was the attribute that had tainted and inspired their Catholic adversaries and fellow travellers like Ormond.[81] Orrery, as he ruminated, concluded that religion and race had fused to range the 'British Protestants' against the 'Irish Roman Catholics of the kingdom of Ireland'. But he admitted how material losses, dispossession after conquest, had completed the polarities.[82] Annesley, also, puzzled over the vital ingredients of his own, and other Irish Protestants', identities. He congratulated himself on having worked indefatigably to guarantee that Ireland, 'the place of my birth should be as much English and Protestant as the stock and country from whence I came'. He depicted 'the English and Protestant interest in Ireland' as locked fast in inevitable conflict with 'the Irish papists'.[83] For Annesley, as for Broghill, such analyses, begun during wartime, were confirmed by the uneasy 1670s and 1680s, and contradicted Ormond's (and the Stuarts') cheery evaluations. Ormond's elastic concept of a political nation composed of 'the English gentry of Ireland' persisted after 1690 among the Tories and proto-unionists, as well as the Jacobites, who saw more danger from dissenters and the Whiggish sons of Commonwealthsmen than from Catholic loyalists. Orrery had first cried up 'the Protestant interest of Ireland' and striven to make it coterminous with the political community of Ireland. His ideological heirs, insisting that their Protestantism more than their Englishness was the source of their trustworthiness, behaved consistently in labouring to transform a Protestant interest into an ascendancy.[84]

---

[81] NLI, MS 8643/9, R. Leigh to G. Lane, 27 October 1666; D. W. Hayton, 'Anglo-Irish attitudes: changing perceptions of national identity among the Protestant ascendancy in Ireland, c. 1690–1750', *Studies in eighteenth-century culture*, 17 (1987), pp. 145–57; P. Walsh, *The Irish colours folded* (London, 1662), p. 11.

[82] Bodl., Carte MSS 44, fos. 230–1; Clarendon State Papers, 79, fo. 90v; R. Boyle, earl of Orrery, *An answer to a scandalous letter . . . by Peter Walsh* (London, 1662), pp. 10, 58; Orrery, *The Irish colours displayed*, pp. 3–7; *Cal. S P Ire., 1660–2*, pp. 167–8, 173–6.

[83] NLI, MS 2481, fo. 3; 8646/1, undated letter of March 1660; BL, Add. MSS 46,937, fo. 155; Sloane MSS 1008, fo. 262; Barnard, 'The Uses of 23 October 1641', p. 918.

[84] D. W. Hayton, 'Ireland and the English ministers, 1707–1716' (unpublished Oxford D Phil thesis, 1975), pp. 120–47.

CHAPTER 12

1659 AND THE ROAD TO RESTORATION

AIDAN CLARKE

THE RESTORATION settlement in Ireland was remarkable for its acceptance of the massive transfer of land carried out by the usurping régimes of the 1650s. Although newcomers had been the initial beneficiaries, many of them were interested only in realizing the value of their assets and much of the confiscated property passed quickly into the hands of established Protestant colonists by purchase and other means. Charles II was confronted by a unified demand from the enlarged Protestant settler community for the preservation of their gains. That community's sense of common cause evolved as the Commonwealth disintegrated after the fall of the Protectorate in May 1659, and the return of the monarchy became increasingly likely. The purpose of this essay is to examine the development of the collaboration between new and old settlers that was to shape the social and political relationships of Restoration Ireland by controlling the local consequences of what happened in England and Scotland and among the Royalists on the continent.

The most direct interplay between events in Ireland and elsewhere arose from the fact that those who competed for power in England needed to secure support in Ireland and to control the apparatus of power there. That competition operated on two levels. The fundamental division, between those who wished to see monarchy restored and those who did not, seemed to lie outside practical politics in 1659. The immediate dispute that unsettled the Commonwealth was among its own supporters and concerned the proper form of government. For most people in Ireland, as in England, the choice between the Protectorate, the Long Parliament and the army was of little significance. There were those, however, though few of them were Irish in any sense, who were committed to the Commonwealth and who supported one or other of its competing factions. There were 'Cromwellians' who believed in the protectoral formula of rule by 'a single person and parliament'. There were Republicans, passionately opposed to the 'single person' and committed to the 'good old cause' of the Long Parliament which had been brought to an end by Oliver Cromwell in 1653. There were those who were indifferent to governmental forms and who believed that the army alone could uphold what had been achieved and that it must not be prevented from doing so, either by opposition from without or dissent from within. These were differences of opinion among a dominant minority. Some form of royalism, complexly divided by differences of interest in the interregnum changes, was the norm in Ireland (see chapter 11 above). Many of the established settlers, however, had come to terms with the régime and took sides as it became destabilized. Some of them no doubt were acting within the system only to subvert it, but others were pragmatically concerned with the need to ensure the most favourable immediate outcome, and not all of these were wholly uncommitted: at its most attenuated, royalism involved unrepentant parliamentarian supporters who believed that the wrong turn had been taken as late as 6 December 1648, when parliamentary authority had been subverted by the army in the purge which had prepared the way for the execution of the king. As events elsewhere altered the scope of political possibility and the dominance of the minority was challenged, the cumulative failure to resolve the immediate issue added strength to the view that only a return to monarchy could restore stability. Preferences about English outcomes were mediated by local circumstances and the different interests began to converge. But the fusion was incomplete until the very end: in Ireland, as in England, some of those who worked towards Restoration were ready to welcome Charles II back unconditionally, but some were not.

In the beginning of the decline, when the lord protector, Richard Cromwell, was disempowered by an officers' coup in late April 1659 and the Protectorate itself was replaced by the reassembly of the surviving members of the purged 'Long Parliament' on 6 May, the reaction in Ireland was muted. The army declined to take sides over Richard and the urgent priority of both officers and civilians was to ensure that the restored Parliament recognized the importance of an immediate validation of the acts and ordinances of the protectoral period, for the legal basis of the settlement in Ireland depended upon them. A carefully chosen group of three, made up of a radical colonel, Richard Lawrence, a conservative administrator, William Bury, and an Old Protestant collaborator, Dr Henry Jones, quondam bishop of Clogher, was sent to press for immediate action.[1] Significantly, their journey proved unnecessary. The case had already been made before they sailed by officers of the Irish army in

---

[1] 'Instructions', TCD, MS 808, fo. 160.

England and appropriate legislation was in preparation. The professed concern of the lord lieutenant, Henry Cromwell, was to ensure that neither the 'common enemy'[2] nor the 'more dangerous, numerous and exasperated people, the Irish Natives and Papists' should be able to exploit the opportunity presented by internal conflict.[3] But his brother had solicited help through members of the Union Parliament aborted by the coup, who returned to Ireland in late April, and he certainly investigated the sources of support in the provinces. The men he chose for this undertaking illustrated both his past policies and his present difficulties: only Lieutenant Colonel Henry Flower, who was sent to Ulster, appeared to fit the straight-forward mould of Cromwellian officer. Munster was entrusted to Lord Broghill, son of the 'great earl of Cork' but close associate of both Oliver and Richard, who commanded only a 'loose company' outside the formal military establishment, and Connacht to its nominal president, the Old Protestant magnate Sir Charles Coote, who had retained a regiment throughout the 1650s, but remained an anomaly in an army largely commanded by colonels from England. As the crisis developed and the return of the Long Parliament brought the Protectorate to an end, Henry was spancelled by his brother's prolonged silence, and the choices altered in a sinister way. The return of monarchy rather than the defence of the Protectorate became a perceived alternative to the rule of Parliament. This was especially the case in Ulster, where the Scots were notoriously disaffected, and where Henry was suspected by one side of collusion with Royalists rather than concern for security and urged by the other to declare for the king. It was also the case at the exiled court, where Charles had hopes of Henry's support and an approach to him was contemplated through Broghill, with whom the Royalists optimistically believed they had made 'some progres in discoursing at distance'.[4]

It was not the case in London. The concern there was to put an end to government by 'a single person and parliament' and to resolve the contradictions of the 1650s by establishing for once and for all the subordination of the army to the Parliament. Both of these priorities applied equally to Ireland. On 7 June, Parliament decided to put the government there into commission and appointed William Steele, Miles Corbett, Colonel Matthew Tomlinson, Colonel John Jones and Robert Goodwin. The first three were sitting members of the Irish Council where

[2] That is, 'the king and his party': John Price, 'The mystery and method of his majesty's happy restauration', in Francis Maseres (ed.), *Select tracts relating to the civil wars in England* (London, 1815), p. 743.

[3] Charles McNeill (ed.), *The Tanner letters* . . . (IMC, 1943), pp. 391–3.

[4] Edward Villiers to Hyde, 11 April 1659 (Bodl., Clarendon MSS 60, fos. 340–1).

they constituted an entrenched opposition to Henry Cromwell; both of the others had had extensive experience of Irish government in the 1650s. None was of Irish provenance. All but Goodwin were implicated in the king's death: Steele, Corbett and Jones were regicides, and Tomlinson had been the officer in charge of Charles before his execution. Only Steele and Corbett were actually in Ireland and they assumed interim powers on 21 June. Their first act was to order the senior officer, Major-General Sir Hardress Waller, to secure Dublin Castle. Colonel Long's garrison was replaced and steps were taken to repair the gates and to block access. Their second act was to order all military forces to return to their depositions of 2 April. This concern to counteract the residual influence of Henry Cromwell mimicked what was happening in London, where the Parliament had already begun the business of re-modelling the army in Ireland. As a preliminary, a Baptist officer who had been cashiered by Henry Cromwell was reinstated and five others who were presently in England, and of whom at least three were Baptists, were confirmed in their commands: four of these had been involved in the overthrow of Richard; the other was the agent, Richard Lawrence. The task was then handed over to a committee, drawn largely from this approved group, which rapidly reviewed the senior positions under the chairmanship of Lord General Fleetwood. Not all of the resulting changes were politically motivated. Fleetwood relinquished his nominal commands, and there was some redeployment, but the net result was a major change in the configuration of army control. Taking transfers and promotions into account, half of the forty-eight regimental command positions changed hands. Religious radicals were favoured. Of the six new colonels, four had been displaced by Henry Cromwell. Among those dismissed were the compromised Henry Flower and all but one of those who had signalled their loyalties by supporting the kingship petition as Members of Parliament in 1657. Significantly, however, the purge faltered in its treatment of two of the three Old Protestant colonels. Robert Phayre, the clergyman's son who governed Cork and befriended Quakers, passed muster with ease, but Sir Charles Coote and Sir Hardress Waller, the only Irish regicide, were neither confirmed in their commands nor dismissed.

A complementary review of the junior officers was left to Edmund Ludlow, who was formally appointed commander-in-chief, a position he had previously held in the early 1650s, on 18 July. Following the principle that the civil authority must have primacy, Parliament turned down a proposal that he should deputize for the Speaker in the commissioning of officers, empowering the commissioners to do so instead, and rejected a move to make him a commissioner. These niceties had little relevance to

Ireland, where the interdependence of government and army had become very close since Henry Cromwell's departure, and the practice did not honour the intention. Soon after his arrival in late July, the commissioners invited Ludlow to join them informally to facilitate the conduct of pressing business arising from the rebellion led by Sir Charles Booth in the north-west of England. The outbreak was all the more sinister because Booth was not a 'cavalier': he had fought against the king and taken part in the politics of the Commonwealth. His rising expressed the impatience of many of those upon whose acquiescence the régime counted, and though the monarchy did not feature in his public declarations there could be no doubt that his demand for a free parliament implied the restoration of the kingship in some form. The Irish government was required to help to suppress the rising as well as to guard against related or opportunistic disturbances. It fulfilled the first of these obligations efficiently and the second draconically. The commander of the horse troops in Ulster was replaced. Catholics were expelled from garrison towns and influential men of doubtful loyalty were placed in preventive custody. The two whom Henry had trusted were singled out for individual treatment (also see chapter 11 above). Ludlow sent for Broghill and two of his majors and required them 'to give satisfaction touching their acquiescence under the present government',[5] as he later reported, passing silently over the anomaly that Broghill's 'loose company' scarcely warranted one major, let alone two. Sir Charles Coote was ordered to remain in Dublin, from where he contrived to manage the escape of the royalist Presbyterian Sir Arthur Forbes from detention in Athlone. According to Forbes, Coote intended to join his forces, which were ready under Sir Francis Gore's command, and 'declare something in order to the King's restauration'.[6] Booth's defeat, on 19 August, put an end to this scheme.

It did not, of course, eliminate the sense of danger, to which the discontent of the cashiered officers was now adding, nor did it simplify the problems of government. Normality was beyond reach because the legitimacy of authority had not been adequately established: the courts were in suspension, the legal basis for the activities of the sheriffs and justices of the peace was unsure, the equity of recent parliamentary taxation was disputed, and the act to settle Irish titles remained in committee. Thus the commissioners had little scope for constructive action, though they managed to create a good deal of alarm by systematically favouring religious radicals in both church and state, and their role was confined to

[5] C. H. Firth (ed.), *The memoirs of Edmund Ludlow* (3 vols., Oxford, 1894), II, p. 107.
[6] Forbes to the Duke of Ormond, Granard Papers, PRONI, H/1/5/1 (undated).

assisting Ludlow to maintain security. His responsibilities were partly managerial, dealing with provisions, pay and demands for arrears, and partly those of a commissar, imposing upon his officers an oath of fidelity to uncover those 'debauched in their principles by the late usurpation of the Cromwels' and inquiring into 'the principles and practices of the private souldiers' to discover moral weakness and papist leanings.[7] At the same time, he made an effort to extend the purge to the 'unregimented' forces which constituted the garrisons of many towns and forts and had escaped Parliament's notice. In September, he also set about organizing supplementary militia forces on a county basis, recruiting experienced army men who were prepared to swear loyalty.

The preoccupation with purging Cromwellian influence was common to Ireland and England: in neither country did it necessarily guarantee the unqualified loyalty of the army to Parliament. The officers in England had deferred to Parliament in May, and Parliament alienated them by continuing to expect deference as its due. Because it highlighted Parliament's dependence upon the army, Booth's rising raised its morale, restored the confidence of the officers, and prompted demands for army autonomy and the fulfilment of Parliament's original promise to prepare new governmental arrangements and dissolve by May 1660. The army perhaps sought no more than partnership with Parliament, but for the majority of members the principle that Parliament should rule was not negotiable. A brief confrontation ended in another coup: the army expelled the members on 13 October and went on to appoint a committee of safety, designed to bring in those who would be prepared to work with the army to achieve a settlement, which was convened on 26 October. Among those named were William Steele and Edmund Ludlow. Steele never served, but Ludlow's participation was to become a significant factor in Irish developments.

Ludlow's intentions are not in doubt. As a committed Republican and Parliamentarian who held high command in the army, he was convinced that the preservation of the Commonwealth depended upon the continued co-operation of the parliamentary and military alliance that had created it, and he worked to reconcile the two, exploring the possibilities of compromise in a way that left him open to the suspicion of collaboration. He had left Ireland as the crisis developed in England, heard news of the coup at Beaumaris, and met one of his absentee officers hurrying to Ireland to solicit army support for the General Council of Officers. His conviction that his influence should be exerted in London rather than from Dublin was

[7] Ludlow, *Memoirs*, II, p. 117.

unaltered, and he did not turn back. His expressed concern paralleled that of Henry Cromwell before him, 'that the common enemy might not be able to take advantage from this sad conjuncture',[8] but his hasty caretaker arrangements had had more to do with threats from within the army than from outside it. The senior officer, Hierome Sankey, who was in England and deeply implicated in the defiance of Parliament, was an unacceptable deputy; the next in line was Waller, whom Ludlow believed to be an opportunist, 'having complied with every party that had been uppermost'[9] and who had not been confirmed in his command. Ludlow's solution was to deputize Commissioner Jones. Already, the officers based around Dublin had been persuaded to denounce what they knew of the English army's demands and had formally acknowledged Parliament as the supreme authority. On his own authority, Ludlow had summarily put his new-modelling arrangements into effect, cashiering and replacing those he distrusted, though his instructions explicitly reserved that power to Parliament. Before he left, he had singled out two men for special attention: he took the trouble to mollify Waller by telling him that Jones had been chosen so that Sankey could be by-passed, and he interviewed Coote, who protested convincingly 'that as he had opposed the late King in his arbitrary designs, so he would continue to act in conformity to those actions, well knowing that if the son should happen to prevail, the English interest would be lost in Ireland, and the Irish restored to the possession of their lands, according to an agreement passed between them'.[10]

Some six years before, from the same vantage point in Ireland, John Jones had accepted the advent of the Protectorate philosophically: 'if ye Governmt be soe Established as may produce the fruits of Righteousness, peace and love to the s[ain]ts', he had written, 'I am not solicitous what forme or shape it hath'.[11] This indifference to issues about which others felt deeply and quarrelled violently qualified him poorly to cope with a developing crisis which was largely concerned with the form that government should take. His concern was with the unity of the army, and it was shared by the majority of his officers, who signed a declaration accepting that the *fait accompli* had been undertaken in good faith under 'necessity and sense of duty' and pledging their solidarity with their brethren in England and Scotland 'that soe we may be in the hand of ye Lord as a threefold cord not easily broken'.[12] Their own union, however,

---

[8] *Ibid.*, p. 129.   [9] *Ibid.*, p. 122.   [10] *Ibid.*, p. 124.
[11] Joseph Meyer (ed.), 'Inedited letters of Cromwell, Col. Jones, Bradshaw and other regicides', *Transactions of the historic society of Lancashire and Cheshire, new series,* 1 (1860–1), pp. 219–20 (where the letter is misdated).
[12] *Ibid.*, pp. 265–6.

was precarious. On the one hand, the reiterated truisms about brotherly love which met renewed efforts from England to secure approval masked an agreement to suspend judgement until the issues were clarified by a promised declaration outlining the army's plans. On the other, it was not obvious how the truculent cashiered officers could be prevented from 'appeareing wth their commands, and attempting a discomposure amongst the fforces'.[13] Jones's despairing hope was that the declaration would prove to 'bee soe comprehensive of good things, and soe suitable to ye spirit of an army of ffreeborn Englishmen and Gospell professors, that it will give universall satisfaction'.[14] That hope was dashed when the declaration arrived early in November. It disappointed even those whom Jones regarded as 'sober men', who complained that what was explicit 'might have been better worded' and what was satisfactory was 'wrapped in gen[era]lls'.[15] But although he recognized that the declaration was not persuasive, Jones was disposed to blame the unpersuaded, and he concluded that those who were not satisfied by it had also been dissatisfied with the recall of Parliament in May. The implication, that the dissidents were Cromwellians rather than Parliamentarians, was clear. Jones was to refine it rapidly as 'the threefold cord' began to unravel.

It is not clear whether it was known in Ireland that the commander in Scotland, George Monck, had encouraged Parliament to resist the demands of the army at an early stage. Certainly, his appeal to Ludlow to support a trenchant declaration in favour of the expelled Parliament 'against ambition and tyranny' seems to have taken Jones by surprise when it reached him at the beginning of November.[16] The intransigence with which Monck spoke of going on 'to the last dropps of my blood' to restore Parliament raised precisely those fears of disunion and division which had become the main preoccupation of the men in charge in Ireland, and Jones and a group of officers, so small as to suggest furtiveness, rebuked him severely. Putting it to him that he was proposing 'a sure way for ye comon Enemie to destroy oure comon Interest as men and Christians', they declared their disapproval of anything that would engage 'any part of the Armyes or fforces of these Nations against their brotheren', and urged him to desist.[17] Though Ludlow denounced this as a 'great alteration' in attitude, for 'they manifestly took part with the army',[18] what was said was entirely consistent with the army's declared priority. The conspiratorial manner hints at a different reality, and Monck had a private source of

---

[13] *Ibid.*, p. 271.   [14] *Ibid.*
[15] *Ibid.*, p. 275.   [16] Ludlow, *Memoirs*, II, p. 449.
[17] 'Inedited letters', pp. 272.   [18] Ludlow, *Memoirs*, II, p. 147.

information in his cousin Henry, who had been preferred by Henry Cromwell and cashiered by Ludlow. From Dublin, Henry assured him that Sir Charles Coote and the former colonel and captain of the lord lieutenant's lifeguard, Sir Theophilus Jones, the son of one bishop and brother of another, 'and a very considerable part of the Army, were resolv'd to Assist him'.[19]

Across the channel events moved quickly. A few members of Parliament co-operated with the army, including Ludlow who served on a sub-committee 'to prepare a form of government', but most did not and nine members of the abrogated Council of State proclaimed themselves as the legitimate government. Attempts to compose the differences between the English and Scots armies failed. The English officers went ahead with a proposal to convene a special council of the whole army to decide upon the form of government, and Ludlow co-operated with them. Monck assured the 'Nine' that he would support them in force if necessary and was commissioned by them as commander of the forces of Scotland and England. Jones had 'noe exact Intelligence how Affaires goe in England, nor what to declare for if there were need',[20] but rumour had it that opinion was moving in favour of a full restoration of the Long Parliament, with the excluded members and the lords re-admitted. The fears that this aroused in him were vividly revealed in his response to an officer-settler in Wexford who wrote to urge that the army must support the restoration of the present Parliament to 'their just rights and privileges': if a full restoration was meant, Jones insisted, 'that is but a faire umbridge devised by the common enemy to disguise a wicked designe to bring in Ch[arles] St[uart]'.[21] The misconstruction seems gratuitous, but may not have been, for his upbraided correspondent was Thomas Scot, son of the republican regicide who was president of the 'Nine'. Jones had taken sides, prompted greatly by developments in Ireland. Outside the army, royalist intrigues were rife, particularly in Ulster where a series of meetings had begun in October at Hillsborough, 'Scottish papers' were being circulated, tax was being withheld, and a 'rising out' had been mounted in Fermanagh. Inside the army, Jones detected a subversive group whose members were either former cavaliers or 'New Royalists' who had been associated with the kingship party and been unhappy with the recall of the Long Parliament in May: he believed that they intended to divide the army in Ireland and

[19] Richard Baker, *A chronicle of the kings of England* (London, 1665), p. 727. C. H. Firth (ed.), *Selections from the papers of William Clarke* . . . (Camden Society, 4 vols., London, 1891–1901), IV, pp. 95–6n.
[20] 'Inedited letters', p. 277.
[21] *Ibid.*, p. 280.

oppose the army in England and that their 'Notion of being for a parliamt' was the same as Booth's.[22] His perception of Anglo-Scottish developments was similar; the real options were those of twelve years earlier and the issue lay between the army and 'Cavaleeres under the maske of a Presbiterian Interest, such as would have the peace established on the Concessions at the Isle of Weight'.[23] This was perhaps a little premature, but it is true that as the Commonwealth came closer to anarchy, the sources of support for restoration were changing: by untraceable degrees, the return of monarchy ceased to be the aspiration of cavaliers and became the practical objective of many who had fought for Parliament in the civil war and who now began to see it as a realistic possibility, and even canvass it as a disguised option, characteristically expressed in a formula which involved the summoning of a free parliament or, more subtly, its preliminary – the undoing of Pride's Purge through the readmission of those who had been excluded. A restoration thus conceived, as going back only to 1648 as its point of departure, was very far from what Royalists had in mind.

The 'Nine' had been able to assure Monck that they had support in the army around London and in the fleet, that Portsmouth would declare for them, and that Ireland would be secured by Coote. On 4 December, a group of them established a provisional government in Portsmouth; on 12 December, a second group was foiled in an attempt on the Tower of London, and on 13 December Admiral Lawson and his captains demanded the renewed sitting of Parliament. At about five o'clock on the same day, Dublin Castle was surprised in the name of Parliament by Captain Bond's foot company. When success was signalled by shots from the top of the castle, horse troops rode through the town with drawn swords shouting 'a parliament, a parliament', and the commissioners and others were rounded up and imprisoned. The immediate leadership of this coup included only one serving senior officer, Major Edward Warren, son of a dean of Ossory and one of Jones's 'New Royalists': associated with him were his brother John, a former lieutenant colonel, William Warden, one of Broghill's majors, and John Bridges who had been removed from command of his English regiment by the army council immediately after the overthrow of Richard. The junior officers involved were Captain Bond and Captain John Joiner, who had been chief cook to Charles I before the war and had been settled for some years in Kilkenny. The wider ramifications of the plot are suggested both by the immediate backing of Dublin and its militia regiments, and by associated coups in a series of garrison towns where governors were overthrown, some by junior officers and others by former

[22] *Ibid.*, p. 281.   [23] *Ibid.*, p. 289.

officers. The only senior officer engaged was Coote, who surprised Galway, took Athlone, and joined the conspirators in Dublin with a force 'chiefly of the English Irish'.[24] As the news spread, most governors went with the tide and preserved their commands by declaring for Parliament, and in Munster mixed forces of veteran parliamentarian and royalist officers and men assembled and did likewise. In Dublin, where Waller lent his support at once, a belligerent declaration calling for the reinstatement of Parliament was prepared and government devolved upon a body which called itself the council of officers, though few of its senior members held current commissions and one, John Cole of Fermanagh, had been cashiered by Parliament in July while another, Theophilus Jones, had been relieved of his command by Ludlow. The external connections suggested by the timing were confirmed by the dispatch of the declaration to the commissioners at Portsmouth with an acknowledgement of their authority, and by the enlistment of Monck's 'old faithfull servant Capt John Campbell' to convey the news to him.[25]

Though plainly related to developments elsewhere, the actions in Ireland were nonetheless pre-emptive. As Waller observed to Monck, what had been done 'must undergoe the hazard to bee judged much by your successe'.[26] As it happened, luck was with them. The soldiers sent to besiege Portsmouth changed sides, the Council of State asserted its authority over the forces in London, and on 24 December General Fleetwood sent the keys of Parliament to the Speaker with an assurance that the members would not be impeded from sitting. They convened on 26 December, the day on which cannonades in Edinburgh and Leith celebrated the news from Ireland, and also the day on which the Council of Officers in Dublin agreed that Ludlow's conduct since leaving Ireland 'hath given just occasion for suspition that hee is noe friend to the Parliament'.[27] By then, both Campbell and Ludlow were on their way back. Ludlow had been at first uncertain what to think of the Irish declaration. Its content could not be faulted, and the signature of his brother-in-law, Major Henry Kempson, was reassuring, but he had doubts about the reliability of a group which combined men of 'known integrity' with men 'who had been very active to support the usurpation of the Cromwels', and which included Theophilus Jones 'who upon all occasions had shewed himself a principal instrument of mischief amongst us'.[28] When Kempson wrote anxiously to say that he 'was

---

[24] That is, the 'New English', Ludlow, *Memoirs*, II, p. 187.
[25] Firth (ed.), *Clarke papers*, IV, p. 203.
[26] *Ibid.*
[27] Ludlow, *Memoirs*, II, p. 471. *Cal. S P Ire.*, *1647–60*, pp. 695–6.
[28] Ludlow, *Memoirs*, II, p. 185.

so unsatisfied with the spirits and principles of these men, that he was very hardly perswaded to sign it',[29] Ludlow accepted his advice to hurry back to Ireland, to support them if they were honest or reduce them if they were not, as he later put it.

The concerns of the officers who assumed control after the *coup d'état* were conditioned by the course of events in England. Initially, to guard against the possibility of reprisal, they needed to consolidate their position in Ireland and to establish formal relations with the army's opponents in England. They set about 'new modelling' the army in their turn by ousting and replacing hostile officers, summoned a convention to raise money to pay it, and proceeded quickly to complete the overthrow of the existing government by drawing up articles of impeachment against Ludlow and the commissioners, who were collectively charged with having 'joyned with that rebellious part of the army in England'.[30] They reported to Portsmouth, explaining firmly that in the interests of security they must remove some officers recently appointed by parliament itself, and offering to send over 3,000 or 4,000 men if needed, and they responded briskly to Monck's request for a regiment of horse. The restoration of the Parliament did not change the priorities, though the arrangements for a convention were prudently discontinued when English misgivings were voiced: it was essential both to gain approval for the alterations in the army command and to persuade Parliament to make alternative governmental arrangements which would sanction their seizure of control by uniting civil and military authority in their hands.[31] Colonel Bridges, with Edward Warren and his brother Abel, a former captain and recent mayor of Kilkenny, represented them formally in London, but they also proceeded indirectly, relying heavily upon General Monck to argue their case and vouch for their dependability. Monck entered England on 2 January, dispersed John Lambert's recalcitrant army units without striking a blow, withdrew his request for assistance from Ireland, and gradually made his way southward to London through January accompanied, among many others, by Captain James Cuffe, agent for Coote, and keeping up a steady correspondence with Broghill and Theophilus Jones. Cuffe's counterpart in Ireland was Sir Joseph Douglas. A well-informed Monck had no doubt that Ireland was in the control of men who thought as he did 'in reference to the ordinances of Magistracy and Ministry, and that love and favour such as are for order and discipline in the Church of God'.[32]

---

[29] *Ibid.*, p. 186.   [30] TCD, MS 844, fo. 648.
[31] HMC, *Leybourne–Popham MSS* (London, 1899), pp. 141–2.
[32] MSS of Lord Oranmore and Browne, HMC, *Various*, VI (London, 1909), pp. 438–9.

At first, the Irish business went smoothly at Westminster. Parliament heard reports on 4 January, approved 'what hath been done' on the following day, and ordered the commissioners to render their account. Before long, doubts were raised as Ludlow challenged this 'dishonourable compliance'.[33] His precipitate arrival off Monkstown on 30 December had presented the officers with no option but to defy him. It cannot be inferred, as Ludlow insisted, that their attitude towards him implied a covert hostility to Parliament itself because his recent activities had been such as to arouse reasonable suspicion. The officers were not alone in suggesting that his duty had required him to be in Ireland, rather than London: his deputy Jones had thought so too. They scored a neat point by suggesting that it was fortunate that Monck had not behaved in the same way, but the core of their distrust was the inference that he had stayed in order to further the army council's scheme for a new parliament. Confirmation of this reading of his actions was provided by the 'too active and encouraging' letters he had sent to Ireland to promote the plan and, still more, by the discovery of a letter of 17 December to Jones in which he had written: 'We seem to be necessitated to look towards the Long Parliament; 'tis to be feared they will be very high, in case they should be brought in without conditions'.[34] Against that background, there was good reason to put an unfavourable complexion on his decision to leave London before the Parliament actually met, and to insist that he should not resume office (or, indeed, leave ship) until Parliament confirmed that this was its wish. That the distrustful reading was the correct one seemed to be confirmed in its turn by Ludlow's refusal to await Parliament's decision.

There ensued a confused and damaging interlude, as Ludlow sailed to the southeast and landed in Duncannon, the only garrison town that had not accepted the authority of the Dublin officers, from which he tried to rally the army to him and destroy the credibility of the army leaders in London, assuring the Speaker that 'although the Parliament's interest be held forth by the officers, another interest is at the bottome'.[35] In a vituperative exchange, the worst of it with Thomas Scot who commanded a besieging force, he asserted the authority of his original commission from Parliament against 'those who for the most part had no commissions from them',[36] and the Dublin officers denounced 'his actings against the Parliament by a power derived from that the Parliament'.[37] He was disconcertingly right on the particular point: only a small minority of those

[33] Ludlow, *Memoirs*, II, p. 200.   [34] *Ibid.*, p. 453.
[35] *Cal. S P, domestic, 1659–60*, p. 310.
[36] Ludlow, *Memoirs*, II, p. 191.   [37] Firth (ed.), *Clarke papers*, IV, pp. 241–3.

who denounced him as members of the council of officers had been officers when he held command. Most of those who had been were now in detention. But without parliamentary confirmation of his authority Ludlow's position was unsustainable, and he returned to London to counter their influence there. The antagonism had already posed problems which Parliament felt unable to adjudicate. Ludlow's sinister warning had to be balanced against a lyrical effusion from Waller who reported that the coup had been so widely supported 'that I may say a nation was born in a day' and that the only hindrance to its success had been the return of Ludlow, whose landing would have 'put all into blood'.[38] The Speaker turned for guidance to Monck, who categorically endorsed the officers: their intention, he affirmed, 'stands uppon the same foote with mine and some of your owne actings: that is, for the restitution of this Parliament to itts present condition'. Improving the opportunity, he suggested that commissioners be appointed to manage both military and civil affairs in Ireland and proposed Broghill, Coote, Waller, Theophilus Jones, Colonel Arthur Hill of Hillsborough, and 'such others as they shall please to join with them'.[39] Parliament was not ready to entrust Ireland to an entirely local group, or to combine civil and military authority, but the need to regularize the position was pressing. On 19 January, in the context of the reception of the charges against Ludlow and the commissioners, it appointed Coote and Waller as commissioners for civil affairs, associating with them three experienced outsiders, none of whom actually came – the existing commissioner, Goodwin, who had never acted, John Weaver, who had been a commissioner in the early 1650s, and Henry Markham, absentee colonel of a foot regiment. If this was satisfactory, as Monck urged, other indications were not. The impeached Miles Corbett remained incongruously in his seat in the Commons and was soon joined by Ludlow, whose obligation to render an account of his actions in Ireland, and by inference to reply to the charges, was continuously postponed. Ludlow professed to believe that he was being prevented from defending himself: the officers from Ireland were convinced that he was being shielded from prosecution. They were further perturbed by the fate of their re-modelling arrangements. On Monck's advice, a committee, comprising Waller, Broghill, Coote, Jones and John Warren, had been appointed to make recommendations and a preliminary list was quickly sent to London for approval. Presumably it reflected the actual position and assigned two regiments to Coote, one each to his three brothers and one to his cousin George St George. The officers

---

[38] HMC, *Report of the manuscripts of the duke of Portland* (London, 1891), I, p. 693.
[39] Ludlow, *Memoirs*, II, pp. 471-2.

now learned that it was likely that these recommendations would be disregarded.

It was not only parliamentary ambivalence that aroused misgivings in Ireland. Though the officers kept in close contact with Monck, and deferred to him, seeking and taking his advice and soliciting his good offices, his caution was becoming increasingly suspect. In the course of his march from York to London he had publicly opposed the return of the secluded members and expressed his preference for 'recruiter' elections which would convert the Parliament into a 'free' one and he had particularly warned Broghill to 'discountenance' the 'eager abettors' of the secluded members who were said to be 'framing petitions in their behalf'.[40] In fact, when he addressed Parliament formally on 6 February, he did not advert to this issue, and he made no effort to conceal his stance on the delicate, unformulated question of whether Parliament's allies in Ireland were to be trusted: they 'will continue faithful', he assured Parliament, 'and thereby Evince, that as well there as here, it is the sober Interest must establish Dominion'.[41] For some days thereafter he deferred to Parliament and forced London to do likewise, symbolically burning its gates on 10 February. On the following day, however, he commanded Parliament to issue writs for new elections within a week, and they complied, with ill grace.

In Dublin, tensions had been surfacing as Waller pitted his authority as senior officer against that of the special appointments committee. That principle rather than status was involved became evident when the name of Monck was invoked to secure his co-operation: 'What is General Monck to me, he said, and further said that he had fought against a single person, and that he would take no more notice of His Excellency the Lord General's orders than of any other single person against whom he had engaged'.[42] The struggle which followed centred upon the question of whether the secluded members should be readmitted to Parliament. Waller prepared an 'engagement' opposing readmission which he wanted the Council of Officers to subscribe and transmit to England. The majority of the officers rejected his proposal, indicated their preference for the return of the purged members, and produced an appropriate declaration. Waller responded by moving for an adjournment to Dublin Castle. When he failed to carry it, he withdrew there with his supporters, Colonel John Warren, who commanded the castle garrison, Colonel Thomas Stanley, an officer-settler

[40] HMC, *Various MSS*, vi, pp. 438–9.
[41] Baker, *A chronicle*, p. 745.
[42] Information against Sir Hardress Waller, TCD, MS 844, fos. 191–5v.

who had been politically active throughout the 1650s and had taken Clonmel in December, Lieutenant Colonel Puckle, who had done verbal battle with Ludlow as governor of Ross, and Henry Flower. Coote and Jones responded by 'riding up and down the streets of Dublin, and declaring for a free Parliament',[43] and Waller and his confederates looked to their defences. Once again, the city and the army acted together.[44] On the following day, the Council of Officers formally adopted a declaration calling for the readmission of the excluded members and arguing that this demand was entirely consistent with their earlier declaration of 14 December, for the privileges of Parliament and the rights and liberties of the people that they had then defended had been violated by Parliament's refusal to admit the excluded members on 27 December.[45] On 18 February, an extraordinary meeting of the Assembly of Dublin endorsed the declaration, 'taking into consideration that a full and free parliament in England is the birthright of the people of England'.[46] On the same day, the castle garrison expressed its satisfaction with the declaration and delivered up Waller and the republican officers.

Waller's justification was that Monck had 'recommended to him the care of preventing – as he said – our declaring for a free Parliament'.[47] If this incongruous appeal to Monck's authority was opportunistic, Waller did not dissimulate his view as a regicide that 'the bringing in of the members formerly secluded in 1648 was to bring in a free Parliament, and that to bring in a free Parliament would be to bring in the King; and that to bring in the King would be to endanger his and all their heads who opposed and cut off the late King's head, and that if the King was brought in by Parliament on any conditions it would be no security to the people'.[48] There is little reason to doubt that the claim to act on Monck's authority was true. What Waller said represented Monck's publicly and privately stated position, which he did not move from until 20 February when he changed tack and decided to admit the purged members on condition that a dissolution should quickly follow, that the republic should be preserved, a Presbyterian church settlement concluded, and supreme military authority vested in himself. Ludlow, who was convinced of Monck's duplicity,

[43] Ludlow, *Memoirs*, II, p. 230.
[44] The claim is explicitly made in T. J., *A letter sent from a merchant in Dublin in Ireland to his friend in London, February 22, 1659* (London, 1660).
[45] HMC, *Leybourne–Popham MSS*, pp. 152–3.
[46] J. T. Gilbert (ed.), *Calendar of ancient records of Dublin in possession of the municipal corporation* (17 vols., Dublin, 1889–1916), IV, pp. 179–80.
[47] HMC, *Leybourne–Popham MSS*, p. 155. *The declaration of Sir Charles Coote . . . and the rest of the council of officers of the army in Ireland* (London, 1659 [1660]).
[48] TCD, MS 844, fos. 191–5v.

recorded that the leaders in Ireland 'moved not a step without his orders and directions'.[49] Monck's admirers, who wished to believe likewise, found it difficult to reconcile the episode with their preconceptions, and reported it confusedly, either fudging the timing or admitting that 'the Design took effect, even a little with the earliest' while ascribing the initiative to Douglas.[50] In fact, Theophilus Jones wrote to Monck on 19 February to explain that Waller had forced their hands 'in this our declaring – not having first therein advised with Your Excellency' and to assure him that the intention was, as in December, to free the Parliament from force 'which is we doubt not what is intended by your Excellency, and what is expected from you'.[51] The explanation may have been disingenuous, for the balance of probabilities suggests that it had been the preparation of the declaration that precipitated Waller's coup.

An additional dimension supports the impression that, as in December, the officers were not prepared to wait upon events at Westminster. The deference of Coote, at least, towards Monck was feigned and the deepest suspicions of Ludlow and the maligned Waller were well founded. At the very time when Monck was burning the gates of London, Sir Arthur Forbes was passing through the city with a message for the king from Coote. As Forbes later told the story, Coote had been disappointed by Monck's failure to respond to the widespread demands for the readmission of the secluded members or a free Parliament which had been made to him on his journey south and had 'resolved to begin the work in Ireland, and to secure all those who were averse to the King's interest, and to invite the King into this kingdom'. Forbes was to seek the king's directions and to say that if the king 'would think fitt to come into Ireland, [Coote] made no question of restoring him to his crown – not knowing, for ought he or I could then conceive, that any other part of the army in the three kingdoms did intend the same thing'. He asked for some ships and horsemen's arms, and nothing else: 'if they carried their business, they doubted not of the King's favour; and if they perished, there was no need of conditions'.[52]

By mid-February, the choices had been reduced to the point where the question itself had changed. The protectoral alternative had never genuinely survived Oliver himself, and had proved illusory under challenge. Its supporters regrouped. Some of them, either falling back on second best or reverting to an earlier occluded preference, revealed

[49] Ludlow, *Memoirs*, II, p. 228.
[50] Price, 'The mystery and method of his majesty's happy restauration', p. 751.
[51] HMC, *Leybourne-Popham MSS*, pp. 155–6.
[52] Forbes to Ormond, PRONI, H/1/5/1. Also see chapter 11 above.

themselves as adherents of the 'good old cause', but the last ditch stand of Waller, Warren and Flower proved to be no more than an early local demonstration of the wider reality that the republican alternative was also disappearing. For most, the question now was, what kind of restoration was there going to be and how could they best influence it to protect their interests. The alternatives were the same as in England: ready compliance or the imposition of conditions. To an extent, obviously, the outcome depended upon English events. Nonetheless, there were genuine local choices to be made, which hinged contingently on how matters went elsewhere. For some time, the resolution in England was indeterminate. When the secluded members came back, they were formally committed to the preservation of the Commonwealth: before they dissolved on 16 March they had legislated for a Presbyterian church settlement, reorganized the militia and agreed upon conditions for the election of a new parliament that were designed to prevent the return of traditional Royalists. The politics were intricate, not least because contacts with the exiled court were numerous, but the intention of the majority was clear, if not publicly spoken: the king was to be invited back by those who had won the Civil War on terms that reflected its result. As elections were conducted and preparations made for the new parliament that was to meet towards the end of April, an organized thrust to that end was mounted. In the interim, however, a royal approach to Monck through Sir John Grenville had proved fertile, and the game had changed: the critical negotiations were no longer with politicians, but with the army leader, whose terms dealt only with the army's concerns. The king's response and counterthrust, the Declaration of Breda on 4 April, cleverly devolved responsibility for the settlement of even these terms to a representative parliament. When the Convention Parliament met, the royal strategy prevailed. On 1 May the Commons accepted that the government of England was of king, lords and commons.

Within that framework, there was a spectrum of choice in Ireland. At one end were those who chose to support the opposition tactics in England and hoped that the opportunity would not be lost to 'ascertayne those just rights by an agreement, which we contended for soe successfully in the warr'.[53] When it came to the point of decision, however, despite Broghill's initial confidence in the military backing for this position, those who wanted conditions were not prepared to carry their convictions to the point of resistance. At the other extreme, the choice was to enter wholeheartedly

---

[53] Broghill's words, T. Birch (ed.), *A collection of the state papers of John Thurloe* . . . (7 vols., London, 1742), VII, p. 912 (hereafter Birch (ed.), *Thurloe state papers*).

into the king's contingency plans. These were never very coherently formulated, because the combination of a volatile situation and slow communications made fine-tuning impossible, but the outlines seem clear enough. Charles could not be sure that the English initiative would prove successful, and he could not be certain that there would be no resistance if it did. From both points of view, it was important to ensure that Ireland was under his control. In the middle of March, at about the same time as overtures to Monck were being made on his behalf, he sent Forbes back to Ireland with letters to Charles Coote, his brother Richard and John King, in which he promised supplies, engaged to come to Ireland unless he should be more needed in England, and entrusted to Coote 'two blank commissions for making him Lord Deputy single, or joyning others with him in the government as he should think fitt'.[54] About 22 March, he wrote in cautious terms to Broghill to 'break the ice' with general assurances of goodwill.[55] It is possible that this crossed an approach to the king by Broghill through his brother Francis which he claimed some years later to have made.[56] At all events, the return of Grenville in late March with news of Monck's willingness to negotiate ended this line of approach.

Between these two choices was the pre-emptive policy of consolidating control in Ireland and registering an earlier compliance than in England. This served the purposes of both factions. There are ample indications that the 'growing party' in Ireland was made up from the outset of a coalition which combined active, cashiered and retired officers with civilians, though in many cases of course, given the events of the two previous decades, that distinction was blurred. The most influential of these, Theophilus Jones's episcopal brother Henry, formerly scout-master-general of the army, is not perhaps the most typical, but the importance of Dr Dudley Loftus and Dr Gorges, Henry Cromwell's secretary, among others, is well attested. In the nature of the circumstances, moreover, a movement which originated in opposition to military rule needed to civilianize itself, just as a movement which was threatened from without and within needed to build up support. A vital step towards the exertion of effective influence by the Protestant community was to fuse the military and civilian through the summoning of a quasi-parliamentary assembly. In this way, the enlarged political nation, united in its commitment to the land settlement, sought to manage the process of restoration in Ireland, ensuring that the event was not merely an English one with Irish consequences, but an associated, in some respects

[54] PRONI, H/1/5/1.
[55] F. J. Routledge (ed.), *Clarendon state papers*, IV (Oxford, 1932), p. 610.
[56] *Cal. S P Ire., 1669–70*, pp. 46–7.

less hesitant, independent initiative in which established and new settlers
came together to contribute to the king's return on the basis of a
programme contained in the Declaration of 16 February, and repeated
almost word for word in an elaborate declaration from Broghill and his
officers in Munster two days later: both looked towards a conservative
church establishment, the advancement of 'the plantacen of Ireland in the
hands of ye Adventurers, and souldiers and other English Protestants', and
the end of taxation without the consent of the Irish Parliament.[57]

That the leaders in Ireland desired the disaggregation of the protectorate
union had been suspected for some time in London, and seemed implicit in
the summoning of the Convention to meet on 24 January to raise money for
the army. Though preparations were 'stopped' in January,[58] they were
resumed in the more defiant mood of February, principally it seems at the
request of the mayor and aldermen of Dublin, and the Convention finally
commenced business on 2 March.[59] In the light of the claim to local
parliamentary rights of taxation, the meeting had a very different
complexion from the original concern with the allocation of contributions
to support the army. The returns, which were roughly based on the old
constituencies except that boroughs sent only one member, favoured the
Old Protestants slightly, but not dramatically, in proportions of three to two
overall, though in Ulster, predictably, it was about four to one. Three-
quarters of the Old Protestant members, who included three peers and a
bishop, were either themselves former members of the Irish Parliament or
belonged to families which had provided members for one or more of the
last three parliaments. Coote was well represented, by family and clients,
while the area of Broghill's influence, Munster, was the only province to
return a minority of Old Protestant members and County Cork, which had
the largest number of seats, returned only two Old Protestant members
out of nine.[60] The contrast reflected differences of alignment and interest
which were to be articulated principally in the religious sphere, where the
broad agreement on the need to suppress the sects and restore order
gave way gradually to muted disagreement about the form of a national
church.

Formally, the balance of influence appeared to move towards those who

[57] Birch (ed.), *Thurloe state papers*, VII, pp. 817–20. *Declaration of Sir Charles Coote* (Dublin, 1660).
[58] John Bridges et al., *A perfect narrative of the grounds and reasons for securing the castle of Dublin for the parliament* (London, 1660), p. 14.
[59] Fergus M. O'Donoghue, 'Parliament in Ireland under Charles II' (unpublished MA thesis, University College Dublin, 1970).
[60] *An account of the chief occurences of Ireland together with some particulars from England from Monday the 12 of March to Monday the 19 of March* (Dublin, 1659/60), pp. 37–8.

sought to impose terms on the king, for on 8 March the Council of State, presided over by the Old Protestant Arthur Annesley, 'who rules the whole affairs of Ireland',[61] devolved the civil government of Ireland to new commissioners, combining Broghill and Coote with two Presbyterians, the Cromwellian Bury and Sir John Clotworthy, an Antrim planter who had been deeply involved in English parliamentary politics in the 1640s and, like Annesley, had been secluded at Pride's Purge. Clotworthy chose to remain in England, but Broghill and Bury continued to 'walke together' until the end.[62] In practice, the tide was against them. It was on 8 March also that the Convention, having endorsed the Declaration of 16 February in general terms, adopted the uncontroversial aim of securing a learned and orthodox ministry 'and no other', supported by tithes and other legal maintenance and settled only in parishes. As the aim was translated into practical decisions, with the assistance of a representative committee of ministers, disagreements appeared, and it was the more conservative view that prevailed. The convention committee dissented from its advisory committee's standards of ministerial fitness and insisted on approving 'divers old prelatical men', and a Presbyterian plan to persuade the Convention to follow the English Parliament in acknowledging the Solemn League and Covenant was scotched by the convention chairman, Sir James Barry. It was later claimed that Clotworthy had determined to by-pass the Convention by going to Breda to argue the Presbyterian case, but was prevented by Monck. As affairs moved to a climax, with the imminent meeting of the English Parliament towards the end of April, the Episcopalians struck decisively, restoring five bishops to their ranks and titles, with annual emoluments of £200, though without jurisdiction.[63]

On secular matters, there seems to have been no such disagreement. The protection of property, a prime concern when the Protectorate fell in May and an outstanding grievance against the Long Parliament in February, was not merely an interest that united all the beneficiaries of the recent redistribution of Irish land, but one which rested on decisions of doubly doubtful legality, since they had no validity in the eyes of either the present authority or any potential successor. Prudence required that what could be done should be done and, towards the end of March, pairing the old and

---

[61] According to Lady Mordaunt, writing on March 9, *Clarendon state papers*, IV, p. 592. Also see chapter 11 above.

[62] Birch (ed.), *Thurloe state papers*, VII, p. 908.

[63] J. I. McGuire, 'The Dublin convention, the Protestant community and the emergence of an ecclesiastical settlement in 1660', in Art Cosgrave and J. I. Maguire (eds.), *Parliament and community. Historical Studies* XIV (Belfast, 1983), pp. 121–45.

the new, the Convention delegated Clotworthy and Sir William Aston, a politically active officer-settler, to present either to Parliament or the Council of State a set of articles seeking the regularization of the arrangements made during the Interregnum. Financial arrangements, with which was bound up the affirmation of the Irish taxpayer's right of consent, occupied a good deal of the Convention's time, and it was likewise on the eve of the English Parliament that the business was completed. A committee to look into both revenue and expenditure had been established during the first week and given comprehensive terms of reference on 12 March. After alternatives to the existing assessment levies were considered in Grand Committee on 29 March, the introduction of a graduated poll-tax with an estimated yield of almost £200,000 was approved on 24 April.

By that stage, tactical disagreements had developed. There had been disquiet in England about the Irish Convention and there seems to have been a feeling that it was particularly inappropriate that it should continue to sit after the Parliament met in England. On the appointed day, 25 April, 'after some high debate about dissolving or adjourning',[64] the Irish Convention agreed to adjourn for a period of six weeks from 27 April, giving the chairman authority to recall the members in an emergency. But many members were unwilling to disband until news was heard from England, the decision was not acted upon, and on 1 May, the day on which the English Parliament endorsed monarchy, the Convention met again. There was no certain news from England, but there was (in Broghill's words) a 'strange report' 'as if there should be a close intended with the kinge, only on an act of indemnity, and a few things of that nature'.[65] On the motion of a prominent adventurer, Henry Whalley, judge advocate of the army in Scotland, whose brother had been a regicide, a declaration was adopted condemning the execution of Charles I (among other things as a breach of the Covenant) and denying that any blame attached to the people of Ireland, since the Irish Parliament 'had not met since 1648': 'Twas not to be stopped, when once mooved', Broghill assured Thurloe.[66] On the day following, the Convention did adjourn for six weeks. The Dublin minute book records that Friday, 4 May, 'was putt apart by authoritie, and to bee kept and observed as a thanksgiveinge day for the restauration of his majestie to his crowne'.[67] The Convention was recalled ten days later when, on Whalley's motion, it formally accepted the Declaration of Breda, and proclaimed Charles II as king: all ministers

[64] Birch (ed.), *Thurloe state papers*, vII, p. 909.   [65] *Ibid.*, p. 911.
[66] *Ibid.*   [67] Gilbert (ed.), *Records*, IV, p. 180.

were ordered to pray for him, and Henry Jones was invited to deliver the sermon at a thanksgiving service. On 20 May, gifts of money were granted to the king and his sons, and a declaration issued for preserving the peace, which was prompted by signs that some of the expropriated were bestirring themselves to recover possession of their estates. On 1 June, after the Convention had appointed a carefully balanced delegation to attend the king and adjourned, Charles signalled the significance of what had happened in Ireland by publishing a proclamation which was similarly designed to disabuse the ingenuous of the notion that the end of the Commonwealth entailed the restoration of things as they had been.[68]

Beneath the surface of the public events of this period were layers of private and secret dealings, for this was a time when it was wise to be reticent, circumspect and ready for any eventuality. For that reason, it is unrealistic to expect to recapture the nuances, and unreasonable to expect everything to fall logically into place. Like Broghill and Charles and Richard Coote, John King was ennobled by Charles II: what comparable services he performed remain unknown. Broghill's later claim to have written to the king late in February 1660 is difficult to reconcile with his recorded words and actions at the time, but it would not have been uncharacteristic for him to have thought it wiser to be prudent than consistent. If so, the event proved him right. That Coote should have offered Charles his unconditional help in February 1660 need not mean that the fears he had spoken of to Ludlow, as to what would happen 'if the son should happen to prevail', were not genuine and lasting: he may have judged it better to rely on rewards than on promises. If so, the event appeared to prove him right too. In reality, however, the question was one of power. The unconditional character of Charles's return was of less significance in Ireland than in England because the Restoration could not materially alter the balance as it had recently evolved. There were unblemished Royalists, most formidably the duke of Ormond, but they were far too few in number to provide a guiltless alternative to those who had assumed control, all of whom had been in some degree complicit with the interregnum régime. The community of interest which was threatened by the return of the *status quo* was narrow, but it extended from whole-hearted Commonwealthsmen to ardent Royalists, and the sources of support for both the return of the king and the retention of the land settlement were the same, and indivisible. The collective momentum which

[68] L. J. Arnold, *The restoration land settlement in County Dublin, 1660–1688* (Dublin, 1993), pp. 37–40.

had been generated before the king's return fuelled the post-Restoration negotiations and ensured that the common aims of old and new settlers were achieved: every Protestant who had joined the royal bandwaggon was confirmed in his acquisitions and empowered to protect them in a Protestant parliament.

CHAPTER 13

CONCLUSION. SETTLING AND UNSETTLING IRELAND: THE CROMWELLIAN AND WILLIAMITE REVOLUTIONS

T. C. BARNARD

THE TERCENTENARY of William III's reconquest of Ireland, unlike that of Cromwell's Irish victories, has stimulated reassessments.[1] These have more often considered how the policies of the 1690s shaped the eighteenth century than how they connected with or completed Cromwellian measures. Thus, with occasional exceptions, little has been made of the continuities in individual experiences or in collective outlooks between the middle and the end of the seventeenth century. Only in respect of the transfers of land from Catholics to Protestants has the Williamite confiscation been treated as ending a process which had begun in the sixteenth century and then accelerated after 1641.[2] Otherwise, although the importance of the fifty years from 1641 in ushering in or tightening Ireland's legal, political and commercial subordination to England is frequently acknowledged, Dr Sean Connolly's recent and powerful account of the emerging Protestant ascendancy is the first to regard these years as formative: when, indeed, the Protestants' predominance was, in swift sequence, created, then challenged and finally saved. But even his study, by opening in the dog days of 1659, rather than in 1641, cannot systematically contrast the earlier with the later crisis.[3]

A few during the Williamite campaign approvingly recalled Cromwell's

---

[1] K. S. Bottigheimer, 'The Glorious Revolution and Ireland', in L. G. Schwoerer (ed.), *The revolution of 1688–1689* (Cambridge, 1992), pp. 234–41; D. W. Hayton, 'The Williamite Revolution in Ireland, 1688–1691', in J. I. Israel (ed.), *The Anglo-Dutch moment: essays on the Glorious Revolution and its world impact* (Cambridge, 1991), pp. 185–212; P. H. Kelly, 'Ireland and the Glorious Revolution: from kingdom to colony', in R. Beddard (ed.), *The revolutions of 1688* (Oxford, 1991), pp. 163–90.

[2] J. G. Simms, *The Williamite confiscation in Ireland, 1690–1703* (London, 1956). A succinct recent account is W. A. Maguire, 'The land settlement', in W. A. Maguire (ed.), *Kings in conflict: the revolutionary war in Ireland and its aftermath 1689–1750* (Belfast, 1990), pp. 139–56.

[3] S. J. Connolly, *Religion, law and power: the making of Protestant Ireland 1660–1760* (Oxford, 1992), especially pp. 5–40.

strategy.[4] Rather more, either silently or inadvertently, repeated what had been tried before. Many of the severities of the Interregnum were eased or abandoned after 1660; in contrast, William III's Irish policies, approved by the Hanoverians, endured for a century. As a result, William III, not Cromwell, would be celebrated (or execrated) as the architect of the Irish Protestant ascendancy.[5]

The turbulent 1680s did not merely mimic the 1640s and 1650s. Apprehensive Protestants foresaw dangers, certainly from James II's accession in 1685, perhaps from Charles II's restoration, and so could prepare themselves in ways impossible in 1641. The Williamite war did not last as long as the earlier rebellion; it killed fewer and destroyed less; nor was it attended with plague and famine. Most historians, if they allow that an undertow of anxiety tugged at both Catholics and Protestants between 1660 and 1688, stress how easily Ireland negotiated the hazards of the Popish Plot and Monmouth's and Argyll's rebellions. A mulish loyalism, it would seem, numbed much of the Protestant community, which, furthermore, was sedated by the spreading prosperity visible in enlarged estates, buoyant trade and new building.[6] Moreover, because the Irish Parliament did not meet between 1666 and 1689, the opportunities for the ambitious or aggrieved to incubate discontent were delayed until 1692. Had the Dublin Parliament sat in the 1670s, as was several times proposed, the politicians who managed and spoke on behalf of an alarmed Protestant interest, notably Orrery, might well have hastened the anti-Catholic laws, which in the event were enacted only after 1695. From 1660, as often before, important Irish policies were decided in London, where desirable offices were distributed and where, increasingly, the army and finances of Ireland were controlled. The flight of the rich and influential from Ireland to England, conspicuous in the 1640s, persisted after the Restoration, especially while the new settlement was being framed in the early 1660s or when in danger of being overturned in the 1670s and 1680s, and obliged

---

[4] Chatsworth House, Derbyshire, Lismore MSS, Miscellaneous volume, labelled '1688–9'; NLI, MS 11,474; Royal Irish Academy, Dublin, MS 1212, p. 74; ibid., MS 24 G 137; Nottingham University Library, Portland MSS, PW A 2690; J. Brady (ed.), 'Remedies proposed for the Church of Ireland (1697)', Archivium Hibernicum, 22 (1959), p. 168; HMC, Report on the manuscripts of the A. G. Finch, esq., (4 vols., London, 1913–65), II, p. 218.

[5] T. C. Barnard, 'Irish images of Cromwell', in R. C. Richardson (ed.), Images of Cromwell: essays by and for Roger Howell (Manchester, 1993), pp. 180–206.

[6] R. Gillespie, 'The Irish Protestants and James II, 1688–1690', IHS, 28 (1992), pp. 124–33. The most serviceable accounts remain: J. G. Simms, Jacobite Ireland 1685–91, (London, 1969); Simms, 'The Restoration, 1660–85' and 'The war of the two kings, 1685–91', in T. W. Moody, F. X. Martin and F. J. Byrne (eds.), A new history of Ireland, III: Early modern Ireland 1534–1691 (Oxford, 1976), pp. 420–53, 478–508.

some notables, such as Anglesey, Conway, Cork, Ranelagh and Sir Robert Southwell, to absent themselves from Dublin for long periods. Even Ormond, ribbed in 1661 for owning no land in England, attending the king as Lord High Steward and advanced in 1682 to an English dukedom, spent £9,000 on the largest mansion in St James's Square in London, yet lacked his own Dublin residence.[7] These arrangements hint how much, between 1641 and 1691, power over Irish affairs had shifted to the English court and Parliament, and so required the more frequent presence of the Anglo-Irish. The London coteries of affluent Protestant ex-patriates and transient visitors were balanced by groups of Catholic suitors. The latter, generally Old English in ancestry and political stance, continued to lobby and argue, as they had over the 'Graces' in the 1620s and at the royal court in the 1640s and 1650s. Their loyalism, reinforced by shared exile with Charles II and the future James II, guaranteed a welcome and a hearing for their spokesmen in the 1660s, and tangible favours for a few, notably those, like Theobald Taaffe, the future earl of Carlingford, or Richard Talbot, ennobled as earl of Tyrconnell, whose affability or swagger had endeared them to the royal brothers. Easy access to the monarch, a ready welcome in the London houses of successive Catholic queens and the willingness of the Stuarts to ease the Irish Catholics' plight *vis-à-vis* landowning, office-holding and religious worship, confirmed the Old English instinct to uphold and exploit English rule.[8]

To identify the dynamic in later seventeenth-century Ireland with the preoccupations and behaviour of a few individuals, no matter how wealthy and powerful, risks overlooking impersonal forces, and of reducing the era to one in which veteran cavaliers wrestled with the compromised Cromwellian survivors.[9] Tempting as it is to linger over the epic contests, of

---

[7] HMC, *Calendar of the manuscripts of the marquis of Ormonde*, ns (8 vols., London, 1902–20), VI, pp. 488, 501, 506; [R. Boyle], earl of Orrery, *The Irish colours displayed* (London, 1662), pp. 9–11; F. H. W. Sheppard (ed.), *Survey of London*, XXIX: *Parish of St James Westminster* (London, 1960), pp. 71, 117–20; T. C. Barnard, 'Housing the Anglo-Irish aristocracy in Dublin and London, 1660–1740' (unpublished paper given at the Aristocratic Town House Conference, Burlington House, 1993).

[8] L. J. Arnold, *The Restoration land settlement in County Dublin, 1660–1688; a history of the administration of the Acts of Settlement and Explanation* (Dublin, 1993), pp. 45–50, 60–1, 72–80, 121–3; P. H. Kelly, '"A light to the blind": the voice of the dispossessed élite in the generation after the defeat at Limerick', *IHS*, 24 (1985), pp. 441–2; Jane H. Ohlmeyer, *Civil war and restoration in the three Stuart kingdoms: the career of Randal MacDonnell, marquis of Antrim 1609–83* (Cambridge, 1993), pp. 266–71; H. O'Sullivan, 'Landownership changes in the county of Louth in the seventeenth century', (unpublished PhD thesis, TCD, 1992), I, pp. 195–236.

[9] Pearse St Public Library, Dublin, Gilbert MSS, 207; K. S. Bottigheimer, 'Kingdom and colony: Ireland in the westward enterprise, 1536–1660', in K. R. Andrews, N. P. Canny and P. E. H. Hair (eds.), *The westward enterprise: English activities in Ireland, the Atlantic and America* (Liverpool, 1978), p. 63.

Ormond against Orrery, Orrery against Anglesey and of Peter Walsh or Tyrconnell *contra mundum*, to do so may exaggerate the role of personal dislike, thwarted ambition and opportunism at the expense of fixed beliefs, and of deeper structural shifts as wealth and power flowed towards the Protestants and England. In addition, the international context of the Irish question altered with the diplomatic *démarche* after the Peace of the Pyrenees in 1659 and Spain's near eclipse.

A further difficulty in deciding the themes around which Ireland's history in the second half of the seventeenth century should best be organized centres on the subtle interplay of past with present and the immaterial with the concrete. Restoration Ireland resounded to plots and panics. Many alarms were imagined; others invented – mysterious rendezvous, dead-letter boxes in ruined abbeys, contracts to kill Protestant prelates or peers, incitement to mass murder.[10] The frights fed on the memories of what had happened in and after 1641, the record of which, artfully contrived to chill Protestants, was constantly improved and updated, and on current worries as papists repossessed property, pleaded in the law courts, practised their religion, and were emboldened by foreign and Stuart friendliness.[11] Just as the past, monotonously rehearsed and ruthlessly reordered by Protestant and Catholic partisans, became an actor in the drama of later Stuart Ireland, so too did the rumours and collective hysteria. Some analysts, eager to impugn the relaxed attitudes of Ormond and of Charles II and James II, meticulously gathered (and sometimes fabricated) evidence of a disordered society; others, with different objectives, reported a placid and prospering Ireland, disturbed only by shifty Cromwellians imbued with republicanism and religious dissent. Since Restoration Ireland did indeed comprehend these several worlds, any satisfying account has both to acknowledge the diversity and contradictions, and to decide whether passivity or truculence had the greater influence over events.

[10] NA, Wyche MSS, 1/34; NLI, MS 13014; Victoria and Albert Museum, London, Orrery MSS, I, fo. 50; II, fos. 33, 35, 39, 41, 43; Southampton University Library, Broadlands MSS, BR 7A/1, 5 and 30 November 1678, 6 December 1679, 14 April 1680, 27 July 1680; Staffordshire C[ounty] RO, Bridgeman MSS, D 1287/A/177; D. Fitzgerald, *A narrative of the Irish Popish Plot* (London, 1680).

[11] NLI, Lane MSS, MS 8644/5; TCD, King MSS, MSS 1995–2008/61; Guildford Muniment Room, Brodrick MSS, 1248/1, fo. 227; Lambeth Palace Library, London, diary of Bishop Simon Digby, MS 3152, 9 December 1688; Midleton Church of Ireland Rectory, County Cork, MS 8, chapter book of Cloyne cathedral from 1663, pp. 9–10; *An apology for the Protestants of Ireland* (London, 1689), pp. 10–11, 19; T. C. Barnard, 'The uses of 23 October 1641 and Irish Protestant celebrations', *English Historical Review*, 106 (1991), pp. 889–920; Barnard, '1641: a bibliographical review', in B. Mac Cuarta (ed.), *Ulster 1641* (Belfast, 1993).

CONCLUSION   269

I

Large losses of lands throughout the seventeenth century progressively
enfeebled the Irish Catholics. The Restoration land settlement moderated,
but did not (as the Catholics had pleaded) reverse the catastrophe of the
1640s and 1650s. Between 1641 and 1688 the Catholics' share of profitable
land dropped from 59 per cent to 22 per cent and was then further
reduced by Williamite confiscations to 14 per cent.[12] In the end, once
William III's victories had completed the enforced redistributions of
the earlier century, the greater Protestant share supported a larger
Protestant population, and drove the prosperous and thrusting to fan out
and colonize institutions and offices until, bit by bit, they monopolized
Ireland's government. In 1641 and again in 1689, some settlers responded
to Catholic provocations with such alacrity that they were accused of
magnifying, if not inventing, the savagery in order to justify new forfeitures.
Thus, reports of robberies around Cork early in 1642 were welcomed,
since, 'they are taken by such neighbours of mine as I wisht might
take them, because I hope to have their lands for it'. Later, in the
1670s, Ormond suspected Orrery of wanting and maybe deliberately
encouraging, 'another rebellion that there may be another redistribution
of lands'. This attitude survived into 1689, when the reconquest of Ireland
was candidly commended to 'all Englishmen', because 'the Protestants
who have estates will add to 'em, and they who have none, will get
some'.[13]

   Despite considerable gains, many Protestants gagged on the Acts of
Settlement and Explanation in the 1660s because they obliged the
disgorging of as much as one-third of their recent acquisitions. Initially
the political processes during which the bills were drafted in London,
debated in Dublin, amplified and amended in England, generated
feverish lobbying and angry protests; next the judicial and administrative
actions by which land claims were adjudicated and property allocated
dismayed many; local difficulties over ousting incumbents and
possessing properties prolonged the unhappiness; continuing uncertainties
obliged numerous landowners to resort to the law courts throughout the
1670s and 1680s; and, finally, the readiness of Charles II and James II to
review both the details and the final shape of the settlement disquieted

---

[12] Simms, *Williamite confiscation*, pp. 14, 22, 59, 195.
[13] Bodl., Add. MSS, C 266, fo. 10v; *The declaration of the Protestant nobility and gentry of the province of Munster* (London, 1689); *Further intelligence from Ireland declared in a letter . . . from Captaine Muschampe* (London, 1642), p. 2.

Protestants.[14] With some justice, therefore, it could be said of the reigns of Charles II and James II, 'the generality of those who enjoy estates on new titles cannot shake off the fear of losing them again'.[15] Shrewd politicians knew that the king must scotch such anxieties by a definitive confirmation of doubtful titles. Initiatives of this sort, however, foundered when the later Stuarts harkened to Catholic grumbles. Even so, it was not until 1687 that some Protestants, unnerved by the Catholics' confidence that soon 'they will have all', extricated themselves from their Irish estates or mused on how best they might defend them.

Catholics, promised much by an expansive Charles II, received too little to please them, but enough to distress their Protestant rivals. Shared exile with the king, his brother and English courtiers, or blatant bribery, assisted a handful of Irish Catholics to generosity. The erratic impact of royal favour determined the variegated patterns of land-holding and the divergent proportions held by Protestants and Catholics in different counties. In Counties Louth and Dublin, for example, the successes of Carlingford and Richard Talbot respectively, the result of high standing at court, inflated the Catholic share of land. Thus, in County Dublin by 1669, ninety-seven papist owners had survived, who enjoyed 35 per cent of the total acreage, or 63 per cent of what they had owned in 1641. In nearby County Wicklow, by contrast, already in 1641 the Catholic share had declined to 35 per cent, and this then fell, as a result of the Cromwellian and Restoration settlements, to a meagre 12 per cent.[16] Elsewhere, in County Kilkenny, if the number of Catholic landlords dropped between 1641 and the 1660s from over 200 to about twenty, nevertheless a strong Catholic group survived there and in Country Tipperary, thanks to its patron, Ormond. In Ormond's great apanage in Kilkenny, the Williamite confiscations reduced the Catholic proportion to a paltry 8 per cent and, eventually, after 1715, the flight and attainder of the second duke of Ormond as a Jacobite, accomplished the final transformation of the local élite into a Protestant ascendancy.[17] Similarly, in County Cork in the 1690s, the dismemberment

[14] For the processes see Arnold, *Restoration land settlement*; Arnold, 'The Irish Court of Claims of 1663', *IHS*, 24 (1985), pp. 417–30; K. S. Bottigheimer, 'The Restoration land settlement in Ireland: a structural view', *ibid.*, 18 (1972), pp. 1–21. The difficulties in the way of satisfaction can be followed in Staffordshire CRO, Dartmouth MSS, D(W) 1778/iii/o/19, partly printed in HMC, *Report on the manuscripts of the earl of Dartmouth* (3 vols., London, 1887–96), III, pp. 107–20.
[15] Bodl., Add. MSS C 33, fo. 71v; NA, M 2460/21; BL, Stowe MSS 745, fo. 47v.
[16] Arnold, *Restoration land settlement*, pp. 109, 138–9, 141–5; O'Sullivan, 'Landownership changes in the county of Louth', I, pp. 333, 372–4.
[17] M. Brennan, 'The changing composition of Kilkenny landowners, 1641–1700', in W. Nolan and K. Whelan (eds.), *Kilkenny: history and society* (Dublin, 1990), pp. 169, 174–5; T. P. Power, 'Land, politics and society in eighteenth-century Tipperary' (unpublished PhD thesis, TCD, 1987), I, pp. 3–4, 90; W. J. Smyth, 'Property, patronage and population: reconstructing the human

CONCLUSION271

of the holding of Clancarty (another connection of Ormond) led hungry squires to scramble for the choicest morsels, and reduced the Catholic percentage of land to about 8, held by some fifteen men.[18] West of the Shannon, where Cromwellian decrees had banished the surviving Catholic proprietors, larger numbers of papist owners clung on throughout the eighteenth century.[19] This confused scene, in which, despite the obvious gains of the Protestants, a few lucky Catholics thrived, together with apprehensions about Stuart thinking on the future of land, accounts for the edginess of the Irish Protestants. The situation also necessitated the constant resort of Protestant and Catholic leaders to London in efforts to shape any fresh measures.

There are no compelling grounds to set aside the traditional criticism of the Stuarts that, by their incessant tinkering with that 'magna carta of this kingdom', the Acts of Settlement and Explanation, they seriously unsettled Ireland.[20] Yet, for all the unease, countervailing forces limited discontent. Protestant incumbents, whatever their misgivings, acted as if secure for all time: they invested in and improved their holdings. The land redistributions had further fragmented an already disunited Protestant interest (see chapter II above).[21] New owners in the distinct categories – letterees, nominees, English adventurers and soldiers, those who had campaigned in Ireland before 1649, Protestants in Connacht and Clare displaced by transplanted Catholics – necessarily competed for an insufficient stock of lands, and acted in unison only when the entire settlement was threatened. Paradoxically, Protestant and Catholic experiences converged, thanks to exile in the 1640s and the late 1680s. The uprooted adjusted rapidly to new lives, even if simultaneously they schemed to retrieve what they had so lately lost. Furthermore, land, though coveted, yielded returns in money, power and status, which by English standards

geography of mid-seventeenth century County Tipperary', in W. Nolan and T. McGrath (eds.) *Tipperary: history and society* (Dublin, 1985), pp. 111–13, 136–7.
[18] D. Dickson, 'An economic history of the Cork region in the eighteenth century', (unpublished PhD thesis, TCD, 1977), I, pp. 65–7.
[19] L. M. Cullen, 'Catholics and the penal laws', *Eighteenth-Century Ireland*, 1 (1986), pp. 23–36; K. J. Harvey, 'The Bellews of Mount Bellew: a Catholic gentry family in the age of penal laws' (unpublished PhD thesis, Pennsylvania State University, 1984); Harvey, 'The family experience: the Bellews of Mount Bellew', in T. P. Power and K. Whelan (eds.), *Endurance and emergence: Catholics in eighteenth-century Ireland* (Dublin, 1990), pp. 171–97; P. Melvin, 'The composition of the Galway gentry', *The Irish Genealogist*, 7 (1986), pp. 81–8.
[20] BL, Add. MSS 28,085, fo. 174; Victoria and Albert Museum, Orrery MSS, II, fo. 16; Bottigheimer, 'The Glorious Revolution and Ireland', pp. 234, 239; Gillespie, 'The Irish Protestants and James II', pp. 131–2.
[21] T. C. Barnard, 'Planters and policies in Cromwellian Ireland', *Past and Present*, 61 (1973), pp. 31–69; Barnard, 'Crises of identity among Irish Protestants, 1641–1685', *ibid.*, 127 (1990), pp. 39–83.

looked meagre. Despite the widespread eagerness to own Irish property, its quantifiable value, in enhanced rents or better returns on investment, can presently only be guessed.[22] Often rentals needed to be supplemented by office or commands. So, while a gulf widened after 1660 between those who owned and those who had forfeited estates, this served to accentuate the differences between those with and without royal favour. In the end, though, Charles II's and James II's tampering with the land acts, itself important in estranging many Irish Protestants, belonged to a more thorough attack on the newly established Protestant ascendancy in office-holding, the law courts, the army and over religious privileges.

II

Freeholds, in Ireland as in England, entitled their possessors to vote in county elections. The changes in ownership during the Interregnum, not any legal disenfranchisement of papists, resulted in an exclusively Protestant House of Commons in 1661. Its members, dreading an imminent restoration of some Catholic proprietors, clamoured for a formal ban of Catholic membership. On this issue, as soon on many others, an intolerant Irish Protestant squirearchy collided with indulgent English rulers. Ormond, exploiting the supine royalism of the majority of Irish MPs, frustrated plans to impose the oath of supremacy, to harry and banish priests, and to stop the continental education of Catholics. Ormond, in resisting so courageously, might have delighted Charles II but he angered those Irish Protestants who already suspected him of strong Catholic leanings.[23] Thwarted, militant Protestants waited for, or themselves tried to create, opportunities to rush anti-Catholic measures on to the statute book. Such struggles polarized Irish politics, and linked them strongly with those of England (especially in the absence of a Dublin Parliament after 1666). Denied other outlets, Irish Protestants exploited or invented plots to remind of the Catholic danger; Ormond and his allies retaliated by attributing treasonable and republican intentions to their opponents. Plots,

---

[22] Barnard, 'Sir William Petty, Irish landowner', in Hugh Lloyd-Jones, Valerie Pearl and Blair Worden (eds.) *History and imagination: essays in honour of H. R. Trevor-Roper* (London, 1981), pp. 201–17; Dickson, 'An economic history of the Cork region', 1, pp. 56–216; R. Gillespie, 'Landed society and the Interregnum in Ireland and Scotland', in P. Roebuck and R. Mitchison (eds.), *Economy and society in Scotland and Ireland 1500–1939* (Edinburgh, 1988), pp. 39, 41; Gillespie, *Settlement and survival on an Ulster estate: the Brownlow leasebook 1667–1711* (Belfast, 1988), p. lix.

[23] Leicestershire CRO, Finch MSS, DG7, 4965, Ire. 10; Bodl., Add. MSS C 33, fos. 54v–4; Carte MSS 69, fo. 374; 221, fo. 156; *Cal. S P Ire., 1660–2*, pp. 224, 268, 291, 445; *ibid. 1663–5*, pp. 65, 85, 91, 115, 232.

real or imaginary, gave form and content to the politics of Ireland after 1660.[24]

The wrangle over whether or not MPs should be required to swear the oath of supremacy illustrated the growing uneasiness of the relationship between Charles II and his loyal deputy, Ormond, on the one part, and the settlers on the other. The oath, demanded of magistrates and office-holders in Ireland since 1560, had been tendered systematically only in the early seventeenth century.[25] Then, the Irish Commons, shocked by the 1641 uprising, imposed the oath on all who still wished to sit. The House and its agents in England quickly promoted a bill which would perpetuate this panicky response.[26] In the event, *de facto* union with England during the 1650s solved the problem by restricting Ireland's representation at Westminster to a group defined by its Protestantism and politics. But when Ireland's representative institutions again appeared in Dublin after 1660, so too did the issue. Catholics, if not outlawed as rebels, resumed their seats in the Lords; the favoured threatened to creep back into the boroughs. Yet, because the Stuarts refused to surrender to extreme Protestant prejudice, not until 1691 did an English act debar Catholics from membership of the Irish Commons; only in 1716 were they excluded from the Lords. Catholic freeholders would not be disenfranchised explicitly until 1729.[27]

Changes in who owned Irish land affected only a part, and indeed the smaller part, of the Irish Commons. The majority of members – 210 of 276 – represented boroughs, and there the Protestant monopoly depended on control of the towns achieved during the 1650s. The returning sovereign publicly promised to alter this, and by so doing antagonized many within

[24] For many examples see PRONI, Belfast, D 1854/3/5, p. 177; NLI, MS 2505; 8643/6; TCD, MS 844, fo. 255; Bodl., Carte MSS 31, fos. 346, 372; 33, fos. 136, 138, 140; 200, fo. 187v; 215, fo. 265; 221, fo. 205; Clarendon State Papers, 79, fos. 90, 107, 181–3, 185v, 251, 270, 275; 84, fos. 186–7; Warwickshire CRO, Newdegate MSS, CR 136/ B280; Victoria and Albert Museum, Orrery MSS, II, fos. 54, 57v, 59; *Mercurius Hibernicus*, 13 (7–14 April 1663), p. 112; Connolly, *Religion, law and power*, pp. 25–32.

[25] *Statutes at large passed in the parliaments held in Ireland* (8 vols., Dublin, 1765), I, p. 279; A. Clarke and R. D. Edwards, 'Pacification, plantation and the Catholic question, 1603–23', in Moody *et al.*, *A new history of Ireland*, III, pp. 200, 212; C. Lennon, *The lords of Dublin in the age of reformation* (Dublin, 1989), pp. 48, 101, 132, 168, 176–7, 196.

[26] *Journals of the House of Commons of the Kingdom of Ireland* (28 vols., Dublin, 1753–91), I, pp. 297, 300–2, 306–9; *The humble propositions of the agents for the Protestants of Ireland (residing at Oxford)* (London, 1644), p. 6; *An ordinance of the Commons assembled in Parliament for a Bill . . . concerning the qualifications of knights, citizens, and burgesses who shall be admitted to sit, in Parliament for the kingdome of Ireland* (Dublin, 1647).

[27] D. Dickson, *New foundations: Ireland 1660–1800* (Dublin, 1988), pp. 40, 73; J. G. Simms, 'Irish Catholics and the parliamentary franchise 1692–1728', in his *War and politics in Ireland, 1649–1730* ed. D. Hayton and G. O'Brien (London, 1986), pp. 225–34. For the allegation that Catholic freeholders, especially in Connacht, had voted in 1661: NLI, MS 16,974, p. 17.

Protestant society.[28] In the early 1670s, when Catholic traders were readmitted into the larger ports and others were encouraged to expect speedy restitution, Dublin, Galway and Limerick were seriously disturbed.[29] Angry Protestant magnates, led by the lord chancellor and archbishop of Dublin, expostulated that the chief towns 'are likely to be composed like Noah's ark of inhabitants of all sorts', and warned how, in the next Parliament, Protestant control would be weakened.[30]

Towns had long possessed a practical as well as symbolic value in schemes for an English Ireland. Conceived as redoubts from which English civility and industry would spread, these centres, turned into Protestant reserves during the Interregnum, after 1660 could look like stagnant havens of the disaffected.[31] Through the 'New Rules' in 1672 the Irish administration was empowered to regulate the affairs of the principal corporations so as to balance the needs of security and prosperity, while rewarding worthy papists.[32] Even before this limited kindness, the towns gave trouble. Trivial squabbles over annual elections or civic leases could be puffed into serious protests by those denied a parliamentary vent for their grievances. The boisterous politics of Dublin throughout the almost continuous crisis of Charles II's and James II's reigns should remind us how much Irish Protestants contributed to, and learnt from, the English opposition to the Stuarts' pro-French and pro-Catholic courses. Dublin, populous and growing, housed an alarming variety of opinions. The Ormondist party, disclosed in 1659 and active in the overthrow of military rule, flourished under Ormond's viceroyalty, when its members outdid one another with florid professions of boundless loyalty (see chapter 11 above).[33]

[28] *Cal. S P Ire. 1660–2*, pp. 356–7, 396; P. Gale, *An inquiry into the ancient corporate system of Ireland* (London, 1834), pp. cxxx–cxxxvi, cxli–cxlii.

[29] Houghton Library, Harvard University, Orrery MSS, 218 22F, letter of S. Foxon to Orrery, 1 April 1667; BL, Add. MSS 19,859, fos. 3v, 5–5v, 14, 17–17v, 21v–22v, 23v, 31v; Stowe MSS 200, fos. 31v, 42v, 43v, 127v, 184, 193, 406, 419v; Bodl., Add. MSS C. 33, fos. 86–86v, 88–88v, 91, 93, 95v, 96; Carte MSS 37, fos. 532v, 537; 147, fos. 179, 182, 185; 220, fo. 142v; Petworth House, West Sussex, Orrery MSS, general series, 28, letters of 14 December 1669, 22 July 1670, 23 September 1670, 27 October 1673; Damer House, Roscrea, County Tipperary, de Vesci MSS, H/15; Victoria and Albert Museum, Orrery MSS, I, fos. 13, 32–7.

[30] Harvard, Orrery MSS, 218 22F, Michael Boyle to Orrery, 17 February 1670[1]. Cf. Chatsworth, Lismore MSS, diary of second earl of Cork, 7 and 9 May 1673.

[31] T. C. Barnard, *Cromwellian Ireland: English government and reform in Ireland 1649–1660* (Oxford, 1975), pp. 50–89; R. Gillespie, 'The origins and development of an Ulster urban network', *IHS*, 24 (1984), pp. 15–29.

[32] *Statutes at large*, III, pp. 205–39.

[33] Bodl., Carte MSS 37, fos. 18, 78, 139; Staffordshire CRO, Bridgeman MSS, D 1287/18/3, Robartes to Bridgeman, 9 October 1669; Barnard, *Cromwellian Ireland*, pp. 81, 88; P. Kilroy, 'Protestant dissent and controversy in Ireland, 1660–1711' (unpublished PhD thesis, TCD, 1991), pp. 28–32, 51–67, 73–6, 88–102; C. McNeill (ed.), *The Tanner letters . . .* (IMC, Dublin, 1943), pp. 457, 459–60.

At the same time, however, Protestant dissent survived even among civic dignitaries, and may have added to political disaffection. In 1668, when dirt had been flung at portraits of the king and queen on public show in the capital, a cavalier gloomily concluded, 'I fear very many hearts are inclined to rebellion'.[34] No doubt he over-reacted; but the Irish government, repeatedly informed of rumoured and, occasionally, actual unrest, had difficulties in winnowing the false from the true, and in assessing how many secretly might admire desperadoes like Blood and Walcott.[35] In the early 1670s, quick changes of governors signalled concessions to the Irish, and were greeted with urban disorders. Even behind such apparently unpolitical acts as an attack by apprentices on a new bridge over the river Liffey lurked wider alarms over the directors and directions of Irish policy.[36] The city threatened to become a battle-ground for the contest between those who favoured giving more to the papists and their opponents, set on (it was rumoured) by English MPs. Late in 1672, the incoming lord lieutenant, Essex, quietened the capital only by deploying more soldiers, issuing a proclamation which solemnly upheld the recent land settlement, and surrendering to the upsurge of anti-popery by banishing priests and introducing the oath of supremacy as a prerequisite for holding municipal office. The restive city bowed before a mixture of cajolery, bribery and *force majeure*.[37] But the political skills and links developed in the 1670s by dissidents were again utilized when Dublin faced the deeper crisis of James II's rule.

In Ireland, as in England, since the Restoration the government had interfered in the municipalities.[38] Until 1685 the 'New Rules' sufficed. Thereafter, with a new parliament in the offing, the Dublin government

---

[34] NLI, MS 8644/1, Sir George Lane to Lady Lane, 10 November 1668.

[35] BL, Stowe MSS 200, fos. 396, 402, 404, 406, 419; 210, fos. 28–9; Bodl., Add. MSS C 33, fos. 49, 66, 67v, 68, 132, 143v; Connolly, *Religion, law and power*, pp. 25–6, 31, 33; A. Marshall, 'Colonel Thomas Blood and the Restoration political scene', *The Historical Journal*, 32 (1989), pp. 561–82.

[36] Bowood House, Wiltshire, Petty MSS, 13/47, 48; Bodl., Carte MSS 37, fos. 578, 586, 66, fos. 285–7v; Add. MSS C 33, fos. 23v, 31, 36; J. T. Gilbert (ed.), *Calendar of the ancient records of Dublin in possession of the municipal corporation* (17 vols., Dublin, 1889–1916), IV, pp. 537–40; J. C. Beckett, 'The Irish viceroyalty in the Restoration period', reprinted in Becket, *Confrontations: studies in Irish history* (London, 1972), pp. 67–86; R. Hutton, *Charles the second, king of England, Scotland and Ireland* (Oxford, 1989), pp. 260–2, 268, 274–5, 281–2.

[37] BL, Stowe MSS 200, fos. 237, 240, 242, 244, 277v; 201, fos. 58, 143; Bodl., Add. MSS C 33, fos. 71v, 77, 78; C 34, fos. 61–5; Leicestershire CRO, Finch MSS, DG7, box 4795, Ire. 10; Gilbert (ed.), *Calendar of the ancient records*, v, pp. 12–17; *The speech of Sr Ellis Leighton Kt. at the Tholsell of Dublin, April the 4th. 1672* (Dublin, 1672), pp. 4–7; R. R. Steele (ed.), *Tudor and Stuart proclamations* (2 vols., Oxford, 1910), II, no. 835 (Ireland).

[38] For English policy see J. Miller, 'The crown and the borough charters in the reign of Charles II', *English Historical Review*, 100 (1985), pp. 53–84; J. H. Sacret, 'The Restoration government and the municipal corporations', *ibid.*, 45 (1930), pp. 232–59.

comprehensively remodelled the boroughs. By *quo warranto* process, the charters of 105 corporations were called in, cancelled and replaced.[39] The main effect was to return almost all towns to Catholic control, and so to prepare the ground for a largely Catholic House of Commons. In Dublin, the oligarchs had capitulated in April 1687 and ostentatiously erased from their journal the earlier order for freemen to subscribe to the oath of supremacy. But it was not enough, and signs of resistance to the *quo warranto* marked out the city for exemplary treatment.[40] A predominantly Catholic corporation was installed. The new lord mayor in 1688 obediently celebrated the Jacobite red-letter days, such as the birth of the Prince of Wales, though his trustees in 1708 were still trying to pay the bills for his inspired hospitality.[41] The new Catholic order in the towns, and particularly in Dublin, warned Protestants how easily their recent gains had been overturned. Merchants and office-holders hastily decamped to England with their assets: an exodus which, exaggerated for political effect, itself added to fears and depressed trade.[42] Trinity College sought to hurry away its silver under the implausible pretence that this was an excellent moment to convert it into cash for buildings.[43] Disbanded Protestant troopers fought with papists who thronged Dublin in the expectation of employment.[44] The capital's Protestant preachers, having lately infused into their parishioners a sharper sense of spirituality, stiffened the Dubliners' morale. The most vigorous among them, William King and Nathanael Foy, stayed when the timid (including all the dissenting pastors) shipped themselves to safety. One minister, perhaps King, in November

[39] Many are to be found in NA, RC 3/1–3/8; NLI, MS 8644/5; and are printed in W. Harris, *The History of the life and reign of William-Henry Prince of . . . Orange* (Dublin, 1749), appendix, pp. iv–xvi.
[40] Bodl., Clarendon State Papers 89, fos. 19–26, 32v, 50v, 59, 64, 98–9; Gilbert (ed.), *Calendar of the ancient records*, v, pp. 389–90, 392–5, 401–2, 406–7, 422–5, 434–6; Simms, *Jacobite Ireland*, pp. 35–6.
[41] Pearse St Library, Gilbert MSS 223, fo. 48; Gilbert (ed.), *Calendar of the ancient records*, v, pp. 449, 460, 475, 482–3, 489; Barnard, 'The uses of 23 October 1641', p. 914, n. 2.
[42] BL, Add. MSS 28,876, fo. 93; Dr Williams's Library, London, Roger Morice Entering book, II, pp. 61, 70; Bodl., Carte MSS 40, fo. 405; Clarendon State Papers 89, fos. 12, 27, 52–3, 59–60, 64–5; Rawlinson MSS A 482, fo. 21v; Southampton University Library, BR 7A/1, 22 January 1686[7]; *An apology for the Protestants of Ireland*, p. 5; T.C. Barnard, 'The political, material and mental culture of the Cork settlers, *c.* 1650–1700', in P. O'Flanagan and C. G. Buttimer (eds.), *Cork: history and society* (Dublin, 1993), pp. 347–9; Gillespie, 'The Irish Protestants and James II', pp. 129–30; J. Miller, 'The earl of Tyrconnell and James II's Irish policy, 1685–1688', *The Historical Journal*, 20 (1977), p. 815.
[43] TCD, Mun. P/1/521; Cambridge University Library, Baumgartner MSS, Add. MSS 1, 60.
[44] NLI, MS 1793, fos. 244–52; T.C. Barnard, 'Athlone, 1685; Limerick, 1710: religious riots or charivaris?', *Studia Hibernica*, 27 (1993); HMC, *Report on the manuscripts of the earl of Egmont*, II, pp. 180–1; HMC, *Report on the manuscripts of the late R. R. Hastings* (4 vols., London, 1928–47), II, p. 392; HMC, *Ormonde*, ns, VIII, p. 346; P. Melvin, 'Sir Paul Rycaut's memoranda and letters from Ireland, 1686–1687', *Analecta Hibernica*, 27 (1972), p. 155.

1688, defended an outspoken sermon of his against detractors by repeating the Scottish saw, 'he that is afraid of a fart will never stand thunder'.[45] The agitations which ruffled many towns, apparently trivial, if studied carefully might reveal the tensions among Irish Protestants and between them and their papist neighbours, links with and imitation of urban discontent in England, and a vibrant, but largely forgotten, political culture.[46] Sometimes a jumpy Dublin government started at shadows (or farts). It, like later scholars, might suppose from the numerous stories of sedition and conspiracy that Dublin and provincial Ireland teetered towards intercommunal violence or rebellion, when the bulk of the population vegetated contentedly. In truth, the equilibrium between loyal languor and incendiarism was an unstable one, so that successive régimes did well to watch closely for incipient unrest.

III

Protestants, dissatisfied with the shakiness of the land settlement, and appalled as papists streamed back into the boroughs, linked these setbacks with another, equally ominous. In the 1660s and 1670s, Catholic barristers assisted their co-religionists through the legal labyrinths; then, after 1685, numerous Catholic judges, magistrates and jurors interpreted and applied the law. Since English plans for Ireland had long rested on the consistent use there of the English law, and because each cut which had emasculated the Catholics required legal procedures, the resilience of this Irish Catholic group at the bar was alarming, involving as it did the reversal of the monopoly achieved by the Protestants in the 1650s.[47] The success of Catholic counsel, as advocates before the English privy council or in the tribunals and courts of Ireland, enraged their Protestant adversaries. Much was blamed on a succession of lord chancellors and law officers, such as Eustace, Archbishop Boyle, Domville, Porter and Fitton, whose sinister Catholic connections or venality predisposed them towards the papists.[48]

---

[45] BL, Stowe MSS 746, fo. 106; Dr Williams's Library, MS 31 J, Roger Morice's chronological account of eminent persons, III, pp. 48, 58: T. C. Barnard, 'Reforming Irish manners: the religious societies in Dublin during the 1690s', *The Historical Journal*, 35 (1992), pp. 806–8; A. Carpenter, 'William King and the threats to the Church of Ireland during the reign of James II', *IHS*, 18 (1972–3), pp. 22–8; H. J. Lawlor (ed.), *The diary of William King, D. D.* (Dublin, 1903).

[46] Barnard, 'Irish images of Cromwell', p. 186; Barnard, 'Athlone, 1685', pp. 61–75.

[47] T.C. Barnard, 'Lawyers and the law in later seventeenth-century Ireland', *IHS*, 28 (1993), pp. 256–82.

[48] BL, Egerton MSS 2618, fo. 100; Bodl, Carte MSS 31, fo. 358; 49, fo. 87; Staffordshire CRO, D 1778/iii/o/19; Arnold, *Restoration land settlement*, pp. 40–2, 76–7, 88–90, 117; Barnard, 'Lawyers and the law', pp. 279–80; HMC, *Egmont*, II, p. 20.

Because the Irish courts did not invariably back Irish Protestant interests, the aggrieved not only berated the judiciary and magistracy, but those like Ormond who had nominated them, and condemned the regular use of laws enacted in England rather than in Ireland and of the king's prerogative to exempt Catholics from disabilities. After 1686, the Catholic barristers, whose skills could mitigate the discriminatory laws against individual Catholics, were promoted to the bench. Protestants, judging according to their usual double standard, having argued that papists objected unreasonably to Protestant-made and administered laws, presumed that they themselves would now be victimized by Catholic judges, sheriffs and jurors.[49] Just as papist lawyers exerted a disproportionate influence over the thinking and actions of the Catholic community after 1660, so, from 1685, their Protestant equivalents, among the earliest to feel the force of Tyrconnell's catholicizing measures, removed to England and concerted the Irish opposition to the gathering Catholic *revanche*.[50] Victory in 1690 allowed revenge. Nevertheless, despite more determined action to turn the law and its practitioners into arms of the Protestant ascendancy, both eluded complete Protestant control.[51]

Protestant apprehensiveness about Irish papists who evaded or manipulated the law paralleled disquiet over the army. Shortly after James II succeeded, Protestants were dismissed without compensation, disarmed and replaced by papists.[52] The militia, the organization of which mirrored and strengthened that of Protestant settlements, though eroded by the commercialization of tenurial relationships and by inertia or complacency, had survived. Its worth, highly estimated by champions of the Protestant interest like Orrery but devalued by Ormond and Essex, was proved during the alarms of 1666 and 1678.[53] Since the 1640s, the defensive

[49] Cork University Library, Southwell MSS, U/55, 10 April 1688; Southampton University Library, BR 7A/1, 13 February 1685[6], 19 February 1687[8]; Barnard, 'Culture of the Cork Settlers', pp. 343–5; Barnard, 'Lawyers and the law', pp. 274–5; Simms, *Jacobite Ireland*, p. 33.

[50] Barnard, 'Culture of the Cork settlers', p. 343; R. Caulfield (ed.), *Journal of the Very Rev. Rowland Davies* (Camden Society, first series, LXVIII, London, 1857), pp. 60–1; S. W. Singer (ed.), *Correspondence of Henry Hyde, earl of Clarendon* (2 vols., London, 1828), II, pp. 239–47.

[51] Barnard, 'Lawyers and the law', pp. 264, 271; C. Kenny, 'The exclusion of Catholics from the legal profession in Ireland, 1537–1829', *IHS*, 25 (1987), pp. 349–55; T. P. Power, 'Conversions among the legal profession in Ireland in the eighteenth century', in D. Hogan and W. N. Osborough (eds.), *Brehons, serjeants and attorneys* (Dublin, 1990), pp. 153–74.

[52] J. Childs, *The army, James II and the Glorious Revolution* (Manchester, 1980), pp. 56–82; Miller, 'Tyrconnell and James II's Irish policy', pp. 813, 818–19; Simms, *Jacobite Ireland*, pp. 33–4.

[53] Warwickshire CRO, CR 136/B280; J. C. Beckett, 'The Irish armed forces 1660–1685', in J. Bossy and P. J. Jupp (eds.), *Essays presented to Michael Roberts* (Belfast, 1976), pp. 41–53; *Sr St John Brodrick's vindication of himself* ([London], 1690), pp. 22–3; K. P. Ferguson, 'The army in Ireland

associations, akin to those of Elizabethan England, Valois France or Covenanting Scotland defined the trustworthy community in terms of exclusive Protestantism.[54] After 1660, however, the militia, because liked by former Cromwellians, and because it necessitated regular gatherings of county notables and freeholders, seemed, at least to the king and Ormond, to constitute an embryonic state within a state. The Stuarts, and their auxiliaries in Ireland, preferred the regular army. Its relationship with the militia was confused: sometimes complementary, occasionally competitive. The Irish Protestants welcomed the army so long as they could command, and be protected by, it; they resented its cost, its being used outside Ireland, its unruliness and its Scots and English officers. From 1649 a disproportionately large army was stationed in Ireland, more often for English rather than Irish needs. In the 1660s and 1670s, Ormond annexed much of the officer-corps to his patronage empire, to the detriment of discipline and preparedness.[55] By the 1680s, Ormond, as his hold on royal favour relaxed, reluctantly and belatedly purged the 'Cromwellian' veterans. Few of those who were displaced had served in the 1650s; they were 'Cromwellian' only in the sense that their titles to lands derived from the Interregnum or that they wistfully remembered Cromwellian stringency towards the Irish. When, in 1686, the new commander, Tyrconnell, remodelled the army more ruthlessly, he turned against the Protestants the principle on which the forces had been reconstituted since 1649: that religion was the surest guide to reliability. By the autumn of 1688, 90 per cent of the army was Catholic. Ormond, the touchy expert on Irish military matters, lost face to his ancient adversary, Tyrconnell, and amongst those clients whom he could no longer promote.[56] Old and set in his habits of loyalty, he merely

from the Restoration to the Act of Union' (unpublished PhD thesis, TCD, 1981), pp. 9–19; R. Loeber and H. Murtagh, 'The reorganization of the Irish militia in 1678–81: documents from Birr Castle', *Irish Sword* (forthcoming); J. G. A. Prim, 'Documents connected with the city of Kilkenny militia . . . ', *Proceedings and Transactions of the Kilkenny and S. E. of Ireland Archaeological Society*, 3 (1854–5), pp. 236–41.

[54] J. C. Beckett, 'The confederation of Kilkenny reviewed', in his *Confrontations*, pp. 47–66; P. Collinson, 'The monarchical republic of Queen Elizabeth I', *Bulletin of the John Rylands Library*, 66 (1986–7), 395–422; E. M. Furgol, 'The military and ministers as agents of Presbyterian imperialism in England and Ireland, 1640–1648', in J. Dwyer, R. A. Mason and A. Murdoch (eds.), *New perspectives on the politics and culture of early modern Scotland* (Edinburgh, 1982), pp. 95–115; M. Greengrass, *France in the age of Henri IV* (London, 1984), pp. 47–56; J. Robertson, *The Scottish Enlightenment and the militia issue* (Edinburgh, 1985), pp. 5–6.

[55] Staffordshire CRO, D 1287/18/3, Lord Robartes to O. Bridgeman, 6, 19, 21, 22, 23, 30 October 1669; Beckett, 'The Irish armed forces', pp. 41–5; Ferguson, 'The army in Ireland', pp. 9–19.

[56] Bodl, Carte MSS 220, fo. 250v; BL, Add. MSS 15,892, fos. 178, 185–85v; 28,938, fo. 289; Ferguson, 'The army in Ireland', p. 17; Miller, 'Tyrconnell and James II's Irish policy', pp. 817–19.

grumbled. Others, led by cashiered Protestants who were often descendants of those who had battled in Ireland in the 1640s – Coote, King, Gore, St George, Boyle and Hamilton – travelled to London or Holland, where they descanted on the rowdiness of Tyrconnell's recruits and the plight of 'the poor English of Ireland'. In England, they joined other refugees, including the barristers, who were soliciting to save Protestant Ireland.[57] Those former officers who stayed in Ireland, frightened by what they took to be the aggression of the Catholics, channelled their military skills into local defensive associations. Thereby the martial traditions of the settlers, most recently directed towards the militia, were preserved (see chapter 11 above).[58] But, as in the 1640s, so in the fresh warfare, the inadequacy of Irish Protestant defences was exposed. Once more Protestant Ireland had to be delivered by armies from outside the island, at a price which included the further extension of English control.

After the 1690s the military continued to be important to how England used Ireland; and in the culture of indigenous Protestant society. Yet, if eighteenth-century Irish Protestants displayed a 'fortress mentality', the large army affected social life and the local economy more than administration or *police*. The vigilant, as in England and Scotland, watched lest a standing army encroach on the civil law.[59] Observers mocked the fondness of Irish Protestants for the militia, both because it was more 'national' than the army, and because gentlemen loved 'having the titles of colonel, major or captain joined to their gentility'.[60] It is difficult to know if the regular musters, parades and exercises retarded, or reflected, the permeation of newer standards of civility and public duty. Leases granted by the Boyles in Munster late in Queen Anne's reign still obliged the tenant to furnish an

[57] NLI, MS 2498/371; BL, Add. MSS 11,759, fo. 92; 28,938, fos. 314–15; *Cal. S P, domestic, 1689–90*, p. 379; Childs, *The army, James II and the Glorious Revolution*, pp. 72–5; Ferguson, 'The army in Ireland', p. 25; P. G. Melvin, 'The Irish army and the Revolution of 1688', *Irish Sword*, 9 (1969–70), pp. 295–7.
[58] NA, M 2541/65; NLI, MS 8646, letter of Neave to Lanesborough; Royal Irish Academy, MS 24 G 4/43, 45; 24 G 5/26; 24 G 6/3; 24 G 7/72; TCD, MS 749/64, 612, 613, 636, 674, 1288; Lambeth Palace Library, MS 3152, 28 and 30 January 1689; Worcester College, Oxford, Clarke Papers, MS 7.8, orders of 3 and 14 July 1691, 7 September 1691; Warwickshire CRO, CR 136/B 291, B 292; HMC, *Thirteenth Report*, appendix, part v, *The manuscripts of the House of Lords, 1690–91* (London, 1892), pp. 161, 181–2; W. G. Wood-Martin, *History of Sligo, county and town* (3 vols., Dublin, 1882–92), III, pp. 101–5.
[59] NA, M 2453/16 November 1697; BL, Add. MSS 38,150, fo. 127v; T. Bartlett, 'Army and society in eighteenth-century Ireland', in Maguire (ed.), *Kings in conflict*, pp. 173–84; Ferguson, 'The army in Ireland', pp. 52–6; J. O'Donovan, 'The militia in Munster 1715–78', in G. O'Brien (ed.), *Parliament, politics and people* (Dublin, 1989), pp. 31–47; Robertson, *The Scottish Enlightenment*, pp. 15–16; L. G. Schwoerer, *"No standing armies!" the antimilitary ideology in seventeenth-century England* (Baltimore, 1974).
[60] Christ Church, Oxford, Wake MSS 12, fo. 370.

CONCLUSION   281

armed horseman and mount.⁶¹ By then this requirement may have
atrophied into an empty formula. On the other hand, Protestant history
and rumours of Jacobite invasions attested to an enduring Catholic danger.
By the eighteenth century, the militia institutionalized the defensive and
companionable aspects of the earlier associations. It was no longer the sole,
or necessarily the most popular, organization to do so: masonic lodges,
hunts, societies dedicated to moral and material betterment (or its
overthrow), Hanover clubs and other friendly societies all catered to
conviviality and the vanities.⁶² But, unlike many of these other, civilian
groups, the militia excluded all but Protestants and could, when required,
serve practical uses. Through the pervasiveness of the militia, and perhaps
through the ubiquity of the officers of the army, the demarcation between
civil and military society was blurred, but not, so far as we can judge, with
any resultant militarization of English government over Ireland. The
eighteenth-century portraits of the menfolk from Irish Protestant families,
peacocks in their vivid uniforms, suggest how the values of military service
permeated this community.⁶³ As the population of Protestant Ireland grew,
and with it the numbers of expectant cadets, the sparse openings offered by
the professions and bureaucracy forced many to seek the prestige and pay
earned from the trade of arms. In following this career, Irish planters
resembled members of landed élites throughout Europe, including the
uprooted Irish Catholics, for whom soldiering offered the best future.⁶⁴

                                         IV

Much that perplexed or upset Irish Protestants after 1641 – a country that
twice dissolved into vicious fighting and contests over who should own land,

---

⁶¹ Cork Archives Institute, Doherty MSS, u/137, box 30, A/4, lease 12 May 1713; NLI, MS 6144;
   Dickson, 'Cork region', I, p. 147; *Seasonable advice to Protestants* (Cork, 1745); C. Smith, *The ancient
   and present state of the county and city of Cork*, second edition (2 vols., Dublin, 1774), I, pp. 58–9.
⁶² PRONI, Shannon MSS, D 2707/C1/1; Cork Archives Institute, U/177, copy of the minute
   book of the Cork city masonic lodge 1726–1731; E. Bowen, *Bowen's court* (London, 1942),
   pp. 97–103; National Gallery of Ireland, *Acquisitions 1986–1988* (Dublin, 1988), pp. 68–71;
   E. C. Nelson, 'The Dublin Florists' Club in the mid-eighteenth century', *Garden History*, 10
   (1982), pp. 142–8.
⁶³ R. Ffolliott, 'The unmistakeable hand of Frederick Buck', *Irish Arts Review*, 1 (1984), pp. 46–50;
   A. Wilton and A. Lyles (eds.), *The great age of British watercolours 1750–1880* (London, 1993),
   plate 56; miniatures at Innis Beg, County Cork.
⁶⁴ L. M. Cullen, 'Catholic social classes under the penal laws', in Power and Whelan (eds.),
   Endurance and emergence, pp. 64–5, 72–6; G. Holmes, *Augustan England: professions, state and society
   1660–1730* (London, 1982), pp. 262–74; M. G. McLaughlin and C. Warner, *The Wild Geese: the
   Irish brigades of France and Spain* (London, 1980); J. C. O'Callaghan, *History of the Irish brigades in the
   service of France* (Glasgow, 1870); J. B. Shaw, *The management of Scottish society 1707–1764* (Edinburgh,
   1983), pp. 6, 8–9.

hold offices and enforce the law – led back to the incontrovertible evidence
of religious difference and conflict. Sometimes the familiar denominations
of Catholic and Protestant served as an easy shorthand, especially after 1641
when race and confession had seemingly converged to rivet the Irish to
popery and the English and Scots to Protestantism.[65] Moreover the divisive
forces released by conquest, dispossession and legalized degradation,
tended to follow and intensify sectarian fissures. Religion could plausibly
explain both the outbreak and character of the wars of the 1640s and
1689–91, and the tempestuous politics of the intervening years. Thus, in
1663, the looming parliamentary storm over the land settlement seemed so
menacing because 'the controversy can be orated to them [the members of
Parliament] to be betwixt English and Protestant and Irish and papist'.[66]
The terminology unfortunately obscured, as may have been intended, the
elision of both religious and ethnic categories. Old English and even Old
Irish – Barrys, Butlers, Fitzgeralds, Frenches and O'Briens – did convert to
Protestantism; numerous Catholics hung on as landowners after 1660; and
newcomers were lost to Catholicism. If the looseness and leakiness of
the sectarian groupings heartened those, from the king and Ormond
downwards, who hoped to build a loyalist coalition in Ireland, based on
the sense of Englishness and irrespective of religious persuasion, they
frightened others for whom the automatic equation of popery with
treachery offered one of the few verities in a world of flux. For many
Protestant analysts, religion best told what had gone wrong in seventeenth-
century Ireland. Continentally trained priests preached rebellion;
Protestants simply because of their faith had been attacked and had seen
their sacred objects violated. Again, after 1685, the vitality and visibility of
the Catholic clergy, impatient to recover church buildings and to harry
Protestant ministers, confirmed the religious inspiration behind the new
affrays. The killing in the churchyard at Kilmallock of the incumbent in
1685 recalled the atrocities familiar from the popular accounts of the 1640s,
and heralded the attacks on Protestant clergy and their churches so
important in 1689[67] (but so little noticed by later historians).[68]

[65] A. Clarke, 'Colonial identity in early-seventeenth century Ireland', in T.W. Moody (ed.) *Nationality and the pursuit of national independence. Historical Studies* XI (Belfast, 1978), pp. 57–71.
[66] Bodl., Clarendon State Papers 79, fo. 100v.
[67] Abbey Leix, de Vesci MSS, H/1, 7 August 1685; HMC, *Ormonde*, ns, VII, pp. 346–7, 364.
[68] Abbey Leix, de Vesci MSS, G/7; PRONI, Dio 4/152, items 1 and 2; Armagh Public Library, Dopping MSS I, 82–5, 87, 89, 91, 92, 98, 108, 109, 111, 112, 114–28, 133–7; Birr Castle, County Offaly, Rosse MSS, a/23, 28 November 1689; Cambridge University Library, Add. MSS I, 95: TCD, MSS 1995–2008/70; St Carthage's, Lismore, County Waterford, chapter book 1663–1829, fo. 23v; BL, Egerton MSS 917, fo. 93; Lambeth Palace Library, MSS 3152, after 9 December 1688; M. Coen, *The wardenship of Galway* (Galway, 1984), p. 21; M. Gilmore,

CONCLUSION 283

Since the majority of Irish Protestants believed themselves to be trapped in inevitable combat with the Catholics, they regretted that the Stuarts, from the 1620s onwards, had not hobbled the papists. Until the 1650s, the one law against the personnel and performance of Catholicism in Ireland was the 1560 Act of Uniformity, but it was enforced only patchily before 1641.[69] Matters changed under the usurper. In 1653, the Dublin government by proclamation extended to Ireland the provisions of an English law of 1585, and required Catholic clergy either to depart or face death. In 1657 a second proclamation insisted that the papal supremacy be repudiated. Severe as these measures sounded, and harsh as were the penalties meted out to the unfortunates who were captured, official rhetoric, intentions and the actuality did not always match. The 1653 order, for example, allowed the Irish council to license priests to stay. Thus, as in the past, the rulers in Dublin and the provinces retained discretion, and once the worst retributive spasm had passed, eased the persecution.[70] Already in 1658 some priests benefited; and in the spring of 1660, the primate himself, O'Reilly, hovered in the capital in the hope of guiding events.[71] Charles II's restoration, with the legal acts of the Interregnum void, presaged better treatment for the Catholics. Protestants, assembled in the Dublin Parliament, countered by asking for laws to continue and extend the Cromwellian severity.[72] Ormond, obedient to the king's and his own instincts, for the moment resisted. Nevertheless, waves of anti-Catholic frenzy – the after-shock of English and European upheavals – obliged the Irish administration to renew measures to expel or silence priests in 1673 and 1678.[73]

'Anthony Dopping and the Church of Ireland, 1685–1695', (unpublished MA thesis, Queen's University Belfast, 1988), pp. 46–55; King, *Diary*, pp. 70–2; William King, *The state of the Protestants of Ireland under the late King James's government* (London, 1691), pp. 213–15.

[69] Clarke and Edwards, 'Pacification, plantation and the catholic question', pp. 191–2, 212, 216–17, 224–5; Lennon, *The lords of Dublin*, pp. 48, 101, 168, 176–7, 183, 196.

[70] BL, Lansdowne MSS 822, fo. 266; Barnard, *Cromwellian Ireland*, pp. 172–3, 180–1; P. J. Corish, 'Two seventeenth-century proclamations against the Catholic clergy', *Archivium Hibernicum*, 39 (1984), pp. 53–7; B. Millett (ed.), 'Calendar of volume 14 of the Fondo di Vienna in propaganda archives, pt. 2', *Collectanea Hibernica*, 30 (1988), pp. 34–5; Steele (ed.), *Proclamations*, ii, nos. 508, 580 (Ireland).

[71] Pearse St Public Library, Gilbert MSS 219, p. 339; T. O Fiaich, 'Edmund O'Reilly, archbishop of Armagh', in Franciscan Fathers (eds.), *Father Luke Wadding commemorative volume* (Dublin, 1957), pp. 192–3.

[72] NA, M 2458/27; NLI, MS 8643/7; BL, Egerton MSS 2618, fo. 100; Bodl., Carte MSS 220, fos. 161, 177v; *Cal. S P Ire., 1663–5*, pp. 65, 66, 91; *Commons Journal, Ireland*, i, pp. 638, 649, 651, 652.

[73] NA, Wyche MSS, I/30; NLI, MS 2490/1; Bodl., Add. MSS C 34, fos. 1v, 38v, 65; Victoria and Albert Museum, Orrery MSS, ii, fos. 31, 35, 41, 47v; Petworth, Orrery MSS, general series, 28, 22 June 1672, 27 October 1673, 24 February 1673[4]; W. P. Burke, *The Irish priests of the penal times (1660–1760)* (Waterford, 1914), pp. 38–41, 66–7; Steele (ed.), *Proclamations*, ii, nos. 844, 845, 850 (Ireland).

The lack of an Irish Protestant Parliament between 1666 and 1692 postponed a comprehensive penal code until after 1695. Then, most notoriously, the Williamite finished the Cromwellian revolution. Furthermore, the mixed motives behind the earlier, also confused the later, campaign. If persecution was to clear Ireland of popish ecclesiastics so as to open it to Protestant missionaries, the latter continued to argue over whether to preach in order to convert or to preach only to the converted. Introversion and inertia, always strong in the Church of Ireland, afflicted its leaders under Charles II. Only in the 1680s did a younger generation tackle an assertive and reinvigorated Catholicism and burnish the reputations of their own local heroes, Bedell and Ussher. From this group, toughened in the Dublin of the 1680s, came the leaders of the 1690s who would back the repressive code with an ambitious, though largely vain, assault on ignorance, irreligion and popery.[74]

Anti-Catholic crusaders, such as Anglesey and Orrery, berated Ormond for his seeming indifference to the threat of popery. In fact, Ormond feigned nonchalance while puzzling how to rule a country in which at least 80 per cent of the inhabitants practised a religion, until 1685, different from that of their monarch. Catholicism, as internally fragmented as Protestantism, encouraged hopes that a group, Gallican in training and outlook, could be attached to a Stuart party which encompassed Protestants and papists.[75] In the 1660s, as in the 1640s, those happy to prefer the king's to the pope's temporal authority were easily outnumbered and overawed by the uncompromising. Ormond, as a result of his known dealings with priests and the failure of his strategy, was denounced, usually by those who also fulminated against how he had profited from the Restoration and protected his Catholic kinsfolk. Yet Ormond faced, even if he never solved, the fundamental weakness of English rule in Ireland, and explored what realists proposed in 1690 and in the eighteenth century: modest gestures towards reliable Catholics, especially those willing to put loyalty to their English monarch before that to the pope.[76] Ormond's courage in addressing this awkward issue contrasted with the deviousness of his strident critics, who, for all their anti-Catholic rhetoric, also cultivated

[74] Barnard, 'Reforming Irish manners', pp. 805, 838; Barnard, 'Protestants and the Irish language, c. 1675–1725', Journal of Ecclesiastical History, 44 (1993), pp. 243–72.
[75] J. Brennan, 'A Gallican interlude in Ireland', Irish Theological Quarterly, 24 (1957), pp. 219–37, 283–309; B. Millett, The Irish Franciscans 1651–1665 (Rome, 1964), pp. 418–63; P. Walsh, The history and vindication of the loyal formulary of the Irish Remonstrance (n.p., 1674).
[76] Royal Irish Academy, MS 24 G 6/33; Victoria and Albert Museum, Ormond MSS, I, fos. 65a, 70; II, fos. 23v–4; Staffordshire CRO, Bridgeman MSS, D 1287/18/3, Bridgeman to Robartes, 18 December 1669; HMC, Dartmouth, I, p. 14; J. G. Simms, 'Williamite peace tactics, 1690–1', in his War and politics, p. 200.

papists. So it was that Orrery's unremitting hatred of the pope and all his engines did not inhibit social (and probably political) dealings with the future Tyrconnell, or the use of Catholic spies.[77] Anglesey's rabid anti-popery was compromised by his daughters' marriages into two prominent Irish Catholic dynasties.[78] Orrery and Anglesey differed from Ormond in using guile and dissimulation to conceal these dangerous intrigues from the anxious Protestants for whom they spoke. Thereby they ran the risk of being unmasked as hypocrites. In addition, this wide gap between private suppleness and public obduracy lends credibility to those who contended that the prospects of material and political gains alone prompted these politicians to mouth robust anti-Catholic opinions. Undoubtedly the settlers like, and led by, Orrery and Anglesey, flourished the more the Catholics were systematically depressed. Yet we should not under-estimate how fiercely many detested Catholicism, both as erroneous and anti-Christian dogma and as a subversive political doctrine.[79] The later Stuarts and their deputies in Ireland resisted the clamour from the 1640s to the 1690s for the Catholics to be definitively disabled, but, by doing so, estranged much of Protestant Ireland.

The penal laws, first sketched in the 1650s and then enacted after 1695, would be applied so flexibly and with so much discretion that some have doubted that they did constitute a coherent code.[80] What mattered to their architects was to have in place safeguards which, when danger again threatened, could be activated. Those who had agreed with the Stuarts and Ormond in questioning the need for such measures, and who had successfully blocked them between 1661 and 1688, though brushed aside in the vengeful euphoria of the 1690s, had their successors in the eighteenth century: at first Tories, who not only queried the efficacy and morality of persecution, but who also viewed Protestant dissenters and republicans, sheltering now among the Whigs, as the worse threat. This divisive issue, of

---

[77] Chatsworth, Cork's diary, 1 March 1668[9], 2 May 1672; Pearse St Public Library, Gilbert MSS 207, p. 15; BL, Stowe MSS 206, fo. 314v; 210, fos. 394, 396; Victoria and Albert Museum, Orrery MSS, II, fos. 47v, 49, 54; T. C. Barnard, 'Land and the limits of loyalty: the second earl of Cork and the first earl of Burlington (1612–1698)', in T. C. Barnard and J. Clark (eds.), *Lord Burlington: architecture, art and life* (London, 1994); Hutton, *Charles the second*, p. 237.
[78] Pearse St Public Library, Gilbert MSS 207, pp. 10–11, 28; Ohlmeyer, *Civil war and restoration*, p. 272.
[79] NLI, MS 2181/13; BL, Add. MSS 4816; Victoria and Albert Museum, Orrery MSS, II, fo. 3; Barnard, 'Crises of identity', pp. 73–5; Barnard, 'Irish images of Cromwell', p. 188; D. Greene, 'The authenticity of Anglesey's memoirs', *Bodleian Library Quarterly*, 9 (1978), pp. 351–7.
[80] Connolly, *Religion, law and power*, pp. 263–313; Cullen, 'Catholics and the penal laws', pp. 23–36.

how best to treat the Catholic majority, continued to animate Irish politics throughout much of the eighteenth century.[81]

Connected with these disagreements were the vexed issues of loyalty and of the nature of Ireland's relationship with England and the English sovereign. Reconquest after 1649 and 1689 ushered in, temporarily at least, closer English control, manifest in the presence of a large English army and also in England deciding Ireland's future. The land settlement, dragged out over most of the century, evolved in Ireland and England. A starker reminder of English power came in 1691, when an act of the Westminster Parliament announced that whoever it recognized as ruler of England should, *ipso facto*, rule Ireland. Such English authoritarianism has been contrasted with the happier situation in 1660 when, it is suggested, the meeting of the Dublin Convention enabled Irish Protestants to invite back Charles II as their king.[82] The absence of a Protestant Parliament in 1689–91 certainly denied Ireland any formal constitutional role in changing monarchs. Informally, however, the sizeable and well-organized exile community in and around London, clever lobbyists and the followers who flocked to William III's colours while he campaigned in Ireland, gave members of the Protestant élite ample opportunities to express their preferences and to influence policy.[83] Furthermore, the role of the Irish Protestants in Charles II's return was negligible; the Convention in May 1660 did little more than proclaim, somewhat belatedly, Charles' hereditary succession to his father in 1649.[84] As for the English tendency after 1689 to arrogate to itself all important Irish matters, this was checked by the regular Dublin Parliaments after 1692. Notwithstanding

[81] Barnard, 'The uses of 23 October 1641', pp. 903–8; T. Bartlett, *The fall and rise of the Irish nation* (Dublin, 1992); D. W. Hayton, 'Ireland and the English ministers, 1707–1716' (unpublished D Phil thesis, Oxford University, 1975), pp. 123–39, 272–93; M. Wall, *Catholic Ireland in the eighteenth century* (Dublin, 1989).
[82] Kelly, 'Ireland and the Glorious Revolution', pp. 163–4.
[83] One contemporary estimated the size of the Irish community in London in 1689 at 5,000. *Animadversions on the proposal for sending back the nobility and gentry of Ireland* (London, 1690), pp. 32–3; R. Bulkeley, *The proposal for sending back the nobility and gentry of Ireland* (London, 1690); Sr St John *Brodrick's vindication*; Caulfield (ed.), *Journal of Rowland Davies*, pp. 60–1; R. Cox, *Hibernia Anglicana* (2 parts, London, 1689–90); D. W. Hayton, 'The propaganda war', in Maguire (ed.), *Kings in conflict*, pp. 106–21; Singer (ed.), *Clarendon correspondence*, II, pp. 239–47, 273, 275, 281–2, 286, 288, 290, 292.
[84] The proclamation, declaring 'whereas by the death of Charles I, the imperial crowns of England, Scotland, France and Ireland did then immediately, solely and rightfully, by inherent birthright and lawful and undoubted succession, descend and come to' Charles II, is dated 14 May 1660. It exists in an apparently unique copy in BL, pressmark 1851 b 48. On 1 May 1660, the Convention had dissociated itself from Charles I's trial. *A Declaration of the General Convention of Ireland, expressing their detestation of the unjust proceedings against the late king . . .* (London, 1660). Cf. Bodl., Carte MSS 44, fo. 664; T. Birch (ed.), *A collection of the state papers of John Thurloe* (7 vols., London, 1742), VII, p. 911.

English pronouncements, the definition of and demarcations between English and Irish competences remained uncertain, and would continue to be disputed until the Act of Union in 1800 apparently closed further debate.

Nevertheless, the act of 1691 has been taken as revealing a process which had gathered pace since 1660, when policy and appointments were increasingly settled in London, and in accord with English priorities. In the 1670s and 1680s, for example, Ireland's defences and finances were more closely overseen from England.[85] If a few of the resulting structures and procedures were new, the essence of the relationship that they articulated – Irish dependence on England – was not. Appointments, from the Irish viceroyalty down to humbler posts in the ports, garrisons and provinces had always been distributed as parts of English patronage. The Irish, knowing this, had quickly learnt the game: in the decades after 1640 they played it, perhaps in larger numbers and with greater finesse than ever before. Like the Scots, the Irish, both Catholic and Protestant, became familiar at court and in the purlieus of Westminster, adepts of political and administrative *arcana*. When they returned to Ireland, much remained to translate patents or promises into concrete benefits. The hazards and haphazardness of this ill-defined but essentially triangular relationship between London, Dublin and the Irish provinces, irritated Irish suitors. Most rounded on feeble patrons. Some, however, formulated sweeping critiques, in which they begged for a return to the rigid rules which, it was claimed, had once governed dealings with Ireland and between the English and Irish governments. The truculent demanded that legislative and executive sovereignty be returned to Ireland, with, for example, a Parliament assembling in Dublin in 1659–61 or in the 1670s; and that viceroys, officials, judges and litigants should not be overruled constantly from London. But, for all their learning, the constitutional theorists wrote for adventitious and topical purposes. Ireland's legislative independence, publicly upheld in the 1640s by the Catholic Old English, by 1660 was proclaimed by Protestant apologists.[86] In the changed atmosphere of the 1670s, Richard Talbot and his lawyer friends, in working in London for a revision of the recent land

---

[85] J. Childs, *The army of Charles II* (London, 1976), pp. 205–6; Dickson, *New foundations*, pp. 14–17; S. Egan, 'Finance and the government of Ireland, 1660–85' (unpublished PhD thesis, TCD, 1983), II, pp. 144–94; Kelly, 'Ireland and the Glorious Revolution', pp. 166–7.

[86] Barnard, 'Planters and policies', pp. 65–7; C. E. J. Caldicott (ed.), 'Patrick Darcy, an argument', in *Camden Miscellany*, XXXI (London, 1992), pp. 197–320; A. Clarke, 'Colonial constitutional attitudes in Ireland, 1640–1660', *Proceedings, Royal Irish Academy*, 90, section C (1990), pp. 357–75; L. O'Malley, 'Patrick Darcy, Galway lawyer and politician', in D. G. O'Cearbhaill (ed.), *Galway: town and gown 1484–1984* (Galway, 1984), pp. 90–109; J. G. Simms, *William Molyneux of Dublin* (Dublin, 1982), pp. 103–5.

acts, argued for the rights of the English Parliament and monarch to conclude the controversy, and manoeuvred the Protestant agents into asserting the powers of the Dublin Parliament.[87]

The numerous inconveniences and ambiguities in the Anglo-Irish relationship provoked monotonous grumbles, but few, either papist or Protestant, wanted to sunder the tie. Indeed there were those who would tighten it, through a formal union which, as in the 1650s, would entitle Irish members to sit at Westminster in an imperial Parliament.[88] Throughout the century, if new settlers chafed against an indifferent or hostile England, they had no alternative ruler in view. After all, between 1638 and 1642, it was not they, but their English and Scottish co-religionists and the Irish papists who had rebelled; similarly, in 1688–9, as Dr Gillespie has recently reminded us, many still adhered to their English sovereign, though a Catholic, especially after he travelled to Ireland (the first monarch to do so since Richard II).[89] Irish Protestants usually submitted, hopeful that their deference might dispel the suspicions of disaffection and slow James's catholicizing impulses.[90] Only when new, and seemingly sympathetic, English régimes offered better to protect their interests, did many Irish Protestants switch: in the later 1640s to Parliament and to Cromwell; in 1689–90, to William III. All, turncoats and loyalists alike, accepted a continuing and intimate English link. Accordingly, to seek in the odd acts of bravado, such as some speeches in the 1660 Convention, or in the more sustained expositions of the lawyers Domville and Molyneux, a proto-nationalism that leads directly to the revolutionary 1790s is to misunderstand the circumstances and attitudes of the seventeenth-century Protestant community. Nor, we should stress, did full-blooded unionism attract many. Rather there was a resigned recognition that Protestant Ireland, created and saved thanks to the

---

[87] Bodl., Carte MSS 69, fo. 369; HMC, *Ormonde*, ns, VII, p. 469. Cf. 'A series of eight anonymous and confidential letters to James II about the state of Ireland', *Notes and Queries*, sixth series, 5, 122 (1882), pp. 361, 402; 123 (1882), pp. 2–4.

[88] Bowood, Petty MSS, B3, B11, B17, B66; F32; Royal Irish Academy, MS 24 G 1/41; Barnard, 'Planters and policies', pp. 64–5; J. Kelly, 'The origins of the Act of Union: an examination of Unionist opinion in Britain and Ireland, 1650–1800', *IHS*, 25 (1986), pp. 236–63.

[89] Gillespie, 'The Irish Protestants and James II', pp. 124–33; Kelly, 'Ireland and the Glorious Revolution', p. 177 and n. 65; J. I. Maguire, 'The Church of Ireland and the Glorious Revolution', in A. Cosgrove and D. McCartney (eds.), *Studies in Irish history presented to R. D. Edwards* (Dublin, 1979), pp. 137–49.

[90] Abbey Leix, G/1, MSS sermons of John Vesey, on Psalm 82:6, 7 and on Luke 12:32; Armagh Public Library, Dopping MSS, 1, 90: Cork University Library, U/55, letters of 28 September 1685 and 19 June 1686; Hovell MSS, private collection in Dublin, letters of 24 February 1684[5], 17 and 28 July 1685; Barnard, 'Culture of the Cork settlers', pp. 347–9; E. Wetenhall, 'The Christian law of the sword', in his *Hexapla Jacobae* (London, 1686), with separate pagination, p. 41.

expeditions of 1649 and 1689, would survive only with English backing. No alternative ruler beckoned; and, environed still by a massive Catholic preponderance, the Irish Protestants could not aspire to form an independent state. Instead they settled for colonizing the state which England had established and preserved for them. So they worked, with skill and gusto, locally and in London, to smooth away the roughnesses. Thanks to their successes they soon assumed that they had made the society in which they lived. Irish Protestants, unless and until they could unite with their Catholic neighbours to separate from England, had to obey their English overlords. This accommodation, sometimes contingent and half-hearted, recalled similar deals struck between *anciens régimes* and provincial élites elsewhere in Europe.[91] Thus, while patriots railed against the English interference, the more regular meetings of the Dublin Parliament, together with the growth of the professions, bureaucracy and armed forces, consoled Irish Protestants for any loss of Ireland's notional autonomy. Much of the day-to-day running of the island – and the profits from it – fell to the Protestants, and soon gave them an ascendancy over the country.

The corollary of the Protestants' military and political triumphs was Catholic defeat. Yet, the resilience and regenerative capacity of the Catholic community, and notably of the Old English of the Pale, dismayed Protestant onlookers. This continuing political potency owed much to the warmth of Charles II's and James II's regard for former affable companions in exile. However, sentiment alone was seldom proof against the more brutal imperatives behind later Stuart conduct, so that, for example, Richard Talbot swung regularly in and out of favour.[92] Solid benefits and ready access to the court, with the expectation of more once James succeeded, locked the Old English into their usual loyalty to the English monarchy. What wrecked this strategy by 1691, as it had in 1649, was that their sovereign ceased to rule England. On each occasion, passionate loyalists forsook Ireland and followed their rightful king to the continent. The calculation of those who had acted thus in the 1650s was correct: Charles II returned, and they – in some measure – were rewarded. Those who took the same route after 1691 could not know that neither James nor his heirs would return. Even so, the appeal and extent of Irish Jacobitism,

[91] W. H. Beik, *Absolutism and society in seventeenth-century France: state power and provincial aristocracy in Languedoc* (Cambridge, 1985); R. Mettam, *Power and faction in Louis XIV's France* (Oxford, 1988).
[92] Pearse St Public Library, Gilbert MSS 207, p. 26; Arnold, *Restoration land settlement*, pp. 72–3, 122–3, 128, 139; P. W. Sergeant, *Little Jennings and fighting Dick Talbot* (2 vols., London, 1913). Talbot's career and connections would repay fresh investigation.

and its embodiment of the traditional thinking of the Old English, are only slowly being investigated.[93]

Some Irish Catholics, in contrast to their Protestant counterparts, could imagine a future outside the orbit of England. Particularly among the Old Irish, loss, long and penurious exile, service in foreign armies or life in continental ports severed any residual ties of affection for England and introduced the refugees to those who might help them back to what they had forfeited. Rebellion in Ireland could succeed, or be suppressed, only with outside aid. The European powers, like England, cared little for Ireland except as it might contribute to their larger designs. Both France and Spain had occasionally fished in these turbulent waters, and, as their own contest reached its climacteric, did so with zest in the 1640s (see chapter 5 above). As a result, Ireland, having first been drawn into, and contributed to, the war of Charles I's three kingdoms, became part of the Thirty Years War, thereby inaugurating what Dr Ohlmeyer has styled a 'War of Five Kingdoms'.[94] Once more, in the 1680s, when the continental struggle between Louis XIV and William of Orange was renewed, England, Scotland and Ireland were soon pulled in.

Periodically in the sixteenth and seventeenth centuries, those Irish keen to cut loose from England, negotiated with the Papacy, the kings of France and Spain and the duke of Lorraine. Earlier the Dutch Revolt had proved the value (as also the perils) of the protective overlordship of a foreign prince.[95] The irredentists' overtures in the 1640s complicated choices and embittered an already fractious Catholic community; they resulted neither in an independent, nor a Spanish or French, Ireland, but better terms for the vanquished when they elected to soldier on the continent.[96]

The eclipse of Spain after 1659 ushered in a strange world less congenial or helpful to skilled Irish diplomatists. Until the 1680s, the Protestant Dutch had borne the brunt of Louis XIV's aggression; then the emperor, Leopold I, awoke to the French design of universal monarchy. Some Irish Catholics,

---

[93] See C. G. Buttimer, 'Gaelic life and contemporary literature in Cork, 1700–1840', in O'Flanagan and Buttimer, *Cork: history and society*, pp. 585–654; Kelly, 'A light to the blind', pp. 431–62; P. Melvin, 'Irish soldiers and plotters in Williamite England', 3 parts, *Irish Sword*, 13 (1978–9), pp. 256–67, 353–68; 14 (1980–1), pp. 271–86; B. Ó Buachalla, 'Irish Jacobite poetry', *The Irish Review*, 12 (1992), pp. 40–9; Ó Buachalla, 'The making of a Cork Jacobite', in O'Flanagan and Buttimer (eds.), *Cork: history and society*, pp. 469–98.

[94] Ohlmeyer, *Civil war and restoration*, pp. 152–73.

[95] A. C. Duke, 'From king and country to king or country? Loyalty and treason in the revolt of the Netherlands', *Transactions, Royal Historical Society*, fifth series, 32 (1982), pp. 113–35; M. P. Holt, *The Duke of Anjou and the politique struggle in the Wars of Religion* (Cambridge, 1986), pp. 93–184.

[96] Brennan, 'A Gallican interlude', pp. 219–37, 283–309; H. F. Kearney, 'Ecclesiastical politics and the counter-reformation in Ireland, 1618–1648', *Journal of Ecclesiastical History*, 11 (1960), pp. 202–12; J. Lowe, 'Charles I and the confederation of Kilkenny', *IHS*, 14 (1964–5), pp. 1–19.

accustomed to the Habsburgs as protectors, sought the Emperor's help.[97] For most, however, France remained the more familiar and useful assistant. The difficulty for Irish Catholics was that France's generally friendly alliances with the later Stuarts diminished the likelihood of French backing for Irish particularism. Thus, when Louis entered the Irish war of 1689–91, he worked for James II's restoration. Dreams of an independent or Catholic Ireland, in so far as France supported them, had to be embodied in a Stuart ruler. During the late 1680s, in contrast to the 1640s, as Dr Hayton has argued, Old English and Old Irish did not pursue violently opposed policies.[98] It would seem that both groupings, owing to the unpropitious international scene, had to focus their hopes on James II, whether as king of Ireland alone, or returned to all three of his kingdoms. Only as the prospects of the Stuarts' restitution faded did the older disagreements – over accommodating themselves to or resolutely opposing English authority – reappear among Irish papists. In the interim, England had allowed the Protestants to establish their ascendancy within Ireland.

[97] G. C. Gibbs, 'The European origins of the Glorious Revolution', in Maguire (ed.), *Kings in conflict*, pp. 9–28; S. P. A. Pincus, 'Popery, trade and the ideological context of the outbreak of the second Anglo-Dutch War', *English Historical Review*, 107 (1992), pp. 1–29; W. Troost, 'William III, Brandenburg and the construction of an anti-French coalition, 1672–1688', in Israel (ed.), *The Anglo-Dutch moment*, pp. 299–334.
[98] Hayton, 'The Williamite revolution in Ireland', pp. 193–4.

SELECT BIBLIOGRAPHY

The dozen or so volumes seminal to any study of the 1640s and 1650s are marked with an asterix (*).

PRINTED SOURCES

Abbott, W. C. (ed.), *The writings and speeches of Oliver Cromwell* (4 vols., Cambridge, Mass., 1947)

Acts of the General Assemblies of the Church of Scotland, 1638–49 (Edinburgh, 1691)

Adair, Patrick, *A true narrative of the rise and progress of the Presbyterian church in Ireland*, ed. W. D. Killen (Belfast, 1866)

*Aiazza, Giuseppe, *The embassy in Ireland of Monsignor G. B. Rinuccini, archbishop of Fermo, in the years 1645–1649* . . . , translated by Annie Hutton (Dublin, 1873)

[Anonymous], 'Commonwealth records' in *Archivium Hibernicum*, 6 (1917) and 7 (1918–21)

[Anonymous], *Memoirs of the right honourable marquis of Clanricard* (Dublin, 1744)

Appleby, John, 'An Irish letter of marque, 1648' in *Irish Sword*, 15 (1982–3)

Berry, H. F. (ed.), *The register of the church of St Michan, Dublin, 1636–85* (Dublin, 1907)

Besse, Joseph, *A collection of the sufferings of the people called Quakers* (2 vols., London, 1753)

*Birch, Thomas (ed.), *A collection of the state papers of John Thurloe, esq.: secretary, first to the council of state, and afterward to the two Protectors Oliver and Richard Cromwell* (7 vols., London, 1742)

Boate, G., *Irelands naturall history* (London, 1652)

Borlase, Edmund, *The history of the execrable Irish rebellion 1641–1662* (London, 1680)

Boyle, Roger, earl of Orrery, *The Irish colours displayed* (London, 1662)

An answer to a scandalous letter . . . by Peter Walsh (London, 1662)

A treatise of the art of war (London, 1677)

Bramhall, John, *Works of John Bramhall . . .* , ed. John Vesey (Dublin, 1676)

Bridges, J., *A perfect narrative* (London, 1660)

Caldicott, C. E. J., 'Patrick Darcy, an argument' in *Camden Miscellany*, XXXI (London, 1992)

Calendar of the Clarendon state papers preserved in the Bodleian Library, ed. O. Ogle, W. H. Bliss and W. D. Macray (3 vols., Oxford, 1869–76); IV, ed. F. J. Routledge (Oxford, 1932)

*Calendar of state papers relating to Ireland
1633–1647 (London, 1901)
Adventurers 1642–1659 (London, 1903)
1647–1660 (London, 1903)
1660–1662 (London, 1905)
1669–1670, with addenda, 1625–1670 (London, 1910)

Calendar of state papers and manuscripts, relating to English affairs, existing in the archives and collections of Venice
1640–1642 (London, 1924)
1642–1643 (London, 1925)
1643–1647 (London, 1926)
1647–1652 (London, 1927)

James Touchet, earl of Castlehaven, *Memoirs . . . his engagement and carriage in the wars of Ireland* (London, 1680; later editions, 1681, 1684; reprinted New York, 1974)

Casway, Jerrold I., 'Unpublished letters and papers of Owen Roe O'Neill' in *Analecta Hibernica*, 29 (1980)

Caulfield, Richard (ed.), *The council book of the corporation of Youghal* (Guildford, 1878)
The council book of the corporation of Kinsale (Guildford, 1879)

Clanricarde, Ulick de Burgh, marquis of, *The memoirs of Ulick, marquis of Clanricarde . . . lord-lieutenant of Ireland and commander in chief of the forces of King Charles . . . during the rebellion* (Dublin, 1757)

Clarendon, Edward Hyde, earl of, *The history of the rebellion and civil wars in England*, ed. W. D. Macray (6 vols., Oxford, 1888; re-issued 1992)

Cotton, Henry, *Fasti Ecclesiae Hibernicae* (6 vols., Dublin, 1845–78)

Cox, Richard, *Hibernia Anglicana, or the history of Ireland from the conquest thereof by the English to this present time* (second edn., 2 vols., London, 1692)

Crist, T. (ed.), *Charles II to Lord Taaffe: letters in exile* (Cambridge, 1974)

Crofton, H. T., *Crofton memoirs* (York, 1911)

Crofton Croker, T. (ed.), *The tour of the French traveller M. de Boullaye le Gouz in Ireland A.D. 1644* (London, 1837)

**Dunlop, Robert (ed.), *Ireland under the Commonwealth: being a selection of documents relating to the government of Ireland, 1651–9* (2 vols., Manchester, 1913)

Elrington, C. R., *The whole works of the Most Reverend James Ussher . . . with a life of the author and an account of his writings* (16 vols., Dublin, 1847)

Fincham, F. W. X. (ed.), 'Letters concerning Sir Maurice Eustace, Lord Chancellor of Ireland' in *English Historical Review*, 35 (1920)

Firth, C. H. (ed.), *The memoirs of Edmund Ludlow, lieutenant-general of the horse in the army of the commonwealth of England 1625–1672* (2 vols., Oxford, 1894)
Clarke papers. Selections from the papers of William Clarke . . . (Camden Society, 4 vols., 1891–1901)

Firth, C. H. and Rait, R. S. (eds.), *Acts and ordinances of the Interregnum, 1642–1660* (3 vols., London, 1911)

French, Nicholas, *A narrative of the earl of Clarendon's settlement and sale of Ireland* . . .
(Louvain, 1668; reprinted in S. H. Bindon (ed.), *The historical works of Nicholas French* (Dublin, 1846))

The unkinde desertor of loyall men and true frinds (1676; reprinted in Bindon (ed.), *Historical works*)

Giblin, Cathaldus, 'Vatican Library: MSS Barberini Latini. A guide to the material of Irish interest on microfilm in the National Library, Dublin' in *Archivium Hibernicum*, 18 (1955)

'Catalogue of material of Irish interest in the collection Nunziatura di Fiandra, Vatican archives' in *Collectanea Hibernica*, 1 (1958)

*Gilbert, J. T. (ed.), *A contemporary history of affairs in Ireland from A.D. 1641 to 1652 containing the* . . . *narrative entitled an 'Aphorismical discovery of treasonable faction'* (3 vols., Dublin, 1879–80)

**History of the Irish confederation and the war in Ireland, 1641–53* . . . (7 vols., Dublin 1882–91)

Calendar of the ancient records of Dublin in possession of the municipal corporation (17 vols., Dublin, 1889–1916)

Gillespie, Raymond (ed.), *Settlement and survival on an Ulster estate: the Brownlow leasebook 1667–1711* (Belfast, 1988)

Gookin, Vincent, *The author and case of transplanting the Irish into Connaught vindicated* (London, 1655)

The great case of transplantation in Ireland discussed (London, 1655)

Grosart, A. B. (ed.), *Lismore papers*, first series (10 vols., London, 1886–8)

Hickson, Mary (ed.), *Ireland in the seventeenth century* (2 vols., London, 1884)

Hill, George (ed.), *The Montgomery manuscripts (1603–1706): Compiled from the family papers by William Montgomery of Rosemont Esquire* (Belfast, 1869)

An historical account of the plantation in Ulster (Belfast, 1877)

Historical Manuscripts Commission, Reports
Fourteenth report, appendix, part VIII. *The manuscripts of the marquis of Ormonde*, OS (2 vols., London, 1885–9)

Report on the manuscripts of the earl of Egmont (2 vols., London, 1905–9)

Calendar of the manuscripts of the marquis of Ormonde, NS (8 vols., London, 1902–20)

Report on the Franciscan manuscripts preserved at the convent, Merchants' Quay, Dublin (Dublin, 1906)

[Hogan, E. (ed.)], *The history of the warr in Ireland* . . . *by a British officer of the regiment of Sir John Clotworthy* (Dublin, 1873)

Hogan, J. (ed.), *Letters and papers relating to the Irish rebellion between 1642–46* (IMC, Dublin, 1936)

Hull, C. H. (ed.), *The economic writings of Sir William Petty* (2 vols., Cambridge, 1899)

Jennings, Brendan (ed.), *Wild Geese in Spanish Flanders 1582–1700. Documents relating to Irish regiments from the Archives Générales du Royaume, Brussels, and other sources* (IMC, Dublin, 1964)

Jones, Henry, *A remonstrance of divers remarkable passages concerning the church and kingdom of Ireland* . . . (London, 1642)

Journals of the House of Commons 1547–1714 (17 vols., London, 1742+)

Journals of the House of Commons of the kingdom of Ireland . . . (1613–1791) (28 vols., Dublin, 1753–91)

Journals of the House of Lords 1578–1714 (vols. II–XIX, London, 1767+)

Journals of the House of Lords [of Ireland] (1634–1800) (8 vols., Dublin, 1779–1800)

Keating, Geoffrey, *Foras feasa ar Éirinn: the history of Ireland,* ed. David Comyn and P. A. Dinneen (4 vols., London, 1902–4)

Keeble, N. H. and Nuttall, G. F. (eds.), *Calendar of the correspondence of Richard Baxter* (2 vols., Oxford, 1991)

Knowler, W. (ed.), *The earl of Strafforde's letters and despatches with an essay towards his life by Sir George Radcliffe . . .* (2 vols., London, 1739)

Larcom, T. A. (ed.), *The Down survey by Dr William Petty 1655–1656* (Dublin, 1851)

Lawrence, Richard, *The interest of England in the Irish transplantation stated* (London, 1655)

England's great interest in the well planting of Ireland (Dublin, 1656)

[Lodge, John, (ed.),] *Desiderata curiosa Hibernica: or a select collection of state papers* (2 vols., Dublin, 1772)

Lowe, John (ed.), *Letter-book of the earl of Clanricarde, 1643–47* (IMC, Dublin, 1983)

Lowry, T. K. (ed.), *The Hamilton manuscripts: containing some account of territories of Upper Clandeboye, Great Ardes, Dufferin in the county of Down, by Sir William Hamilton, afterward Viscount Clandeboye* (Belfast, 1867)

MacLysaght, E. (ed.), *Calendar of the Orrery papers* (Dublin, 1941)

'Commonwealth state accounts 1650–1656' in *Analecta Hibernica,* 15 (1944)

McNeill, Charles (ed.), *The Tanner letters. Documents of Irish affairs in the sixteenth and seventeenth centuries extracted from the Thomas Tanner collection in the Bodleian Library, Oxford* (IMC, Dublin, 1943)

Massari, Dionysius, 'My Irish campaign' in *The Catholic Bulletin,* 4 (1916), 7 (1917), 8 (1918), 9 (1919), 10 (1920)

Meyer, Joseph (ed.), 'Inedited letters of Cromwell, Col. Jones, Bradshaw and other regicides' in *Transactions of the Historic Society of Lancashire and Cheshire,* new series, 1 (1860–1)

Millett, Benignus (ed.), 'Calendar of volume 1 of the Scritture riferite nei congressi, Irlanda in propaganda archives' in *Collectanea Hibernica,* 6–7 (1963–4)

'Calendar of volume 14 of the Fondo di Vienna in propaganda archives, pt. 2' in *Collectanea Hibernica,* 30 (1988)

Mills, James (ed.), *The register of St John the Evangelist, Dublin, 1619–99* (Dublin, 1906)

Morrice, Thomas, *A collection of the state letters of Roger Boyle, first earl of Orrery* (Dublin, 1743)

Nalson, J. (ed.), *An impartial collection of the great affairs of state* (2 vols., London, 1682–3)

*O'Ferrall, Richard and O'Connell, Robert, *Commentarius Rinuccinianus, de sedis apostolicae legatione ad foederatos Hiberniae catholicos per annos 1645–9,* ed. Revd Stanislaus Kavanagh (IMC, 6 vols., Dublin, 1932–49)

O'Hart, J. (ed.), *Irish landed gentry when Cromwell came to Ireland* (Dublin, 1887)

O'Meagher, J. Casimir (ed.), 'Diary of Dr Jones, scout-master general to the army of the Commonwealth . . .' in *Journal, Royal Society of Antiquaries of Ireland,* fifth series, 3 (1893)

O' Rahilly, Cecile (ed.), *Five seventeenth century political poems* (Dublin, 1952, reprinted, 1977)

Pender, Séamus (ed.), *A census of Ireland c. 1659* (IMC, Dublin, 1939)

Russell, C. W. and Prendergast, J. P., *Account of the Carte collection of historical papers* (London, 1871)

Rutt, J. R. (ed.), *Diary of Thomas Burton, esq.*, (London, 1828)

Scrope, R. and Monkhouse, T. (eds.), *State papers collected by Edward, earl of Clarendon, commencing 1621* (3 vols., Oxford, 1767–86)

Seymour, St John D., *Adventures and experiences of a seventeenth century clergyman. Edited from the original manuscript* (Dublin, 1909)

Simington, R. C. (ed.), *The civil survey A.D. 1654–56* (IMC, 10 vols., Dublin, 1931–62)

The transplantation to Connaught 1654–1658 (IMC, Shannon, 1970)

Singer, S. W. (ed.), *The correspondence of Henry Hyde, earl of Clarendon . . .* (2 vols., London, 1828)

State of the papist and protestant proprietors in the kingdom of Ireland (London, 1689)

The statutes at large passed in the parliaments held in Ireland . . . 1310–1761 (8 vols., Dublin, 1765)

Steele, R. R. (ed.), *Tudor and Stuart proclamations* (2 vols., Oxford, 1910)

Storey, George, *A continuation of the impartial history of the war of Ireland* (London, 1698)

Temple, Sir John, *The Irish rebellion: or the history of the beginning and first progress of the general rebellion raised within the kingdom of Ireland upon the three and twentieth day of October 1641* (expanded version, London, 1646)

Walsh, P., *The Irish colours folded* (London, 1662)

Whitelocke, Bulstrode, *Memorials of the English affairs from the beginning of the reign of Charles I to the happy restoration of King Charles II* (later edn., 4 vols., Oxford, 1853)

Young, R. M. (ed.), *The town book of the corporation of Belfast 1613–1816* (Belfast, 1896)

Historical notices of old Belfast and its vicinity (Belfast, 1896)

'A diary of the proceedings of the Leinster army, under Governor Jones . . . ' in *Ulster Journal of Archaeology*, second series, 3 (1897)

Adamson, J. S. A., 'The baronial context of the English civil war' in *Transactions, Royal Historical Society*, fifth series, 40 (1990)

Andrews, J. H., *Plantation acres: an historical study of the Irish land surveyor and his maps* (Omagh, 1985)

Asch, Ronald (ed.), *Three nations – a common history? England, Scotland, Ireland and British history c. 1600–1920* (Arbeitskreis Deutsche England-Forschung, XXIII, Bochum, 1993)

Arnold, L. J., 'The Cromwellian settlement of County Dublin, 1652–1660' in *Journal, Royal Society of Antiquities in Ireland*, 101 (1971)

'The Irish Court of Claims of 1663' in *IHS*, 24 (1985)

The Restoration land settlement in County Dublin (Dublin, 1993)

Aston, T. (ed.), *Crisis in Europe 1560–1660: essays from 'Past and Present'* (London, 1965)

Aylmer, G. E., 'Presidential address: collective mentalities in mid-seventeenth century England: II. Royalist attitudes' in *Transactions, Royal Historical Society*, 37 (1987),

Bagwell, Richard, *Ireland under the Stuarts and during the Interregnum* (3 vols., London, 1909–16; reprint, 1963)

Barnard, T. C., 'Lord Broghill, Vincent Gookin and the Cork elections of 1659' in *English Historical Review*, 88 (1973)

'Planters and policies in Cromwellian Ireland' in *Past and Present*, 61 (1973)

**Cromwellian Ireland: English government and reform in Ireland 1649–1660* (Oxford, 1975)

'Sir William Petty, his Irish estates and Irish population' in *Irish Economic and Social History*, 6 (1979)

'Sir William Petty, Irish landowner' in Hugh Lloyd-Jones, Valerie Pearl and Blair Worden (eds.), *History and imagination: essays in honour of H. R. Trevor-Roper* (London, 1981)

'Crises of identity among Irish Protestants 1641–1685' in *Past and Present*, 127 (1990)

'The uses of 23 October 1641 and the Irish Protestant celebrations' in *English Historical Review*, 106 (1991)

'Irish images of Cromwell' in R. C. Richardson (ed.), *Images of Cromwell: essays by and for Roger Howell* (Manchester, 1993)

'Lawyers and the law in later seventeenth century Ireland' in *IHS*, 29 (1993)

'The political, material and mental culture of the Cork settlers, c. 1650–1700' in P. O'Flanagan and Cornelius Buttimer (eds.), *Cork: history and society* (Dublin, 1993)

'1641: a bibliographical essay' in Brian Mac Cuarta (ed.), *Ulster 1641* (Belfast, 1993)

'Athlone, 1685; Limerick, 1710: religious riots or charivaris?' in *Studia Hibernica*, 27 (1993)

'The Hartlib circle and the cult and culture of improvement in Ireland' in M. Greengrass, M. P. Leslie and T. Raylor (eds.), *Samuel Hartlib and universal reformation: studies in intellectual communication* (Cambridge, 1994)

'Land and the limits of loyalty: the second earl of Cork and first earl of Burlington (1612–1698)' in T. C. Barnard and J. Clark (eds.), *Lord Burlington: architecture, art and life* (London, 1994)

Bartlett, Thomas, 'Review article: A new history of Ireland' in *Past and Present*, 116 (1987)

Baumber, Michael L., 'The navy and the civil war in Ireland, 1641–1643' in *Mariner's Mirror*, 57 (1971)

'The navy and the civil war in Ireland, 1643–1646' in *Mariner's Mirror*, 75 (1989)

*Beckett, J. C., 'The confederation of Kilkenny reviewed', in Michael Roberts (ed.), *Historical Studies*, II (London, 1959)

The cavalier duke. A life of James Butler first duke of Ormond, 1610–1688 (Belfast, 1990)

Beckles, Hilary, 'A riotous and unruly lot: Irish indentured servants and freemen in the English West Indies, 1644–1713' in *William and Mary Quarterly*, 47 (1990)

Bergeron, L. and Cullen, L. M. (eds.), *Culture et pratiques politiques en France et en Irlande XVIe–XVIIIe siècles* (Paris, 1991)

Bigby, D. A., *Anglo-French relations, 1641–9* (London, 1933)
Birch, Thomas (ed.), *An inquiry into the share which Charles I had in the transactions of the earl of Glamorgan* (London, 1756)
Blackwood, B. G., *The Lancashire gentry and the great rebellion, 1640–1660* (Manchester, 1978)
Blake, J. W., 'Transportation from Ireland to America, 1653–60', *IHS*, 3 (1942–43)
Bolton, F. R., *The Caroline tradition of the Church of Ireland* (London, 1958)
Bottigheimer, K.S., 'Civil war in Ireland: the reality in Munster' in *Emory University Quarterly*, 22 (spring, 1966)
'English money and Irish land. The "Adventurers" in the Cromwellian settlement of Ireland' in *Journal of British Studies*, 7 (1967)
*English money and Irish land. The 'Adventurers' in the Cromwellian settlement of Ireland (Oxford, 1971)
'The Restoration land settlement in Ireland: a structural view' in *IHS*, 18 (1972)
'Kingdom and colony: Ireland in the westward enterprise, 1536–1660' in K. R. Andrews, N. P. Canny and P. E. H. Hair (eds.), *The westward enterprise: English activities in Ireland, the Atlantic and America, 1480–1650* (Liverpool, 1978)
Boyd, Andrew, 'Rinuccini and civil war in Ireland, 1644–9' in *History Today*, 41 (Feb. 1991)
Bradshaw, Brendan, Hadfield, Andrew and Maley, Willy (eds.), *Representing Ireland: literature and the origins of conflict, 1634–1660* (Cambridge, 1993)
Brady, Ciaran and Gillespie, Raymond (eds.), *Natives and newcomers. Essays on the making of Irish colonial society 1534–1641* (Dublin, 1986)
Brennan, Monica, 'The changing composition of Kilkenny landowners, 1641–1700' in William Nolan and Kevin Whelan (eds.), *Kilkenny: history and society. Interdisciplinary essays on the history of an Irish county* (Dublin, 1990)
Brooke, Peter, *Ulster Presbyterianism* (Dublin, 1987)
Brún de, Pádraig, Ó Buachalla, Breandán and Ó Concheanainn, Tomás, *Nua-dhuanaire I* (Dublin, 1986, reprinted, 1991)
Bryan, D., 'Colonel Richard Grace' in *Irish Sword*, 4 (1959–60)
Burke, James, 'The New Model Army and the problem of siege warfare' in *IHS*, 27 (1990–1)
Butler, W. F. T., *Confiscations in Irish history* (London, 1977 edition)
Canny, Nicholas P., 'The formation of the Irish mind: religion, politics and Gaelic Irish literature, 1580–1750' in *Past and Present*, 95 (May 1982)
The upstart earl: a study of the social and mental world of Richard Boyle, first earl of Cork, 1566–1643 (Cambridge, 1982)
Kingdom and colony. Ireland in the Atlantic world 1560–1800 (Baltimore, 1988)
'In defense of the constitution? The nature of the Irish revolt in the seventeenth century' in L. Bergeron and L. M. Cullen (eds.), *Culture et pratiques politiques en France et en Irlande XVIe –XVIIIe siècles* (Paris, 1991)
'The marginal kingdom: Ireland as a problem in the first British empire' in Bernard Bailyn and Philip D. Morgan (eds.), *Strangers within the realm: cultural margins of the first British empire* (Chapel Hill, 1991)
'Irish resistance to empire? 1641, 1690 and 1798' in Lawrence Stone (ed.), *An imperial state at war* (London, 1994)

'The 1641 depositions as a source for the writing of social history: County Cork as a case study' in P. O'Flanagan and Cornelius Buttimer (eds.), *Cork: history and society* (Dublin, 1993)

'English migration into and across the Atlantic during the seventeenth and eighteenth centuries' in Nicholas Canny (ed.), *Europeans on the move: studies on European migration, 1500–1800* (Oxford, 1994)

Canny, Nicholas and Pagden, Anthony (eds.), *Colonial identity in the Atlantic world 1500–1800* (Princeton, 1987)

Carles, Pierre, 'Troupes Irlandaises au service de la France, 1635–1815' in *Etudes Irlandaises*, ns 8 (Dec. 1983)

Carlin, Norah, 'The Levellers and the conquest of Ireland in 1649' in *The Historical Journal*, 30 (1987)

*Carte, Thomas, *History of the life of James, first duke of Ormonde* (3 vols., London, 1735–6; second edn., 6 vols., Oxford, 1851)

Casway, Jerrold I., 'Owen Roe O'Neill's return to Ireland in 1642: the diplomatic background' in *Studia Hibernica*, 9 (1969)

'George Monck and the controversial catholic truce of 1649' in *Studia Hibernica*, 16 (1976)

Owen Roe O'Neill and the struggle for Catholic Ireland (Philadelphia, 1984)

'Two Phelim O'Neills' in *Seanchas Ardmhacha*, 11 (1985)

'The Belturbet council and election of March 1650' in *Clogher Record*, 22 (1986)

Clarke, Aidan, 'The earl of Antrim and the first Bishops' War' in *Irish Sword*, 6 (1963)

The Old English in Ireland 1625–1642 (Ithaca and London, 1966)

'Ireland and the general crisis' in *Past and Present*, 48 (1970)

*'The genesis of the Ulster rising of 1641' in P. Roebuck (ed.), *Plantation to partition. Essays in Ulster history in honour of J. L. McCracken* (Belfast, 1981)

*'The 1641 depositions' in P. Fox (ed.), *Treasures of the library of Trinity College Dublin* (Dublin, 1986)

'Sir Piers Crosby, 1590–1646: Wentworth's "tawney ribbon"' in *IHS*, 26 (1988)

'Varieties of uniformity: The first century of the Church of Ireland' in W. D. Sheils and Diane Wood (eds.), *The churches, Ireland and the Irish*. (Studies in Church History, xxv, Oxford, 1989)

'Colonial constitutional attitudes in Ireland, 1640–1660' in *Proceedings, Royal Irish Academy*, section C, 90 (1990)

'The 1641 rebellion and anti-popery in Ireland' in Brian Mac Cuarta (ed.), *Ulster 1641* (Belfast, 1993)

Connolly, S. J., *Religion, law and power: The making of Protestant Ireland, 1660–1760* (Oxford, 1992)

Corish, Patrick J., 'Bishop Nicholas French and the second Ormond peace, 1648–1649' in *IHS*, 6 (1948)

'Rinuccini's censure of May 22 1648' in *Irish Theological Quarterly*, 18 (1951)

'Two contemporary historians of the confederation of Kilkenny: John Lynch and Richard O'Ferrall' in *IHS*, 8 (1953)

'John Callaghan and the controversy among the Irish in Paris' in *Irish Theological Quarterly*, 21 (1954)

'Ireland's first papal nuncio' in *Irish Ecclesiastical Record*, fifth series, 81 (Jan–June 1954)

'The crisis in Ireland in 1648: the nuncio and the supreme council: conclusions' in *Irish Theological Quarterly*, 22 (1955)

Corish, Patrick (ed.), *Radicals, rebels and establishments. Historical Studies*, XV (Belfast, 1985)

Cosgrove, A. and Maguire, J. I.(eds.), *Parliament and community. Historical Studies*, XIV (Belfast, 1983)

Crawford, E. M. (ed.), *Famine: the Irish experience* (Edinburgh, 1989)

Cregan, Donal F., 'Daniel O'Neill, a royalist agent in Ireland, 1644–1650' in *IHS*, 2 (1941)

'Some members of the confederation of Kilkenny' in S. O'Brien (ed.), *Measgra i gCuimhne Mhichíl Uí Chleirigh* (Dublin, 1944)

'The confederation of Kilkenny: its organization, personnel and history' (unpublished PhD thesis, NUI, 1947)

'An Irish cavalier: Daniel O'Neill' in *Studia Hibernica*, 3 (1963)

'An Irish cavalier: Daniel O'Neill in the civil wars 1642–51' in *Studia Hibernica*, 4 (1965)

'An Irish cavalier: Daniel O'Neill in exile and restoration 1651–1664' in *Studia Hibernica*, 5 (1965)

*'The confederation of Kilkenny' in Brian Farrell (ed.), *Irish parliamentary tradition* (Dublin, 1973)

Cullen, L. M., 'The Irish diaspora of the seventeenth and eighteenth centuries' in Nicholas Canny (ed.), *Europeans on the move: studies on European migration, 1500–1800* (Oxford, 1994)

Cullen, L. M., and Furet, François (eds.), *Ireland and France, 17th–20th centuries: towards a comparative study of rural history* (Paris, 1980)

Cunningham, Bernadette, 'Native culture and political change in Ireland, 1580–1640' in Ciaran Brady and Raymond Gillespie (eds.), *Natives and newcomers: essays on the making of Irish colonial society, 1534–1641* (Dublin, 1986)

Curtin, Benventura, *see* MacCurtain, Benevenuta

Dudley Edwards, R., 'The Irish Catholics and the puritan revolution' in Franciscan Fathers (eds.), *Father Luke Wadding, commemorative volume* (Dublin, 1957)

Duffy, P. J., 'The evolution of estate properties in South Ulster, 1600–1900' in William Smyth and Kevin Whelan (eds.), *Common ground: essays on the historical geography of Ireland presented to T. Jones Hughes* (Cork, 1988)

Duggan, Lucy, 'The Irish brigade with Montrose' in *Irish Ecclesiastical Record*, fifth series, 89 (Jan.–June 1958)

Dunne, T. J., 'The Gaelic response to conquest and colonization: the evidence of the poetry' in *Studia Hibernica*, 20 (1980)

Dwyer, J., Mason, R. S., Murdoch, A.(eds.), *New perspectives on the politics and culture of early modern Scotland* (Edinburgh, 1982)

Elkin, Robert E., 'The interactions between the Irish rebellion and the English civil wars' (unpublished PhD thesis, University of Illinois at Urbana-Champaign, 1961)

Ellis, Steven, '"Not mere English". The British perspective, 1400–1650' in *History Today*, 38 (Dec. 1988)

Esson, D. M. R., *The curse of Cromwell: a history of the ironside conquest of Ireland 1649–1653* (Totowa, New Jersey, 1971)

Farrell, Brian (ed.), *Irish parliamentary tradition* (Dublin, 1973)

Firth, C. H., 'Account of money spent in the reconquest and settlement of Ireland, 1646–56' in *English Historical Review*, 14 (1899)

Cromwell's army: a history of the English soldier during the civil wars, the commonwealth and protectorate (London, 1902; reprinted London, 1992)

Firth, C. H. and Davies, G., *The regimental history of Cromwell's army* (2 vols., Oxford, 1940; reprinted, 1991)

Fissel, Mark Charles (ed.), *War and government in Britain 1598–1650* (Manchester and New York, 1991)

Fitzpatrick, Thomas, *The bloody bridge and other papers relating to the insurrection of 1641* (Dublin, 1903; reissued, 1970)

'The Ulster civil war, 1641. "The king's commission" in the County Fermanagh' in *Ulster Journal of Archaeology*, second series, 13 (1907), 14 (1908), 15 (1909)

Waterford during the civil war (1641–1653) (Waterford, 1912)

Ford, Alan, *The Protestant Reformation in Ireland* (Frankfurt, 1985)

Furgol, Edward M., 'The military and ministers as agents of Presbyterian imperialism in England and Ireland 1640–48' in J. Dwyer, R. S. Mason, A. Murdoch (eds.), *New perspectives on the politics and culture of early modern Scotland* (Edinburgh, 1982)

A regimental history of the covenanting armies, 1639–1651 (Edinburgh, 1990)

Gardiner, Samuel R., *History of England from the accession of James I to the outbreak of the civil war, 1603–1642* (10 vols., London, 1863–81; new edn., 10 vols., 1883–4)

'Charles I and the earl of Glamorgan' in *English Historical Review*, 2 (1887)

History of the great civil war, 1642–1649 (new edn., 4 vols., London, 1893; reprint, 1987)

'The transplantation to Connaught' in *English Historical Review*, 14 (1899)

History of the commonwealth and protectorate 1649–1660 (new edn., 4 vols., London, 1903; reprint 1988)

Gentles, Ian, *The New Model Army in England, Ireland and Scotland 1645–1653* (Oxford, 1992)

Gilbert, Sir John T., *A history of Dublin* (3 vols., 1854–59; reprint, Dublin, 1978)

Gillespie, Raymond, *Colonial Ulster: the settlement of East Ulster 1600–1641* (Cork, 1985)

'Mayo and the rising of 1641' in *Cathair na Mart*, 5 (1985)

'The end of an era: Ulster and the outbreak of the 1641 rising' in Ciaran Brady and Raymond Gillespie (eds.), *Natives and newcomers: essays on the making of Irish colonial society, 1534–1641* (Dublin, 1986)

'Landed society and the Interregnum in Ireland and Scotland' in Rosalind Mitchison and Peter Roebuck (eds.), *Economy and society in Scotland and Ireland, 1500–1939* (Edinburgh, 1988)

'The Presbyterian revolution in Ulster, 1600–1690' in W. J. Sheils and Diana Wood (eds.), *The churches, Ireland and the Irish* (Studies in Church History, xxv, Oxford, 1989)

302   SELECT BIBLIOGRAPHY

The transformation of the Irish economy, 1550–1700 (Dundalk, 1991)
'An army sent from God: Scots at war in Ireland, 1642–9' in Norman MacDougall (ed.), *Scotland and war AD 79–1918* (Maryland, 1991)
'A question of survival: The O'Farrells of Longford in the seventeenth century' in Raymond Gillespie and Gerard Moran (eds.), *Longford: essays in county history* (Dublin, 1991)
'Owen Roe O'Neill' in Gerard O'Brien and Peter Roebuck (eds.), *Nine Ulster lives* (Belfast, 1992)
'Destabilizing Ulster, 1641–2' in Brian Mac Cuarta (ed.), *Ulster 1641* (Belfast, 1993)
Gillespie, Raymond and Moran, Gerald (eds.), *'A various country': essays in Mayo history 1500–1900* (Westport, Mayo, 1987)
Longford: essays in county history (Dublin, 1991)
Goldstrom, J. M., and Clarkson, L. A. (eds.), *Irish population, economy and society: essays in honour of the late K. H. Connell* (Oxford, 1981)
Gouhier, Pierre, 'Mercenaires Irlandais au service de la France (1635–1664)' in *Irish Sword*, 7 (1965)
Gowen, Margaret, 'Seventeenth-century artillery forts in Ulster' in *Clogher Record*, 10, (1980)
Greaves R. L., and Zaller, Robert, *Biographical dictionary of British radicals in the seventeenth century* (3 vols., Harvester, 1982–4)
Habbakuk, H. J., 'Landowners and the civil war' in *Economic History Review*, second series, 18 (1965)
Hamilton, Charles L., 'Scotland, Ireland and the English Civil War' in *Albion*, 7 (1975)
Hardinge, W. H., 'On the circumstances attending the outbreak of the civil war in Ireland' in *Transactions, Royal Irish Academy*, 24 (1866)
Hayes-McCoy, G. A., *Irish battles. A military history of Ireland* (Belfast, 1989) especially the chapters on Benburb and Rathmines
Hayton, David, 'Anglo-Irish attitudes: changing perceptions of national identity among the Protestant ascendancy in Ireland, *ca.* 1690–1750' in *Studies in Eighteenth Century Culture*, 17 (1987)
Hazlett, Hugh, 'A history of the military forces operating in Ireland, 1641–9' (unpublished PhD thesis, Queen's University, Belfast, 1938)
*The financing of the British armies in Ireland, 1641–9' in *IHS*, 1 (Mar. 1938)
*The recruitment and organization of the Scottish army in Ulster, 1642–9' in H. A. Cronne, T. W. Moody and D. B. Quinn (eds.), *Essays in British and Irish history in honour of James Eadie Todd* (London, 1949)
Henry, Gráinne, *The Irish military community in Spanish Flanders, 1585–1621* (Dublin, 1992)
'Ulster exiles in Europe, 1605–1641' in Brian Mac Cuarta (ed.), *Ulster 1641* (Belfast, 1993)
Hill, Christopher, 'Seventeenth-century English radicals and Ireland' in *A nation of change and novelty. Radical politics, religion and literature in seventeenth-century England* (London, 1990)
Hill, Jacqueline, R., 'Popery and protestantism, civil and religious liberty. The disputed lessons of Irish history' in *Past and Present*, 118 (Feb. 1988)

'1641 and the quest for Catholic emancipation, 1691–1829' in Brian Mac Cuarta (ed.), *Ulster 1641* (Belfast, 1993)

Hill, James Michael, *Celtic warfare 1595–1763* (Edinburgh, 1986)

Holiday, P. G., 'Land sales and repurchases in Yorkshire after the civil wars, 1650–1670' in *Northern History*, 5 (1970)

Hollick, Clive, 'Owen Roe O'Neill's Ulster army of the confederacy, May–August 1646', *Irish Sword*, 18 (1991)

Hynes, Michael, *The mission of Rinuccini, 1645–49* (Louvain, 1932)

'The Irish republic in the seventeenth century' in *The Catholic Historical Review*, 23 (1937)

Irwin, L., 'The earl of Orrery and the military problems of Restoration Munster' in *Irish Sword*, 13 (1977–9)

*Kearney, Hugh F., *Strafford in Ireland 1633–41: a study in absolutism* (Manchester, 1959; second edn., Cambridge, 1989)

Kelly, J. J., 'Colonel Richard Grace' in *Irish Ecclesiastical Record*, fourth series, 26 (1909)

Kenyon, John P., *The civil wars in England* (New York, 1988)

Kerr, A. W. M., *An Ironside of Ireland: the remarkable career of Lieut-General Michael Jones, governor of Dublin and commander of the parliamentary forces in Leinster, 1647–9* (London, 1923)

Kilroy, Phil, 'Women and the Reformation in seventeenth-century Ireland' in Margaret MacCurtain and Mary O'Dowd (eds.), *Women in early modern Ireland* (Dublin, 1991)

'Protestantism in Ulster, 1610–1641' in Brian Mac Cuarta (ed.), *Ulster 1641* (Belfast, 1993)

Protestant dissent and controversy in Ireland (Cork, 1994)

King, D. W., 'The succession of Colonels in the army of Ireland, 1658–9' in *Journal of the Society for Army Historical Research*, 55 (spring, 1977)

Knox, R. B., *James Ussher. Archbishop of Armagh* (Cardiff, 1967)

Lenihan, Pádraig 'The Leinster army and the battle of Dungan's Hill' in *Irish Sword*, 71 (spring, 1991)

*Lindley, Keith, 'The impact of the 1641 rebellion upon England and Wales 1641–5' in *IHS*, 18 (Sept. 1972)

Lodge, J., *The peerage of Ireland* (Dublin, 1789)

Loupès, P., 'Le jardin irlandais des supplices: la grande rebellion de 1641 vue à travers les pamphlets anglais' in L. Bergeron and L. M. Cullen (eds.), *Culture et pratiques politiques en France et en Irlande XVIe –XVIIIe siècles* (Paris, 1991)

Love, Walter D., 'Civil war in Ireland: appearances in three centuries of historical writing' in *Emory University Quarterly*, 22 (1966)

*Lowe, John, 'Some aspects of the wars in Ireland, 1641–1649' in *Irish Sword*, 4 (1959)

'The campaign of the Irish royalist army in Cheshire, November 1643 to January 1644' in *Transactions of the Lancashire and Cheshire Historical Society*, 3 (1959)

'The negotiations between Charles I and the confederation of Kilkenny, 1642–9' (unpublished PhD thesis, University of London, 1960)

'The earl of Antrim and Irish aid to Montrose in 1644' in *Irish Sword*, 4 (1960)

*'Charles I and the confederation of Kilkenny, 1643–1649' in *IHS*, 14 (1964–5)

'The Glamorgan mission to Ireland 1645–6' in *Studia Hibernica*, 4 (1964)

Lynch, K. M., *Roger Boyle, first earl of Orrery* (Knoxville, 1965)

McAdoo, Henry, *John Bramhall and Anglicanism, 1663–1963* (Dublin, 1964)

Macafee, W. and Morgan, V., 'Population in Ulster, 1660–1760' in Peter Roebuck (ed.), *Plantation to partition: essays in Ulster history in honour of J. L. McCracken* (Belfast, 1981)

McCarthy, William P., 'The royalist collapse in Munster 1650–1652' in *Irish Sword*, 6 (summer, 1964)

MacCarthy-Morrogh, Michael, *The Munster plantation. English migration to southern Ireland 1583–1641* (Oxford, 1986)

Mac Cuarta, Brian (ed.), *Ulster 1641* (Belfast, 1993)

MacCurtain, Benevenuta [a.k.a. Margaret q.v.], 'Dominic O'Daly: an Irish diplomat' in *Studia Hibernica*, 5 (1965)

MacCurtain, Margaret and O'Dowd, Mary (eds.), *Women in early modern Ireland* (Dublin, 1991)

McDonnell, John, *The Ulster civil war of 1641 and its consequences; with the history of the Irish brigade under Montrose in 1644–46* (Dublin, 1879)

MacGillivray, Royce, 'Edmund Borlase, historian of the Irish rebellion' in *Studia Hibernica*, 9 (1969)

MacGiolla Eáin, E. (ed.), *Dánta, amhráin is caointe Sheathrúin Céitinn* (Dublin, 1900)

McKenny, Kevin, 'A seventeenth century "real estate company". The 1649 Officers and the Irish land settlements, 1641–1681' (unpublished MA thesis, NUI, Maynooth, 1989).

Maguire, J. I., 'The Dublin Convention, the Protestant community and the emergence of an ecclesiastical settlement in 1660' in A. Cosgrove and J. I. Maguire (eds.), *Parliament and community. Historical Studies*, XIV (Belfast, 1983)

Maguire, N. K., 'Regicide and reparation: the autobiographical drama of Roger Boyle, earl of Orrery' in *English Literary Renaissance*, 21 (1991)

Malcolm, Joyce Lee, 'All the king's men: the impact of the crown's Irish soldiers on the English civil war', *IHS*, 21 (Mar. 1979)

Marshall, John J., 'Sir Phelim O'Neill 1604–1652[-3]' in *Ulster Journal of Archaeology*, second series, 10 (1904)

Meehan, C. P., *The confederation of Kilkenny* (Dublin, 1860)

Meehan, J., 'Catalogue of the high sheriffs of the county of Leitrim' in *Journal, Royal Society of Antiquaries of Ireland*, 38 (1909 for 1908)

Miller, Amos, 'Sir Richard Grenville, governor of Trim and the character of the English soldier in Ireland, 1642–3' in *Ríocht na Mídhe*, 5 (1973)

Miller, John, 'The earl of Tyrconnell and James II's Irish policy' in *The Historical Journal*, 20 (1977)

Mitchison, Rosalind, and Roebuck, Peter (eds.), *Economy and society in Scotland and Ireland, 1500–1939* (Edinburgh, 1988)

*Moody, T. W., Martin, F. X., and Byrne, F. J. (eds.), *A new history of Ireland*, III: *Early modern Ireland 1534–1691* (Oxford, 1976; reprinted with corrections, 1978), especially the chapters by Patrick Corish on the 1640s and 1650s

A new history of Ireland, IX: *Maps, genealogies, lists* (Oxford, 1984)

SELECT BIBLIOGRAPHY 305

Morrill, John S. (ed.), *Reactions to the English civil war 1642–1649* (London, 1982)
Oliver Cromwell and the English revolution (London, 1990)
The Scottish national covenant in its British context 1638–51 (Edinburgh, 1990)
The impact of the English civil war (London, 1991)
Morrissey, Thomas J., 'The strange letters of Mathew Hartegan, S. J., 1644–45' in *Irish Theological Quarterly*, 37 (1970)
Murphy, J. A., 'The expulsion of the Irish from Cork in 1644' in *Journal of the Cork Historical and Archaeological Society*, 69 (1964)
'Inchiquin's change of religion' in *Journal of the Cork Historical and Archaeological Society*, 72 (1967)
*'The politics of the Munster Protestants, 1641–1649' in *Journal of the Cork Historical and Archaeological Society*, 76 (1971)
Neely W. G., *Kilkenny. An urban history 1391–1843* (Belfast, 1989)
Ní Ch'eallacháin, Máire, *Filíocht Phádraigín Haicéad* (Dublin, 1962)
Nolan, William and Whelan, Kevin (eds.), *Kilkenny: history and society. Interdisciplinary essays on the history of an Irish county* (Dublin, 1990)
Nutall, G. F., *Visible saints* (Oxford, 1957)
Ó Buachalla, B., 'Irish Jacobite poetry' in *The Irish Review*, 12 (1992)
'James our true king. The ideology of Irish royalism in the seventeenth century', in D. George Boyce, Robert Eccleshall and Vincent Geoghegan (eds.), *Political thought in Ireland since the seventeenth century* (London and New York, 1993)
Ó Danachair, C., 'Montrose's Irish regiments' in *Irish Sword*, 4 (1959)
Ó Doibhlin, E., 'The Cromwellian settlement and its aftermath' in *Seanchas Ardmhacha*, 4 (1961)
Ó Donnchadha, Tadhg (ed.), 'Cín lae Ó Mealláin' in *Analecta Hibernica*, 6 (1931)
O'Dowd, Mary, 'Women and war in Ireland in the 1640s' in MacCurtain, Margaret and O'Dowd, Mary (eds.), *Women in early modern Ireland* (Dublin, 1991)
Power, politics and land: early modern Sligo (1568–1688) (Belfast, 1991)
Ó Dúshláine, Tadhg, *An Eoruip agus litríocht na Gaeilge 1600–1650* (Dublin, 1987)
O Fiaich, Tomás, 'Edmund O'Reilly, archbishop of Armagh, 1657–1669' in *Father Luke Wadding*, ed. Franciscan Fathers (Dublin, 1957)
'Republicanism and separatism in the seventeenth century' in *Léachtaí Cholm Cille*, 2 (1971)
O'Flanagan, P. and Buttimer, Cornelius G. (ed.), *Cork: history and society* (Dublin, 1993)
O'Hart, J., *Irish landed gentry when Cromwell came to Ireland* (Dublin, 1887)
O'Mahoney, S. F., 'The Irish discalced Carmelites, 1625–53' (unpublished PhD thesis, TCD, 1978)
O'Malley, Liam 'Patrick Darcy, Galway lawyer and politician, 1598–1668' in Diarmuid Ó Cearbhaill (ed.), *Galway: town and gown 1484–1984* (Dublin, 1984)
Ó Mórdha, P. B., 'The battle of Clones, 1643' in *Clogher Record*, 4 (1962)
Ó Mórdha, Séamus P., 'Hugh O'Reilly (1581?–1653), a reforming primate' in *Breifne*, 4 (1970)
'Heber MacMahon, soldier bishop of the confederation of Kilkenny' in Joseph Duffy (ed.), *Clogher record album. A diocesan history* (Monaghan, 1975)

Ó Murchadha, Ciarán, 'Land and society in seventeenth century Clare' (unpublished PhD thesis, NUI, Galway, 1982)

O Riordan, Michelle, 'Historical perspectives on Gaelic poetry of the "hidden Ireland"' in *The Irish Review*, 4 (Cork, 1988)

The Gaelic mind and the collapse of the Gaelic world (Cork, 1990)

'A seventeenth-century "political poem"' in Myrtle Hill and Sarah Barber (eds.), *Aspects of Irish studies* (Belfast, 1990)

'The native Ulster *mentalité* as revealed in Gaelic sources 1600–1650' in Brian Mac Cuarta (ed.), *Ulster 1641* (Belfast, 1993)

O'Riordan, S., 'Rinuccini in Galway 1647–1649' in *Journal of the Galway Archaeological and Historical Society*, 23, nos. 1 and 2 (1948)

Ó Siochrú, Mícheál,'The confederation of Kilkenny' in *History Ireland*, 2 (summer, 1994)

O'Sullivan, Harold, 'The Cromwellian and Restoration settlements in the civil parish of Dundalk, 1649–1673' in *Louth Archaeological and Historical Journal*, 19 (1977)

'Land ownership changes in the county of Louth in the seventeenth century' (unpublished PhD thesis, TCD, 1992)

O'Sullivan, William, 'The only gold coinage issued in Ireland (1646)' in *British Numismatic Journal*, 33 (1964)

Ohlmeyer, Jane H., '"The Dunkirk of Ireland": Wexford privateers during the 1640s' in *Journal of the Wexford Historical Society*, 12 (1988–9)

'Irish privateers during the civil war, 1642–50' in *Mariner's Mirror*, 76 (May 1990)

'The "Antrim plot" of 1641 – a myth?' in *The Historical Journal*, 35 (1992); also see the reply by Michael Perceval-Maxwell and Ohlmeyer's rejoinder in *The Historical Journal*, 37 (1994)

Civil war and restoration in the three Stuart kingdoms: the career of Randal MacDonnell, marquis of Antrim 1609–1683 (Cambridge, 1993)

'A Stuart turn-kilt: Randal MacDonnell, marquis of Antrim' in *History Today*, 43 (Mar. 1993)

'The war of religions (1603–1660)' in Thomas Bartlett and Keith Jeffery (eds.), *A military history of Ireland* (Cambridge, forthcoming, 1995)

Parker, Geoffrey, *The Army of Flanders and the Spanish road 1567–1659: the logistics of Spanish victory and defeat in the Low Countries' wars* (Cambridge, 1972; third edn., 1989)

The Thirty Years War (London, 1984)

The Military Revolution: military innovation and the rise of the west, 1500–1800 (Cambridge, 1988)

Perceval-Maxwell, Michael, 'Strafford, the Ulster Scots and the covenanters', *IHS*, 18 (1973)

'The Ulster rising of 1641, and the depositions' in *IHS*, 21 (Sept. 1978)

'The adoption of the Solemn League and Covenant by the Scots in Ulster' in *Scotia: American–Canadian Journal of Scottish Studies*, 2 (1978)

'Protestant faction, the impeachment of Strafford and the origins of the Irish civil war' in *Canadian Journal of History*, 17 (1982)

'Ireland and Scotland, 1638 to 1648', John Morrill (ed.), *The Scottish national covenant in its British context* (Edinburgh, 1990)

'Ireland and the monarchy in the early Stuart multiple kingdom' in *The Historical Journal*, 34 (1991)

'Ulster 1641 in the context of political developments in the three kingdoms' in Brian Mac Cuarta (ed.), *Ulster 1641* (Belfast, 1993)

The outbreak of the Irish rebellion of 1641 (Dublin, 1994)

Perry, Nicholas, 'The infantry of the confederate Leinster army 1642–1647' in *Irish Sword*, 15 (winter, 1983)

Petrie, Charles, 'Ireland in Spanish and French strategy 1558–1815' in *Irish Sword*, 6 (summer, 1964)

Pinkerton, William, 'Unpublished poems relating to Ulster in 1642–43' in *Ulster Journal of Archaeology*, 8 (1860)

Prendergast, J. P., 'Records of the Kilkenny confederate assembly, AD 1642–1650' in *Journal, Royal Society of Antiquaries of Ireland*, 1 (1849–51)

The Cromwellian settlement of Ireland (revised edn., London, 1870; third edn. Dublin, 1922)

Ramsey, Robert W., *Henry Cromwell* (London, 1933)

Henry Ireton (London, 1949)

Reay, B., *The Quakers and the English revolution* (London, 1985)

Reid, J. S., *History of the Presbyterian church in Ireland*, ed. W. D. Killen (3 vols., Belfast, 1867)

Richardson, R. C. (ed.), *Images of Cromwell: essays by and for Roger Howell* (Manchester, 1993)

Roebuck, Peter, 'The making of an Ulster great estate: the Chichesters, barons of Belfast and viscounts of Carrickfergus, 1599–1648' in *Proceedings, Royal Irish Academy*, section C, 79 (1979)

'Landlord indebtedness in Ulster in the seventeenth and eighteenth centuries' in J. M. Goldstrom and L. A. Clarkson (eds.), *Irish population, economy and society: essays in honour of the late K. H. Connell* (Oxford, 1981)

Roebuck, Peter (ed.) *Plantation to partition: essays in Ulster history in honour of J. L. McCracken* (Belfast, 1981)

Rogers, P. G., *The fifth monarchy men* (London, 1966)

Russell, Conrad, 'The British problem and the English civil war' in *History*, 72 (1987)

'The British background to the Irish rebellion of 1641' in *Historical Research*, 61 (1988)

The causes of the English civil war (Oxford, 1990)

The fall of the British monarchies 1637–1642 (Oxford, 1991)

Ryder, Ian, *An English army for Ireland* (London, 1987)

Seymour, St John D., *The puritans in Ireland, 1649–1661* (Oxford, 1921)

Samuel Winter (Dublin, 1941)

Simms, Hilary, 'Violence in County Armagh, 1641' in Brian Mac Cuarta (ed.), *Ulster 1641* (Belfast, 1993)

Simms, J. G., *War and politics in Ireland, 1649–1730*, ed. David Hayton and G. O'Brien (London, 1986) especially chapter 1 on Drogheda, chapter 2 on Waterford and chapter 3 on Limerick.

Simington, R. C., 'A census of Ireland *c.* 1659' in *Analecta Hibernica*, 12 (1943)

Simon, James, *An essay towards an historical account of Irish coins* (Dublin, 1810)

Smyth, William, 'Society and settlement in seventeenth century Ireland: the evidence of the "1659 census"' in William Smyth and Kevin Whelan (eds.), *Common ground: essays on the historical geography of Ireland presented to T. Jones Hughes* (Cork, 1988)

'Territorial, social and settlement hierarchies in seventeenth century Kilkenny' in William Nolan and Kevin Whelan (eds.), *Kilkenny: history and society. Interdisciplinary essays on the history of an Irish county* (Dublin, 1990)

'Making the documents of conquest speak: the transformation of property, society and settlement in seventeenth-century counties Tipperary and Kilkenny' in P. Gulliver and M. Silverman (eds.), *Approaching the past* (New York, 1992)

Smyth, William and Whelan, Kevin (eds.), *Common ground: essays on the historical geography of Ireland presented to T. Jones Hughes* (Cork, 1988)

Smout, T. C., Landsman, N. C. and Devine, T. M., 'Scottish emigration in the seventeenth and eighteenth centuries' in Nicholas Canny (ed.), *Europeans on the move: studies on European migration, 1500–1800* (Oxford, 1994)

Sparks, May, 'Archbishop Rinuccini, papal nuncio' in *Old Kilkenny Review, Journal of the Kilkenny Archaeological Society*, 8 (1954)

Stevenson, David, 'The desertion of the Irish by Coll Keitach's sons, 1642' in *IHS*, 21 (1978)

Scottish covenanters and Irish confederates: Scottish–Irish relations in the mid-seventeenth century (Belfast, 1981)

'The century of the three kingdoms' in *History Today*, 35 (Mar. 1985)

'Cromwell, Scotland and Ireland', John Morrill (ed.), *Oliver Cromwell and the English revolution* (London, 1990)

Stradling, Robert, *The Spanish monarchy and Irish mercenaries: The Wild Geese in Spain, 1618–68* (Dublin, 1994)

Stranks, C. J., *The life and writings of Jeremy Taylor* (London, 1952)

Talon, Geraldine, 'Books of survey and distribution, County Westmeath: a comparative survey, with reference to their administrative context and chronological sequence' in *Analecta Hibernica*, 28 (1978)

Thirsk, Joan, 'The sale of the royalist lands during the Interregnum' in *Economic History Review*, second series, 5 (1953)

Trevett, Christine, *Women and Quakerism in the seventeenth century* (York, 1991)

Urwick, William, *Independency in Dublin of the olden time* (Dublin, 1862)

The early history of Trinity College, Dublin, 1591–1660 (London, 1892)

Vann, Richard T. and Eversley, David, *Friends in life and death. The British and Irish Quakers in the demographic transition* (Cambridge, 1992)

Wedgwood, C.V., *The king's war* (New York, 1959)

Westerkamp, Marilyn, *Triumph of the laity, Scots–Irish piety and the Great Awakening, 1625–1760* (Oxford, 1988)

Wheeler, J. S. 'Logistics and supply in Cromwell's conquest of Ireland' in Mark Charles Fissel (ed.), *War and government in Britain 1598–1650* (Manchester and New York, 1991)

Whelan, Kevin and Nolan, William (eds.), *Wexford: history and society. Interdisciplinary essays on the history of an Irish county* (Dublin, 1987)

White, B. R., *The English Baptists of the seventeenth century* (London, 1985)

Woodward, Donald, 'The overseas trade of Chester, 1600–50' in *Transactions of the Historic Society of Lancashire and Cheshire*, 12 (1970)

Woolrych, A., *From commonwealth to protectorate* (Oxford, 1982)

INDEX

The following abbreviations are used:

abp	archbishop	LL	lord lieutenant
bp	bishop	LD	lord deputy
Co.	County	n	note
d.	died	OFM	Franciscan
LJ	lord justice	RC	Roman Catholic

Act for the Settling of Ireland (1652), 193, 269, 271
Act of Attainder (1657), 224
Act of Bangor (1654), 206
Act of Settlement (1662), 269, 271
Act of Uniformity, 283
Act of Union (1800), 287
Adamson, John, 8, 17
'adventurers', 22n, 130, 130n, 131, 133, 134, 136n, 137n, 138, 151, 181, 192, 193n, 260
Adventurers Act (1642), 130, 192, 193
'Aiste Dháibhí Cúndún' [Dáibhí Cundún's poem], 113, 119
Albemarle, duke of, see Monck, George
Alexander VII, pope, 106
Alger, Robert, 197
ambassadors, 93n
Amsterdam, Dutch Republic, 9, 170
An aphorismical discovery of treasonable faction, 91, 115, 118, 123, 125
Andalusia, Spain, 12
Anglesey, earl of, see Annesley, Arthur
Anglo-Irish, see Old English
Anglo-Irish relations, see Britain
Anglo-Scottish relations, 129, 131, 134, 135, 138, 142, 143-4, 147-8, 156-8
Anne of Austria, 91
Annesley, Arthur (d. 1686), earl of Anglesey, 6, 22, 88, 136n, 147n, 221, 232, 237, 238, 240, 261, 267, 268, 284, 285
'An Síogaí Rómhánach' [The Roman Fairy], 113, 115, 116, 124, 125

Antrim, county, 43, 44, 73, 179, 182, 205
Antrim, earls of, see MacDonnell, Alexander and Randal
Antrim, town, 78
Arcloyne Castle, Co. Cork, 81
Argyll, Scotland, 125n
Argyll, earls of, see Campbell, Archibald
aristocracy, 12, 13, 114, 118, 119-20, 121, 123, 223, 227
Arklow, Co. Wicklow, 67
Armagh, city, 29, 30, 47, 217
Armagh, county, 34, 35, 37, 52, 179, 207n, 223
armed forces, 7, 13, 14, 43-65; 'British'/anti-Catholic coalition, 44-7, 50, 130-4, 166, 220; size of, 45, 45n, 50-1, 55, 56, 58
armed forces of Dublin government, 44-6, 72, 220, 275, 278-9; cost after the Restoration, 275; cost during 1640s, 169, 171, 220; 'new army', see Wentworth, Thomas
armed forces of English parliament in Ireland, 43, 44-6, 55, 56, 146, 213, 214, 231, 233-4, 235, 242, 244-6, 247, 249-51, 252, 253-6; size of, 45, 45n, 50-1, 53, 55, 56, 58, 60, 61, 62, 169, 279; strategy of, 56-61, 62-5; see also parliament; New Model Army
armed forces of Irish, see Kilkenny, Confederation of
Army of Flanders, 41, 71, 72n, 91, 100, 104
artillery, 67; see also firearms
Artully, Co. Kerry, 75
Askeaton Castle, Co. Limerick, 74

Printed in Great Britain
by Amazon

26792567R00212